The MARKETING *of* NATIONS

A Strategic Approach to Building National Wealth

PHILIP KOTLER
SOMKID JATUSRIPITAK
SUVIT MAESINCEE

THE FREE PRESS

New York   London   Toronto   Sydney   Singapore

THE FREE PRESS
A Division of Simon & Schuster Inc.
1230 Avenue of the Americas
New York, NY 10020

Manufactured in the United States of America

10   9   8   7   6   5   4   3   2

Library of Congress Cataloging-in-Publication Data

Kotler, Philip.
   The marketing of nations : a strategic approach to building
national wealth / Philip Kotler, Somkid Jatusripitak, Suvit Maesincee.
     p.   cm.
   Includes bibliographical references and index.
    1. Economic development.   2. Economic policy.   3. Industrial policy.
I. Somkid Jatusripitak.   II. Suvit Maesincee, 1961–   .
III. Title.
HD75 IN PROCESS
338.9—dc21   97-1285
                                                      CIP

ISBN 0–684–83488–X

The author acknowledges, with thanks, permission to quote or adapt material from the following
sources:

Harvard Business Review: Gary Hamel and C. K. Prahalad, "Strategic Intent," May–June 1989,
pp. 70–71; Alfred D. Chandler, "The Enduring Logic of Industrial Success," March–April 1990,
pp. 130–140; C. K. Prahalad and Gary Hamel, "The Core Competence of the Corporation,"
May–June 1990, pp. 79–91; Joel Bleeke and David Ernst, "The Way to Win in Cross-Border Alliances," Nov.–Dec. 1991, pp. 127–135. Copyrights © 1989, 1990, 1990, 1991 by the President and
Fellows of Harvard College; all rights reserved.

Business-Government Relations in Australia, ed. Stephen Bell and John Wanna. Copyright © 1992
by Harcourt Brace and Company, Australia.

Technology and the Wealth of Nations, ed. Nathan Rosenberg, Ralph Landau, and David C. Mowery. Copyright © 1992 by the Board of Trustees of the Leland Stanford Junior University.

Hungary: An Economy in Transition, ed. Istvan P. Szekely and David M. G. Newbery, Copyright ©
1993 by Cambridge University Press.

To my wonderful wife, Nancy, and to my splendid daughters, sons-in-law, and grandchildren, who have brought so much joy into my life

Philip Kotler

To Thailand, my beloved country

Somkid Jatusripitak

To my parents, my wife, Pagagrong, and my daughter Erica

Suvit Maesincee

We also dedicate this book to all the economists, social scientists, and business theorists who are working diligently to understand and define how nations can improve the health and wealth of their citizens

Philip Kotler, Somkid Jatusripitak, and Suvit Maesincee

CONTENTS

PREFACE

The reader who opens this book will very likely question the reason for yet another study of economic development. How, exactly, does this study differ from others on the subject? And for whom specifically is it intended? The following paragraphs attempt to answer these questions.

Why another book on economic development? Literally thousands of books and articles have been written on the subject of economic development and ways to improve the wealth of nations. Various economic development textbooks offer a broad view of all the factors that might affect a nation's economic condition and progress or lack of progress. And there are many treatises and monographs that put forth well-reasoned arguments favoring one economic development prescription over another.

Many contemporary proposals for solutions to the problem of economic development derive from one or more classic views about the nature of economic society and prosperity. The most notable of these views are as follow.

Thomas Mun (1571–1641), one of the earliest economic writers on building national wealth, articulated the *mercantilist* view, contending that England must sell to other countries more than she bought from them. He advised the English government to reduce the people's consumption of foreign goods by raising their prices and putting up protectionist tariffs; to develop home industries to supply most necessities; and to encourage companies to sell as many English goods abroad as possible. These prescriptions were seen as the best way to build gold reserves in the nation. Mercantilists saw gold, not goods, as the measure of a nation's wealth.

François Quesnay (1694–1774) advanced the *physiocratic* view that wealth consists not in the quantity of accumulated gold in the nation but in the quantity of raw materials enjoyed by the nation; in particular, the surplus of agricultural and mineral products over their cost of production. Quesnay saw manufacturing and trade as relatively sterile activities, at best creating artificial wealth.

Adam Smith (1725–1790), in his famous treatise *An Inquiry into the Nature and the Causes of the Wealth of Nations,* advanced the view that nations best created value and wealth by using the principle of the division of labor, each worker becoming a specialist and therefore more productive at a single task. Under those circumstances, no one person could make everything he needed; he would gain goods through using the exchange value that he earned by working. Adam Smith saw exchange, private property, and free markets as the foundation for building national wealth.

Karl Marx (1818–1883), in *Das Kapital,* opposed this view and argued that free markets lead to recurrent business cycles and the steady impoverishment of the masses. He held that a nation's economy would perform better if private property was expropriated and managed by the state in the interests of the proletariat. Under the dictatorship of the proletariat, workers would be paid their true labor value, and the economy would be planned and managed to serve their interests.

John Maynard Keynes (1883–1946) saw flaws in both the free market and the planned economy. He advocated a positive role to be played by the government in reducing the severity of the business cycle through the adroit management of the money supply and fiscal policy.

Friedrich von Hayek (1899–1992), on the other hand, held that when government played an active role in owning or regulating business it would stultify economic growth, lead to ultimate domestic disaster, pave the way for totalitarianism, and lead the nation down *The Road to Serf-*

dom. His thesis has been much amplified by Milton Friedman (1912–), who is today's most articulate opponent of government ownership and/or regulation of the economy, seeing it as the source of great distortions and costs to the whole society.

These themes of the great economists concerning the proper way to build the wealth of a nation have been embroidered, refined, and debated in countless writings, speeches, and forums. Important contributions for understanding the economic development process have been made by such economists as J. Schumpeter, R. F. Harrod, E. D. Domar, S. Kuznets, C. Clark, W. Rostow, J. K. Galbraith, and others. Economic development agencies such as the World Bank and the International Monetary Fund have their own theories as well to guide their decisions on which countries and economic development projects to fund.

What is different about this book? This book does not present a unique prescription on how economies are supposed to build their wealth and national welfare. There is no single prescription that all countries should follow. We have witnessed spectacular economic growth in countries as dissimilar as Singapore, Hong Kong, Japan, and South Korea, just as in the last century, the path to strong growth took different forms in England, Germany, and the United States.

For this reason, what is needed instead is a systematic methodology that a particular nation can apply to assess its starting conditions, its major opportunities, its strengths and weaknesses, and the most promising available paths to achieving economic progress or economic revitalization. If the focus here was a business firm instead of a nation, we would call this methodology *strategic market management.* We wish to take the view that a nation can be thought of as running a business and, as such, can benefit from adopting a strategic market management approach. This is not to ignore the much greater cultural and political complexity of running a nation. Nor is this the same as saying that a nation should run itself as a planned economy, as did the countries in the Soviet bloc. Strategic market management is a continuous self-correcting process that consistently considers where the nation is heading, where it wants to be heading, and how best it can get there.

This book differs from other treatments of economic development in the following ways:

1. It applies the concepts, theories, and tools of strategic market management to guide a nation in its pursuit of economic wealth building.
2. It integrates the development of a nation's macro policies with the realities of the behavior of a nation's micro-units, such as consumers, producers, suppliers, and distributors. Too often, national policies fail to recognize the perceptions, preferences, and behavioral dynamics of actual actors in the marketplace who will respond to the national policies in often unexpected ways.
3. It covers more than strictly economic factors and forces as determinants of economic development. It recognizes the critical role played by a country's culture and politics and pleads for an alignment of economic policies with the nation's culture and politics.
4. It covers the economic growth problems facing highly industrialized nations as well as developing nations. That is, economic development is a challenge facing all nations.
5. It does not propose one most efficient path to development. Rather it presents the issues that every nation must consider in deciding on its own best path to development.

Who are the intended readers? The authors have addressed this book to the following primary audiences:

1. Government and political leaders who are involved in planning for a nation's prosperity.
2. The economic ministries and development officials within the government that are officially charged with developing and carrying out economic policies.
3. Economists and officials in the World Bank, the International Monetary Fund, the World Trade Organization, OECD, UNDP, and other international and regional economic organizations contributing consulting and/or funds in support of national projects and development.
4. Economists and economic development scholars who are interested in examining how strategic market management theory might be blended with economic development theory.
5. Strategic market management scholars and practitioners who might

want to further elaborate and apply their ideas to the level of the most complex of organizations, namely, the nation.

6. General lay readers who care about their nation's course of economic development and want a better understanding of the factors that affect national wealth and welfare.

Every book is a beginning, not an ending. Nothing conclusive can be written about a subject as broad and complex as a nation's economic development. We will regard this book as successful it if raises important questions in the minds of the readers and leads them to join in the common search for the answers.

We owe a great debt to all the economists and economic development experts who are cited throughout the book. We relied heavily on their wisdom and insights.

In addition, we are especially indebted to Professor Subbiah Kannappan of Michigan State University, a leading economic development scholar, who gave generously of his time to carefully review the manuscript and, in the course of doing so, to provide important perspectives and themes. Many improvements were due to his suggestions; at the same time, the authors take full responsibility for the final results.

Philip Kotler
Somkid Jatusripitak
Suvit Maesincee

Part I

UNDERSTANDING THE CHALLENGE OF NATIONAL ECONOMIC DEVELOPMENT

Chapter 1

Challenges to Building a Nation's Wealth

A s the earth and its 5.3 billion inhabitants spin toward the twenty-first century, many questions can be raised about the current state of mankind. Although there has been undeniable progress in our technological capabilities since Galileo and Newton, we can question whether our ability to govern ourselves intelligently has reached any higher plane than found in the Middle Ages. Two bloody world wars in the twentieth century, the ubiquitous presence of poverty amidst plenty, tribal conflicts between neighbors living side by side in Africa, Europe, and elsewhere . . . all suggest a deep flaw in the human condition and human governance.

When Adam Smith wrote his *Wealth of Nations* in 1776, he created a revolution in economic thought comparable to the American Revolution's impact on political thought. Smith outlined a system of economic arrangements and behavior—denominated today as "capitalism"—which promised to boost economic productivity substantially and to disperse its gains widely among the working population. Britain's flourishing in the nineteenth century, its Industrial Revolution, helped build a wealthy class and middle class, but left behind many millions of ill-paid, ill-fed workers. No wonder workers organized eventually into unions for self-protection against what seemed to be an uncaring entrepreneurial class and society.

Karl Marx's writings came at the perfect time, supplying a convincing logic and plan to transform the power of capital into serving the broader interests of mankind. The workers were held to be the creators of wealth and therefore the proper heirs to wealth, against their exploiting property owners. The proletariat, it was argued, had every right to overthrow the capitalists and landlords, take things into their own hands, and govern the society in the interests of all of its members, not just the privileged few.

But this philosophy, called "communism," had a dark side. By concentrating power into the hands of a few, by creating one political party representing the "dictatorship of the proletariat," people lost their political freedom. Officials of the Communist Party in countries such as the Soviet Union, North Korea, and East Germany, lived comfortable and privileged lives, while the economic level of most workers showed little or no improvement. In fact, not only did the workers lose political freedom, but they fell further and further behind their brethren in other countries in economic welfare. The gap between the average incomes and living conditions in Western Europe and Eastern Europe grew wider and wider.

Consider a more recent case, the difference in wealth that two contrasting economic systems produced in South and North Korea in 1994:[1]

- South Korea's gross domestic product per capita, $6,568; North Korea's $1,000.
- South Korea's economic growth, 8.8%; North Korea's, −5%.
- South Korea's exports, $81 billion; North Korea's exports, $1 billion.

Yet it would be an oversimplification to attribute differences in national economic performance to two polar systems for organizing national economies. So many other factors come into play: different natural resource endowments, levels of education, cultural attitudes toward work and wealth, government effectiveness and laws, and so on. Various countries—Singapore, Hong Kong, Malaysia, Taiwan, among them—in recent times have made huge gains in economic welfare while operating under quite different systems of economic and political organization. So we must look deeper into the conditions that help nations produce high economic growth. Adam Smith described only one strand in a complex combination of strands that must be woven together by a nation in its pursuit of economic progress.

Over the last fifty years, much good research has been done on the conditions that contribute to economic development. There are major theories propounded by Harrod, Domar, Rostow, Kuznets, Chenery, Lewis, Rosenstein-Rodan, Nurkse, Hirschman, Galbraith, and Drucker. There are major studies of the development history and strategies of specific countries, such as Japan, South Korea, Taiwan, Singapore, India, China, Chile, and Italy. There are deep studies of the role of specific factors such as achievement motivation, culture of productivity, government industrial policy, nation industrial structure, educational investment, and so on.

Then why another study? We believe that this one differs from previous studies in a number of ways:

1. This study takes on a strategic planning approach to the problem of building national wealth. A nation's leaders must develop a vision, missions, policies, and structures to guide the day-to-day efforts to grow the nation's economy. Just as companies apply strategic planning concepts and tools to guide their company's future course, national leaders must apply strategic planning concepts and tools to guide their nation's development. This study provides national planners with a step-by-step process to determine the economic pathway that will best achieve their economic development objectives.

2. This study provides operational management guidance to government and business leaders. There is typically a large gap between what government officials set as policies at the national level and the actual workings of the business system at the local level. National policies must be grounded in a deep understanding of the actual behavior of producers, distributors, and consumers in the marketplace. We think that some popular theories of economic development fail to connect with the realities of the local and global marketplace.

3. This study synthesizes economic, political, and cultural factors into a broad theory of economic development, rather than overrelying on any one set of forces that drive growth. Too often, economists don't work with social scientists although both may be studying economic development. Economists consider the social factors to be "untidy." But these factors all play a role in our framework. As a result, readers will gain a

broader picture of potential stimulants to economic progress and can better anticipate arguments and counterarguments favoring one course of economic development or another. The idea of a single unique development path for all countries has to be rejected.

4. This study examines the economic development problems of all nations, not only the so-called Third World nations. All nations face intense global competition, threatening to undo their established industries and create joblessness and lost wealth. Even within advanced industrial nations, such as the United States and the United Kingdom, large neighborhoods and regions resembling Third World conditions will be found.

This chapter examines the major challenges facing today's nations in building a viable economy. We will first describe the major problems facing nations, then look at the changing forces that are producing these problems as well as opportunities, and finally consider the objectives that most nations seek in pursuing economic development. In the next chapter, we will examine the major dilemmas and trade-offs faced by nations trying to improve their situation.

PROBLEMS PLAGUING NATIONS

No nation today is free from problems, even though the nature, depth, and range of issues vary widely. The former Eastern bloc countries are struggling with a historically unprecedented task, namely, converting from a centrally planned economy to a market economy. In the interim, some vocal groups within the former Soviet bloc countries yearn to restore the old centrally planned economy, even though it did little to improve their material living standards. They are forgetting the endless queues, the shoddy goods, the poor services that were endemic in these societies. Certainly Poland, Hungary, and the Czech Republic are making some headway, albeit with different formulas, while Romania, Bulgaria, and indeed the Russian republics are falling pathetically behind. What will happen to some of the countries in this part of the world is anyone's guess.

Many African nations are mired in problems, ranging from corruption, food shortages, low literacy and productivity to AIDS and other diseases and ethnic conflicts. Economists have proposed solutions for the less developed countries for fifty years now, and massive injections of aid from the World Bank and International Monetary Fund have streamed into Third World countries. Given the lack of development, either the economists' advice has been ignored, or what is worse, it has been accepted and implemented, but turned out to be inadequate, or even counterproductive.

Even the wealthier West has its share of problems. Western Europe's gross national product (GNP) has stagnated, joblessness is as high as 25 percent in countries such as Ireland and Spain, and capital seems to be fleeing to the greener pastures of the buoyant Far East. Nor are the prospects for job creation very promising as European companies turn to downsizing their workforces and reengineering their antiquated organizations. The United States, today's dominant world power, has by contrast a manageable unemployment and inflation rate, but suffers from urban blight, deteriorating infrastructure, and poverty amidst plenty. Some rural areas and inner-city areas resemble Third World zones in terms of the pitiably low income levels and living conditions.

The major bright spot in the global economy is the example of several nations in the Far East. First there was Japan, then the Five Tigers of Taiwan, South Korea, Hong Kong, Singapore, and Malaysia. Now Indonesia and China are picking up development steam, each reporting a double-digit annual growth in GNP. The economic spark has also been lit in India under its new government. Yet even these flourishing economies must carefully manage their growth and avoid inheriting problems that the West experienced—problems of unmanageable traffic congestion and air pollution, of urban slums, of workers unprotected by safety conditions and social benefits, and so on.

Here we will single out and examine four major problems plaguing many nations: low levels of living; the problem of population growth; a lack of jobs; and a deteriorating infrastructure.

Low Levels of Living

In too many nations, general levels of living for the vast majority of people are still very low. Figure 1.1 illustrates the per capita income gap between rich and poor nations, as of 1990. Switzerland had over 270 times the per capita income of Ethiopia, one of the world's poorest countries. Furthermore, the gap between rich and poor nations has been progressively widening.[2]

There is also a large and often widening gap between the rich and poor within individual nations. The income gap is generally greater in less developed nations than in industrial nations.[3]

> *If we compare the share of national income that accrues to the poorest 40% of the country's population with that of the richest 20%, we find that countries like Taiwan, Hong Kong, South Korea, Indonesia, Canada, Japan, and Sweden have relatively lesser inequalities; others like India, Malaysia, Tanzania, Chile, Costa Rica, and Libya have moderate inequality; and yet others like Brazil, Ecuador, Colombia, Jamaica, Mexico, Venezuela,*

FIGURE 1.1

Per Capita Gross National Product in Selected Countries, 1990 ($U.S. at official exchange rates)

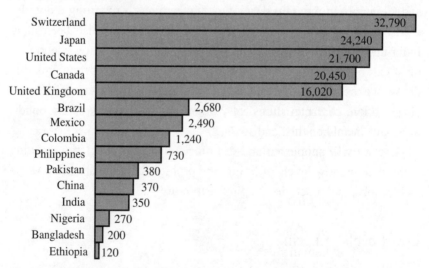

Source: World Bank, *World Development Report, 1992: Development and the Environment* (New York: Oxford University Press, 1992), Table 1.

> *Kenya, Sierra Leone, South Africa, and Guatemala have drastic income inequality in their overall income distribution.*[4]

Apart from struggling with poverty, many people in Third World nations fight a constant battle against malnutrition, disease, and poor health. In 1990, the average number of physicians per 100,000 people was only 4.8 in the least developed countries compared with 210 in the industrial countries.[5] Every year, about 17 million people die from infectious and parasitic diseases. Moreover, more than 80 percent of the 12–13 million HIV-infected people are in the Third World.[6]

The infant mortality rate is 99 per 1,000 births on average in the least developed countries, compared with about 74 in developing countries and only 11 in industrial countries. Average life expectancy is about 52 years in the least developed countries compared with 61 and 75 years among developing countries and industrial nations respectively.[7]

Malnutrition is another major problem in the Third World. About 800 million people in the Third World still do not get enough food. In terms of per capita daily protein consumption, it is 97 grams per day in the United States, compared with 63 and 43 grams per day in Brazil and Ghana respectively.[8]

As for the spread of educational opportunities, literacy levels remain relatively low in the Third World—literacy rates in the less developed and developing countries average only 45 percent and 64 percent of the population respectively, in contrast with 99 percent for the industrial nations.[9]

As Professor Todaro has argued, "most important is the interaction of all the above characteristics. They tend to reinforce and perpetuate the pervasive problems of 'poverty, ignorance, and disease' that restrict the lives of so many people in the Third World."[10]

The Population Growth Problem

About 4.1 billion of the world's 5.3 billion people live in the Third World, most of them in poverty. The world population in the year 2010 is estimated to be 7.2 billion people, of which almost 5.9 billion will be living in the Third World (see Figure 1.2).[11]

The explosive birth rate found in many Third World nations means that these nations have the burden of supporting millions of people younger than fifteen. At present, millions of children are working in farms, factories, street corners, and in garbage dumps in many large cities in Asia, Central America, and Latin America. Surely, enhancing educational opportunities is a way to make schooling a real alternative for these children.[12] However, the immediate challenge is, how will the nation build enough schools? And some years later, how will the nation provide enough jobs?

While the explosive population growth is the main problem facing Third World nations, many industrial nations confront the opposite problem of stagnant or even negative population growth as well as an aging population. The segment of the U.S. population with the highest growth rate is seventy-five years old and above. Japan's demographics makes it

FIGURE 1.2

World Growth Population, 1750–2100 (billion)

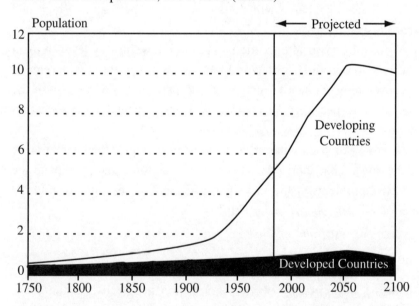

Source: Energy Technology Cooperation for Sustainable Economic Development (Lanham, MD: University Press of America, 1993); based on Petesch, *North-South Environmental Strategies, Costs, and Bargains,* 1992.

the nation with the world's oldest population.[13] Old people, like the very young, tend to consume resources and place higher demands on health and social services. Thus, for these "high elderly-dependent" countries, how will the working population generate enough surplus to support the retired population and the not-yet-of-age population?

For the past decade, the French have had 1.9 children per family, well under the 2.1 figure considered necessary to prevent a substantive reduction in current population. The French government has tried to stop the dramatic decline in the nation's population growth rate by encouraging families to have more than two children. If the decline in the growth rate is not halted, France will become underpopulated, underproductive, and top-heavy with senior citizens who will overtax the social security system.[14]

The Job Shortage Problem

Technology improves productivity but may reduce the number of jobs. The growth in GDP and unemployment in many countries indicates that employment has consistently lagged behind economic growth. This phenomenon, called "jobless growth" (see Figure 1.3) is witnessed in both industrial and developing countries

Between 1973 and 1987, employment in countries like France, Germany and the UK actually fell, even though they had fairly respectable GDP growth rates. Three-quarters of the rise in output in these countries came from increases in total productivity, with the rest from increased capital investment—without creating new jobs.

The developing countries have also experienced jobless growth. The labor force in developing countries will continue to increase by 2.3% a year in the 1990s, requiring an additional 260 million jobs. Women's participation in the labor force is likely to increase. And there will be a steady migration of people

FIGURE 1.3

Jobless Growth: GDP and Employment, 1975–2000

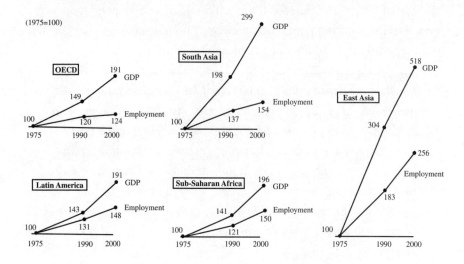

Source: UNDP, *Human Development Report 1993* (New York: Oxford University Press, 1993), Figure 3.2, p. 36.

> *to urban areas in search of work; the annual rate of net migration is likely to be about 4.6% by the year 2000. Taking into account the number of people unemployed or underemployed, the total requirement for the next decade is around one billion new jobs.*[15]

Even though almost all nations are coping with the job shortage problem, relative to those of industrial countries, levels of labor productivity remain extremely low in developing countries. This is mainly due to the lack of "complementary" factor inputs such as physical capital and human capital.[16]

The Infrastructure Problem

Adequate infrastructure, well employed, not only promotes economic growth but also enhances living standards. But throughout the developing nations, the physical infrastructure is poor.

In Bangladesh, the railway and road networks are not only inad-equate, but also in an unsatisfactory state of maintenance. In-land waterways, which are important means of transport, are insufficiently developed. Energy consumption is low at 43 kilo-grams of coal equivalent per head. Only about 8% of the villages have access to electricity.[17]

Third World economies are victims of a vicious cycle (see Figure 1.4). A severe fiscal crisis plagues governments bedeviled by chronic and huge budget deficits. These deficits partly came from bankruptcy of state-owned enterprises, ill-considered increases in social spending, and over-growth of the public sector. To sustain the deficits, these governments incurred heavy debt burdens. This forced them to cut back sharply on in-vestment in both physical and social infrastructure.[18] The poor infrastruc-ture leads to low investment formation. This in turn leads to low wages and low employment rates, which lead to low consumption and poor mo-tivation. These last two result in low productivity.

Poor productivity, in turn, means poor profits which, on the one hand, will discourage potential investors from investing more, and on the other

FIGURE 1.4

The Vicious Circle of Poverty and Backwardness

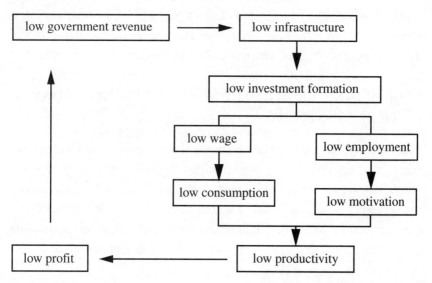

hand, affect the revenue received by the government. Diminished government revenues means that only a slim budget can be assigned to build up the nation's infrastructure. This catastrophic cycle will continue unless an effective wealth-building strategy is applied to rescue the economy as a whole.

High growth also leads to infrastructure problems. In high-growth developing nations, congestion has become an increasingly punishing tax on business and leisure.

In Bangkok, the high rate of "unmanaged" growth threatens to throttle further growth. Because the supply of infrastructure has failed to keep pace with the demands placed upon it, the capacity of this city has come under increasing strain.[19]

Industrial countries also face an infrastructure problem, namely, the deterioration of their physical infrastructure. As travel time increases, infrastructure has become a hot political topic.

In America, the Clinton Administration promises to spend $80 billion on renovating the country's roads, creating a new high-speed rail network linking America's major cities and developing new technologies to expand the capacity of the existing infrastructure.[20]

The 1980s marked a period of diminishing public investment in infrastructure. At the end of the 1990s, however, infrastructure development will be one of the biggest challenges facing almost all governments.

MAJOR FORCES AND TRENDS AFFECTING TODAY'S NATION-STATES

The four problems described above are the result of more fundamental forces that are producing discontinuities in global affairs. At least six forces can be identified: (1) global interdependence; (2) protectionism and growing economic blocs; (3) transnationalization of multinational corporations (MNCs); (4) rapid technological advances; (5) conflicting politics and tribalism; and (6) growth of environmental concerns.

Global Interdependence

Since World War II, the international economic system has evolved into a truly *global* economy—an interdependent system of trade, investment, and development that connects nearly all regions of the world. The rules of the game are typically established and altered by both bilateral and multilateral negotiations and agreements among companies, industries, nations, and regions.[21]

In the new context, national and regional economies remain vitally interconnected but no one player can impose its will on the rest of the world. Multiplicities of opportunities and threats are derived from cooperation and collaboration on the one hand and competition and conflict on the other.[22] Global interdependence thus increasingly results in ad hoc alliances.

The EC, for example, is presently suffering from a huge trade deficit with Japan and complains about Japanese market barriers. However, it is cooperating with the U.S. in trying to link international trade rules with issues such as social and labor rights.[23]

Under global interdependence, the worse choice that a country can make is *autarchy* (self-sufficiency). Brazil and India lag behind in many key technologies (e.g., computers) because they opted for many years to do it themselves. No country can make everything it needs; it must import the things that are better or cheaper from elsewhere. And it needs to pay for these imports with goods that it can export as a result of making these items better or cheaper.[24]

Protectionism and Growing Economic Blocs

At the same time that tariffs are being reduced as part of the Tokyo Round of trade negotiations, the number of nontariff barriers has grown rapidly since the mid-1970s and has now become more important than tariffs as an impediment to international trade. There are various forms of nontariff barriers, ranging from import licensing requirements that may be applied in a discriminatory fashion, to import quotas, to a variety of surveillance practices, quarantines, and arbitrary requirements and standards, to outright prohibitions against the exports of a particular nation. Ironically, tariffs are preferred to nontariff barriers in that they simply tax imports rather than artificially limit them.[25]

Economic blocs also represent a form of protectionism. While liberalization in the General Agreement on Tariffs and Trade (GATT) is generally applied on a most-favored-nation (MFN) basis, economic blocs explicitly discriminate against the rest of the world by providing trade preferential arrangements only to the member states. However, Article XXIV of the GATT allows for the establishment of economic blocs, with certain specified provisos.[26]

Presently, there are more than one hundred regional blocs in existence. The establishment of an economic bloc may either *create* trade or *divert* trade. The trade liberalization within a region reduces transaction costs and trade-related barriers, thus fostering intra- and inter-industry specialization. The resulting economies of scale further encourage industrial efficiency and economic growth. Increased intraregional trade can be derived from both new trade creation and third-country import substitution (that is, trade diverted by the bloc preferences). The trade diversion occurs when the latter effect is greater than the former, making the world economic welfare as a whole worse off.[27]

Given global interdependence, protectionism, and growing economic blocs, one crucial issue will be the bilateral, regional, and multilateral management of international trade so that each is congruent with the others.

Transnationalization of MNCs

The globalization of industry and trade is a new reality for economic development. The emergence of global industries—automobiles, electronics, pharmaceuticals, chemicals, and petroleum and petrochemicals—creates new networks of international division of labor. Both industrial and developing economies are involved, and increasingly integrated with each other.[28]

MNCs have evolved from loose international organizations to highly programmed, globe-spanning supercompanies, many of which have larger turnover than the GNPs of most countries. Some have political influence in their countries and can influence a nation's economic policy and industrial development and job creation.[29]

As John Stopford and Susan Strange put it: "While nation-states retain power to disrupt, manage or distort trade by controlling entry to the 'national' market, they cannot so easily control production which is aimed at a 'world' market and which does not necessarily take place within their countries."[30] As a result, the role of the nation-state in international economic activities is changed substantially from direct influence to bargaining and negotiating only. In addition, the costs that nations face in protecting their territory can be as high as, if not higher than, those of trade protection.[31]

When the Brazilian government introduced its Informatics Laws to prevent the international computer enterprises from producing in Brazil, it imposed a very high cost on those local enterprises needing to use the latest and best computers in order to keep up with their competitors.[32]

Rapid Technological Advances

At present, the world is evolving from an industrial era to an information era. During the first period of the industrial era, the focus shifted from agriculture to industry. This was the turning point where capital-intensive industries received more emphasis than the unskilled labor-intensive industries that had formerly predominated. In the information era, the emphasis shifted from capital-intensive industries to knowledge-intensive ones. The critical area of competition will be in developing the technology to create high value-added products and high-wage jobs. The stiff competition will take place in eight industrial domains: microelectronics, biotechnology, advanced materials, telecommunications, civil aviation, robotics, machine tools, and computer software. Table 1.1 shows thirty emerging technologies and their sectorial impacts.

Technology improves productivity, resulting in a decrease of the labor cost as a proportion of total cost in many industries (e.g., fabricating, information technology industries). At the same time, technology and

TABLE 1.1

Thirty Emerging Technologies and Their Sectorial Impacts

Technology	Sector of Impact
Genetic engineering	Agriculture, Manufacturing (pharmaceuticals), Services (health) Forestry, Mining
Enhanced chips/ gallium arsenide	Manufacturing (electronic & scientific equipment), Communication, Defense
Artificial intelligence	Services, Manufacturing
Cell/tissue culture	Services (health), Manufacturing (pharmaceuticals, food), Agriculture, Forestry
Microcomputers	Services, Manufacturing, Defense
CAD/CAM/CAP/CAE	Manufacturing, Services, Communications
Robotics	Manufacturing, Mining
Composite materials	Manufacturing (automobile, aircraft)
Remote sensing	Forestry, Agriculture, Mining, Services, Defense
Imaging	Manufacturing (electronics) Services, Mining, Communications
Fiber optics	Communications, Manufacturing (electronics)
Monoclonal antibodies	Agriculture, Manufacturing (pharmaceutical), Services (health)
Computer software	Manufacturing, Services, Communications, Defense
Advanced polymers	Manufacturing
Lasers	Manufacturing (electronics, transportation, medical instruments), Services, Communications
Synthetic fuels	Manufacturing (refining), Energy, Services (transportation)
Coal technologies	Mining, Manufacturing
Food irradiation	Manufacturing (food, chemicals), Agriculture
Telecommunication	Communication, Services, Construction

Surface chemistry/ plasma technologies	Manufacturing, Energy, Agriculture, Services
Biomass	Manufacturing (chemicals), Agriculture, Energy, Forestry
Hydrogen energy technologies	Manufacturing, Utilities, Energy
Separation and membrane technologies	Manufacturing (food, chemical)
Fermentation	Manufacturing (food), Agriculture
Structural ceramics	Manufacturing (metal, transportation)
Optoelectronic/ storage systems	Communications, Manufacturing (electronics)
Construction technologies	Construction, Mining
Speech recognition	Manufacturing, Services
Photovoltaics	Manufacturing (electronics), Communications
New alloys	Mining, Manufacturing (transportation)

Source: From Hamid Noori, *Managing the Dynamics of New Technology: Issues in Manufacturing Management* (New York: Prentice-Hall, 1990), Exhibit 2.1, p. 20.

modern design allow firms to save on materials. These are the major threats for many developing countries that have based their export strategy on cheap labor and/or material costs. In addition, many MNCs have recently shifted back their labor-intensive operations from developing countries to industrial countries.[33]

These state-of-the-art technologies, however, contribute to Third World development as well. As Sam Pitroda argued, high technology is *already* an essential element in many development activities such as water sourcing, sanitation, agriculture, and construction. If a community needed, say, widespread immunizations or replacement of a power grid, a telephone seems to be an indispensable tool in getting the job done. It is critical if the job were tied to a natural disaster such as flood or drought. In addition, information technology not only reduces cultural barriers and alleviates economic inequalities but also compensates for intellectual disparities. However, human factors will be of increasing concern because of the inability of many people in the workforce to cope with these new technologies.[34]

Conflicting Politics and Tribalism

The end of the Cold War has brought to the forefront internal conflicts within nations whose roots are economic and ethnic.[35] Here it is important to distinguish between a plural society and a multinational state in which culturally, and often linguistically, distinct groups of people are concentrated in different regions of the country (e.g., Canada, India, Yugoslavia, Rwanda, Nigeria, Ethiopia, and Eritrea). The enduring tensions underlie political processes and rivalries, and when not contained, erupt into open "ethnic" conflicts. Between 1989 and 1992, eighty-two conflicts erupted, of which seventy-nine were internal conflicts equivalent to civil wars. Such countries as Somalia, Iraq, Afghanistan, and Cambodia appear in danger of further turmoil. Currently disintegration is most evident in Sri Lanka and the former Yugoslavia.[36]

> *When Yugoslavia broke up in 1991–1992, several other republics declared their independence as separate states. Two of these, Croatia and Bosnia, had sizable minority populations of ethnic Serbs. Serbia seized effective control (through local Serbian militias) of significant areas of Croatia and Bosnia that contained Serbian communities or linked such populations geographically. Non-Serbian populations in these areas were driven out or massacred—"ethnic cleansing."*[37]

Secessionist movements and claims of regional self-determination tend to erupt more frequently in a multinational state than in a plural society. In a plural society, by contrast, many cultural and ethnic groups live side by side throughout most or all of the country (as in the United States). Yet certain groups may confront persistent discrimination and antagonism. The interrelations among groups become very tense when there are large economic and social disparities, and may spill over into the broader political arena.[38]

> *In many East African countries, there is a substantial number of Asian, particularly Indian inhabitants, many of whom are employed in economic activities and tend to be comparatively affluent. Like the Chinese in Indonesia or the Jews in Europe, they are highly urbanized and relatively well educated. Their different*

culture and physical appearance, together with their relative prosperity, have bred xenophobia and jealousy among the African majority. In 1973, some 30,000 Asians were expelled from Uganda, causing a detrimental brain drain from which Uganda has not yet recuperated. More recently, many Asians in Kenya became victims of hostile xenophobic feelings.[39]

In contrast, "tribal societies"—fundamentally multinational states—in which one particular tribe has more political and economic power than the others, are inevitably faced with geopolitically rooted tensions and instability. A recent example of such instability is provided by Rwanda, in which the Hutu majority are discriminated against by the Tutsi minority.

In sum, too much ethnic polarization is likely to foster conflict, political unrest, and possible political fragmentation, all of which are major impediments in creating national wealth.[40]

Growth of Environmental Concerns

Ecological degradation is one of the most critical issues determining the future of humanity. Fortunately, there is growing awareness of the earth's fragility and vulnerability to many kinds of pollution, loss of irreplaceable resources, and other catastrophes. However, it is the rich countries that are more concerned with the adverse effects of further growth on the environment, and that pass more environmental protection laws than the poor countries. The poor countries, on the other hand, try desperately to raise living standards, with little regard for pollution and other adverse effects of growth.[41]

At present, environmental issues have surfaced in trade discussions. The rich countries, for example, complain about being at a disadvantage compared to the cheaper costs of producing in the poorer countries where environmental laws are still relaxed or do not exist. Yet poorer nations would see environmental laws and enforcement as threatening to retard their economic development efforts.

THE OBJECTIVES OF NATIONS

The traditional quest of policymakers is to increase the amount of goods and services their nations produce. This type of thinking, however, could mean that many policymakers ignore factors that are critical to the long-term health of their nations' economies.

Four factors should be included in evaluating a nation's wealth:

1. *Natural Capital*—the value of land, water, minerals, timber, and other natural resources.
2. *Physical Capital*—the value of machinery, buildings, and public works.
3. *Human Capital*—the productive value of people.
4. *Social Capital*—the value of families, communities, and various organizations that glue a society together.

A nation that ignores or fails adequately to upgrade and invest in any of these areas confronts the risk of weakening the long-term health of its economy in favor of short-term gains. The World Bank has recently recalculated wealth to include a nation's natural capital, physical capital, human capital, and social capital. The rankings of the wealth of nations have changed, as shown in Figure 1.5[42]

In the face of the formidable problems facing nations, and the complex underlying forces, nations have to clarify what they can realistically hope to accomplish. A nation's wealth creation, to a great extent, should be both a physical reality and a state of mind in which society has the drives and means to pursue a better life.[43] People of all nations aspire to a good economy, a good society, and a good political process.

A Good Economy

The main objective here is to raise the level of GNP per capita by stimulating economic growth so that poverty is reduced and material standards of living are improved. A pattern of broad-based economic growth should focus on uplifting the growth of income levels of "target" poverty groups that are the vast majority segments of populations.[44]

Coupled with pursuing economic growth, nations should seek to improve their international competitiveness. For many poor countries, this involves strengthening their access to global markets, the flows of capital, and technology transfer.

Internally, nations desire a high level of employment and stable price levels. They also want a high quality of products and services to be available and distributed across all population classes.

FIGURE 1.5

Ranking Wealth of the World

Per capita income has been the traditional measure of nations' wealth. But the World Bank has recalculated wealth to include a nation's natural resources; machinery, buildings, highways and other "produced assets"; human resources; and so-called social capital—the value added by families and communities. The bank's formula changes the rankings:

Top 15 ranked by per capita income (and rank by new measure):	Top 15 ranked by World Bank's "estimated wealth" per capita formula (and rank by per capita income measure)
1. Luxembourg (3) $36,650	1. Australia (23) $835,000
2. Switzerland (4) $36,330	2. Canada (17) $704,000
3. Japan (5) $29,770	3. Luxembourg (1) $658,000
4. Sweden (6) $27,600	4. Switzerland (2) $642,000
5. Denmark (10) $26,470	5. Japan (3) $583,000
6. Norway (11) $25,510	6. Sweden (4) $491,000
7. Iceland (7) $24,550	7. Iceland (7) $486,000
8. Austria (16) $23,330	8. Qatar (20) $472,000
9. United States (12) $23,280	9. United Arab Emirates
10. France (13) $22,800	(12) $468,000
11. Germany (15) $22,240	10. Denmark (5) $461,000
12. United Arab	11. Norway (8) $423,000
Emirates (9) $22,180	12. United States (9) $420,000
13. Belgium (18) $21,680	13. France (10) $413,000
14. Netherlands (19) $21,050	14. Kuwait (19) $404,000
15. Italy (20) $20,800	15. Germany (11) $397,000

Source: World Bank, 1995.

Without sustained and continuous economic progress at the individual and societal level, human potential will not be realized. One clearly has to "have enough in order to be more." Rising per capita incomes, the elimination of absolute poverty, greater education and employment opportunities, and lessening income inequalities therefore constitute the "necessary," albeit not sufficient, goals for development.

A Good Society

One of the misleading practices in national accounting is to measure a nation's wealth and well-being in terms of its GNP performance. This takes too narrow a view. One's life is affected not only by one's income but by one's longevity, safety, environment, health, freedom from crime, drugs, violence, and family breakdown.

Somehow a country's well-being must include measures of its social health. In this regard, the U.S. has serious social problems:

- *In 1990 there was one violent crime every 17 seconds, and a crime against property every two seconds. Most Americans can expect to face theft three or more times in their lives.*
- *In 1960 nine in every thousand marriages ended in divorce, and only 5% of children were born to unmarried women. By the 1990s, this had risen to 21 divorces in a thousand, and some 27% of children were born to unmarried women.*
- *Drug abuse places a large burden on society. While the actual costs are unknown, they have been estimated at some $60 billion, half of which represents lost productivity by drug users; a third, the costs of drug-related crime; and the remainder, expenditure on welfare and health care services.*[45]

Thus, apart from its quantity, the *quality* of high GNP growth is a concern. There are two objectives: (1) for individuals, the objectives are to raise the level of living, including good health, better education, more job opportunities, and greater attention to cultural and humanistic values; (2) for society as a whole, the objectives are social cohesion, justice, good environment, security, and peace.

A Good Political Process

People everywhere want good government. At a minimum, this means that citizens must be able to influence the conduct and operations of government. They must be able to vote people into positions of power and vote them out as well. Democracy is a powerful force for instilling good government.

Over the last two centuries, democracy has become more and more widespread as a form of government. . . . Many nations do not yet have democratic governments (the most important of these is China). And existing democracies are imperfect in various ways—from political apathy in the United States and corruption in Japan to autocratic traditions in Russia. Nonetheless, the trend is toward democratization in most of the world's regions.[46]

Apart from democratization, another political imperative is to expand the range of economic and social choices available to individuals. Wealth can enable a person to gain greater control over nature and one's physical environment. It also gives the person the freedom to choose greater leisure, to have more goods and services, and even to have less if he or she so wishes.

However, the relationship between democracy and economic performance is by no means clear-cut. China is the fastest-growing country, but clearly not a democracy. Singapore, a capitalist economy, is a complex case:

Singapore's government has consistently denied its citizens some rather fundamental civil liberties, such as a free press and the right to a speedy trial. The circulations of the Asian Wall Street Journal *and the* Far Eastern Economic Review *were cut severely after disputes with the government over coverage of various political developments in Singapore. In Singapore, citizens cannot own satellite dishes, since they are not supposed to receive unauthorized broadcasts. They cannot bring in unapproved magazines from abroad. The government has repeatedly justified these restrictions on the grounds of maintaining harmony and preventing social breakdown.*

One government opponent, Chia Thye Poh, was jailed for 23 years under the country's draconian Internal Security Act without ever being tried or formally charged. The government targeted other opposition politicians for criminal or tax investigations. The New York Times Magazine *ran a 1988 cover story titled "City of Fear," referring not to Beirut or Bucharest but to Singapore.*[47]

Keen social observers such as Dahrendorf, Barro, Galbraith, Friedman, and Drucker make a strong argument for the interrelationship between freedom and development. A recent United Nations Development

Programme (UNDP) study revealed a high correlation between human freedom and human development—countries that rank high on the freedom index also rank high on the developmental scale. Potential freedom unleashes the creative energies of people, resulting in higher levels of income and progress.[48]

Although a good economy, good society, and good political process are all desirable, they are difficult to achieve. In fact, they are in a trade-off relationship with each other in many cases. Some of the major trade-offs are:

- More freedom means less social cohesion and less security.
- A healthy environment may require a slower income growth.
- Technology transfer means high dependence in international relations.
- High income growth and equal income distribution are difficult to reconcile; the goals of human capital growth may conflict with the goals of saving and capital formation.
- An overvalued exchange rate, meant to keep import prices low to help consumers, may ultimately lead to a currency crisis.
- International competitiveness of our nation is often built at the expense of other nations, leading them to retaliate.
- High employment and stable prices do not always go together.

THESIS OF THIS BOOK AND A ROAD MAP

Economic development is not a problem that belongs only to economists to model; social, cultural, and political factors must also be taken into account in arriving at a full picture of a nation's opportunity potentials. This book holds that the key to economic development is to build the nation's vision and macro-policies on a firm understanding of how organizations and individuals initiate behavior and respond to stimuli. The assumption that businesses are pure profit maximizers and consumers are pure utility maximizers can carry the analysis only so far. Indeed, these assumptions can distort the analysis by precluding major cultural and political differences that shape how firms and citizens respond to economic development initiatives.[49]

We see a positive role for government to play in setting favorable macro-policies and in establishing micro-support programs that help businesses realize their full potential in creating wealth. A nation's government, in partnership with business and various social groups, must achieve a national wealth-building strategy and consensus if it hopes to succeed in the highly competitive global marketplace.

How Nations Can Create Wealth

One way to think about a nation's wealth potential (in terms of GNP) is to focus on the distribution of GNP expenditures on goods and services by different sectors—household, business, government, and foreign. The consumption of goods and services by individuals and households is termed *personal consumption expenditure*. The second major category of a nation's wealth is *gross private domestic investment*—the purchase of goods and services by the business sector. The fixed part of these investments comprises the purchases of new capital goods, such as factories, machinery, and equipment. The third category is *government spending*, comprising government consumption expenditures and public investment.

Some of the goods and services produced in an economy are *exported* to foreign users. Foreign-produced goods and services are also *imported* into the economy. The foreign sector therefore records in GNP as the trade balance: the spending by foreigners on domestic product (exports) less the domestic spending on foreign product (imports).

The other component of the foreign sector records in GNP as *net factor income from abroad*. This component includes the net return on investment, the net interest income, and net labor income from abroad. Figure 1.6 provides a picture of these wealth categories and expenditure flows.[50]

We can also view a nation's wealth in terms of *inputs, throughputs*, and *outputs*. The input component comprises factors of production (both capital and labor). Such factors of production can be inflowing from abroad (by means of inward investment), recycling within the economy (by means of local reinvestment), or outflowing from the economy (by means of outward investment).

These factors of production are then used as inputs for domestic production. One of the key production tasks is to maximize the output/input ratio (productivity). The outputs of this production serve domestic consumption and exports. However, when domestic demand exceeds domestic production, this gap is usually filled by imports.

FIGURE 1.6

Nation's Wealth Components and Expenditure Flows

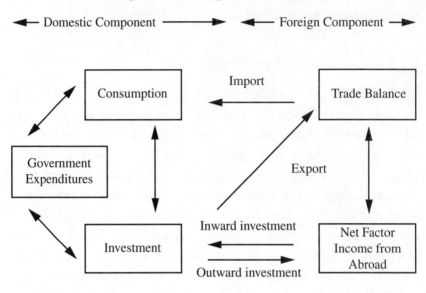

The Role of the Public Sector in the Nation's Wealth-Building Strategy

Government has substantial effects on everyday business and personal choices through such measures as the provision of physical and social infrastructure, fiscal and monetary policy, investment policy, industry policy, trade policy, and so forth. Government policies encourage or discourage growth and employment prospects through the effects such policies have on people's choices to save, invest, work, and use their leisure.

The objective should be to ensure that incentives created by government policies maximize economic development. Public policies related to the nation's economic process are illustrated in Figure 1.7.

To elaborate, the nation's investment policies strengthen the input component of its economic process, particularly inward investment and local investment. The nation's industry policies enhance the nation's industrial competitiveness in the global marketplace. The nation's industrial portfolio is developed to serve both domestic and export markets, and to reduce imports. Thus, trade policies take on a major role here.

The three primary public policies cannot work efficiently unless they

FIGURE 1.7

Government's Primary Policies Toward the Nation's
Wealth-Building Strategy

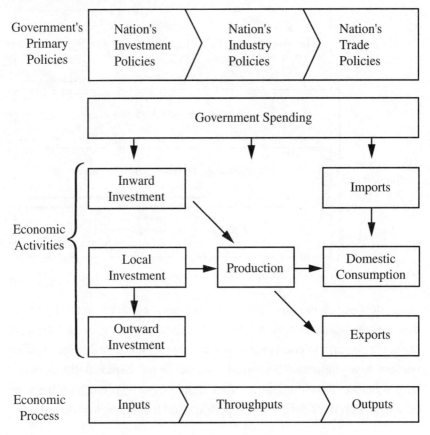

are pursued in a supportive environment, with an adequate infrastructure, an appropriate institutional framework, and a stable macroeconomic groundwork. Thus, to assist in creating the nation's wealth, government activities should be composed of both primary and support policies, as shown in Figure 1.8.

The Role of the Private Sector in the Nation's Wealth-Building Strategy

The private sector plays a major role in developing a nation's wealth. The government's and companies' policies should be compatible (see Figure 1.9).

FIGURE 1.8

Government's Primary and Support Policies Toward the Nation's Wealth-Building Strategy

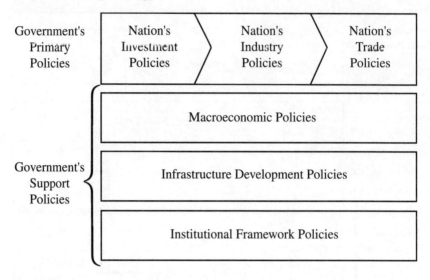

To elaborate, companies should pursue business development policies that are consistent with the nation's investment and industry policies. By the same token, the company's product development policies should be consistent with the nation's industry and trade policies. Finally, the company's market development policies should be congruent with both the company's product development policies and the nation's trade policies.

FIGURE 1.9

Government-Business Relationship in Building the Nation's Wealth

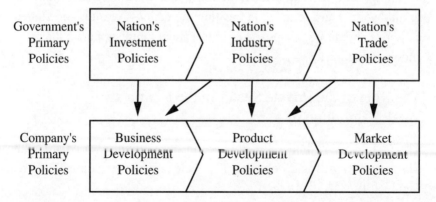

These company-level primary policies require a set of support policies, including financial policies, business infrastructure policies, and liaison and legal-related policies. The company's financial policies (e.g.,
sources and uses of fund) should be consistent with the nation's macroeconomic policies (e.g., inflation, interest, and foreign exchange rates).
Likewise, the width and depth of the company's infrastructure (human
resources, technical know-how, related and supporting industries) are determined by the nation's infrastructure development policies (education,
university-industry R&D cooperation, small and medium business development). Finally, the nation's institutional framework (e.g., government
regulation, deregulation, and re-regulation) inevitably affects the company's liaison and legal-related activities (e.g., mergers and acquisitions,
employee benefits).

In summary, both public and private sectors require coordination to
create the nation's wealth.

This book comprises four parts. Part I deals with *understanding the
challenge of national economic development.* In Chapter 2, we illustrate
the major dilemmas and trade-offs in public policy toward economic development. Chapter 3 examines eight basic pathways of development,
conceptualized from different groups of countries. There is no one best
pathway of development. By assessing the advantages and difficulties of
each pathway, policymakers can choose the pathway that makes the most
sense.

Part II deals with *formulating the nation's strategic thrust.* The notions
of strategic groups of nations and of strengths, weaknesses, opportunities, and threats (SWOT) analysis are applied at the national level. In
Chapter 4, we classify different groups of nations by their economic status. Each strategic group of nations has its own competitive conditions
and opportunities in the world economy. Assessing the nation's strengths
and weaknesses takes place in Chapter 5, followed by assessing the nation's opportunities and threats in Chapter 6. Three assessments—the
competitive and cooperative patterns, the nation's strengths and weaknesses, and the nation's opportunities and threats—are the foundations
upon which to form the national strategic thrust, which is discussed in
Chapter 7.

Part III deals with *developing the nation's strategic posture.* Given the
nation's strategic thrust, a set of government primary and support poli-

cies must be developed. Chapter 8 examines the government's primary policies, beginning with investment policies. Then the development of the nation's industrial clusters, industrial portfolio, and trade policies are discussed in chapters 9, 10, and 11, respectively. Following these primary policies, government support policies are discussed, beginning with macroeconomic policies in Chapter 12, then infrastructure development policies in Chapter 13, and institutional framework in Chapter 14. All these support policies are critical because they can either impede or facilitate the creation of wealth.

In Part IV, the focus shifts *from the government to the business enterprises*. Chapter 15 discusses coordinating a company's business policies with the nation's public policies. The ways to nourish a company's growth under these circumstances are discussed in Chapter 16, and strategic alliances and their implications are dealt with in Chapter 17.

However, the nation's plan for creating wealth cannot be achieved unless it is effectively implemented. Thus, the final chapter deals with issues in the strategic implementation of the nation's wealth creation strategies. The main focus is on how policymakers can coherently integrate the nation's strategic vision with its strategic postures, and how the government can work with companies to help them achieve their wealth-building strategies.

Chapter 2

Major Dilemmas and Trade-Offs in Public Policy Toward Economic Development

One would think that economic development policymakers could follow a simple logic to arrive at a set of feasible strategies. Starting from the recognition of constraints and opportunities, they would proceed to define a broad set of national wealth-building strategies.

Unfortunately, along the way they would confront major dilemmas and trade-offs at every juncture. In this chapter we examine and illustrate the eight major issues facing economic development policymakers:

1. Growth versus income distribution orientation
2. Sectoral balance versus sectoral imbalance
3. Shock therapy versus gradualism
4. High employment versus high inflation
5. State ownership versus private ownership
6. Large private companies versus small entrepreneurs
7. Interventionism versus free markets
8. Inward investment facilitation versus bootstrapping

GROWTH VERSUS INCOME DISTRIBUTION

Since the 1970s, there has been a significant change in perception regarding the ultimate goals of economic development. In the industrial countries, the focus has shifted from the relentless pursuit of growth toward more concern for the many unintended consequences for the environment: the greenhouse effect; the disposal of nuclear waste; the deteriorating ozone layer; the erosion of the earth's surface with deforestation; and so forth.[1]

In the poor countries, by contrast, a main concern focused on the trade-off between growth and income distribution. That development requires some concentration of capital is obvious. The basic issue, however, is how eventually to spread the fruits of rapid economic growth to the vast majority of people.[2] In Brazil, income disparities between the rich and the poor rank about the worst in the world. This simply reflects the inability of Brazilian society to reach national consensus on the direction of the nation's wealth creation. In other developing countries, the gap between the rich and the poor is widening. In Indonesia, the poorest 20 percent of the people receive only 8.8 percent of national income; in Sri Lanka,[3] only 4.8 percent. Rapid economic growth does not always reduce the scale of widespread absolute poverty.[4]

The former great appeal of Marxian economics for developing countries lay in its seeming solution to the income distribution dilemma. By the state taking over the means of production and redistributing incomes "From each according to his ability, to each according to his needs," Marx offered the hope of reconciling high economic growth and equitable income distribution. In practice, however, Marxian economics led to low economic growth and lower living standards for all except the privileged.

Arguments Relating Income Distribution and Growth

There are two schools of thought on the relationship between growth and income distribution. One school suggests that unequal distributions are inevitable at early stages of development and in fact facilitate rapid economic growth. The rationale is that high personal and corporate incomes are necessary conditions of saving, which support investment and economic growth. When national and per capita incomes reach a certain level, redistributions of income should then be achieved through tax and subsidy mechanisms, as well as expenditures favoring the poor.[5]

The other school of thought argues that low levels of living for the poor would lower their health, energy, incentives, and economic productivity, and thus lead to a slower-growing economy.[6] Also, the demand for locally produced necessity goods will increase as the income level of the poor increases. Rising demands for local goods, in turn, induce local investment, production, and employment. Citizens then feel more involved in the development process, allowing them to realize their full potential and make their best contribution to society.[7]

Professor Michael Todaro adds another reason to support this argument.[8] He argues that, unlike the rich in the now developed countries, the rich in presently developing countries have a low propensity to save or invest in their local economy. They spend a significant portion of their incomes instead on luxury goods or seek "safe havens" abroad in the form of capital flight. Such "savings" and "investments" do not contribute to the nation's wealth creation.[9]

In fact, some economic policies play a critical role in determining income inequality. For example, the promotion of labor-intensive industries helps spread the benefits of growth more equitably, while price support policies and the promotion of large-scale firms tend to negatively affect the distribution of income. In addition, price stability appears to be positively associated with improvement in income distribution.[10]

SECTORAL BALANCE VERSUS SECTORAL IMBALANCE: INDUSTRY VERSUS AGRICULTURE

In a balanced growth strategy, agriculture and industry are balanced by relying on the income elasticities of demand for each sector's output.[11] By contrast, unbalanced growth strategy focuses on the strength of forward and backward linkages as a guide to investment priorities. In practice, many planners have concentrated resources on industrial sectors while ignoring the agricultural and other industrial sectors.

Arguments for Sectoral Balanced Growth

Agriculture plays an important role in economic development. Countries lacking agricultural reform risk serious bottlenecks to development.[12]

Britain in the eighteenth century, and China and Japan in recent times, provide clear examples of balanced growth, with agriculture as a leading sector.

In Great Britain of the 1740s, an increase in farm productivity based on scientific farming, better crops, rotations, and so forth helped foster the Industrial Revolution. During the nineteenth century, there was a shortage of labor as industry grew rapidly, and this spurred a further improvement in Britain's agricultural efficiency, namely, "high farming"— deep plowing, draining heavy fields, and some irrigation. But the most critical factor was the repeal of the Corn Laws, in which imports of grain were prohibited unless its price had increased to a certain level. Britain then relied on free trade: industrial goods were exported, food was imported, and sectors were balanced by trade.[13]

In China after Mao's death, the strategy of "walking on two legs" was abandoned, and agricultural and rural growth was encouraged. Between 1979 and 1984, the liberalized economy encouraged reforms in the rural areas and growth of agriculture and rural industry. Labor-intensive industry in rural areas absorbed labor and avoided open unemployment, especially during the agricultural slack season (by 1991, these rural industries were the most rapidly expanding segment of the industrial sector—producing 31 percent of industrial output value and more than 22 percent employment of the labor force).[14] The workers switched between working the land and manufacturing. This took advantage of labor as an abundant factor, raised output, and redistributed income (see China model in Chapter 3).[15]

In the case of Japan, its farmers were heavily taxed. The heavy taxes forced Japanese farmers to become more productive. Japan also imported some rice to stabilize its food markets, and took measures to protect its inefficient farmers.[16]

Arguments for Sectoral Unbalanced Growth

In contrast, the Soviet Union historically pursued a policy of unbalanced growth, as evidenced by the periodic campaigns to discredit the wealthy peasants, collectivize farming, extend grain production to new land, and so forth. By using an unbalanced strategy, particular bottlenecks in certain key sectors were reduced or eliminated. Scarce capital and managerial talent were concentrated in these key sectors. This gave the USSR its peculiar nature of planning by "campaigning." The first three Five-Year Plans emphasized heavy industry. The emphasis changed from machine building in the first Five-Year Plan to metallurgy, machine building, fuel, energy, and chemicals in the second and third Five-Year Plans. This emphasis on key sectors yielded high growth rates. While sectors that promoted further growth (e.g., capital goods) were emphasized, sectors that did not contribute to growth (e.g., consumption) were neglected.[17]

As Soviet economic planning became more sophisticated, "campaign" planning turned out to be less appropriate. When the number of goods and industries proliferated, "balanced" growth became more critical. Failure to pull up lagging sectors—particularly agriculture—resulted in severe shortage problems and slowed the Soviet Union's growth rate.[18]

SHOCK THERAPY VERSUS GRADUALISM

Many economic reforms being introduced in former Socialist countries envisage a complete transformation from a command economy to a market economy. However, there are marked differences among individual countries. Some countries started their economic reforms earlier than others. Early starters included Hungary, Poland, the Czech Republic, and the Slovak Republic; late starters included Russia, Albania, Bulgaria, and Romania. There have also been differences in the speed of reform—the "shock therapy" of Poland and the Czech Republic, in contrast with the "gradualism" approach of Hungary.[19]

There are arguments for both shock therapy and gradualism. Some economists argue that gradual changes are too often absorbed and their effects are easily neutralized by the current structures of a central planned economy. Thus, despite many partial changes, the basic features of the command economy (the intervention in the allocation of inputs and the structure of outputs; related monopolization; pervasive price controls; dependence of enterprise managers on party and state bodies; and severe regulations and restrictions imposed on the private sector) largely remain unchanged. By contrast, shock therapy provides stronger incentives to the new economic system, thus accelerating the reallocation of resources and raising economic efficiency more quickly. In addition, shock therapy reduces the uncertainties facing the public with regard to the new rules of the game in the economy.[20]

Shock therapy seems especially appropriate in countries with high and long-lasting inflation (such as Poland) because it serves to break the inflationary expectations of enterprises and workers. Shock therapy, however, has some disadvantages. It imposes a heavy burden in terms of a sharp reduction of real wages, outputs, employment, and consumption. A tight and radical reform may create social tensions, which can lead to adverse consequences. Shock therapy, thus, cannot work efficiently unless people are willing to accept such sacrifices.[21]

This was the case in Poland where the Mazowiecki-led government found popular support for the shock therapy started at the beginning of 1990. This shock therapy included: (1) drastic cuts in the budget, including reductions in consumer subsidies; (2) increased interest rates to restrict credit growth; (3) fixed exchange rate to the U.S. dollar; and (4) fully liberalized foreign trade. Indeed, Polish citizens accepted this drastic reduction of real wages and incomes, but a people's willingness to sacrifice the present for a better future should neither be overestimated nor overstrained.[22]

There are certain limits in implementing shock therapy. Massive real income losses may induce demands for wage increases, resulting in a new wage-price spiral. By the same token, a tight fiscal and monetary policy may lead to a chain of enterprise bankruptcies. In addition, secondary effects such as a decline in demand for goods produced by the efficient sectors may exacerbate recession tendencies and lead to a sharp increase in unemployment.[23]

A number of factors, as Professors Gabrisch and Laski have suggested (1991), determine whether policymakers prefer the shock therapy or gradualist approach: their economic "ideology"; their perception of economic interactions; their risk preference; the expected political support from people; and the specific kind of problems they are facing. Shock therapy is justified if the disequilibria in the economy are of a greater order. Otherwise, a gradualist approach might be preferred so as to avoid the risks of strong sacrifice-demanding measures.[24]

HIGH EMPLOYMENT VERSUS HIGH INFLATION

Some nations may face a situation of high employment and high inflation. To reduce the inflation, policymakers need to reduce demand. But reducing demand is also likely to create some unemployment. This presents a serious dilemma for policymakers. If they pursue an expansionary policy, there will be less unemployment, at least for a while, but at the expense of more inflation. If they choose a contractionary policy, there may be less inflation, at an expense of more unemployment. In neither case will the situation be satisfactory. The aim of demand management, therefore, is to strike some equilibrium between employment and inflation.[25]

Prior to the mid-1960s, many countries' conditions were not very far from this ideal. Starting in the mid-1960s, the rates of inflation and unemployment rose higher, and since 1973 they have been breaking historical records. Professor A. W. H. Philips attempted in 1958 to address this relationship: the lower the rate of unemployment, the higher the rate of inflation, and vice versa. He estimated the percentages and this became known as the *Philips curve*. But the Philips curve has been challenged on both empirical and theoretical grounds.[26]

However, many countries' experiences show that over the long run, there is no positive trade-off between the two rates. Indeed, the trade-off is negative in that inflation undermines competitiveness and growth. A new phenomenon appeared, known as *stagflation*, in that inflation remained high even while levels of unemployment rose. Economists offer different explanations of this phenomenon. Some emphasize the role of inflationary expectations in the wage- and price-setting process. Some believe that wage negotiation plays a vital role since long-term wage contracts may induce future inflation. Some stress the importance of price and labor wage controls in curbing inflation, particularly in times of low unemployment. Several economies adopted price control programs in the 1970s to curb inflation. On the other hand, some have advocated a basic change in the wage-setting process.[27]

STATE OWNERSHIP VERSUS PRIVATE OWNERSHIP

State-owned enterprises can be categorized into four groups:

- Enterprises wholly owned and operated by the state. Most of these are capital- and technology-intensive operations that contribute to economic progress or to national security (e.g., mining or petroleum production).
- Public services owned and provided by local or national governments, such as airlines, railways, telecommunications networks, health and educational services.
- Enterprises partially owned by the state; the structure and degree of control vary widely across these enterprises.
- Enterprises owned but not operated by the government.[28]

The Growing Indebtedness of State-Owned Enterprises (SOEs)

State-owned enterprises are showing a growing indebtedness as a result of several factors:

1. SOEs were usually set up for multiple purposes and to serve multiple interest groups. Most SOEs face conflicting pressures from various parties and find it is difficult to reconcile multiple and conflicting objectives. Thus, managerial staffing was frequently based on political considerations rather than on managerial ability.[29]

2. SOEs are governed by competing objectives such as employment creation, redistribution of income, and regional development, rather than by overriding economic objectives such as profit maximization and efficiency. As a result, the national treasury often has to make up for the growing negative cash flow in operating the SOEs.[30]

3. Government pricing and labor policies are usually incongruent with the efficient operation of SOEs. This makes it impossible to overcome the high overhead costs incurred by the SOEs.[31]

4. Many governments fail to develop effective means for supervising and evaluating the performances of SOEs. Most projects are often initiated through many ministries.[32]

These problems are worsened by corruption, as in the notorious Malaysian case when a major highway contract was awarded to a construction company with limited experience, but owned by the ruling political party. The inherent conflicts embodied in the creation of SOEs subsequently led to their demise in many countries.[33]

Can State-Owned Enterprises Be Run Efficiently?

SOEs in the developing countries are often thought to be inefficient. This claim, however, requires deeper examination. Furthermore, efficiency is not a simple concept and merits careful specification.

Ajit Singh, for example, argues that there are several economic rationales for operating SOEs in developing countries: incomplete markets; externalities; the lack of entrepreneurship; and so on. In addition, operationally, nations have a longer time horizon than private-sector enterprises.[34] SOEs do not necessarily perform less efficiently. The critical factor is not ownership itself, but rather the nature of the competitive condition in which enterprises, either public or private, operate. For example, in South Korea, the Pohange Steel Company (Posco) is publicly operated and highly efficient, whereas the Steel Authority in India is also publicly owned but poorly operated.[35]

As Singh argues, if other influential factors (such as age, size, and type of industry) are controlled, and if more appropriate criteria for measuring performance are employed rather than just profitability, there is no reason to reprove SOEs severely as being less efficient.[36]

LARGE PRIVATE COMPANIES VERSUS SMALL ENTREPRENEURS

The benefits of large firms are self-evident. Their greater access to financial resources enables large firms to internalize various functional activities—ranging from R&D, production, and marketing to services—for which economies of scale and scope follow.[37] However, there are some factors pointing to the probable faster growth of small firms:

- vertical disintegration of large firms to escape unions and high wages;
- closures occurring among some large firms;
- sectoral shifts from manufacturing (with its generally larger facilities) to the service sector (with its generally smaller facilities);
- the strategic downsizing of large conglomerates as part of a retreat into core competences.[38]

Many governments are paying increasing attention to the potential contributions of smaller firms. Smaller firms meet the need to diversify the economy in order to insulate it against macroeconomic fluctuations and crises. Smaller firms can adapt more quickly to changing economic circumstances. And smaller firms may decrease the amount of income inequality.

It remains debatable whether small businesses have a greater potential for job creation. Bennett Harrison shows that this popular conception might be misleading and incorrect. Even though there are large numbers of small businesses proliferating in industrial countries, the largest business enterprises constantly account for the great majority of jobs; they dominate the coordination of activities across the firm's value chain; they control large financial resources; they help develop and diffuse new technology; they have scale economies; and they typically pay higher wages and benefits.[39]

Evidence of Small Private Enterprises

In the United States, small firms with 100 to 500 employees represent the fastest-growing sector in the economy.[40] Approximately 355,000 U.S. manufacturers with fewer than 500 employees account for about 46 percent of the value added in U.S.-manufactured products. Moreover, the competitiveness of major U.S. manufacturing firms depends on these small suppliers.[41]

About 75 percent of manufacturing employment in Japan is in small and medium-size companies, compared to about 35 percent in the United States. These small suppliers provide the flexibility and high quality that help strengthen the competitive advantage of Japan's large corporations.[42]

In Germany, small and medium-size companies, known as the *Mittel-*

stand, have an excellent export performance that contradicts their small scale and low profile. Many have more than 50 percent market share worldwide. Their dominance is achieved by a relentless focus and pursuit of niche market segments.[43]

Italy was the fastest-growing European economy in the first half of the 1980s. In the area of central and northeast Italy known as the *Terza Italia*, small manufacturing firms predominate, and their productivity has exceeded that of the rest of the country.[44]

Consider the region of Emilia-Romagna in north-central Italy. With a population of only 4 million, it has about 90,000 small manufacturing companies, most with 50 employees or less. These companies account for about 40% of the region's employment and span a variety of industries, including machine tools, automatic machinery, motorcycles, automobiles, electronic controls, and apparel. Although manufacturing businesses in Emilia-Romagna are tiny, through networks they can compete globally in state-of-the-art technology niches.[45]

Developing countries also have increasing numbers of small enterprises. During the 1980s in Kenya, more than 1,500 new private limited-liability companies were registered each year.[46]

Evidence of Large Private Enterprises

Yet there are nations whose economic development mainly depends on large-scale private enterprises. South Korea provides an excellent example. The top five *chaebol*—groups of South Korean conglomerate firms—account for approximately half of the national output. In 1990, the turnovers of all the affiliate companies of the top thirty *chaebol* came to 127 trillion won ($180 billion), equivalent to 76 percent of the country's GNP.[47]

The formation of *chaebol* depends mainly on government support, including privileged access to domestic lending and foreign borrowing, bargain-price acquisition of public properties, noncompetitive awarding of government contracts, and so on. By the end of 1990, the top thirty *chaebol* received a significant proportion of available credit at preferential interest rates of 129 trillion won, compared with shareholders' equity of only 32 trillion won, forcing smaller companies to borrow at higher rates on the unofficial market.[48]

The advantage of *chaebol* is scale-related—that capital-intensive industries will benefit from the efficiency caused by large production volumes and a concentration of capital.[49] On the other hand, the major disadvantage of the *chaebol* model is greater monopoly of business, which widens the unequal income distribution. The vast majority of the South Korean working class have not gained any substantial benefits flowing from three decades of rapid growth. The standard of living of this group dramatically declined in the 1980s.[50] Moreover, small and medium-sized enterprises cannot easily develop because the *chaebol* dominate all industries from consumer to industrial goods. Material wealth is circulated within the upper half of the population. Here development was accompanied by increased income inequality.[51]

As a result, the South Korean government recently began to limit the power of the country's *chaebol*. In early 1991, the South Korean government forced the *chaebol* to choose up to three core businesses that would be given easier access to credit than the rest of the group. The objective was to force *chaebol* to specialize in an effort to improve efficiency and to impose some discipline on their sprawling businesses.[52]

INTERVENTIONISM VERSUS FREE MARKETS

A mainstream view in economics is that the fundamental problem is how best to allocate scarce resources such as capital, skilled labor, and raw materials to competing ends. This is seen as best advanced under a free trade regime with perfect competition among private firms, while state intervention is seen as reducing economic efficiencies. Free trade and competition bring about an efficient price structure and choices through price mechanisms.[53]

The most familiar case for free trade arises from the Ricardian and neo-Ricardian principle of comparative advantage. Ricardian theory of trade explains comparative advantage in terms of a single key factor of production (e.g., labor productivity or natural resource endowments) or

technological differences. Production is assumed to exhibit constant return to scale.[54] Subsequent contributions by Eli Heckscher and Bertil
Ohlin directed attention to the relative abundance of inputs and biases in
input-output relationships. They argued that, in a world of internationally
immobile inputs, nations that have a relative abundance of capital would
export a relatively capital-intensive input mix, while importing the labor-
intensive goods they need from nations with abundant labor but little
capital.[55]

---

*The principle of comparative advantage is well illustrated by
Denmark, a small European country with 5 million people and a
$120 billion economy (GDP)—$23,000 per capita. Denmark has
few domestic energy sources, almost no mineral resources, and
modest amounts of land for agriculture. It has to import most
raw materials and many of the manufactured products on which
its economy depends. To pay for these imports, Denmark spe-
cializes in two export products for which it has a comparative
advantage on European and world markets. One is butter, which
does not require large amounts of land, energy, or raw materials
but requires a specialized and skilled dairy industry. The other is
Lego™—the children's toy bricks. Manufacturing Lego is not
easy: the bricks must fit together precisely even after years of
harsh treatment. By creating the superior product Denmark
gained predominance in the world market for children's plastic
building bricks. By specializing in export products where it has a
comparative advantage—butter and Lego—Denmark balances
its trade and pays for its various imports.[56]*

Since World War II, however, there has been growing concern about
the competitiveness and performance of nation-states and their business
enterprises. Trade between countries is not simply drawn from their respective comparative advantages; rather, advantages from trade seem to
be drawn from differentiation, economies of scale, and so forth.[57] This
more sophisticated trade theory reinforces the call for "strategic trade
policies," which factor in economies of scale, monopolistic competition,
monopoly pricing, and government intervention in improving national

welfare by means of positive externalities and profit shifting.[58] These two factors are described below.

Positive Externalities. Positive externalities describe a situation where an economy can benefit from an action that might be too costly for an individual firm to undertake, thus resulting in so-called market failure. These positive externalities usually occur in high-tech industries.[59]

> *For instance, suppose a firm's R&D activities would generate benefits for itself and others (e.g., spillover effects towards suppliers, consumers, workers), in excess of its cost, but the innovating firm's share of benefits would be inadequate to cover its costs. It would, then, make sense for the government to encourage the firm to undertake those activities as long as the social benefits from these activities outweigh the social costs.[60]*

Profit Shifting. Profit shifting describes a situation in which there are a small number of firms competing in an oligopolistic market structure and earning excess rents or profits. In such markets, the use of import tariffs or export subsidies, for example, can strengthen the competitive position of domestic firms and help them obtain a significant proportion of the industry's excess profits. Profit shifting, thus, is based on the assumption that a domestic government seeks to maximize national welfare, not the world welfare.[61]

Strategic trade policies are based on certain assumptions about the characteristics that industries should have if their targeting is likely to increase national welfare. Professor Barbara Spencer suggests that an industry that will prove a promising candidate for targeting should possess one or more of the following characteristics:

1. It earns supernormal profits, which requires that there be barriers to entry.

2. A subsidy leads foreign rivals to cut back output, implying that the industry is normally subject to stiff foreign competition or potential competition.

3. It is at least as concentrated as the rival foreign industry.

4. Factor prices do not increase much in response to domestic targeting, which is more likely if the industry does not have a strong union or if no key input is in fixed supply.

5. It has a fundamental cost advantage relative to foreign competition.

6. It gains substantial scale or learning economies from increased production, implying that the products or the process may be new.

7. There is a minimum spillover of new domestic technology to rival foreign firms.

8. R&D and capital costs form a significant proportion of industry costs, indicating that they are important factors in firm rivalry.

9. R&D and capital subsidies will raise entry barriers to foreign firms.[62]

These only emphasize the many difficulties in implementing strategic trade policies:

- Identifying the appropriate industries for targeting requires an ability to assess markets in which excess profits or rents are being made. However, it is difficult to distinguish ex-post (realized) from ex-ante (planned) profits.
- Even when appropriate industries can be reliably identified, it is difficult to select the right policy in support of indigenous firms.
- The applicability of strategic trade policy is further limited in many developing countries since few firms have operated in the kinds of industries in which these conditions arise.
- Strategic trade policy is a game that a country's trade rivals can also play and make all sides end up losers.[63]

Because of these implementation problems, most economists fear that such ideas, rather than enhancing national welfare, may do damage by encouraging interventionist governments to adopt poorly designed measures hiding behind the intellectual respectability that these ideas provide.[64] In practice, government intervention often takes place in economies lacking a basic infrastructure and institutional framework, where it is difficult to implement workable measures. Paradoxically, the need for government intervention may also lessen as these economies grow richer and develop their infrastructure and institutional frameworks.

INWARD INVESTMENT FACILITATION VERSUS BOOTSTRAPPING

Since the end of World War II, almost all the world's largest corporations have been expanding from national enterprises to multinational corporations. These MNCs have greatly extended the scope of their functional activities to most areas of the global economy.

MNCs influence the wealth creation of the host economy. They affect the host country's level of employment, the composition of factors of production, the domestic industrial structure, and the country's external balance of trade. Depending upon one's perspective, MNCs can be viewed, according to Professor Philip King, either as a mechanism for development or as an agent of imperialism.[65]

Drawing in foreign domestic investment can be thought of as a way of filling in certain GNP gaps. The first is the "resource" or "saving-investment" gap between desired investment and local savings. The second is a "foreign exchange" or "trade" gap between foreign exchange requirements and those obtained from net export earnings plus net foreign aid. An inflow of foreign capital can improve the balance of payment's current account by alleviating part or all of the deficit. The third is the "management and skill" gap, in which management, entrepreneurship, technology, and skill need to be filled by the local operations of MNCs via training programs to local staffs. The fourth is the "efficiency" gap. Foreign investment forces local firms to become more efficient and innovative. Finally, the fifth is a "tax" gap between targeted government tax revenues and actual taxes obtained. Tax revenue levied from MNCs may help governments mobilize public financial resources for development projects.[66]

However, the gap-filling pro-foreign investment positions outlined above are attacked by the following arguments:

• Economically, although MNCs provide capital, they can lower domestic savings and investment rates by inhibiting competition through exclusive production contracts with host governments; by failing to reinvest a significant proportion of their profits; and by retarding the growth potential of indigenous firms that might act as their suppliers by importing these intermediate goods from overseas affiliates instead.[67]

• Sociologically, MNC activities tend to reinforce dualistic economic structures by promoting the interests of the small number of well-paid, modern-sector workers. MNCs also worsen income distribution by widening wage differentials. In addition, they exacerbate the imbalance between rural and urban economic opportunities by primarily locating in urban centers, resulting in strong rural-to-urban migration.[68]

• Technologically, even though foreign investment may contribute positively to local employment, it may replace engineering jobs with manual ones.[69] Some MNCs build low-skill "screwdriver" operations to assemble imported components within the host country's tariff-protected walls. Frequently, their products compete directly with those of indigenous firms that may employ skilled workers and engineers. Another aspect of the problem concerns worker safety. Industrial disasters, such as the one that occurred at the Union Carbide plant in Bhopal, India, in 1984, have cast doubt on the safety practices of MNCs.[70]

• Fiscally, despite their contribution to public revenue in the form of corporate taxes, these amounts may be considerably less than the value granted to the MNCs by tax rebates, excessive investment allowances, disguised public subsidies, and tariff protection. Moreover, MNCs can avoid much local taxation via "transfer pricing"—a mechanism that artificially inflates the price MNCs pay for intermediate goods purchased from overseas affiliates, thus leading them to report lower profits in their local operations. As long as corporate tax rates differ across countries, host governments can exert little control over this transfer pricing. As a result, the private profits of MNCs may outpace the social benefits.[71]

• Politically, some MNCs not only gain control over local assets and employment but also can exert considerable influence on the country's political decisions. Consider the 1970s ITT experience in Chile: "Shortly after Salvador Allende, a left-wing politician who opposed foreign investment, was elected to power in Chile in 1974, ITT lobbied the American CIA to fund a political group opposed to Allende. The company also encouraged U.S. aid to the Chilean military (which strongly opposed Allende) and it systematically delayed shipments of spare parts to the Allende government in order to destabilize the regime."[72]

• Ethically, some MNCs produce notoriously inappropriate products (primarily to serve the need of local elites). Inappropriate processes and technologies may also complement inappropriate consumption patterns. One of the classic cases is the Nestlé Corporation:

> *Nestlé Corporation marketed infant formula as a modern, more nutritious formula for infants in the Third World. Many have objected to Nestlé's approach because mothers' natural supply of milk is more nutritious than any artificial formula. To add to the problem, because of their low purchasing power, many mothers often dilute the formula by using contaminated water, resulting in increased malnutrition and infant mortality.*[73]

SUMMARY

A nation's wealth-building strategy must acknowledge the existence of numerous trade-offs: growth versus income distribution; sectoral balance versus sectoral imbalance; shock therapy versus gradualism; high employment versus high inflation; state ownership versus private ownership; large private companies versus small entrepreneurs; interventionism versus open markets; and facilitating inward investment versus bootstrapping.

The choices of policies and administrative actions are partly influenced by the nation's culture, attitudes, and values (e.g., countries with individualistic cultures are likely to choose free trade policies, whereas countries with communitarian cultures are likely to choose managed trade policies; are partly affected by the nation's stage of economic development (e.g., the less developed countries usually focus on growth-oriented strategies while the developed countries usually focus on equality-oriented strategies); and are partly determined by the nation's factor endowments (e.g., there is evidence that large countries, such as Brazil, are likely to pursue import substitution protectionism whereas small countries, such as Hong Kong, are likely to pursue export promotion strategies). Thus, when considering which choice of policies and administrative action to select, many factors must be taken into account beyond the pros and cons of the policy choices per se.

Chapter 3

Distinguishing Alternative Pathways to Development

There are a multitude of economic pathways that countries can take in their pursuit of development. Most countries have settled for some form of capitalist order. Yet a monolithic concept of capitalism no longer exists, perhaps never did. Today's global economy is one of "capitalistic diversity."[1] Even beyond the three versions found in the "triad"—American, European, and Japanese—there are further variations that are distinctively East Asian, Latin American, and reflections of other countries. In East and Southeast Asia, for example, Singapore chose to develop an infrastructure conducive to high technology and service. Hong Kong chose to operate as a laissez-faire economy, while South Korea and Taiwan followed the Japanese model. In Latin America, Chile initiated a strategy of liberalization before any other Latin American country.

In Europe, state-sponsored technological ventures have had some success. France represents the prototype of a country setting very ambitious technoeconomic goals and constructing a whole set of state mechanisms to support these goals. India's mixed planned economy, labeled "Socialist," has been basically capitalist, despite large public-sector investments in industry and banking and administrative regulations: agriculture, services, foreign trade, and even industry have seen major growth of privately owned enterprise which are reflected in, and reinforced by, recent changes at the national level.

In the former Socialist countries, decentralized decision making and market transactions are replacing centralized planning and command allocations. Yet the nature and rate of change varies. Even before the breakdown of communism, China and the Soviet Union took different pathways of development. China pursued a strategy of heavy industrial development but decentralized approaches to primary-sector development, while in the Soviet Union all sectors were under centralized planning and large-scale bureaucratic directions. Recently, China and the former Soviet Union are again pursuing different paths toward a market economy. China liberalized its economic system without changing its political system, while in the Soviet Union the political system fell apart even as it started dismantling its economic superhouse.

The other former Socialist states in Eastern Europe are also pursuing a variety of development strategies. The major policy debate in Eastern Europe is between the gradualists, like those in Hungary, and the shock therapists, like those in Czechoslovakia and Poland.

This chapter will examine and compare eight alternative pathways to development. We first categorize the groups of countries by the stage of market economy development (existing market economies versus market economies in transition: see Figure 3.1). In existing market economies, two main criteria—*type of intervention* (fundamental versus selective) and *trade orientation* (inward versus outward)—are used to contrast alternative pathways of development. On the other hand, in those market economies in transition, two different criteria—*pattern of growth* (balance versus unbalance) and *time frame* (gradualism versus shock therapy)—are used. By these means, we identify eight representative pathways of development.

Distinguishing pathways of development will help policymakers, first, to assess the advantages and drawbacks of each pathway subject to the nation's unique set of opportunities, constraints, and competitive conditions; and second, to select the best economic development pathway for that nation.

FIGURE 3-1

Alternative Pathways to Development

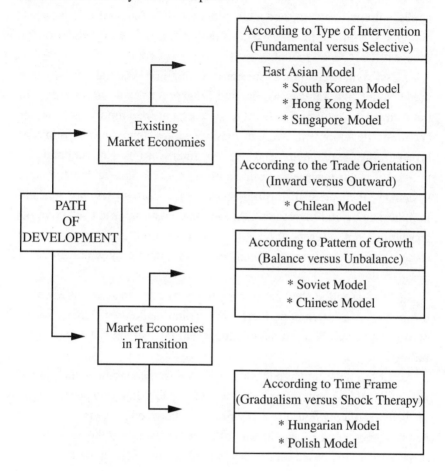

MARKET ECONOMY DEVELOPMENT: THE EAST ASIAN MODELS

East Asian countries are thought to have industrialized following the Japanese "model" of development. Several arguments have contributed to this hypothesis. One is the *late starter* theme. Japan may be viewed either as the last of the major countries to undergo an industrial transformation or as the first of the developing countries to industrialize. The East Asian countries were also late starters. They began to industrialize in the 1950s and 1960s. Some key features contributing to the notion of a Japanese–East Asian model of industrial development include an emphasis on export performance, high savings and investment rates, dynamic entrepreneurship, and high productivity of capital and labor. A common Confucian ideology is also regarded as a key ingredient of the Japanese–East Asian model.[2]

In East Asian economies, one must distinguish between the Japanese model states like Taiwan, Korea, and Singapore, versus Hong Kong. In the former, the major objective for government intervention is to foster economic development. We can classify policy interventions into two broad groups: *fundamental* and *selective* interventions. Key fundamental policies include macroeconomic stability, a stable and secure financial system, limited price distortions, openness to foreign technology, and high human capital investment. Among the most important selective interventions are discretionary industrial promotion, assisted export-led trade policies, and strategic financing (low interest rates and directed credit).[3]

Such interventions had necessarily to be selective to assure success, as information was often poor, there were capital market deficiencies, and a considerable variability in the incidence and intensity of the potential for failure.[4]

According to John Page (1994), in East Asian economies, the policymakers create *economic contests* that deliberately link competition with the benefits of cooperation among firms and between government and the business sector.[5] The basic feature of each contest is that the government provides rewards based on the firm's performance, which are monitored by the government and competing firms. The initiatives range from very simple nonmarket allocation rules (e.g., access to rationed credit for exporters) to very complex government-business investment coordination.[6] Economic contests, however, require a high-quality civil service, which has the capacity to monitor performance and which is insulated from political interference.

Two elements greatly contributed to East Asia's rapid growth. The first was getting the fundamentals right. Good macroeconomic management provided the stable groundwork for private investment. Price distortions had to be minimized. Policies were needed to enhance the integrity of the banking system, to assist the financial sector's capture of nontraditional savers, and to encourage personal and corporate savings. Education policies stressing universal primary and secondary education were needed to increase labor force skills. Foreign investment policies were needed to acquire and license foreign knowledge and technologies. Public investment had to complement private investment and promote an export orientation. Agricultural policies had to encourage productivity improvements and avoid excessive taxes in the rural economy.[7]

Secondly, policy interventions had to be carefully chosen. All interventions incur costs, but these costs were generally curbed within certain limits. Given the outright importance of macroeconomic stability and export growth in East Asian countries, subsidies were provided within fiscally responsible bounds and international interest rates were used as a benchmark for domestic interest rate controls. Policy interventions that were not congruent with these objectives were either discarded or modified.[8]

At the same time, there were large differences among East Asian countries in the pattern and extent of interventions. Hong Kong is a clear example of the success of a free market approach to economic development. Singapore exemplifies a blend of the free market approach with some state interventions designed mainly to promote foreign investment or higher-technology firms. Korea and Taiwan (and Japan in the 1960s and 1970s), by contrast, are examples of the selective intervention approach.

The Selectivist Approach: The South Korean Model

Within only a few decades, South Korea has transformed from a poor agrarian economy to a dynamic industrial economy. Korea's economic development can be divided into four distinctive stages. These are: Reconstruction (1950–61); export-oriented industrialization (1962–72); heavy and chemical industries promotion (1973–80); and trade liberalization in the 1980s.[9]

Reconstruction (1950–61). The Korean War reduced the nation's already weak industrial base to almost nothing. Due to the extremely low level of living, the national savings rate was lower than 5 percent, resulting in the typical vicious circle of poverty, as depicted below:

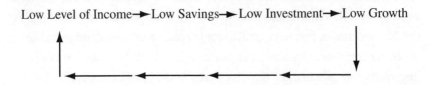

Low Level of Income→Low Savings→Low Investment→Low Growth

In this period, foreign aid took a major role in fulfilling the gap between investment and saving. Import substitution policy was limited to a few consumer and intermediate goods industries. Due to the small internal market and the large capital requirements of many investment projects, import substitution policy soon reached its limit.

During this period, the government tightly controlled various price instruments, particularly interest rates and foreign exchange rates. To some extent, the government kept the Korean currency overvalued, and the official interest rates were manipulated to a level far below that of the curb market rate.

At the same time, agricultural land reform contributed to the improvement in income distribution. Since the traditional capitalist class had been destroyed, however, the government, not the private sector, played a vital role in the reconstruction of industry.[10]

Export-Oriented Industrialization (1962–72). This period was the critical turning point in Korea's economic history. Liberalization and policy reforms were introduced and expanded.

The first reform was liberalizing the foreign exchange rate, which resulted in sharply depreciating the won. Subsequently, the official deposit rate was raised from 11 percent to 30 percent in 1965. In 1967, the Korean government took a significant step toward the free trade regime by adopting a so-called *negative list system of import licensing*. This system insulated exporters from the adverse effect of import protection by enabling them to obtain essential productive inputs rapidly and at near-world prices. Moreover, capital was made available to exporters at rates lower than normal bank lending rates for rationed domestic credit. It is worth noting that the Korean government provided the input and credit facilities to all exporters without discrimination.[11]

Heavy and Chemical Industries Promotion (1973–80). During the 1970s, three major external shocks affected the Korean economy. The first was the opening of U.S.–China diplomatic relations, which caused the political imbalance in the region, at least in the short run. The others were the 1973 oil shock and the rising protectionism in the world market. This led the Korean government to pursue sufficiency in diversified sectors, from agriculture to national defense, as a priority national goal. In addition, in the international market, Korean exports began to lose their price competitiveness because other developing countries (particularly the ASEAN countries) with cheaper labor had aggressively invaded many labor-intensive industrial segments. This led Korea to shift its emphasis from labor-intensive export industries to heavy and chemical industries, including steel, metal products, shipbuilding, machinery, automobiles, and petrochemicals.[12]

To establish the heavy and chemical industries, various selective and discriminatory policies were applied, including import protection, substantial subsidies through long-term lending, tax holidays, and accelerated depreciation. Investment capital from both domestic and foreign sources was directly funneled to these sectors, usually at a cost of funds even less than the already low official rates.[13]

Though the heavy and chemical industrialization policy in this period spawned many successful projects, it also contributed to an economic crisis in 1980 and, on average, provided low economic returns.[14] This policy brought about various adverse effects, including an inflationary spiral, a worsening of income distribution, an increase in the foreign debt, and the existence of many helpless manufacturers in heavy industrial sectors.[15]

The second oil crisis brought to the surface all the problems that had accumulated during the heavy and chemical industrialization period. An economic crisis in the year 1980 was the worst in Korea's modern economic history, with a negative growth rate, hyperinflation, and a huge increase in the current account deficit. As a result, a drastic restructuring of some industries began, followed by a new liberalizing policy.[16]

Trade Liberalization in the 1980s. In the early 1980s, the Korean government decided to cope with the economic crisis by means of stabilization and liberalization strategies. Almost all direct and indirect subsidies were removed. Many selective interventions were phased out. The targeting of strategic industries, which was the main instrument in promoting heavy industrialization in the 1970s, was discontinued. Instead, Korea's industrial policy moved toward providing fundamental support for labor force training and R&D investment.[17]

To maintain price stability, the government dramatically cut public spending and tightly controlled monetary growth. As a result of these measures and the trade liberalization, the Korean economy and its exports grew at a rapid pace during the 1980s.[18]

The Fundamentalist Approach: The Hong Kong Model

Hong Kong, by contrast, intervened the least selectively, though it provided the "fundamentals." The development pathway included free pursuit of international trade, few business regulations, and no state-owned enterprises. Taxes were low and uniform across activities (the personal income tax was 15 percent, and the business profit tax was 15.5 percent). The government limited its role to providing physical and social infrastructure: the airport, port facilities, some transportation systems, extensive low-rent housing facilities, and the water supply. Health care for young women and children is subsidized. Primary education is free, and secondary education is heavily subsidized. The government also supported some higher education and training programs.

Hong Kong's only natural resource is its harbor. Before World War II, one of Hong Kong's main industries was shipbuilding and repair. Its initial industrialization was enhanced by the large presence of expatriate British trading and financial enterprises (which over time transmitted their skills and information to locals), and an influx of textile entrepreneurs and technicians from Shanghai who had already undergone a learning process.[19] After World War II, Hong Kong businesses invested in the textile industry, specifically spinning, weaving, and knitting mills. They also invested in plastic molding.

As an entrepot trade center, Hong Kong boasted a large number of banks and merchant trading houses providing financial and international marketing facilities to the nascent textile industry. The free trade status helped ensure that Hong Kong's manufacturers were able to compete with foreign counterparts on equal terms.[20]

By 1954, Hong Kong had become a major producer of cotton yarns and gray cotton piece goods. Its growing plastic industry supported entry into consumer goods such as plastic housewares and toys. Hong Kong businesses also started to produce other low-tech goods, such as flashlights, batteries, and enamelware. In the 1960s, Hong Kong's textile industry moved into producing simple garments as a result of mastering bleaching, finishing, and dyeing technologies. Local businesses also moved into higher-tech areas such as electronic products, computer memories, and scientific instruments. Hong Kong became a major producer of watches, clocks, cameras, and microscopes.

Hong Kong's economic development illustrates an evolution from basic industries (textiles and plastics) toward manufacturing downstream products. Furthermore, there is a movement from low-tech to high-tech capabilities. From the 1970s, Hong Kong's economy shifted toward that of a newly industrialized nation. Various industries had diversified and upgraded their operations. The more capital- and skill-intensive clothing industry increased its share of manufactured output in the same period sharply, from 3 percent to 29 percent, while its share of employment as a percentage of total manufacturing employment declined from 32 percent in 1950 to 14 percent in 1980. Such upgrading of industries constituted a shift of the composition of factors of production: manufacturing declined while trading increased. Furthermore, services increased their added value by shifting from the unskilled type to sophisticated business, financial, and industrial services.[21]

However, Hong Kong businesses basically produced goods for other companies rather than marketing these goods under Hong Kong brand names. The same was initially the case for Japan, which acted primarily as a supplier of private label products. The difference is that Japan soon started to put its own names on its products and in the process developed extremely advanced marketing skills.

One of the unique features of Hong Kong's industrial development is that almost all its business enterprises have been started with the entrepreneur's own capital. Entry barriers to industry thus remained low and encouraged the proliferation of small, specialized enterprises. As a result, manufacturing enterprises employing fewer than twenty workers constitute the majority of Hong Kong companies (as is the case also in Taiwan, but not Singapore and South Korea). Most of these enterprises are doing simple processing and assembling. The main advantages of such industrial development are: (1) Vertical takeoff and a fast-paced industrialization take place since it does not require much capital accumulation; (2) the mobilization and utilization of all available manpower, skill, and technology are maximized; and (3) the pitfalls of a dual economy are avoided, since large numbers of small enterprises are directly and indirectly integrated into the world market through the subcontracting system. However, one of the main disadvantages of such industrial development is that Hong Kong has lower labor productivity and a lower value-added per unit labor cost across various industrial sectors.[22]

Subsequent growth in Hong Kong's economy has been driven by the rapid accumulation of human and physical capital as well as by the drastic changes in the composition of output, particularly the upgrading of the manufacturing sector and the emergence of a new services sector.[23]

High-Technology and Service Development Approach: The Singapore Model

Like Hong Kong, Singapore has no natural resources except its harbor. It is also a modern city-state that has successfully developed from an entrepot trade center into a high-technology manufacturer, and increasingly into a provider of sophisticated services.[24]

In spite of these similarities, Singapore and Hong Kong followed different development strategies. Whereas there is a relative small government intervention in Hong Kong's industrial growth, the Singapore government has been far more selectivist by intervening heavily in the direction of industrial development—focusing on labor-intensive industries in the 1960s, and then shifting to more capital- and skilled-intensive sectors.[25]

With the state having a strong influence on the direction of industrial development, Singapore's pattern of industrial development is viewed as being in line with that of Korea (while Hong Kong is in line with Taiwan). However, the contrast is associated with the different patterns of foreign investment. Unlike Korea, Singapore during the 1970s and early 1980s relied much more on foreign investment than on foreign loans.[26] There is a conception that foreign investment will ensure a continuously higher standard of living for Singapore's citizens and a competitive position in the global marketplace.[27]

The Industrialization Process. After Singapore's independence in 1959, the government encouraged industrial development through an import substitution strategy. But by the late 1960s, trade liberalization was pursued, and export subsidies were introduced to equalize incentives across different activities and ensure that local producers had become competitive in relation to their foreign counterparts. On the one hand, most import duties have been set at 5 percent since 1981, and the last quota was removed in 1988, making Singapore a truly free trade economy. On the other hand, additional export promotion measures, such as the development of overseas marketing services, were undertaken.[28]

The shift in the trade regime toward greater outward orientation was accompanied by labor law revisions enhancing the country's attractiveness to foreign investors. Other related policy measures included the removal of restrictions on the number of establishments, equity participation, the repatriation of profits, local-content requirements, and requirements to employ nationals. Singapore's government spent greatly on public infrastructure. Tax incentives were introduced to encourage inward foreign debt investment. Thus, Singapore encouraged foreign investment by matching local productive factors with foreign technical and managerial know-how.[29]

Singapore's Second Industrial Revolution. With an upturn in international investment in 1978, Singapore's government attempted to resolve the contradiction between labor-intensive and capital-intensive manufacturing and address the rapid inflow of foreign labor. It embarked on the so-called Second Industrial Revolution, aiming at transforming Singapore toward a higher value-adding economy, thereby escaping from the competition with cheaper wage countries and decreasing its reliance on labor expansion for growth.[30]

The key feature of this new strategy was the radical turnaround in wage policy. On the one hand, the wage costs were raised in order to discourage low-skill, labor-intensive investments; other related measures such as tariff revisions and restrictions on imported labor were also undertaken.[31] On the other hand, the policymakers have actively encouraged the relocation of low-wage activities to neighboring countries for the purpose of supporting their industrial development and assuring Singapore's producers of access to low-cost intermediate inputs.[32]

At the same time, the government provided a range of policy instruments (e.g., extremely generous tax and fiscal incentives) to foster a drastic shift in investment toward more capital-intensive, higher value-added production. It also progressively upgraded the physical infrastructure needed to support growth.[33]

To achieve the desired shift in the manufacturing sector, the government set about fostering both the quantity and the quality of skilled labor. It also introduced an array of incentives and assistance to facilitate a wider adoption of labor replacement production techniques. Emphasis was placed on parts and component manufacturing (e.g., aircraft, automotive components, and precision equipment). Moreover, the government defined Singapore's strategic location as a basis for further higher value-added industrial expansion. This could be accomplished through industrial servicing or by positioning Singapore as the center of the waterways and air routes in the region. Along the value chains, Singapore would not only seek to produce many higher value-added products for advanced industrial markets, but it would also service the immediate region as a supplier of medium-technology products and services.[34]

Apart from the manufacturing sector, Singapore has placed increasing emphasis on developing its service sector. In particular, the government has focused on developing Singapore as a sophisticated financial capital and a medical capital of Southeast Asia.[35]

Key Success Factors of East Asian Models

The success of the East Asian models of economic development arose out of a special set of political conditions that are not likely to be duplicated elsewhere. The East Asian governments were able to make policy decisions based primarily on economic rationales rather than on the political and rent-seeking rationales so often found elsewhere in the developing world. The key answer is that in East Asia:

1. the ideologies of the elites were congruent with growth oriented policies
2. non-economic elites were included in the wealth sharing programs as beneficiaries of growth

3. the honest bureaucracies and economic technocrats were insulated from narrow political pressures.[36]

The redistribution of income that occurred in Japan, Korea, and Taiwan was more the result of historical accident than deliberate policy. Events such as Japan's defeat in war, the U.S. military occupation in Japan and Korea, Korea's war destruction, and so on, made possible a thoroughgoing land reform program and eliminated the property ownership of the urban elite in 1945–53. Subsequent growth did not really affect this egalitarian base, in spite of the fact that growth policies were not primarily designed to achieve this goal. Korea, for example, did not expend more concern on social welfare until it reached the period of rapid development. Singapore is an exception, in that its government pursued growth for the purpose of improving the life of most Singaporeans.[37]

Where did the honest bureaucracies and economic technocrats insulated from narrow political pressures come from? As Professor Dwight Perkins points out:

These countries recognize that if they failed in economic terms, their societies were going to be swallowed up by external powers and they knew it. Reinforcing this awareness was the fact that political power in each society rested on a combat-hardened army (Korea, Japan), an army-party elite isolated from the rest of society (Taiwan), and general populist support from the beneficiaries of the social welfare system (Singapore). Nowhere in this list does one find the local landlord elites and other baronies that plague the politics of the Philippines and parts of Latin America. Nor are there the deep ethnic splits found throughout Africa, splits that have much to do with why coherent national economic policies, as contrasted to narrow strategies to favor specific groups, are so difficult to achieve. Korea, Taiwan, Japan, Hong Kong, and Singapore are all ethnically quite homogeneous.[38]

Professor Perkins also points out that one unique feature that makes economic performance in East Asia different from that of other developing countries may lie more in the ideologies or mind-sets of the elites than in any true self-interest rooted in the social structure. He argues that "somehow these East Asian countries have recognized the importance of not killing off the goose that laid the golden eggs of sustained development and have been able to avoid economic policies that would do precisely that." The very fact of the East Asian success has certainly forced other developing countries to rethink their basic assumptions regarding how best to achieve their development goals.[39]

Apart from the "Four Tigers"—Singapore, Hong Kong, Taiwan, and South Korea—a few other nations have had some success in industrializing. However, their paths of development are not as widely applicable as that of the Four Tigers. Israel, for example, has built up its economy in an atypical pathway. Unlike the Asian newly industrialized countries (NICs), it received sustained foreign capital from several sources—U.S. foreign aid, contributions from Zionists in foreign countries, and German reparations. Like the Asian NICs, Israel provided a heavy government support in key industries. To foster its competitiveness, Israel has developed a few niches in world markets (e.g., in cut diamonds and military technology).[40]

FREE MARKET DEVELOPMENT:
THE CHILEAN MODEL

The evidence of the benefit of an outward-oriented trade policy has produced increasing disenchantment with the inward-oriented approach and greater demand for trade policy reforms.

Chile, under the reign of General Pinochet, who came to power in 1973, was the pioneer in pursuing free market policy in Latin America. In 1973, Chile was one of the most protected countries in the world through a complex tariff and nontariff structure, a distorted multiple exchange rate system, quotas, permits, exemptions, and special regimes. Within six years, Chile had been transformed into one of the most open economies by establishing a uniform tariff of 10 percent and eliminating all nontariff barriers. In addition, several structural reforms were introduced within the context of an anti-inflationary stabilization program. These included fiscal reform, price liberalization, privatization, deregulation and liberalization of the capital market, labor reform, and the opening of the capital account. It took this stabilization program eight years to lower the triple-digit annual inflation rate to a single-digit one.[41]

Trade Liberalization in Chile

The intense political pressures following a trade liberalization program have deterred many governments from pursuing trade reform. The Chilean case is worth studying because it provides a fourteen-year picture of the effects of trade reform on economic growth in general and industrial development in particular.

The drastic trade reforms in Chile between 1973 and 1980 led to a major restructuring of industry. In the immediate term, the protected industrial sectors found it hard to compete with foreign counterparts. The resulting bankruptcies and unemployment in these sectors were not immediately offset by the growth in the export sector.[42]

By contrast, in the medium and long term, trade liberalization has generated a series of positive consequences. Resources were reallocated more efficiently in line with the country's comparative advantages. Consumer welfare was increased through access to higher-quality, lower-cost goods. Local producers had more discipline since they were compelled to boost their efficiency in the face of foreign competition. Furthermore, local producers had adopted worldwide efficiency standards.[43] As a result, Chilean exports expanded considerably. Exports in 1980 were almost five times higher than in 1971. Interestingly, remarkable increases were recorded by the manufacturing sector, whose 1980 exports were twelve times of those in 1971.[44]

A significantly depreciated exchange rate was a crucial factor in fostering the impressive growth in exports. It is worth noting that when Chile pegged the Chilean peso to the U.S. dollar to reduce inflation in April 1980, the peso was overvalued and the nation's manufacturers faced increased difficulty in exporting, while importers found it easier to import manufactured goods. The result was a huge trade deficit in 1980 and 1981. The ease of borrowing money from the international financial community also led to a tripling of Chile's foreign debt during 1978–82.[45]

As a consequence, a massive devaluation occurred in 1982, resulting in a 14 percent decline in the economy for the year. Many large Chilean firms declared bankruptcy, and unemployment rose sharply, to 35 percent of the workforce. A coherent outward-oriented policy did not take place again until 1985. The previous Chilean twelve years' experience led to two conclusions: (1) the exchange rate must be allowed to move with market forces; and (2), although an outward-oriented policy can foster growth, it also exposes an economy to significant risks. Chile's policy-makers had to consider the long-term impact of global forces and trends on the economy and deliberately adjust its economic policy to fit with external as well as internal forces.[46]

The Chilean model, showing an economy switching from a strongly inward-oriented to an outward-oriented economy, is highly instructive for many Third World countries—and particularly those of Latin America. As the economic aftereffects of the twin oil shocks finally came due in the mid-1980s, almost all Latin American governments faced the inevitable realization: not protectionism nor statism but liberalization can create national wealth. As late starters, not pioneers, the other Latin American countries can benefit from the accumulated experience, policy errors, and sacrifices that accompanied economic liberalization in Chile.[47]

PRIMARY-SECTOR DEVELOPMENT: THE CHINA MODEL

In the 1950s, China's industrialization path followed that of the Soviet Union, emphasizing central planning and heavy industry targeting, including Mao's Great Leap Forward campaign. This changed significantly in 1978–79, when China introduced economic liberalization policies, aimed at establishing a system of *market socialism* with elements of guided capitalism. Although the major reforms took place in the agricultural sector, there was also significant progress in manufacturing, trading, consumer goods, and foreign trade. The growth has been led by exports.[48]

Under this regime, a more autonomous and efficient government structure was developed. Enterprises were freed from administrative controls. Price controls were abolished. State-owned enterprises were encouraged to keep in line with the market demand, price, and quality. In addition, small private businesses were allowed.[49]

Capitalism with Chinese Characteristics

Unlike the Soviet Union's strategy, China's changes were in economics, not politics. The first of China's three waves of reform was directed by Deng Xiaoping in the late 1970s and early 1980s. Two main elements were present. First, structural reforms of agriculture were introduced by combining marketing and privatization policies. The state gave restricted de facto private property rights in land and farm capital to peasant families, subject to the obligation that a certain portion of their output had to be delivered to the state at state-set prices plus the payment of some communal levies. By these means, the peasants were free to make decisions on production. Furthermore, all surplus above their contractual and tax obligations is free—the peasants can consume this surplus themselves or sell it at relatively free market prices.[50]

This program of marketing and privatization led to a substantial rise in output and productivity. In the first half of the 1980s, real value added in agriculture increased by 7 percent a year, while the number of people working the land decreased. This made everyone in China better off; peasant prosperity increased while consumers received a better quality and quantity of food. China created a committed reform constituency containing three-quarters of its population. The economic genius of the reforms was that it laid the groundwork for sustained growth of the agricultural sector, and generated enough surplus of rural savings to finance industrial development. The political distinction of the reforms was that China captured this surplus not by milking the rural sector, as mistaken Stalin-like industrialization drives usually did, but by making peasants prosper.[51]

The second element of the reforms was the *open-door policy*. The central government's monopoly over foreign trade was abolished. Four "special economic zones" were established, aimed to draw in foreign capital and know-how. The open-door policy has reshaped the Chinese economy, bringing it the same benefits that the export-led growth of the East Asian tigers achieved.[52]

From Agricultural Development to Industrial Development

After the success of the agricultural reform, the Chinese policymakers shifted their reform efforts in 1984 and 1987 to industry. The government altered the industrial property structure by (1) transforming many medium-sized state enterprises to the less rigidly and bureaucratically controlled cooperative sector; (2) extending the scope of private ownership of small-to-medium enterprises; and (3) experimenting with alternative forms of property ownership (e.g., state-cooperative, cooperative, private, state-foreign private). In the late 1980s, the denationalization of all industry and the privatization of state-owned enterprises were proposed.[53]

In industry, the emphasis also shifted to the long-neglected consumer goods and services sector. Imports of foreign consumer goods were allowed. This eased pent-up demand and helped convert increasing incomes of both the peasantry and the urban workers into wanted goods.[54] China was creating an economy that looked less and less like its former ideological counterparts in the Soviet Union and Eastern Europe, and more and more resembled that of its East Asian neighbors.[55]

The most significant change in China's reform is its efficiency improvement. During the period of the Great Leap Forward and the so-called Cultural Revolution (between the mid-1950s and the mid-1970s), its "total factor productivity" did not increase substantially in spite of its 5.6 percent real GDP growth a year. In fact, all of China's pre-reform growth derived from adding more inputs, particularly capital (both saving and investment rates ran at around 35 percent of GDP), not from deploying them more efficiently. By these means, Chinese economic growth can be sustained for a long period of time, but not forever.[56]

However, some current indicators show that the Chinese economy is becoming more competitive and efficient. First, the total factor productivity of China's private firms rose from zero in the pre-reform years to almost 5 percent a year during the 1980s (the same figure for state firms was 2.5 percent). Second, the profitability of both state and nonstate enterprises declined while their productivity rose. Third, returns in the state and nonstate sectors are beginning to converge. In addition, the variation of rates of return across industries is also narrowing—from 7–98 percent in 1980 to 8–23 percent in 1989. All these factors imply an overall decrease in monopoly power and profits and an equalization of returns across enterprises, industries, and regions.[57]

HEAVY INDUSTRY DEVELOPMENT: THE CLASSICAL SOVIET MODEL

The Soviet model of economic administration has been the prototype of all command economies. Planning and management in the classic Soviet model are characterized by the following features:

- Almost all the economic decisions are centralized. These decisions directly affect the rate of investment, which in turn determines the growth rate, the distribution of capital among economic sectors, and the allocation of funds into collective and individual consumption.
- Due to the vertical links between different parts of the economic system, the imperative form of transmitting decisions is downward—lower levels of the hierarchy usually receive plan tasks as orders that must be carried out regardless of the prevailing economic climate.
- There is a predominance of economic planning in terms of physical units to minimize the risk that enterprises will carry out undesirable substitution in production.
- Money plays an insignificant role within the state sector. Interfirm transfers are carried out according to plan. Since unplanned transactions are illegal, an enterprise has no need of active money beyond the wage bill.[58]

The main features of the classical Soviet model of economic administration may be summarized as follows:

1. Industry is the key driver in the development program, while agricultural investment is maintained to the minimum necessary to allow agriculture to supply industry with food, raw materials, and expanding resources of labor supply.
2. An import-substitution trade policy is pursued.
3. Very high investment and savings rates are maintained.
4. An unbalanced growth pattern is employed by allocating a significant proportion of investment capital to heavy industry. Certain scarce raw materials and technologies are critical in operating heavy industries. The former Soviet Union, having abundant minerals and energy, could accomplish this goal without affecting its balance of payments.
5. In choosing among productive techniques, the most advanced technology is employed. Meanwhile, critical inputs such as capital and skilled labor are economized.
6. To build up a stock of human capital, emphasis is placed upon vocational and technical training by using the factory itself as a major training center.[59]

The Advantages and Disadvantages of the Classical Soviet Model

The classical Soviet model exhibits a set of advantages and disadvantages. According to Martin Janicke, its main advantages are:

1. Annual, medium-term, and perhaps longer-term plans are drawn up with the formal broad participation of all stakeholders that have an important interest.
2. All appropriate public interests can be comprehensively represented in the organization and information system.
3. There is no mass unemployment.
4. Political pressures involving the threat to take capital elsewhere (or not to invest) no longer exist, because capital is owned by the state.
5. The system does not rely on wasteful consumption for growth, and wasteful overproduction is a rare occurrence.
6. There is a relatively marked equality of opportunities in many sectors except the power center, resulting in a lower degree of social problems than under capitalism.
7. The educational system aims to adjust training to the needs of the society. The problem of lack of skills is less acute than in most capitalist countries.[60]

But there are also a number of disadvantages to the classic Soviet model:

1. The planning machinery constantly becomes enmeshed in production details. An unwillingness to use prices as aggregators in detailed formulations implies ever-increasing planning complexity as the variety of goods produced in the economy increases.

2. A top-downward orientation of production and motivation leads to a lack of flexibility with regard to consumers, citizens, or new requirements.

3. The system discourages the economic payoffs of information and services and their potential for innovation. To some extent, a mania for secrecy and palliation, typical of oligarchic structures, results in self-deception, information gaps, and delayed reaction to problems. Moreover, various factors inhibit the innovative thrust—the effects of

deep-seated defects, a lack of organizational freedom and legal rights, and insufficient media support for interests that run counter to the prevailing approach.

4. It is not uncommon to see an overrepresentation of the powerful traditional industries in the planning hierarchy. The main lobbyist for each industry is typically the responsible minister of the industry, with his bureaucracy of specialists in a narrow range of products. Thus, under the Soviet regime, vertical concentration, rather than horizontally concentrated conglomerates with their greater flexibility, dominates the industrial structure.

5. An emphasis on plant profitability calculations under the tight planning mechanism leads to the neglect of other factors, such as investment in environmental protection.

6. The heavy emphasis on industry causes the communes and regions to stay in a weaker position.[61]

The Soviet Economic Performance

Ideally, given its factor endowment advantages, the former Soviet Union ought to be an economic superpower. Yet all this potential is mainly weakened by the inoperable economic system.[62] The economic planning in the Soviet-type economy affects the social opportunity set primarily through the cost of transactions. Transaction costs that are relevant to the Soviet-type economy are the volume of human and nonhuman resources employed in order to prepare economic plans; monitor their execution; maintain and protect the rules of the game; and cheat and lie to bureaucratic superiors.[63] Those costs severely limit the potential growth rate of the Soviet economy.

From the 1960s onward, the Soviet Union was unable to catch up with the trend of shifting away from traditional heavy, capital-intensive industries toward high value-added, knowledge-intensive, and consumer-driven industries.[64]

Developing a consumer-driven economy requires dismantling central planning, while a knowledge-intensive society implies an end to censorship, tight controls, party orthodoxy, and monop-

> *oly. Investing in new growth sectors means diverting funds from farm support, from food subsidies, and above all from the military. In fact, spending on these areas continued to rise, leaving nothing for modernizing older industries and decaying infrastructure, let alone for new technologies. The Soviet economy thus became trapped, deep-frozen in an economic "long cycle," that was tied to industries and inputs of the 1930s.*[65]

RESTRUCTURING A FULL-FLEDGED MARKET-TYPE ECONOMY

Gradualism: The Hungarian Model

Like other central planned economies, from the late 1950s the Hungarian economy had grown quite rapidly. But growth had slowed down by the late 1960s. By the 1980s, the country coped with several severe crises. Many Hungarians eventually realized that the only way to overcome these crises required a strong commitment to transforming the country's command economy into a market-driven system.[66]

The restoring of macroeconomic stability is a critical step in the Hungarian transformation process. Hungary aimed to lessen its reliance on external savings by cutting the deficit on the current account vis-à-vis the rest of the world. The improvement of the external balance was, to a great extent, accomplished by concerted government policy actions enforcing tight measures on the domestic markets, at the cost of zero GDP growth and a temporary drop in the level of real household consumption. Domestic demand management successfully curbed imports to a level that generated a positive current account.

As a result of increasing hard currency export revenues and further improvements in the economic structure, the foreign debt-service ratio drastically declined. Meanwhile, international (hard) currency reserves substantially increased, enabling Hungary to continue the real appreciation of its currency (HUF). The continuing real appreciation will further ease inflationary pressure and attract foreign investors. The rationale for the latter is that investment will be cheaper now than later, and the dollar value of future returns will be higher.[67]

Despite a strongly appreciating domestic currency and very high interest rates, Hungary has been remarkably successful in weathering the collapse of Soviet bloc trade by dramatically increasing its exports to the West, implying that Hungarian firms were greatly able to improve their cost efficiency and product quality. After the 1968 reforms, most enterprises were quite responsive to market signals (such as exchange rates, taxes, subsidies). This responsiveness, however, was partially obscured by the opacity of the legal and tax system. As taxes are made more uniform and exchange rates are unified and changed in line with trade deficits, these market responses will show up at the aggregate level.[68]

Hungary, instead of applying the "shock therapy" approach of Poland and Czechoslovakia, has adopted a "gradual" approach to reforming its institutions, the tax system, and the foreign trade regime. Unlike Poland and Czechoslovakia, Hungary's privatization program has been state-guided and incremental, aimed at selling enterprises rather than giving them away to the populace. The new State Property Agency (SPA) is now established as the body which nominally "holds" state assets, and its mission is supervising the privatization process.[69]

Compared with its neighbors, Hungary's economic performance is impressive. In Hungary, the rapid development of its private sector was accompanied by further critical steps in the creation of the legal and institutional framework of a market economy. A large number of basic laws and deregulation were carried out. In contrast to its neighbors, almost all the basic institutions, regulations, and legislation of a market economy now exist in Hungary. As a result, foreign direct investment is increasing. In addition, Hungary has also regained secured access to international capital markets.[70]

Shock Therapy: The Polish Model

Compared with its neighboring countries, Poland had most of the peculiar characteristics of industrialized Communist countries. A vast majority of the population was rural-based, working in agriculture. Education levels were relatively low. The rates of population growth and of infant mortality were high. Furthermore, most of the country's physical capital had been either destroyed or damaged during the war. The loss of a large number of intelligentsia meant a major loss of human capital.

The "Balcerowicz Plan." When the Solidarity government took office in 1989, the nation was experiencing an economic crisis: declining output, widespread shortages, and price increases close to hyperinflation. The new government acted responsively to stabilize the economy by launching a path-breaking economic reform program. The program pursued three main policies. (1) *Economic liberalization*: all the legal and administrative changes needed to create the institutions of private property (in areas ranging from agricultural land transfer to urban land taxation), establish legislation, develop the financial system, improve the telecommunication infrastructure, and encourage market competition. (2) *Macroeconomic stabilization*: measures to limit budget deficits, reduce the growth of the money supply, as well as set up a uniform currency exchange rate so as to develop a new monetary system based on a convertible currency and stable prices. (3) *Privatization*: a wide range of measures aimed at transferring ownership of state property to the private sector.[71]

Poland's strategy has been to introduce these three main policies of reform as rapidly as possible. The rationale for comprehensiveness and speed in introducing reforms is clear-cut (see Chapter 2).[72]

Among the three policies, privatization is the most challenging and time-consuming. Most of the privatization was initially carried out in the wholesale and retail trade, and then extended to broader areas, including manufacturing. As a result, the availability of goods and the quality of services improved significantly.[73]

At the same time, the urban private sector, particularly in services, was growing rapidly. During 1991–92 there were around 1.56 million private businesses in Poland. And about 58 percent of the employed workforce was in the private sector, including family farming.[74]

To attract foreign direct investment, many restrictions were relaxed. Most licensing requirements were abolished. Full repatriation of all profits and of capital gains was guaranteed. The minimum investment clause was eliminated. However, the tax holiday conditions remained tight so as not to give foreign capital an unfair advantage over domestic capital.[75] As a result, only small-scale foreign investment increased. The major impediments to attracting large-scale foreign investment were the inability to determine who was the owner of appropriate terrains in a "greenfield" project, as well as the unwillingness of local authorities to issue the necessary permits. In addition, Poland was perceived as a high political risk country. All this frustrated potential investors, who decided to look for greener fields elsewhere.[76]

Alternatively, foreign capital could be attracted to acquire an existing state-owned enterprise (SOE). But there are several obstacles. The potential acquirer must acquire the assets of the enterprise—including the management, the Workers' Council, and the union—with special conditions, e.g., worker dismissal is not allowed for a two-year period. Since foreign investors must also receive approval of the funding organ (in most cases, the Ministry of Industry) and of the Ministry of Ownership Transformation, negotiations tend to be lengthy and costly. Despite these obstacles, several foreign firms, ranging from consumer goods companies to automobile manufacturers, acquired SOEs. But in relation to the size of the Polish economy, such foreign acquisitions were insignificant.[77]

The Consequence of Reforms. "Shock therapy" was Poland's initial step toward a market economy. On the one hand, it brought a number of immediate benefits—substantially reduced inflation, lessened shortages, and increased exports to Western countries. On the other hand, shock therapy initially produced a drastic decline in economic activity: the shrinkage in GDP, the drop in industrial output, and rising unemployment.[78]

Recently, however, the Polish economy has started to recover. Inflation declined considerably. Economic and industrial growth turned positive. Efficiency increased in both the public and the private sectors, and almost all industrial firms operated without subsidies.[79]

Professor Mark Schaffer suggests two major possible scenarios for Poland. Optimistically, if macroeconomic stability continues and the economy remains relatively depoliticized, then Poland could be considered for membership in the European Union by the end of the 1990s. If, pessimistically, macroeconomic stability cannot be maintained and the economy is repoliticized, then it will take a possibly lengthy time for

BOX 3.1

Possible Models for North Korea

In communist regimes, three models for change have been conceived in recent times. The East European model is not likely to succeed in North Korea because there has been little experience of civil liberty there. Nor is the Soviet scenario feasible, since it is difficult to believe that a leader like Gorbachev, who was seen as having a rational vision, and a group of progressive thinkers can emerge to confront the existing order in North Korea. Unfortunately, Kim Il Sung has eliminated most dissident, reform-inclined intellectuals and civilian leaders.

The fact that the Pyongyang regime has set aside the Najin-Sunbong area (621 square kilometers) for special economic zones clearly emulates the Chinese experience, as does the revision of the 1984 Joint Venture Law. In addition, a tentative corporatization/privatization is observed in the August Third Movement, which was placed outside of central planning as a means of providing incentives for increased production. Although the incentives are at local government rather than individual levels, they are being institutionalized through "direct sales stores" where locally produced goods are sold directly to local customers, by-passing centralized control. However, North Korea has a long way to go before it can adopt substantial reforms as national commitments. In the PRC, Deng paved the way for major economic reforms in the late 1970s, leading to an economic boom in the coastal areas.

If North Korea pursues Chinese-style reform, it will face a number of dilemmas. Even if it welcomed foreign investment and economic assistance from Japan and the United States, it would remain bitter about wartime crimes and imperialism. Pyong-Yang still repeats the same rhetoric about the struggle against imperialism and the idea of one nation and self-reliance. The reality is that economic recovery in North Korea, in the form of trade, aid, and investment links with the United States and Japan, will come about only when the country is seen as realistically committed to the pursuit of peace with the Republic of Korea and to the abandonment of its highly suspect nuclear weapons research program. Currently, the North appears to be trying to buy time while searching for some way out of its dilemma short of drastically reforming its system.

Quoted from Pan Suk Kim, "Will North Korea Blink?: Matters of Grave Danger," *Asian Survey* (March 1994), pp. 270–271, with minor changes.

Poland to join the European Union. Poland, thus far, has managed its economy in line with the direct path to Europe. (See Box 3.1 for a discussion of North Korea's possible pathways to economic development.)[80]

SUMMARY

This chapter examined eight development pathways illustrated by several different countries. Each model has its merits and drawbacks. There is no one best pathway for nations to pursue since each faces a unique set of opportunities, constraints, and competitive conditions. However, by assessing the advantages and drawbacks of each pathway, subject to a nation's unique set of opportunities, constraints, and competitive conditions, the economic development policymakers are in a better position to select the most appropriate development pathway for that nation.

Part II

FORMULATING THE NATION'S STRATEGIC VISION

Chapter 4

Strategic Groups of Nations and the Global Competitive Structure

I n an increasingly interdependent global economy, a nation's international trade is of critical importance. This leads us to look at its competitive position in a world of many suppliers and buyers, and varying
national endowments, economic policies, and trade strategies. Sometimes these lead to specific trading relationships and articulate national
strategies: examples include Japan, Europe, and the United States, the
advanced trading countries. China as a fast-growing national economy
is emerging with its own distinctive strategy. Others like India, Indonesia,
Brazil, and Zimbabwe are also attracted by the allure of a national
strategy.

We classify the many economies covered in this chapter into groups of
nations whose national trade strategies are somewhat similar. These
might reflect national stages of development, conscious trade policies,
and ongoing economic performance. In some cases, these may lead to
game-theoretic contests between individual countries, a group of countries, or contrasting positions in world forums. The strategic group might
be distinguished by its relative strengths and weaknesses as well as by
opportunities and threats. Although manufacturing is the most publicized—or specific items like automobiles or oil—the scope is much

wider and includes agricultural services, finance, and so on. This is a classification as of today, but is subject to change as economies undergo change, in part as a result of the trade and marketing strategies they pursue.

In this chapter, we first introduce the notion of national evolution. Nations exhibit different features in different stages of development. These stages and features have been identified by different observers; we have chosen to examine the stages of Walt Rostow (1964) and Michael Porter (1990). After examining these stages, we describe eight strategic groups of nations.

THE STAGES IN NATION EVOLUTION

Rostow's Five Stages of Economic Development[1]

Walt Rostow proposed one of the best known models for classifying countries by stage of economic development. He identified five stages of development—growth is the movement from one stage to another, and countries in the first three stages are considered to be underdeveloped. Each stage is described and illustrated below.

Traditional Society. In a traditional society, economic change and improvements are not sufficient to increase output per capita. Most of the economy is oriented toward producing primary products such as agriculture, fuel, forestry, and raw materials. The majority of people live and work in rural sectors. Literacy is low, as is the level of per capita output. Little economic exchange in organized markets takes place.

Transitional Society. A society in transition has formed contacts with other cultures. The contacts include various transfers of more developed nations' values, attitudes, institutions, best practices, technology, foreign aid, and foreign direct investment. However, these transfers are sometimes thought to create a situation of vulnerability in which forces largely outside the control of the country in transition can have decisive and dominating influences on its overall economic and social well-being. The development of physical and social infrastructure has begun in a small but important way. This stage is the precondition for takeoff.

Takeoff Society. In the takeoff stage, nations experience an accelerated growth rate. Improvements in production lead to expansion of supporting and related industries. The country's capital stock is very active and dynamic. In this stage, some key sectors generate sufficient capital and plow back a high level of profits to finance further growth.

In addition to domestic savings, nations need to obtain foreign exchange to finance many development projects. Although foreign direct investment and foreign aid are a significant source of foreign exchange, exports typically account for a very high percentage of the annual flow of total foreign currency earnings. In this stage, physical and social infrastructure have been intensively developed to sustain steady development.

Technological Maturity. In this stage, the economy is effectively applying modern technology to the full range of its economic activities. Unskilled labor and capital-intensive industries are replaced by more skilled labor and more advanced technology-intensive industries. At this point, productivity and wages increase very rapidly and the economy is highly dependent on global economy.

High Mass Consumption. In this fifth stage, per capita income has increased to levels that provide purchasing power beyond the basic necessities. Consumers now start shifting their attention from the quantity of goods to the quality of their lives.[2]

Porter's Stages of National Competitive Development

Michael Porter (1990) uses a theory of competitive advantage to explain economic development within nations and national differences in growth and prosperity. He identifies a four-stage development process. The characteristics of each are summarized in Table 4.1 below.

National prosperity, in Porter's view, is highly associated with the "upgrading" of competitive advantage. In the beginning, a nation tries to exploit its factor conditions to drive its development. At the next stage, the nation starts attracting foreign technology and investing in capital equipment, while encouraging more savings. Labor- and resource-intensive industries are replaced by industries that are more capital- and technology-intensive. The most successful companies are able to

TABLE 4.1

The Stages of National Competitive Development

Driver of Development	Source of Competitive Advantage	Examples
Factor conditions	Basic factors of production (e.g., natural resources, geographical location, unskilled labor)	Canada, Australia, Singapore, South Korea before 1980
Investment	Investment in capital equipment, and transfer of technology from overseas; also requires presence of and national consensus in favor of investment over consumption	Japan during 1960s. South Korea during 1980s
Innovation	All four determinants of national advantage interact to drive the creation of new technology	Japan since late 1970s. Italy since early 1970s; Sweden and Germany during most of the post-war period
Wealth	Emphasis on managing existing wealth causes the dynamics of the diamond to reverse: competitive advantage erodes as innovation is stifled, investment in advanced factors slows, rivalry ebbs, and individual motivation wanes	U.K. during post-war period; U.S.A., Switzerland, Sweden, and Germany since 1980

Source: Robert M. Grant, "Porter's 'Competitive Advantage of Nations': An Assessment," *Strategic Management Journal,* 12 (1991), Table 1, p. 540.

produce higher value added through product and service differentiation. These companies concentrate on knowledge activities overseas.

At a further stage, the nation turns to innovation as a major driver of its national wealth. If it succeeds, it may move into still another stage marked by the effort to manage and preserve its existing wealth. Its investment and innovation activity might slow down and the nation's competitive advantage may begin to erode.[3]

STRATEGIC GROUPS OF NATIONS AND THE GLOBAL COMPETITIVE STRUCTURE

Nations can be classified into the following eight strategic groups (see Figure 4.1), using two strategic dimensions—*the level of wealth position* and *the degree of industrialization.*[4]

1. The Industrial Giants
2. The Rising Stars
3. The Latin Americans
4. The Populous Countries
5. The Former Socialists
6. The Industrial Nichers
7. The Commodity Nichers
8. The Subsistents

The Industrial Giants

This group (the United States, Germany, France, the United Kingdom, Italy, and Japan) possesses the highest economic power. Table 4.2 illustrates the economic indicators of the countries in the group.

FIGURE 4.1

Strategic Groups of Nations

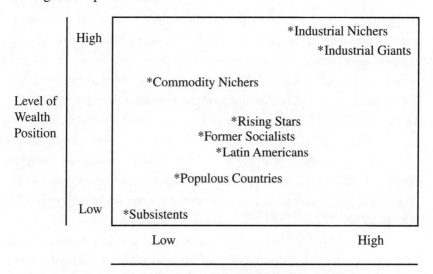

TABLE 4.2

The Industrial Giants

Country	Population *(million)*	GDP *(U.S.$ billion)*	Per capita GDP *(U.S.$ million)*
United States	248.76	5,163.7	20,758
Germany	78.66	1,337.7	17,006
France	56.14	955.9	17,020
United Kingdom	57.02	831.7	14,540
Italy	57.52	865.8	15,063
Japan	123.12	2,833.7	23,016

Source: Philip R. Cateora, *International Marketing* (Homewood, IL: Irwin, 1993), Exhibit 9.1, p. 264; Exhibit 9.6, p. 287; and Exhibit 8.12, p. 251.

Internal Cooperation. Countries in this group play a vital role in the world community. Through the G7 mechanism, they cope with international trade conflicts, alleviate or annul international debts of which they are the major lenders, help restore the economies in former Communist countries, and deal with global pollution and resource degradation problems.

Competition. The nations in this group compete with each other for world leadership in the economic, political, and technological spheres. Japan stepped into the economic superpower position as the economies of the United States and EC-4 nations stagnated. This led twelve countries in the European Community group to establish the European Single Market in 1992 in order to strengthen their competitiveness vis-à-vis Japan and the United States. The United States, after losing global dominance in one industry after another (e.g., textiles, steel, automobiles, consumer electronics, home appliances, and telecommunications equipment), requested other countries to implement a free trade policy through the GATT mechanism, and also formed the North American Free Trade Agreement (the United States, Canada, and Mexico). In response, Japan extended its investments in the EC and the United States. It also extended its strategic alliances with the Asian NICs and Southeast Asian countries.

Economic Performance. Figure 4.2 compares the performance—in terms of *GDP growth, inflation, unemployment,* and *balance-of-payment position* as a percentage of GDP—of the six industrial giant nations in 1980–90 with their positions in 1967–73 before the oil crisis. The four performance dimensions are joined up to form a diamond for each nation: the bigger the nation's diamond, the better its economic performance.

In the 1960s and early 1970s, most countries performed relatively well on the four dimensions. Japan and Germany possessed the largest diamonds. But after the oil crisis, their growth stagnated, and inflation and un-

FIGURE 4.2

Economic Performance of the Industrial Giants, 1980–90

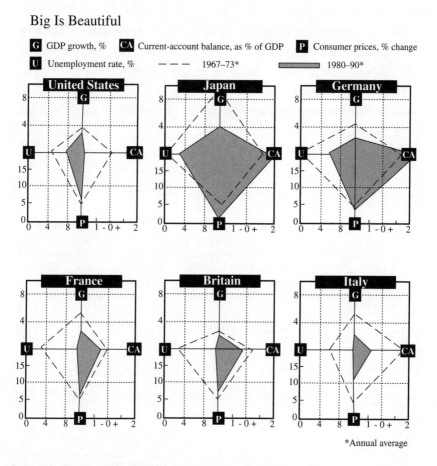

Big Is Beautiful

Source: "An Economy's Best Friend," *The Economist,* Nov. 16, 1991, p. 87.

employment rose. All countries—particularly Britain and Italy—saw their diamonds shrink dramatically during 1974–79 (not shown). Only two countries—Japan and Germany—regained their sparkle during the 1980s. Unemployment appeared to rise everywhere. The diamonds of the other four countries remained smaller in the 1980s than before 1974. Due to its huge current account deficit, America's shrank compared with the 1970s. Britain, France, and Italy all coped with a higher unemployment rate, Italy is the only country whose diamond shrunk from every direction.[5]

Future Competitiveness. One interesting question is which nations in this group will be best able to respond to the coming challenges of other strategic groups of nations, particularly the new emerging economies from East Asia. Table 4.3 ranks these six countries on the basis of five factors—the higher the score in parentheses (0, 1, 2), the more favorable the outlook for that country.

The first indicator is labor market flexibility (see column 1). The more flexible the labor market, the more quickly workers who lose their jobs to Third World competition will move to other growth sectors. America gets the highest score, followed by Britain and Japan. Britain's labor market reforms have moved it closer to the American system. For Japan,

TABLE 4.3

The League of Nations

	Labour market flexibility	Employ-ment in manu-facturing 1993	Adults with upper-secondary education % 1991	High-tech exports, % 1992	Pension-fund assets as % of GDP, 1992	Total score out of ten
United States	(2)	16 (2)	83 (2)	38 (2)	56 (2)	10
Japan	(1)	24 (1)	67 (1)	36 (2)	20 (1)	6
Britain	(1)	20 (1)	65 (1)	31 (1)	62 (2)	6
Germany	(0)	31 (0)	82 (2)	21 (0)	6 (0)	2
France	(0)	21 (1)	51 (1)	24 (0)	3 (0)	2
Italy	(0)	22 (1)	28 (0)	15 (0)	1 (0)	1

Source: "Survey of the Global Economy," *The Economist*, Oct. 1, 1994, Table 18, p. 38.

its commitment to lifetime employment is the major impediment, resulting in high labor market inflexibility. Continental European countries get
no scores due to their strict employment protection laws, minimum
wages, and overgenerous unemployment benefits, all of which make
labor markets inflexible.

The second indicator reflects the percentages of the workforce still
employed in manufacturing (see column 2): the higher the number, the
bigger the adjustment the country faces in response to competition from
the newly emerging economies. America scores top marks, while Germany is at the other extreme. German manufacturing accounts for more
than 30 percent of total employment. Sizable barriers to competition in
services will also affect Germany's future competitiveness.

The third indicator is the quality of education (column 3), indicating
whether workers are well equipped for the industries of the future (the
scoring is based on the percentage of adults with at least an upper secondary education). America and Germany perform excellently. Italy is
the lowest. It is worth noting that the quality of training is not incorporated in this indicator. In the past, Germany and Japan had managed the
transition between school and work better than did the United States and
Britain. More recently, however, Germany's apprenticeship schemes
have shown a slow response to changes in technology.

The fourth indicator shows high-tech goods as a share of total manufacturing exports (column 4). America and Japan score top marks: high-
tech goods account for more than one-third of their exports, compared
with 31 percent in Britain, around 20 percent in France and Germany,
and only 15 percent in Italy.

The last indicator measures pension fund assets as a percentage of GDP
(column 5). Pensioners in countries with highly developed private pension
funds like America and Britain will enjoy the advantage of high returns on
investments in emerging markets. By contrast, pension fund assets are
equivalent to 6 percent or less of GDP in France, Germany, and Italy.

The overall score (column 6) reflects a nation's potential ability to respond to the "challenge" coming from the new emerging economies.
America comes out on top, followed closely by Japan and Britain. In
contrast, Germany, France, and Italy lag a long way behind.

For future growth and prosperity, economies must shift from declining
sectors to more-skill-intensive goods and services. The United States
seems to perform better at this strategy than Europe. Another advantage

is that American consumer goods are likely to have strong appeal for millions of new consumers. By contrast, with its rigid labor markets and trailing high-tech industries, Continental Europe may have a very high possibility of pursuing protectionist policies over the next decade. Jobless rates are still high while labor market reforms are lagging, thus pointing to further unemployment.[6]

The Rising Stars

The "rising stars"—comprising the "Four Tigers"—South Korea, Taiwan, Hong Kong, and Singapore—and "three later tigers"—Thailand, Malaysia, and Indonesia—are a highly diverse group of economies, differing in natural resources, population size, culture, and economic policy.[7] Table 4.4 illustrates some economic indicators of the countries in this group.

The key feature of this group is that all these economies had rapid, sustained growth during 1960–90. These countries were also characterized by unusually rapid export growth and strong and dynamic agricultural

TABLE 4.4

The Rising Stars

Country	Population *(million)*	GDP *(U.S.$ billion)*	Per Capita GDP *(U.S.$ million)*
South Korea	42.38	211.9	4,999*
Taiwan	20.10	151.5	7,538*
Hong Kong	5.76	62.9	10,918*
Singapore	2.68	28.4	10,582*
Thailand	55.70	45.6	893†
Malaysia	17.89	32.2	1,991†
Indonesia	184.28	69.7	405†

*Data drawn from the *International Trade Statistics Yearbook,* op. cit.

†Data drawn from *The World Market Atlas* (New York: Business International, 1992).

Source: From Cateora, *International Marketing,* Exhibit 9.1, p. 264; Exhibit 9.6, p. 287; and Exhibit 8.12, p. 251.

sectors. Moreover, the rising stars have experienced much higher per capita income growth while income distribution has been more equal than in other developing countries. Figure 4.3 shows the link between growth of GDP per capita during 1965–90 and the ratio of the top to the bottom quintile of the income distribution. According to Figure 4.3, the Four Tigers showed exceptional growth and high income equality.[8]

Three growth-related factors explain why the rising stars differ from

FIGURE 4.3

Income Inequality and Growth of GDP, 1965–89

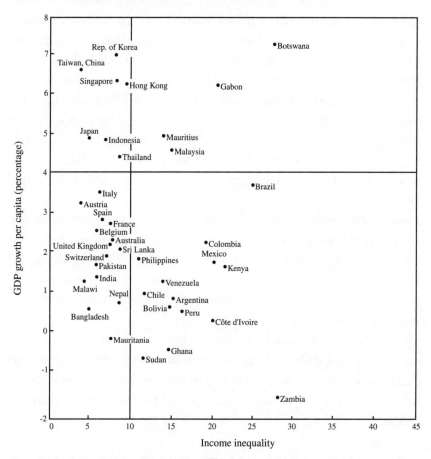

*Income inequality is measured by the ratio of the income shares of the richest 20% and the poorest 20% of the population.

Source: John M. Page, "The East Asian Miracle: An Introduction," *World Development*, vol. 22, no. 4 (1994), Figure 2, p. 616 (based on World Bank data).

other groups of nations. First is the high investment rate during 1960–90 supported by the rapid growth in domestic saving. Second is the high and rising stock of human capital supported by universal primary and secondary education. These two factors account for a substantial amount of the growth in the rising stars. Differences in growth rates between the rising stars and other groups of nations largely reflect differences in the rates of savings and capital accumulation.

The third factor—changes in total factors productivity (TFP)—is also important. The TFP performance of the rising stars as a group exceeds that for most other countries (Figure 4.4). According to John Page, we can categorize the rising stars into two distinct groups: *investment-driven* economies and *productivity-driven* economies. The investment-driven economies—Indonesia, Malaysia, and Singapore—have relatively low TFP growth rates and small relative contributions of TFP to output growth. In contrast, the productivity-driven economies—Korea, Hong Kong, Thailand, and Taiwan—have relatively high TFP growth rates and higher contributions of TFP to output growth. Thus, East Asia's superior performance can be derived from three main sources: (1) capital allocating to high return investments; (2) the quick absorption of Western technology; and (3) value productivity as compared to physical productivity.[9]

Export Development Strategy. Having a small internal market is a major weakness that forces these "tigers" and "little tigers" to rely on export development as a basis for their industrialization. By using export-led industrialization strategies, the group's share of industrial and manufacturing sectors in their GDP has increased dramatically, while the agricultural share in their GDP has declined.

Since the 1970s, most of the tigers have diversified their exports to lessen their vulnerability to price and demand fluctuations in their exported goods. The production and export of resource- and labor-intensive goods had decreased considerably, replaced by many capital-intensive products.

Intraregional Trade. Intraregional trade among the Four Tigers is gradually increasing, though less than that among the "later tiger" nations. The share of this intraregional trade was 8.7 percent in 1973, 10.0 percent in 1981, and 10.5 percent in 1988.[10] As Marcus Noland points out, "it is un-

FIGURE 4.4

Total Factor Productivity Growth and Part of Growth Due to Growth of Factor Inputs, 1960–89

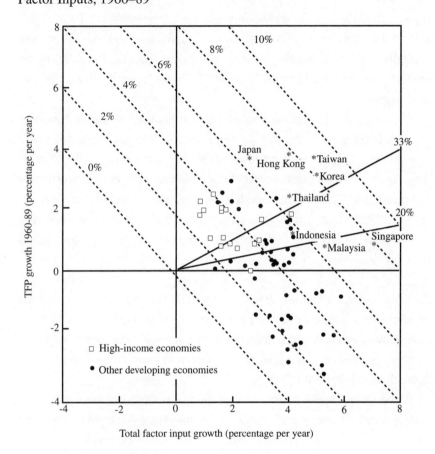

Total factor input growth (percentage per year)

*Dashed lines represent total average GDP growth rate, 1960-89. Solid rays represent the contribution to total growth by TFP growth.

Source: Page, op. cit., Figure 4, p. 618 (based on Nehru and Dhareshwar, 1993, and World Bank data).

likely that the 'four tigers' would enter into preferential trade arrangements among themselves, if for no other reason than that Hong Kong and Singapore are practically free traders and there is consequently little scope for trade preferences."[11]

Intraregional Investment. Intraregional investment flows in the rising stars is closely linked to the so-called *flying geese* regional pattern of manufacturing production. This pattern of development began with the 1960s emergence of the Four Tigers specializing in the production and exports of labor-intensive goods. During the 1970s, while Japan increasingly shifted its focus to technology-intensive industries, the Four Tigers shifted their emphasis from labor-intensive industries toward skilled- and capital-intensive industries. During this same period, the later tigers shifted from resource-intensive industries more toward labor-intensive industries.

The intraregional production and investment activities of the Four Tigers accelerated in the late 1980s. Japanese yen appreciation, rising real wages, and labor shortages shifted the comparative advantage in labor-intensive industries toward the next-tier economies. It is worth noting that in the "flying geese" path to development, foreign direct investment and technology transfers were the critical factors as each nation typically looked to more advanced neighbors for technology and capital imports.[12]

Future Prospect and Some Impediments. The four NICs have succeeded in transforming local productive potential into competitively priced products demanded on world markets and establishing self-sustaining development. Now each of the four must confront the transformation toward a more democratic political system.[13]

Is the Four Tigers' success in adopting outward-oriented policies a model for the "later tiger" nations? Thailand and Malaysia have been viewed as potential fifth and sixth "tigers." They received substantial foreign investment in the 1980s and created a sizable middle class. Indonesia set the goal to become a NIC by 1994. It failed, but has made substantial progress in attracting foreign investment.[14]

It is worth noting that, although "little tigers" have recently registered impressive increases in manufactures exports, in many cases the relevant technology and skills have not been integrated into the broad-based economy. In Malaysia, for example, export manufacture has been largely confined to the foreign processing zones, with few backward or forward linkages to the rest of the economy. This lack of integration has limited the ability of the later tigers to absorb technology and skills from abroad.[15]

The Latin Americans

Table 4.5 illustrates some economic indicators of the countries in the Latin American group.

Latin American countries have a shared history (e.g., import substitution), common problems (e.g., inflation), and same solutions (foreign debts).[16] Since 1930, they had begun to develop their import substitution industries—starting from basic production technologies and rising to middle and moderately high technologies. They adopted this kind of industrialization strategy because they believed that the sizes of their domestic markets and natural resources were sufficient to support industrial expansion.[17] However, their domestic markets were saturated faster than expected, and it became necessary to export surplus products to neighboring countries such as those in Central America: El Salvador, Honduras, Guatemala, Nicaragua. Brazil, for example, exports to Bolivia,

TABLE 4.5

The Latin Americans

Country	Population (million)	GDP (U.S.$ billion)	Per Capita GDP (U.S.$ million)
Argentina	32.32	82.4	2,647
Brazil	150.37	326.3	2,306
Chile	13.17	18.9	1,511
Mexico	88.60	139.9	1,686
Peru	21.55	45.2	2,183
Uruguay	3.09	7.5	2,452
Venezuela	19.74	49.6	2,716
Ecuador	10.59	10.6	1,069
Colombia	32.98	36.2	1,209
Paraguay	4.28	4.5	1,155
Bolivia	7.31	3.9	588

Source: Ibid., Exhibit 9.3, p. 281.

Peru, and Paraguay. Apparently part of the strategic intent of the stronger countries in this group is to pursue regional power.

Because of excessively high tariff barriers and limited internal barriers, the gap between many Latin American countries and international productivity levels constantly widened, making it unlikely that these countries could accomplish the original goal of gradual integration into the global economy.[18]

As for inflation, Latin American countries possess two characteristics that distinguish their inflation from that in other countries: prices rose to hyperinflation levels and the inflation's causes seem to be structural rather than monetarist. The external debt problems of Latin American countries began in the nineteenth century, when borrowing took place to develop resource-intensive industries. In the 1940s and 1950s, borrowing took place to finance the import substitution trade policy. The twin 1970s oil crises intensified the debt problem. After the second oil shock, the resulting world recession led to a decline in world trade and consequently a collapse in the exports of the Latin American countries.[19]

In the mid-1980s, the saturation in the domestic market and the decrease in the purchasing power of regional trading partners led to high external debt and stagnation in these economies. The successful experiences of Asian NICs led most Latin American governments to realize that outward-oriented, not inward-oriented, policies should be the appropriate strategy in building their national wealth.

The Populous Countries

There are some distinctive differentiating characteristics in the development strategies of the two most populous countries, China and India. China adopted a Communist path to development, marked by major upheavals, whereas India followed the model of a mixed economy, which gradually expanded the role of the state bureaucracy. China's Great Leap Forward of 1958–60 marked the first major shift and ended in production disasters, severe starvation, and massive famine. A stable economic regime followed, with emphasis on heavy industrial development, controls on internal migration, and regional self-sufficiency. Administered prices, selective decentralization, and an "iron rice bowl" policy, which guaranteed basic food needs to all covered workers, were some of the mechanisms employed in national planning. After Mao's reign ended in 1976, China pursued more market-oriented policies and made greater use of market incentives. India also emphasized heavy industry development in the state sector, but allocations to agriculture and consumer goods were more generous, and it relied more generally on market prices.[20]

Table 4.6 illustrates some economic indicators of the two countries in this group.

India and China eventually shifted their trade and investment policies from inward orientation to outward orientation. In 1956, India issued an industrialization policy which emphasized the development of heavy industries in the public sector, leaving the other areas open for private enterprise. Foreign direct investment was not encouraged, equity participation was limited to less than 50 percent, sensitive security fields were barred, and preference was given to modern technology.

A complex system of licensing (e.g., for new plants and plant expansion) was used to influence private investments in the capital and intermediate-goods industries. High tariffs, and tight quotas on imports, particularly for consumer goods, were applied to protect local producers. Controlled allocations of foreign exchange in time became the chief means of control. There was little incentive to export. Only small enterprises that provided consumer goods for the domestic market were really free from government control.[21]

In the 1980s, India took the first steps toward relaxing this framework of controls. In 1991, to cope with a balance-of-payments crisis, the new Indian government initiated more sweeping reforms, which accelerated the shift from a protected, licensed economy to a decontrolled, delicensed, and deregulated one, and so reduced the range of discretionary,

TABLE 4.6

The Populous Countries

Country	Population (million)	GDP (U.S.$ billion)	Per Capita GDP (U.S.$ million)
India	811.82	236.5	291
China	1,119.70	422.5	377

Source: Ibid., Exhibit 8.9, p. 242.

ad hoc demand. These reforms included: (1) devaluing the currency to make it partly convertible; (2) reducing tight restrictions on imports and lowering import duties on capital goods; (3) cutting the number of subsidies; (4) progressively liberalizing interest rates; (5) abolishing production licenses for most industries; (6) easing restrictions on repatriating dividends and royalties; (7) establishing a partial tax exemption on profits from export sales and revising the system of personal taxes; (8) allowing a partial sale of shares in selected public enterprises; and (9) reducing restrictions on foreign trading companies.[22] The monetary and financial-sector reforms, however, including currency convertibility, were slow in maturing. Unlike China, India had always had a well-established central fiscal and reserve bank system.

China's shift from autarchy to outward-oriented growth after 1978 goes a long way toward explaining the doubling of its rate of growth in GNP. After 1984, the government promoted the growth of nonpublic business enterprises either in urban areas or in special economic zones. By 1991, these nonpublic business enterprises accounted for 47 percent of total industrial value. On the government side, there has been administrative reform—with a steady decentralization of responsibility for infrastructure and social services to lower levels of government.[23] As a result, the number of rural people living in absolute poverty has fallen sharply over the past two decades.[24]

As the Chinese and Indian economies move rapidly toward greater reliance on free markets in the 1990s, a major concern is that the changes will bring in their train greater income inequality, rising inflation, and continued environmental damage.[25] The fear is also that corruption may take new forms as lobbyists for special favors and quick decisions seek to influence the political process even as discretionary decision making is on the wane in many areas.

In the political sphere, China's economic reforms of the 1980s occurred while bypassing democratization. The harsh repression that culminated in the Tiananmen Square massacre in June 1989 impeded the pace of economic reform and social progress. If China were able to reconcile the issue of political democracy and economic reform, it could well become one of the world's major economic powers.[26]

If the pace of momentum continues, China will have a larger GDP than the U.S. by 2003. Even if its 1980s growth rate halved,

> *it would pass the U.S. in 2014. It is possible that China will be the world's largest economy by the year 2020, a position which will inevitably give it very much more influence in world politics.*[27]

India is not much behind in the revised calculation of GNP size and is also poised to move ahead, but not as dramatically as China. An uncertain element is the political evolution of India after the end of the Congress Party's dominance.

It is worth noting that other populous countries, such as Bangladesh and Pakistan, are still deeply mired in poverty and backwardness. Both have little prospect for capital accumulation in the coming years. Bangladesh is extremely poor, with no foothold to get accumulation started. Military-influenced Pakistan faces political instability. As for Vietnam, as one of the populous Socialist states, it is trying to follow China's reform model.[28]

The Former Socialists

When the Communist regime took over in Russia in 1917, it gave priority to developing heavy industry and military strength. Later, under Stalin's reign, priorities were shifted to consumer goods, agriculture, light industries, and construction. GNP growth rose 5.9 percent, 5.0 percent, 5.3 percent, 3.7 percent, and 2.6 percent, respectively, in the successive Five-Year Plans from 1950 to 1975. Per capita consumption grew at an average of 3.0 percent per annum during 1950–80. However, these rises were accompanied by a steep hike in the cost of real resources. The growth rate started to diminish when stagnation set in during the 1980s. Though there was a huge surplus of unnecessary goods, there were shortages of necessary consumer goods, especially food. These products, however, could be obtained from "black" markets, but at excessive prices.

Indeed, command economies can, on the one hand, boast of efforts to develop equitable income and orderly development. On the other hand, they exhibit a sluggishness in the areas of technology, personal ambition, and risk taking. The failure of centrally planned policies to advance economic growth and create national wealth led most of these economies in the 1990s to adopt the market economy model to guide their economic and industrial development.

Table 4.7 illustrates some economic indicators of the countries in the former Socialist group.

Hungary stands out as an early persistent reformer even under the Communist regime. After the defeat of the Communists, the new government cautiously reshaped the reform program, with gradual reduction of subsidies, some tightening of monetary policy, and a continuing liberalization of foreign trade and foreign exchange.[29]

The former Soviet Union made its first serious attempt to utilize market forces in 1987, by giving state-owned enterprises greater flexibility and more incentives to improve efficiency. After the collapse of the USSR in 1991, Russia adopted "shock therapy" to energize the economy. By 1992, it had liberalized trade within the economy, removing price controls, drastically cutting government spending, making the currency partly convertible, and adopting a value-added tax. Unfortunately, the ex-

TABLE 4.7

The Former Socialists

Country	Population *(million)*	GDP *(U.S.$ billion)*	Per Capita GDP *(U.S.$ million)*
Czechoslovakia	15.65	50.5	3,225*
Hungary	10.38	28.9	2,783*
Poland	37.85	82.2	2,172*
Albania	3.20	2.0	625*
Bulgaria	8.99	36.2	4,030*
Romania	23.15	42.1	1,819*
Yugoslavia	23.69	73.0	3,083*
Estonia	1.6	8.9	5,523†
Latvia	2.7	16.3	6,013†
Lithuania	3.8	19.7	5,543†

*Data drawn from "Indicators of Market Size for 117 Countries, Part II," *Business International*, July 8, 1991.

†Data drawn from *Fortune*, Oct. 21, 1991, pp. 68–74.

Source: Ibid., Exhibit 8.5, p. 237, and Exhibit 8.9, p. 238.

tent of reform was limited by various political considerations. The central bank was injecting loans to industry at negative real interest rates, inducing inflation and jeopardizing the stabilization program. Meanwhile, the government failed to reach its deficit targets. Liberalization of foreign trade was pursued and access to hard currency was undertaken, although with many restrictions. Progress was impeded by the ethnic conflicts along the country's southern rim, which disrupted trade and investment.[30]

In 1993, Czechoslovakia split into the Czech Republic and Slovakia. The former is presently a growing economy and hopes to join the European Union, while the latter stumbles economically and elects nationalistic leaders.[31]

In Poland and in Yugoslavia, the situation has been similar at the beginning, but it is strikingly different today, mainly for political reasons. At the start, extreme disequilibrium led to hyperinflation in 1989. In both countries, reform programs started in 1990, with macroeconomic discipline to curb inflationary pressures. Over time, however, differences emerged. When serious economic and political strains had intensified in both countries, Polish monetary policy seemed to be too restrictive, while that of Yugoslavia was too lax. The breakup of Yugoslavia put an end to its reform program.[32]

The Balkan peninsula is marked by bitter ethnic conflicts and civil wars that threaten to pull the whole region away from ties to the new Europe. While the neighboring countries of Hungary and Poland embrace free market reforms, Bulgaria and Romania are slow to emerge from the days of totalitarian rule.[33]

The early stages of economic transformation from a centrally planned to a market-based economy are very traumatic, with economic contraction much greater than expected. Employment fell in Eastern Europe while inflation rose drastically.[34] According to Otto Hieronymi (1990), it appears that for the next few years at least, Russia and Eastern Europe will be coping with very difficult circumstances, including:

- General political uncertainties
- Declining real income for much of the population
- The announcement of a severe austerity program
- Widespread realization of the debt problem and the fear of its impact on the nation's modernization and growth

- Fear of the failure of Soviet reform and of a subsequent backlash that could affect the other former socialist states
- Relatively slow change in the real economy, compared with the substantial changes "on paper"
- Substantial price increases for basic goods and growing fear of inflation
- Fear of unemployment
- A feeling of inadequacy resulting from the general technology gap between the former socialists and the OECD countries
- Apprehension that the entrenched rulers are trying to save their privileges and are maneuvering to retain power
- The proliferation of opposition parties and vocal dissension among the leaders
- Unfamiliarity with a market economy and apprehension about adjustment to it
- Confusion about the privatization program and fears of speculative capital imports
- The rescinding of foreign exchange travel allowances
- Constant warnings of economic difficulties and pessimistic comments by former government officials about the general economic and political situation[35]

The lack of a coherent vision about the future economic order is the main source of pessimism among countries in this group.

The Industrial Nichers

This group includes smaller industrial nations such as Belgium, the Netherlands, Switzerland, Norway, Sweden, and Israel. Table 4.8 illustrates some economic indicators of the countries in the industrial nichers' group.

A major disadvantage of smaller nations is that their domestic market is not large enough to permit as rapid a development of scale economies that would lead to further price reductions and further expansion of the market. Also, industrial nichers must face competitive threats both from larger industrial countries and from newly industrialized countries (NICs). Technological advances in the larger countries have led to increased competitive pressure on small industrial country firms. At the

TABLE 4.8

The Industrial Nichers

Country	Population *(million)*	GDP *(U.S.$ billion)*	Per Capita GDP *(U.S.$ million)*
Belgium	9.85	156.8	15,794
Denmark	5.14	106.2	20,694
Luxembourg	0.38	8.0	21,110
Netherlands	14.83	223.7	15,084
Austria	7.62	126.5	16,598
Finland	4.96	115.5	23,278
Iceland	0.25	5.2	20,611
Norway	4.23	90.9	21,488
Sweden	8.50	189.9	22,342
Switzerland	6.65	177.2	26,639

Source: Ibid., Exhibit 9.1, p. 264.

same time, the newly industrialized countries are increasing their competitive pressure in other industrial segments which are driven by price competition. This is the "small-country squeeze," as illustrated in Figure 4.5. The competitive threat to small industrialized economies can be defined as follows:

1. Markets for products which are relatively simple and based on mature technologies (Area A) are increasingly dominated by the NICs.
2. Markets where the products are very complex and/or based on new technologies (Area C) are increasingly dominated by the industrial superpowers.
3. Area C is itself increasing as more traditional sectors are adopting new technology.
4. Area B, which is the natural domain of the small industrialized countries, is therefore being squeezed from two directions.[36]

In addition, small industrial countries tend to have relatively fewer firms with worldwide capabilities. Among these countries, primarily

FIGURE 4.5

The Small-Country Squeeze

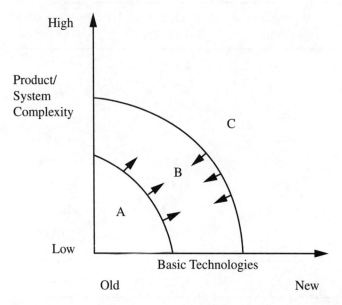

Source: Christopher Freeman and Bengt-Ake Lundvall, eds., *Small Countries Facing the Technological Revolution* (New York: Pinter Publishers, 1988), Figure 2.1, p. 49 (based on Stankiewicz, 1982).

Dutch- and Swiss-based companies have been successful in conducting world-scale R&D and in orienting production toward the world market. However, to be successful in this way requires certain productive capabilities—of technology and of management skills. Swiss companies, for example, are not able to develop and upgrade their technological capabilities quickly enough and are losing their footholds in many industrial sectors. The Swiss watch industry has suffered major export declines because it overlooked the potentials of electronic and digital watches, and underestimated the aggressive moves by Japanese competitors.[37]

The Commodity Nichers

The economies of countries among the commodity nichers' group—Saudi Arabia, Kuwait, United Arab Emirates, Qatar, Oman, Bahrain, and so on—thrive on petroleum. This group hurt the global economy with its two oil crises. These incidents spurred oil-consuming countries to seek energy-conserving measures; to explore other forms of energy such as solar energy; and to explore new oil sources, for example, in the North Sea. Those efforts, together with the failure in cartelizing oil production among OPEC members, caused global oil prices to drop, thus decreasing earnings for the commodity nichers.

Table 4.9 illustrates some economic indicators of certain countries in this group.

With similar resources and structure, countries in this group share a common strategic outlook. They are all trying to shift from oil overdependence and public-sector-driven growth to private-sector initiatives and a diversified industrial base. The general objectives of the evolving development strategy in the region include:

- Diversifying the region's economic structure in order to minimize its exposure to external factors by creating an industrial and technological base that is self-sustaining and independent from the oil sector.
- Increasing the added value of their natural resources through downstream processing.
- Fulfilling the domestic demand as much as possible while increasing exports by capitalizing on the region's relative advantage in certain products.
- Enhancing regional cooperation.
- Developing and increasing human productivity and enhancing the relation between reward and productivity.[38]

TABLE 4.9

The Commodity Nichers

Country	Population *(million)*	GDP *(U.S.$ billion)*	Per Capita GDP *(U.S.$ million)*
Saudi Arabia	16.10	96.9	6,020
Kuwait	2.04	18.1	9,751
Iraq	18.92	50.7	2,971
Iran	54.61	197.7	3,853
Syria	12.53	32.4	2,884

Source: Ibid., Exhibit 9.7, p. 287; and Michael P. Todaro, *Economic Development in the Third World*, 5th edn (White Plains, NY: Longmans, 1994), p. 650; *The World Market Atlas*, 1992.

Unfortunately, the recent Gulf crisis greatly affected political stability and imposed heavy financial burdens on the commodity nicher countries. However, the constructive subsiding of conflict between countries in this group and Israel will notably contribute to regional peace, which is an important factor in the creation of national wealth in the region.

The Subsistents

About half of the world's countries are classified as *less developing nations*, many of which are in Africa and South Asia. In the economic aspect, the most common characteristics of this group of countries are: a sharp economic decline; a drop in per capita incomes; rapid growth in population; a decrease in export revenues; and the curtailment of foreign investment.[39] As for the social aspect, a sharp decline in school enrollment, increases in malnutrition, and high maternal and child mortality are all too common in this group of countries. These are mainly attributed to the severe cuts in health and education expenditures. But the most disturbing problem, particularly in Africa, has been the widespread growth of the human immunodeficiency virus (HIV). This problem has tragically affected the quality of their human resources and its impact will last for generations.[40]

Table 4.10 illustrates some economic indicators of some countries in the subsistents' group.

IDENTIFYING THE NATION'S COMPETITORS AND ALLIANCES

Given the global competitive structure and strategic groups of nations, each nation's policymakers must proceed to formulate their country's competitive and cooperative strategies. They will then have a better sense of which countries they can effectively compete with and which countries they can cooperate with in the global marketplace.

The policymakers must decide which competitors to compete against most vigorously. This choice is aided by assessing the nation's strengths and weaknesses (see Chapter 5) and opportunities and threats (see Chapter 6). A nation can focus its attacks on one of the following several classes of competitors.

TABLE 4.10

The Subsistents

Country	Population (million)	GDP (U.S.$ billion)	Per Capita GDP (U.S.$ million)
Ethiopia	49.24	5.3	121
Kenya	24.03	8.3	373
Sudan	25.02	9.2	398
Uganda	18.79	2.5	148
Zambia	8.45	1.9	252
Niger	7.73	2.2	333
Nigeria	108.54	20.9	205

Source: Cateora, *International Marketing,* Exhibit 9.4, p. 284.

Strong versus Weak Competitors

Most nations aim their shots at their weaker competitors. This requires fewer resources and time per world market share point gained. But in the process, the nation may achieve little in the way of improved capabilities. A nation should also compete with strong competitors to sharpen its skills. Furthermore, even strong competitors have some weaknesses, and the nation may prove to be a worthy competitor.

Close versus Distant Competitors

Most nations usually compete with other nations that are similar (e.g., Singapore competes with Hong Kong, not with South Korea).

The two dimensions—strong versus weak and close versus distant— can be combined together to form a nation's competitive patterns. Figure 4.6 illustrates Thailand's competitive patterns.

Almost all countries shown in Figure 4.6 are competing with Thailand in two major domains: foreign direct investment attraction and exports. Due to the similar resource endowment, many ASEAN member states are direct competitors for both foreign direct investment attraction and exports. Countries like China and Vietnam, which have ample reserves of

FIGURE 4.6

Thailand's Competitive Patterns

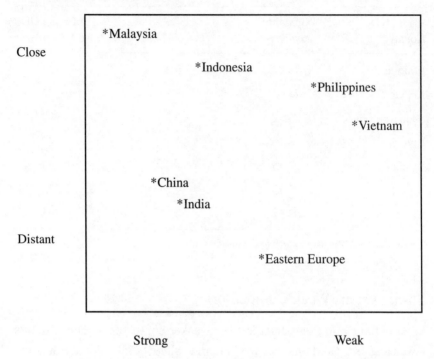

low-cost labor, are now the competitors for many Thai factory-driven export industries. The emergence of Eastern European countries as market economies creates more choices to many MNCs for their foreign direct investment.

The same notion can be applied to determine cooperative arrangements. Nations can focus on one of the following several classes of alliances.

Strong versus Weak Alliances

Many nations prefer to collaborate with weaker allies: reasons include enhancing their bargaining power within the whole group; gaining bargaining power for a weaker group; gaining access to the natural resources of weaker partners; and so on. A nation may also collaborate with strong allies in order to access aid, capital, technology, and markets.

Close versus Distant Alliances

Many nations prefer to collaborate with competitors who resemble them most: they may share a common language, culture, and way of doing business.

The two dimensions—strong versus weak and close versus distant—can be combined together to form a nation's cooperative patterns. Figure 4.7 illustrates Thailand's cooperative patterns.

From Figure 4.7, Japan, the United States, the European Union, and ASEAN nations are still close and strong partners for the Thai export industries. Trade with ASEAN was limited until recently, but these countries together now constitute Thailand's second-largest market after the United States (the bulk of exports to ASEAN are computers and computer parts, integrated circuits, and electrical appliances, mostly to Singapore). Also from Figure 4.7, Japan and Asian NICs are the close and strong partners for Thailand's inward foreign direct investment. Many

FIGURE 4.7

Thailand's Cooperative Patterns

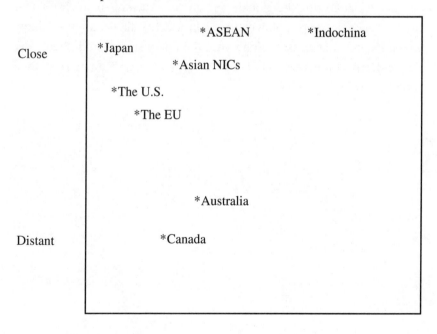

other industrial nations like Canada and Australia are relatively strong but distant partners, while Indochina countries such as Laos, Cambodia, and Vietnam are close but relatively weak partners for the Thai economy. The latter are potential countries for Thai's exports and outward foreign direct investment.

SUMMARY

Different nations are at different levels of development. In this chapter, we first described and illustrated Rostow's stages of economic development—traditional society, transitional society, takeoff stage, technology maturity, and high mass consumption, followed by Porter's stages of national competitive development—factor-driven, investment-driven, innovation-driven, and wealth-driven developments.

The second section described major strategic groups of nations classified by using their level of wealth and degree of industrialization. Eight strategic groups of nations were identified: the Industrial Giants, the Rising Stars, the Latin Americans, the Populous Countries, the Former Socialists, the Industrial Nichers, the Commodity Nichers, and the Subsistents. By analyzing the global competitive structure and their own nation's strategic group, policymakers can identify their nation's relative strengths and weaknesses, along with the opportunities and threats that derive from competing and cooperating within and among strategic groups.

Chapter 5

Assessing the Nation's Strengths and Weaknesses

W hy is one country prospering and another country stagnating? Some people answer, "Natural resources." Yet Argentina, Brazil, Nigeria, and Russia have abundant natural resources but low standards of living. Japan, Switzerland, and Singapore have very limited natural resources and little land but have achieved a high standard of living.

Consider the relative position of two countries, Argentina and Singapore. Before the outbreak of World War I, Argentina was the second-richest country in the world—after only the United States—in terms of per capita income. Unfortunately, its poor and incapable government reduced Argentina's economy presently to only a tenth that of Switzerland. If its international competitiveness had been maintained, its economy would now be the size of Britain or Italy. By contrast, Singapore took only two decades to shift from a developing to a developed nation. By 1990, Singapore's GDP per capita reached $12,310, up from $950 in 1970. It enjoys low unemployment, high budget surpluses, low pollution, and relatively few social problems. By the end of the century, Singapore aims to reach Switzerland's living standards.[1]

Changes in global forces and trends provide specific opportunities and threats to nations. The degree to which each nation captures the opportu-

nities or copes with the threats depends on its inherent capabilities. All
the elements of a nation's capabilities are shown in Figure 5.1 below.

1. These elements include the social (e.g., culture, attitudes, and values; social cohesion); the economic (e.g., factor endowments, industrial organization); and the political (e.g., leadership).
2. The quality of these elements can either be inherited, such as certain
   factor endowments (like natural resources), or created, such as a nation's industrial organization.
3. It can also be either static (a nation's culture, attitudes, and values)
   or dynamic (government leadership, industrial organization).
4. Some of these elements are more structural (factor endowments),
   some are more behavioral (government leadership), some are the
   combination of these two (a nation's industrial organization).

Therefore, policymakers should be concerned with their nation's capabilities not just in terms of scope and intensity, but also the substitution

FIGURE 5.1

The Nation's Capabilities

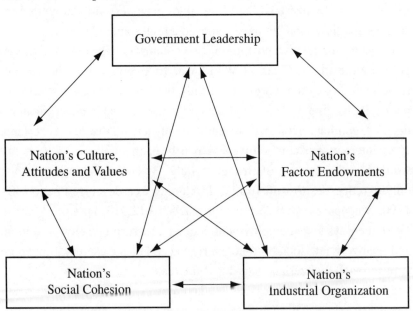

and synergistic effects among these elements over time. This chapter will examine each of these elements in turn.

A NATION'S CULTURE, ATTITUDES, AND VALUES

In recent publications, Professor Michael Porter (1990) argued that some nations achieve competitive advantages, but he did not explain why some achieve this and others do not. Differences in economic performance may result, in part, from differences in national culture. Cultural influence has become more important since many empirical studies of socioeconomic factors (e.g., education, population growth, nutrition, capital investment, and technological innovation) fail to explain these performance differences. The study by Professors Franke, Hofstede, and Bond has revealed the potential of cultural influences in explaining economic phenomena. They found that cultural factors explain more than 50 percent of the differences in economic growth rates f\or the periods 1965–80 and 1980–87.[2]

Individualistic Versus Communitarian Capitalism

Cultures in the contemporary world can be seen as combinations and variations of two ideal types: *individualism* and *communitarianism*. Individualism suggests an atomistic conception of society, emphasizing individual initiative, decision making, and achievement. The interests of the community are driven by self-interested competition among many, preferably small proprietors. Communitarianism, by contrast, takes a more organic view, emphasizing the value of belonging to groups and organizations which make decisions and which protect people in exchange for their loyalty.[3]

According to Lester Thurow, the economic competition between communism and capitalism is over. Now it is a competition between different versions of capitalism. Specifically, the individualistic variants of capitalism (e.g., British-American) are going to confront the communitarian form of capitalism (e.g., Japanese, East Asian, and German).[4]

Britons and Americans usually think in terms of clear-cut dichotomies: free trade, free markets, and competition are good, while protectionism,

BOX 5.1

Dealing with International Competition

Consider how the U.S. can compete against Japan. The U.S. managers cannot emulate the Japanese style of cooperation, nor can they hope to establish such webs of interdependencies as the Japanese use to lower costs. Not only can the Americans not cooperate in this manner due to their individualistic orientation, but many such forms of cooperation are also considered illegal in the U.S. Thus, Americans have to find other culturally acceptable ways to enhance their competitive position. The key goal is cost containment and enhancing the quality of products to achieve a competitive edge. One way the United States can achieve this is by inspiring and encouraging innovation, technological breakthroughs, and creativity. Such a strategy is also congruent with the American culture of individualism because individuals who creatively contribute ideas to attain the goal are recognized and rewarded for their individual talents, skills, and contributions. Thus, it becomes clear that trying to enhance U.S. competitiveness through the adaptation of collectivistic Japanese techniques such as quality circles is just the opposite of what U.S. managers should do—unless these techniques are considerably modified to encourage and reward individual work. America achieved greatness through the entrepreneurial spirit of individuals working to creatively build their companies: "the American way." American competitiveness can be enhanced by capitalizing on the American cultural values of individualism and growth.

Quoted from Coral R. Snodgrass and Uma Sekaran, "The Cultural Components of Strategic Decision Making in the International Arena," in Anant R. Negandhi and Arun Savara, eds., *International Strategic Management* (Toronto: Lexington Books, 1989). pp. 147–148, with minor changes.

government intervention, and cooperation are bad. As a result, each individual firm naturally struggles to maximize profits and avoid pursuing collaboration with others. Cooperation is often prohibited by its antitrust laws (see Box 5.1). By contrast, Japan's competitive advantages are more subtle than such dichotomies suggest. The Japanese government protects its companies, but just until they become competitive internationally. The government directs the vision, but allows private companies freely to develop; their companies compete fiercely but they also cooperate closely. The bottom line of all these activities is to create harmony (*wa*)—what Westerners see as contradictions.[5]

In sum, these different versions of capitalism have significant effects on everything from labor relations and industry policy to public education.[6] According to Ezra Vogel (1987), the issues that government and business policymakers must confront in the international context are as follows:

1. How will membership in this global system be defined and enforced? Who will decide which communities have a stake in the outcome? How will community need be defined?

2. By what procedures will consensus be achieved? To what extent can policies be imposed by leaders in the name of efficiency and meritocratic norms? To what extent will government be responsive to the demands of various groups? To what extent will the right to manage come from ownership and property rights? To what extent from local groups, communities, and governments?

3. How will national governments be intertwined in the governance of global systems?

4. How will the role of various specialized organizations be coordinated? How will a system be devised that is sufficiently flexible to adjust to changing circumstances?

5. What will be the underlying principles of the new global culture that will serve as a basis for people from different cultural backgrounds to work together?[7]

Attitudes and Values

Apart from the overall culture, the people's specific attitudes and values also affect a nation's economic conduct and performance. For economic conduct, countries like India, China, and the larger Latin American countries provide good examples. During the last decade or so, large countries attempted to make themselves the center of *regional power*. These countries viewed the world economy on a regional basis instead of on a global basis. They adopted *inward-oriented* strategies instead of *outward-oriented* strategies. Because the size of their domestic market and that of neighboring countries was not large enough to take all their output, they failed. The result was high-cost domestic industries that required continued protectionism to survive.

In some countries, antibusiness sentiment is the factor that holds back economic development. Government and labor policies are often antibusiness. Iran, in spite of its educated population and natural resources, has regressed economically following the Ayatollah Khomeini's fundamentalist religious movement, which imposed an isolationistic and militaristic character on the Iranian economy.

One of the major explanations of Britain's economic decline in the last century is a set of attitudes and values associated with the "English way of life," emphasizing nonmaterial and nonindustrial qualities. Stable, cozy, and spiritual values are prevalent in British society. The British genius stressed preserving, harmonizing, and moralizing; the British character was conservative. As Paul Herbig points out, "its greatest task and achievement . . . lay in taming and civilizing the dangerous engines of progress that it had unwitting unleashed" in the Industrial Revolution. Further, an industrial career was less esteemed in Britain than elsewhere. To stimulate a mass desire for goods seemed repugnant. Even more than selling, manufacturing itself was depreciated: in Britain, manufacturing was the worst paid industry and the least likely to offer high management positions.[8]

Another kind of national attitude that is associated with economic performance is the *nationalistic attitude*. France is a case in point. Together with Britain, France is the last nation in Europe to shed a sense of superiority. The French missed their great opportunity in 1958 to become the center of a new Europe. Even though French companies export substantially, they failed to develop true MNCs. There are only a handful of French companies in Europe. France left the strategic window wide open for its more dynamic and farsighted Dutch, German, Swiss, Swedish, and American counterparts. With a low level of cosmopolitanism, there are too few Frenchmen abroad, and too few executives speak foreign languages. In their provincial vision, many French leaders as well as the media reject imports and applaud their government in pursuing tariff and nontariff measures. In sum, the French people are too satisfied with their lifestyle and too skeptical about the benefits of a new style of global leadership.[9]

A different national attitude is the *saving attitude*. According to Hamish McRae, "it is about deferred gratification—putting off pleasure today for some greater good in the long term." The United States is a case in point. The United States saved less than any other industrial nation during the second half of the 1980s. This low saving rate was influenced by the self-confidence of its society; it was also associated with its sense of security. To elaborate, unlike its Continental European and Japanese counterparts, the United States has never been invaded by a hostile power, and is fortified by a history of economic ascendancy. For many reasons, America's low saving rate diminishes its competitiveness in the global economy.[10]

Still another national attitude has to do with *state intervention and controls*. New Zealand under its former prime minister, Sir Robert Muldoon, is a case in point. During that time, no one except the government was allowed to broadcast television programs. Workers had to belong to a trade union. A government license had to be obtained to import goods. Motivation and incentives to work more were discouraged since the top tax rate was 66 cents on the dollar.[11]

If one wanted to rent a television set he was obliged by law to put down six months' rent in advance. If one wanted to invest in or set up a business overseas he had to renounce his nationality to get his money out of the country. He needed a permit to subscribe to an overseas journal. He was not allowed to truck goods more than 40 miles without the permission of the Railways. It was illegal to sell petrol below a minimum price. It was against the law to make carpets from anything other than wool. To buy margarine, he had to have a doctor's prescription.[12]

When New Zealand finally dismantled this regulatory apparatus in the early 1990s, its economy moved into positive growth.

For government, businesses, and the community at large, changing the country's attitudes and values is one of the most difficult tasks since it requires national consensus to get rid of limiting ideologies and misconceptions. However, we are seeing change in some countries.

A NATION'S SOCIAL COHESION

The second factor that can represent a strength or a weakness is the nation's degree of social cohesion. In multicultural nations containing different languages and religions, there are almost always sociocultural tensions and conflicts. As military threats have lessened, future conflicts may well be between cultural groups rather than states. Current examples include the internal conflicts and tensions in Bosnia, India, Iraq, Liberia, Somalia, and Sri Lanka. Industrial countries are not excluded: we witness conflict in Canada and Belgium. In the United States and Germany, examples range from black riots in Los Angeles to neo-Nazi attacks on immigrants and asylum seekers in Germany.[13]

Minorities often find it difficult to participate fully in societies that are influenced by the dominant groups. This exclusion is implicitly embedded in everyday practice. A UN report points out:

> *In the U.S., where everyone is "created free and equal," there is a marked difference between the white and black populations. These disadvantages start at birth. The infant mortality rate for blacks is 19 per 1,000 live births, comparing with 8 for whites. Black children are much more likely than white children to grow up in single-parent homes—in 1990, 19% of white children were growing up in single-parent households, compared with 54% of black children. Children in black families are also more likely to grow up in poverty. The real GDP per capita for blacks in 1990 was around $17,000, compared with $22,000 for whites.*[14]

For other countries, power and wealth are highly concentrated in minorities. In Syria, the state is ruled by a small minority: Hafez Al-Assad's Alawite sect makes up less than 10 percent of the population. In Iraq, the Sunni dominate the Shiite majority. In South Africa, wealth is concentrated in the minority whites, leaving the blacks as a marginalized majority who live below the poverty line.[15]

This does not imply that social cohesion is high in a single-tribal nation. Modern life creates new social classes. Severe poverty and regional disparities have become commonplace. While division among classes and interest groups is growing, the success of a nation's wealth creation depends on whether these groups can pull together or tend to drift apart. Like any strategy, national wealth creation is more likely to succeed if all groups are participating and have strong commitment to the national policy. This requires deliberate internal marketing of the benefits of social cohesion in creating national wealth.[16]

A NATION'S ECONOMY: FACTOR ENDOWMENTS

A nation's economic endowments include its natural resources, population size, human capital, physical capital, technology, and infrastructure. Shortfalls can be met by imports, which may be paid for by exports of other products or by foreign credit.

Natural Resources

Countries with rich natural resources and large geographical areas are often thought to prevail in the economic contest. Historically, geographical and natural resources provided the Dutch and the British access to economic leadership. With greater natural advantages in land, minerals, and energy resources, the United States achieved subsequent leadership. This notion, however, is no longer valid in the contemporary world. The former Soviet Union, with rich resources and large geographical areas, did not achieve a higher standard of living. Per capita GDP in Australia is lower than in Japan, even though Australian natural resources per capita are over 150 times greater. Past experience in successful adaptation to resource scarcity either domestically or by importation casts doubts about whether resource constraints necessarily limit growth in the long run.[17]

New Zealand and Hong Kong, which in 1991 had roughly the same GNP per capita, have generated their wealth quite differently. New Zealand has plentiful land but few people, and is therefore a low-cost producer of agricultural goods—nearly 20% of its exports come from primary goods (e.g., timber, minerals); and in meat, dairy products, fish, fruit, vegetables and beverages, the proportion rises nearly 70%. Hong Kong, by contrast, has hardly any land and the densest population of any territory on earth, and is therefore a manufacture and entrepot trader, with 90% of its exports being manufactured goods.[18]

Population Size and Demographic Changes

There is a wide range of views as to the effects of rapid population growth on economic performance. Those who argue for net gains flowing from rapid population growth suggest that

- On the demand side, a large population means a large potential market size. On the supply side, this large population encourages efficiency via economies of scale.
- A large population fosters a high division of labor, resulting in specialization and, hence, more efficient production.
- A larger population contributes more talented people.
- Greater population induces the development of new technology for dealing with any potential adverse effects of rapid population growth. This includes agricultural innovation and increases food productivity.[19]

Those who maintain the opposite view put forth arguments concerning the negative effects of population growth at both aggregate and individual levels. At the aggregate level:

- Greater population demands substantial government expenditures to maintain physical and social infrastructure. It also requires government to create more jobs in securing adequate employment.
- Rapid population growth implies a growing percentage of very young children heavily dependent on a shrinking percentage of working-age people.
- Increasing population density in rural areas may lead to diseconomies of scale in agricultural production if plots of land have to be divided into smaller parcels.
- In many developing countries, population growth rates are usually too high for agricultural innovation to keep pace with the demand for food.
- The higher the population growth, the higher the severe environmental degradation.

At the individual level, a large family size may lead to fewer resources per child and greater demands on children to work at an early age. These factors can be detrimental to the development of children, both physically and mentally, which in turn limits their potential to create the wealth of their nation.[20]

Human Capital

The contribution of human capital toward national wealth creation is straightforward. The higher the average level of skill and knowledge, the easier it is for working-age individuals to understand, apply, and gain the fruits of technical progress, and hence, the higher the living standards of nations.[21]

A nation must invest in mass education and also diversify the subjects taught. China and India are very good examples of different educational systems. While China is changing its educational system from focusing mainly on passing exams to enter elite universities to mass education, India still maintains the same educational system in which only the elite can obtain better education. India's educational system not only hinders its national wealth-building performance but also deepens the unequal distribution of wealth, which brings about much intranational conflict and tension.[22]

In some countries—Thailand, for example—the current educational system does not support the nation's economy-building strategy in the long run. Countries that are pursuing industrialization certainly require more scientists and engineers. Yet more students may be electing to take social science training, which results in the country having to import scientific and engineering help from abroad.

Physical Capital

Physical capital can be classified into three main categories: *residential stock*, *inventories*, and *nonresidential capital stock*. Among these three, nonresidential capital stock plays the major role in the growth process. Table 5.1 shows the growth of nonresidential gross capital stock per employee among the industrial countries. Since 1890, the United Kingdom is noted to have the slowest growth of capital per employee (2.1 percent a year). By contrast, the United States nonresidential capital per employee was more than double that of the United Kingdom in 1890. As a result, since 1890 the United States had overtaken the United Kingdom in terms of productivity. But by the late 1980s, when its growth of capital per employee had slowed down, the United States had begun to lose its superiority to Japan, which has constantly increased its growth in capital stock per employee over time (4.2 percent a year since 1890).

Technology

Technology is one of the most critical elements in creating national wealth. It is usually embodied in physical capital investment, and en-

TABLE 5.1

Gross Nonresidential Fixed Capital Stock Per Person Employed, 1890–1987 ($ at 1985 U.S. relative prices)

	1890	1913	1950	1973	1987
France	n.a.	(9,600)	14,800	43,309	80,604
Germany	(9,611)	(13,483)	16,291	55,421	89,154
Japan	1,454	2,264	6,609	33,101	78,681
Netherlands	n.a.	n.a.	20,181	59,459	80,897
UK	7,634	9,780	13,923	39,100	58,139
USA	16,402	35,485	48,118	70,677	85,023

Source: Angus Maddison, *Dynamic Forces in Capitalist Development: A Long-Run Comparative View* (New York: Oxford University Press, 1991), Table 3.9, p. 66. Gross capital stock (nonresidential structures and equipment) and employment estimates derived from sources indicated in Appendices C and D. For Germany 1890–1950 and France 1913–50 standardized gross capital stock estimates were not available so net stock movements were used as a proxy from national sources cited in A. Maddison, "Growth and Slowdown in Advanced Capitalist Economies," *Journal of Economic Literature* (June 1987), Table A.16. Capital stocks in national currencies were revalued at 1985 prices using implicit deflators for the relevant types of investment. Conversion into dollars was made by using 1985 purchasing power parities for investment goods supplied by Eurostat. The valuation basis is therefore comparable with that used for GDP.

hances the quality and productivity of using natural resources and human capital.[23] Some countries cannot compete internationally because they are at a disadvantage in investment capital, productivity, or producing value-added goods in relation to other countries with new industrial technologies. Although some countries have shifted their structure toward more capital-intensive or skilled labor-intensive industries, they still employ unskilled labor and use primitive technology. The lack of both physical and human resources suppresses the level of industrial and technological development.[24]

Governments usually play a major role in supporting a nation's technical progress. France, for example, has constantly used the power of the state to catch up in technologies with lumpy and risky front end investments (e.g., energy, defense, telecommunications, space, marine exploration). These efforts will gain support from a broad national consensus, since they produce positive spillover effects in such key industrial areas as semiconductors, computers, lasers, and so on, where French corporations are too weak to be competitive internationally.[25]

Infrastructure

The nation's wealth creation is facilitated by an adequate infrastructure. Developing countries face this problem differently. Bangladesh, for example, lacks most necessary infrastructure. As a result, the nation cannot pull itself out of poverty and backwardness. Countries of recent high economic growth, such as Thailand, are facing infrastructure bottlenecks, especially in transportation and telecommunications. They are inadequate to support the next period of economic expansion.

By contrast, France is on a par with its most advanced counterparts in terms of transport, communications, and energy infrastructure—even ahead in some areas. Physical and social infrastructure continue to be built in French cities other than Paris to draw business investments.[26]

The Role of Factor Endowments in National Wealth Building.

To understand the role of factor endowments in creating national wealth, it is necessary to distinguish among types of factors. According to Porter (1990), two important distinctions stand out. The first is between *basic* and *advanced* factors. The second is their specificity: *generalized* versus *specialized* factors.[27]

Basic factors are passively inherited, or require relatively modest or unsophisticated investment to build up. Examples include natural resources, climate, location, unskilled and semiskilled labor, and physical capital. By contrast, advanced factors are more critical since their development demands large and continuous investments in both human and physical capital. Examples include technical progress, highly educated personnel, and modern communications infrastructure. It is worth noting that advanced factors are often built upon basic factors, implying that basic factor pools must be of sufficient quantity and quality for the creation of related advanced factors.

For the second distinction, generalized factors include the transportation and communication systems, a supply of unskilled labor, and other general resources. By contrast, specialized factors involve narrowly skilled personnel, infrastructure with specific properties, specific knowledge, and other factors pertinent to a limited range of industries. Specialized factors require more focused—and often riskier—private and social investment. Compared with generalized factors, specialized factors provide more decisive and sustainable bases for competitive advantage. They are, however, often built upon the generalized factors.

In sum, both advanced and specialized factors are critical in enhancing the international competitiveness of the nation. The quantity and quality of advanced and specialized factors determine the possibility and rate for reaching higher-order competitive advantage (e.g., differentiation, proprietary production technique). They also determine the possibility and rate of upgrading.

A NATION'S INDUSTRIAL ORGANIZATION

Industrial organization is a key factor in a nation's international competitiveness. In some nations such as the United States, the economic and industrial sector is competitive, characterized by free entry and exit due to laws regulating restraint of trade, an infrastructure of schooling, information, and credit that encourages resource mobility, and a national tradition of enterprise. Departures from the ideal, such as price fixing, are viewed as unfair and in fact are often illegal. By contrast, there is a very different structure and process in nations where industrial groups dominate the industrial sector. Each industrial group is a key power center, active in almost all industries.[28]

An example is the *keiretsu* industrial groups in Japan. Historically, the Japanese government encouraged the building of *keiretsu* for two primary reasons: First, interlocking ownership and close buyer-supplier relationships could be used as organizational barriers to keep out foreign imports and investment. Second, the government wanted to concentrate the country's scarce resources in industries that have high potential in enhancing Japan's long-term economic prosperity. It is believed that these groups, with their strong bank support and diversified risk, were best able to develop such strategic industries.[29]

The Japanese *keiretsu*'s firms are financed by its group bank and through cross-shareholding of each others' stock. Since a firm's capital formation is achieved through the group bank and its affiliate companies, its dependency on the other group companies is very high.[30]

The Japanese approach is being imitated successfully by many East Asian countries. The well-known one is Korea's *chaebol* (see Chapter 2). A *chaebol* can be defined as "a business group consisting of large companies which are owned and managed by family members in many diversified industrial sectors." There are presently over fifty *chaebol* groups of varying sizes in Korea. The Korean *chaebol* have played a crucial role in the development of the Korean economy. The Korean government encouraged these companies to pursue risk-taking, growth-oriented strategies. The low-cost funds and bank credit provided by the government enabled these groups to expand their business with relatively small amounts of equity.[31] Massive industrial projects were often carried out aggressively by Korean *chaebol*. These *chaebol* increased their size in order to gain the capacity to undertake such major projects.[32] Like the Japanese *keiretsu*, *chaebol* finance new ventures with cross-shareholding among member companies, thus maintaining control within the whole group of companies.[33]

Taiwan also has industrial groups, known as *jituangiye*. Compared with *keiretsu* and *chaebol*, *jituangiye* are relatively uninfluential. *Jituangiye* business investments are mostly financed through private sources. Due to limitations in private financing, their scale tends to be small.[34]

Table 5.2 illustrates the organizational characteristics of these three Asian countries' businesses. It appears that these organizational characteristics partially reflect the differences in organizational size and structure among the three countries. Major differences stem from the way in which business firms are financed.[35]

The competitive success of East Asian industrial groups, however, suggests the following question. Does it point to a new irrefutable logic of industrial economics that must be heeded by all firms that hope to compete in the global marketplace?

Not necessarily. In the 1970s and 1980s, industrial districts in Europe such as the Third Italy, Baden-Württemberg in southern Germany, West Jutland in Denmark, and southwest Flanders in Belgium attained profound international competitiveness, even though they contained groups of small

TABLE 5.2

Organizational Characteristics of Business Groups

	Japan	Korea	Taiwan
Ownership Pattern	Shareholding of group firms	State-financed family groups	Family ownership partnerships
Intragroup Network	Shareholding & mutual influence	Hierarchical structure	Multipositions of core personnel
Intergroup Network	Shareholding & joint ventures	Coordination by government banks	Investment by private sources
Subcontract	Structured	Insignificant	Highly flexible
Investment Pattern	Vertical & horizontal	Vertical & horizontal	Vertical & horizontal
Financing Pattern	Bank-financed group activities	State-financed sector growth	Private source and reinvestment

Source: Gary G. Hamilton and Marco Orru, "Organizational Structure of East Asian Companies," in Kae H. Chung and Hak Chong Lee, eds., *Korean Managerial Dynamics* (New York: Praeger, 1989), Table 4.4, p. 46.

firms. These groups of entrepreneurial firms actively pursued a strategy that reaps many of the advantages of big ones. These advantages include continuous innovation; they deploy flexible production processes and specialization, matched by a high degree of cooperation and coordination.[36] Firms in industrial districts cooperate along the value chain, ranging from pooling funds for R&D to setting up joint training centers, promoting dialogue between producers and users of capital equipment, and providing specialized export and legal services. By such means, small firms gain access to facilities and expertise they could never afford on their own.[37]

According to Hubert Schmitz and Bernard Musyck, the European industrial district experience points toward a new model of a nation's industrial organization which:

1. emphasizes delegation of functions to a diverse range of governmental and non-governmental institutions;
2. operates through institutions close to the enterprises;
3. extends the concern with entrepreneurship from the private to the public sector; and

4. stresses self-help through business associations and producer consortia.[38]

The structures of the industrial groups are closely related to national public policies. Industrial groups can work efficiently only in environments with limited antitrust policies. Industrial organizations such as industrial groups represent an important element in enhancing the international competitiveness of any nation-state.[39]

GOVERNMENT LEADERSHIP

The vision of a nation's political leader can vitally affect that nation's economic performance. This is typically overlooked by development economists, who accord no role to leadership in their "production function" modeling of economic development, or prefer to treat leadership as an exogenous function. According to Vaclav Klaus, prime minister of the Czech Republic, "the potential leaders must formulate and sell to citizens of the country a positive vision of a future society." Ronald Reagan's "supply-side revolution," Gorbachev's *perestroika*, Rajiv Gandhi's "push toward the twenty-first century," and Deng Xiaoping's New China all create roles for "managerial visionaries" to emerge—those who can convincingly paint a vision of the future for their nations.[40]

In East Asia, according to Anis Chowdhury and Iyanatul Islam, while the governments may not have played the role of an "engine of growth," they have certainly played the role of a "handmaiden of growth" by carrying out necessary policy reforms that create and maintain an environment conducive to rapid economic growth.[41] More interestingly, countries in East Asia are characterized by:

1. an elite bureaucracy staffed by the best managerial talent;
2. an authoritarian political system in which the bureaucracy has sufficient scope to take policy initiatives; and
3. close government–big business cooperation in the policymaking process.[42]

According to Nikhilesh Dholakia, "these countries' government and business seem suffused with managerial visionaries who have portrayed visions of future development in their respective fields, then gone ahead and achieved these visions."[43]

Singapore's current character has been dominated and shaped by one man—Lee Kuan Yew. In 1959, when he came to power, Lee inherited a parliamentary system of government from the British but over the years altered it significantly, in order, some say, to perpetuate his own rule. A believer in democracy—up to a point—Lee said in his most telling quote: "We decide what is right. Never mind what the people think."[44]

For other regions, a lack of vision and strategic foresight retards industrial development.

In Latin America, governments, administrations and political parties made little attempt to prepare society for the process of industrialization. They attached little importance to institutional development; Latin America remained "undermanaged." The public service sector was expanded, but the quality of the health and education systems usually left a great deal to be desired. R&D was neglected: most enterprises took an interest in it only when it came to adapting imported technologies to domestic conditions and the smaller domestic markets. Government made no attempt to initiate a systematic technological learning process.[45]

Apart from vision, another aspect of political leadership is the power to overcome obstacles and implement its policy choices. This may distinguish the "weak" from the "strong" governments. Consider how two countries, Brazil and South Korea, dealt with the problem of spiraling debt and reduced inflow of foreign capital during the 1980s. Brazil, in fear of a reduced capital inflow, cut investment even more severely than it cut consumption. In South Korea, which had more confidence in its ability to control social unrest, the government raised domestic saving and stepped up domestic investment to replace foreign borrowings, even though this led to a sharp cut in real wages and consumption. As a result, growth rates declined substantially in Brazil while they stayed high in South Korea. As Stopford and Strange argued, "Brazil's policy choice in the 1980s reflected in part the relative weakness of its government in the aftermath of the transition to civilian rule. Weak states usually resort to approaches that can be regarded as making policy by default."[46]

> *A problem of many Latin American countries was government's inability to reduce the mounting deficits of the state-owned enterprises. Nationalization in the raw material sector in the 1960s and 1970s led to a decline in investment activity and a drop in foreign exchange earnings. At the same time, these governments were demanding a new international economic order so that they might improve the sales potential of their raw materials and increase their foreign exchange earnings. They kept pointing to "external factors" to conceal the governments' own weaknesses.*[47]

Except for dictatorships, most countries have weak governments representing compromised positions. The government head leads a coalition of parties and cannot move too far from the center, even if this is warranted. In many countries, government's role is further weakened by rampant corruption where parliamentarians maximize their own interests, not the public interest.

In general, four major problems created by the government can impede the nation's wealth creation potential: (1) corruption; (2) military overspending; (3) resource misallocation; and (4) political instability.

Corruption

A high degree of corruption is detrimental to the wealth creation of many nations. Corruption in government takes many forms. But according to Michael Beenstock, all forms of corruption share "the secret and usually illegal abuse of conferred monopoly status." Beenstock distinguished three specific types of corruption:

> . . . extortionary corruption *in which payment is demanded for performing legal acts,* subversive corruption *where bribery secures illegal actions, and* benign corruption *in which the salaries of the lower-grade civil servants are modestly augmented by additional payments that in many ways resemble tips or gratuities.*[48]

Corruption introduces distortions in the efficiency of resource allocation. When inferior products/services are chosen, the society is worse off.

Even when the best products are selected, the existence of a bribe means a higher incurred cost.[49] Corruption not only creates a concentration of unproductive wealth, much of which flies out of the country, but also corrodes the nation's culture, attitudes, and values.

Yet, in a bureaucratically rigid economy, corruption often serves a useful role in getting things going. Office clerks were tipped to get papers moved. Petitions to be processed needed to get to the right desk. Even public-sector firms and state governments resorted to the device. Sometimes it was not payments but favors. Often officials avoided decisions because of fears they would be accused of corruption. Corruption under these circumstances would have been a small price compared to the cost of nondecision, wastage, and so on.

Military Overspending

Military overspending is another major impediment to the nation's wealth creation caused by the government. A superpower's superior position usually erodes when it spends its economic wealth on the military and wars. In the contemporary world, the United States and the former Soviet Union are inevitably losing their relative economic power, just as Spain, The Netherlands, France, and England lost theirs in the past. A significant proportion of their resources is diverted from creating productive assets and allocated rather for military purposes.

High military spending is also found in many developing countries. Many of the Gulf states, for example, have spent an inordinate amount on military goods at a cost that depleted most of the national resources which could have been spent on creating national wealth.

Resource Misallocation

Stagnation in the creation of national wealth partly results from the misallocation of resources. Valuable resources are oversupplied to some industrial sectors and undersupplied to others. The nation therefore suffers from an imbalance in its industrial competitiveness. Australia, for example, possesses a high potential for producing several industrial goods because it has both factor and company competitiveness. However, the country focuses on agricultural production and produces more wool than any other country. The United States, too, has concentrated its resources on three main industrial sectors—agriculture, medicine, and defense—instead of distributing more to commercial-industrial sectors that could create greater strength in their global competitiveness.[50]

Misallocation of resources in the Soviet-type economies arises from two major sources. First there is the gap between the *planned* combination of outputs and the *actual* demand for outputs by the society. Second, there is a contraction in the social opportunity set. The lack of incentives along with the high transaction costs are major reasons underlying the economic inefficiency of Soviet-type economies (see Chapter 3).[51]

Political Instability

A high degree of political instability discourages private investment and causes capital flight. Many countries have suffered economically because of weak and incompetent governments. The inability to exercise state leadership often leads to coups and countercoups, loss of foreign investments, and, hence, a lower standard of living.

There is a high potential for political instability in the Middle East, where many countries have no constitution, no religious freedom, no elected parliament, and no formal justice system. Political and social suppressions inevitably lead to political instability. Consider Egypt: even though it looks like a country with modern democracy, there are still no free general elections. Open criticism of the regime is prohibited and press censorship has been reinstated.[52]

In East Asian countries, even though traditional monarchs had been replaced by republics, most of them are in practice governed by a single-party rule. This is the case with the ruling party governments in China and Taiwan. Singapore has blocked most substantial opposition from political involvement, while the South Korean government often declares all political opposition illegal.[53]

Single-party ruling governments does not mean that political instability is absent from the scene. Yet there are benefits. As Roy Hofheinz and Kent Calder argue, "once established, the East Asian people, particularly the private sector, are more comfortable to know that their governments do not change. Perhaps this helps explain why East Asian governments seem more familiar with, and sometimes more competent at, economic policy than in the West."[54]

ASSESSING A NATION'S STRENGTHS AND WEAKNESSES: THE CASE OF SOUTH KOREA

Here we will apply and illustrate our framework for strength and weakness analysis in the case of one country: South Korea. South Korea is committed to rapid economic growth through industrialization and has enjoyed a high rate of growth, undergoing fundamental structural changes from a predominantly agricultural to an industrial economy. What major factors might explain Korea's successful recent economic growth? On the one hand, we must examine its capabilities: the nation's attitudes and values; the nation's government leadership and industrial organization; and its qualitative and quantitative changes in the factor endowments (i.e., physical capital, wage and labor supply, and human capital). On the other hand, we must note the external conditions at the time.

The Nation's Attitudes and Values

South Korea's grand strategy is to imitate Japan's path to development, driven by the principle of "Do what the Japanese have done, but do it cheaper and faster." The *imitation* strategy has been drawn from the Korean value of "that's good enough" and by the aggressiveness of "first start and then let's see" practices. Interestingly, these beliefs and values are extremely different from those of North Korea, even though the two countries share the same culture (see Box 5.2).[55]

Government Leadership

The role of South Korea's government in choosing an economic development strategy was critical. In the early stages of development, the market itself is unable to choose the best "strategy." In such circumstances, as Taewon Kwack has argued, choosing the right strategy is far more important than choosing a right set of policy measures to implement the selected strategy. In fact, an outward orientation is not always superior to an inward orientation. However, because of South Korea's small internal market and limited factor endowments, the outward-oriented development strategy suited South Korea better than an inward-oriented strategy.[56]

The scarcity of capital caused South Korea's domestic rate of return to be much higher than in the world's financial markets. However, the official domestic interest rate had been kept very low (except for the period 1965–71). The resulting high level of domestic investment demand generated a large gap between investments and savings, which was filled by foreign loans.[57]

The foreign exchange rate policy, accompanied with various financial incentives, also contributed to the success of the outward-oriented strategy. Clearly, overvaluation in foreign exchange was adopted during the import substitution phases (1950s and 1970s). However, in the export-promotion phase (1960s) and in the liberalization stage (1980s), the exchange rate policy aimed at improving the balance of payments. During that time, incentives to promote exports were supplied throughout all the stages.[58]

An additional feature contributing to South Korea's success was its group of top-quality bureaucracies. They carried a strong strategic intent of exploiting the benefits of economies of scale through exports. Furthermore, the stability of domestic politics as well as the relatively high probity of most Korean political and business leaders were two major factors alleviating capital flight.[59]

Resources were not allocated solely at the discretion of the government, however. Although the government made the decision to allocate more resources to the export sector, it was the market that decided on the composition of the export sector. It is worth noting that this division of roles between government and business in resource allocation was very helpful in reaching the second-best solution, particularly where some kinds of market failure still existed.[60]

Industrial Organization

Korea's *chaebol* have long dominated the Korean economy, particularly in the 1960s and 1970s. In the past, the Korean government had used the *chaebol* as a key driver of the industrialization process. However, the

---

BOX 5.2

North Korean Attitudes and Values

Countries sharing a common culture but which have developed different beliefs and values can emerge with different levels of wealth creation. This clearly happened in the contrasting fortunes of East and West Germany, as well as North and South Korea. Here we will examine the case of North Korea.

North Korea's strategy has been stubbornly guided by what it calls *juche sasang*, or the ideology of self-identity, creativity, and autonomy. This thought system encompasses the idea of *juche* in ideology, the idea of *chaju* (independence) in political work, and the idea of *chawi* (self-defense) in military affairs. Juche was first used by Kim Il Sung when he addressed his party's propaganda and agitation workers around the end of 1955, stressing "juche in ideology." Juche meant self-reliance in the economic area.

The basic strategy of self-reliance calls for the economy to rely on domestic resources in all sectors for 60–70% of supplies. When key raw materials are not available, the strategy is to substitute other domestic resources and to minimize dependency on other nations. The juche idea is to build one's country with its people's labor and own

---

major Korean *chaebol* have recently been forced to undergo crucial organizational transformations that have gradually replaced personal and political styles of leadership with more strategic and rational ones. The government's new attempt to change the *chaebol* is to encourage specialization. Specialization was the primary reason for the government decree in 1991 that the top thirty *chaebol* should each select three core businesses. Since 1986, each *chaebol* has been forced to comply with controls on its domestic borrowing. The new policy will exempt these controls for the three businesses each *chaebol* chooses. Moreover, interest rate deregulation is now being considered by the government. If *chaebol* had to pay a market price for borrowed money, they would soon be

national resources. North Korea aimed to build self-sufficient agriculture, on the one hand, and to drive industrialization through heavy-industries-first development, on the other.

The strategies employed by South and North Korea produced extraordinarily different results. South Korea practiced state capitalism, in which the state owned and operated some key enterprises and financial institutions, at the same time allowing primarily private enterprises, interlocked businesses, and a market-driven economy. The state communism of North Korea achieved initial fast development by state ownership of the means of production, relying on mass mobilization policies such as socialization of industries and land and collectivization of agriculture. The self-sufficiency principle, however, impeded further economic progress. South Korea's strategy, on the other hand, was more flexible, pluralistic and pragmatic than Communist Korea's self-sufficiency. Capitalist South Korea worked effectively within the fluent international capitalist environment by controlling foreign investment and national financial mechanisms rather than by state ownership of the means of production.

Quoted from Byoung-Lo Philo Kim, *Two Koreas in Development: A Comparative Study of Principles and Strategies of Capitalist and Communist Third World Development* (New Brunswick, NJ: Transaction Publishers, 1992), pp. 133–137 and 194–195, with minor changes.

---

forced to dump unproductive assets. By these means, capital would be allocated more efficiently.[61]

Physical Capital

About 20 percent of the past GNP growth came from the increase in physical capital input. This is very natural because Korea's industrialization required high investment. Interestingly, as a result of the abundant investment opportunities, the high domestic real rate of return on capital alleviated the negative effects generated by government intervention in the allocation of investment resources.[62]

Wage and Labor Supply

In the early 1960s, Korea had a substantial labor surplus. These low wage rates played a vital role in maintaining the competitiveness of its export goods.

Although South Korea's relative unit labor cost has been growing rapidly, it was able to maintain price competitiveness in the world market. R. Dornbusch and Y. C. Park (1987) provide a good explanation of this phenomenon:

> *Imports of new technology decrease unit labor cost in the front line industries by raising productivity, and these industries emerge as new exporters. However, the wage level in these sectors increase as does the wage level of traditional sectors whose productivity is unchanged. Consequently, the unit labor cost of the traditional export industries rise, causing them to lose competitiveness in the export market. In this process, the average unit labor cost rises while the front line industries' costs go down. Thus, the apparent conflict between a rapid rise in the average unit labor cost and the maintenance of export competitiveness is reconciled. This explanation is supported by the rapid upscale transformation of the composition of Korea's exports.*[63]

Human Capital

In the rural sector, equal and wide access to productive assets through land reform in the 1950s provided the incentive and opportunity for the development of human capital.

South Korea adopted an investment strategy that balanced human resource development with increased physical capital and technology transfer. A strong emphasis on education and health helped to create a large productive labor force with strong knowledge and talents.[64]

External Conditions

The world economic environment should also be taken into account. Dornbush and Park (1987) argue that, compared with Latin American countries, South Korea (as well as other Asian NICs) was fortunate. South Korea suffered much less deterioration in terms of trade during the second oil and interest rate shocks. All these factors combined to enhance Korea's high economic growth.[65]

IDENTIFYING A NATION'S STRENGTHS AND WEAKNESSES

It is one thing to discern attractive opportunities in the world economy; it is another to have the necessary competencies to succeed in these opportunities. Each nation needs to evaluate its strengths and weakness periodically. This can be done by using the form shown in Figure 5.2. Policymakers must review the nation's capabilities. The factors listed under each are illustrative rather than exhaustive. Each factor is rated as to whether it is a major strength, minor strength, neutral factor, minor weakness, or major weakness.

Included with the factors are their importance weights. In examining its pattern of strengths and weaknesses, a nation does not have to correct all its weaknesses nor gloat about all its strengths. Not all weaknesses are important, nor do all strengths have an equal weight in determining outcomes. The big question is whether the nation should limit itself to those opportunities where it now possesses the required strengths (e.g., the flood of raw material exports by the former Soviet Union to earn hard currency) or should consider attractive opportunities where it might have to acquire or develop certain strengths (e.g., creating innovation-driven societies in many Asian NICs).

Sometimes a nation does poorly not because it lacks the required strengths but because the government policymakers and business leaders do not work together as a team. Thus, internal marketing is needed to build more teamwork before using external marketing in the global marketplace to create wealth.

SUMMARY

In today's world of interdependence and a constantly changing environment, creating or sustaining a nation's wealth is possible only when the nation's capability portfolio is driven forward in the right direction where

FIGURE 5.2

Nation's Strength/Weakness Analysis

	Importance Weight	Performance				
		Major Strength	Minor Strength	Neutral Factor	Minor Weakness	Major Weakness

Culture, attitudes, and values
*culture of
  productivity
*entrepreneurial
  spirit
*attitude
  toward saving
*family value						

Social cohesion
*distribution of
  wealth
*distribution of
  power
*cultural
  homogeneity						

Factor endowments *natural resources *human capital *technology level *age distribution of population						

Industrial organization
*competitive
  intensity
*cooperative norms
*industry
  diversification
*industry
  specialization
*state-owned
  enterprises						

Government leadership *visionary leadership						

FIGURE 5.2 (continued)
*government strategic
 support
*administrative
 efficiency
*policy consistency
*political stability

---

it fits in with the general and competitive environment of the world economy. The nation's capabilities can be subsumed under five main categories: (1) culture, attitudes, and values; (2) social cohesion; (3) factor endowments; (4) industrial organization; and (5) government leadership. Economic development policymakers must be concerned with a nation's capabilities not just in terms of the level and importance of each element, but also in terms of the substitution and synergistic effects among these elements over time.

Chapter 6

Assessing the Nation's Opportunities and Threats

A fter the Cold War ended, the world's focus turned from struggles in the political and military spheres to competition and cooperation in the economic sphere. Six fundamental forces underlie this awareness: the fact of global interdependence; the widespread protectionism and growth of regional blocs; the transnationalization of MNCs; the rapid technological advances; the internal conflict within nations; and the growth of environmental concerns. These forces affect nations in varying degrees.

This chapter examines how a nation can identify its major opportunities and threats. We start by comparing two nations—Britain and Japan—the former as an example of a failure to exploit its opportunities; the latter as an example of successfully coping with a threat. Afterwards, we will examine current opportunities and threats that derive from each of the major global forces and trends. These opportunities and threats, when matched with a nation's capabilities, provide the basis for policymakers to formulate that nation's strategic thrust (to be discussed in Chapter 7).

A TALE OF TWO NATIONS

Britain's Failure in Exploiting Its Opportunities[1]

Britain is a good example of a country that failed to sustain its pioneering advantage. In the last half of the nineteenth century, Great Britain was the center of the Industrial Revolution and enjoyed a disproportionate record of scientific and technological progress. Its growth should have been self-sustaining. However, it lost its leading position in industry after industry to emerging industrial powers such as Germany, France, and eventually the United States. By the turn of the century, Britain absolutely lagged behind these other nations with respect to the major innovations that it had introduced during the second half of the nineteenth century.

Chemicals was the most technologically advanced of all the industries developed in this period, providing a wide range of new products such as medicines, fertilizers, textiles, film, and the industry's first major innovation—synthetic dyes. Ironically, the first synthetic dyes were invented in 1856 by an Englishman, William Perkin. During the 1860s and 1870s, Britain had almost every comparative advantage in the new industry. On the supply side, Britain had the largest supplies of high-quality coal, which is the main dye-producing raw material. On the demand side, Britain's gigantic textile industry was the largest downstream market for the new dyes. What it lacked was primarily experienced chemists. This problem could have been easily solved by hiring trained German chemists. Given its advantages, British entrepreneurs should have dominated the dyemaking industry. Instead, German industrialists such as Bayer, BASF, and Hoechst took the lead by heavily investing in the whole value chain. As a result, Germany's competitive advantage (trained chemists) overwhelmed Britain's economic comparative advantages (demand and supply strengths).

The same missed opportunity occurred in heavy and light machinery, steel, electrical equipment, copper, and other metals. Britain was a pioneer in the metal industry, but its first mover advantage was eroded by Germans and Americans who made substantial investments in the industry. In machinery (the new industry of the Second Industrial Revolution), German producers aggressively acquired the lead in manufacturing heavy processing machines and equipment. Americans took a near-global monopoly in sewing, agriculture, and other light machinery produced by fabricating and assembling standardized parts. This high-volume production process was already known, by the 1880s, as "the American system of manufacturing."

Japanese Success in Exploiting Opportunities

Now let's examine how the Japanese, in contrast to the British, brilliantly exploited their opportunities.

After World War II ended in 1945, the Japanese government needed to set urgent priorities to restore the country from its desperate condition following the war. In the first phase of reindustrialization during the early postwar period, Japanese firms pursued a strategy of producing low-price, high-quality products for the mass market. Japan's major exports came from industries such as textiles, home appliances, and sundries.[2]

In the mid-1960s, Japanese labor costs began to rise dramatically. Heavy and chemical industries (e.g., steel, shipbuilding, heavy machinery, petrochemical, and synthetic fibers) began to replace labor-intensive industries, which moved their investment to the low-cost countries in East Asia.

Japan's limited space, however, constrained further expansion of these industries. These resource- and energy-intensive industries reached their peak in the early 1970s. The 1974 oil crisis propelled Japan to shift from resource- and energy-intensive industrial sectors to more knowledge-intensive industrial sectors (notably automobiles and electronics products). This began the third phase of Japan's reindustrialization. Like the labor-intensive industries, heavy and chemical industries moved their investment abroad.[3]

The West's commitment to free trade and its tolerant reaction to Japan's expansionist and exclusionary trade practices provided the Japanese with a unique opportunity to pursue mercantilist policies. Lack of retaliatory duties, tariffs, and quotas created very little pressure for Japan to pursue foreign direct investment.[4]

In the third phase of industrialization, Japan's drastic expanding trade surplus quickly led to trade conflicts and a sharp appreciation of the yen. To avoid protectionism, starting in the mid-1970s, Japanese companies began to invest heavily in foreign assembly plants. At the same time, they constantly upgraded their home-based industries, producing higher value-added goods.[5]

IDENTIFYING A NATION'S OPPORTUNITIES AND THREATS

Clearly, countries differ in their capabilities to identify and respond to opportunities and threats. This was evident in contrasting Britain and Japan. Here we will define opportunities and threats more precisely.

An opportunity can be defined as an arena *in which a nation can create or obtain additional wealth*. The nation's success probability depends on whether its capabilities exceed those of the competition in meeting *key success requirements* for operating in the target area. Mere capabilities do not constitute a national competitive advantage. The best-performing nation will be the one that can *create the greatest wealth attainment by delivering the greatest value to its customers* in the global marketplace.

Looking at Figure 6.1, the nation's best opportunities would be those in the upper-left cell; and policymakers should prepare plans to pursue

FIGURE 6.1

Opportunity Matrix

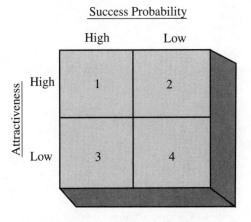

Source: Philip Kotler, *Marketing Management: Analysis, Planning, Implementation and Control,* 9th edn (Upper Saddle River, NJ: Prentice Hall, 1997), Figure 3.8, p. 82.

these opportunities. The opportunities in the lower-right cell are too minor to consider. The opportunities in the upper-right cell and lower-left cell should be monitored in the event that any improve their attractiveness and probability of success.

By contrast, a nation's threats are *challenges posed by unfavorable trends or developments economically, politically, or socially* that would lead, in the absence of the nation's defensive action, to a deterioration in wealth.

Threats should be classified according to their *seriousness* and *probability of occurrence*. Figure 6.2 illustrates several threats facing the nation. The threats in the upper-left cell are major threats, since they can seriously hurt the nation and have a high probability of occurrence. For these threats, the nation needs to prepare contingency plans that spell out what defensive steps it can take before or during each threat's occurrence. The threats in the lower-right cell are very minor and can be ignored. The threats in the upper-right and lower-right cell do not require contingency planning, but do need to be carefully monitored in the event they grow more critical.

Figure 6.3 provides examples of opportunities and threats that are derived from each element of global forces and trends, for a particular nation or group of nations.

FIGURE 6.2
Threat Matrix

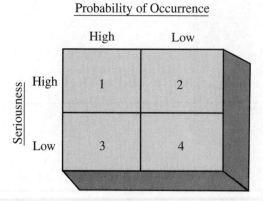

Probability of Occurrence

	High	Low
High	1	2
Low	3	4

Seriousness

Source: Ibid.

FIGURE 6.3

Global Forces and Trends

Global Forces and Trends	Implications
Global Interdependence	*Exploiting Opportunities from Other Nations' Threats
	*Exploiting Opportunities from Other Nations' Moves
	*Vulnerability to External Developments
	*Pursuing Import Liberalization Policies
Protectionism and Growing Economic Blocs	*Enhancing the Nation's Competitiveness Through Economic Alignment
	*The Rise of the Regional Economies
Transnationalization of MNCs	*Increasing the International Division of Labor
	*Developing a Nation's Multinational Corporations
Conflicting Politics and Tribalism	*Preparing for the State Reunification
	*Changing the Nation's Alliances
Rapid Technological Advances	*Creating Technological Muscles Through Cooperation
	*Finding Technological Niches in the Global Market
	*Coping with Comparative Advantage Reversal
Growth of Environmental Concerns	*Exporting of Environmentally Helpful and Friendly Products

Each of these opportunities and threats is illustrated in the text that follows.

EXPLOITING OPPORTUNITIES FROM OTHER NATIONS' THREATS

Singapore presents a good example of a country that is poised to benefit from a threat facing another country, in this case, Hong Kong.[6] Hong Kong faces the challenge of how to cope with the transfer of sovereignty from the United Kingdom to China in 1997. The draft of the Basic Law, which set out the rules governing Hong Kong's affairs for at least a half century after 1997, seems to give the Chinese government sweeping powers. There is no way to know whether China will allow Hong Kong to run under its current economic and political system. The unclear political future has led to the flight of capital and people from Hong Kong, which is likely to rise even further above the current high levels. In fact, Hong Kong's economy has become increasingly integrated with parts of southern China through trade and investment links. Surely, these interdependencies could be threatened with the eruption of political instability in China.[7]

Singapore, on the other hand, hopes to exploit the uncertainties hanging over the future of Hong Kong. In 1989, Singapore made drastic changes in its emigration laws in order to attract capital and labor from Hong Kong. Singapore is attempting to expand its role as an international financial center. With the exception of the foreign exchange and commodity futures markets, so far, its financial markets are small. Funds under management in Hong Kong are nearly ten times those of Singapore. Moreover, the regulatory environment in Hong Kong is considerably more liberal than that in Singapore, allowing Hong Kong to be well integrated into the world capital markets. Nonetheless, Singapore may be expected to take advantage of the financial uncertainties concerning Hong Kong's future.[8]

EXPLOITING OPPORTUNITIES FROM OTHER NATIONS' MOVES[9]

Hong Kong itself faces a new opportunity resulting from China's planned joining of the World Trade Organization. As the eleventh-largest trading nation in the world, China decided to sign the Final Act Embodying the Results of the Uruguay Round of Multinational Trade Negotiations (Final Act) and the Agreement Establishing the Multilateral Trade Organization (MTO Agreement) in Morocco in April 1994, thus taking one step closer to regaining its GATT Contracting Party status. On the other hand, China will automatically assume all the basic obligations of the GATT—unify its tax systems, reform its price and foreign trade systems, and reduce its customs duties. Meanwhile, China will enjoy the rights granted to it—the Generalized System of Preferences (GSP) benefits for certain exports and certain exemption clauses, such as protecting infant industries.

Hong Kong is China's top foreign investor, contributing more than 60 percent of China's total foreign investment. It also serves as a conduit between China and the rest of the world. Given this position, Hong Kong would benefit greatly from China's GATT Contracting Party status. Evidently, in 1993, when China reduced its tariff duties on 3,371 categories of merchandise, Hong Kong saved approximately 6.44 billion HK dollars in the first half of 1993, resulting in a 6.6 percent increase in its export competitiveness. Furthermore, China's recent opening up of its service market gives Hong Kong a great opportunity in providing strong financial and business services.

VULNERABILITY TO EXTERNAL DEVELOPMENTS

South Korea illustrates the vulnerability of a nation even when it has achieved a high level of exports. Korea's exports are highly concentrated, a large amount going to the United States. Korea's growing trade surplus vis-à-vis the United States is now raising the possibility of the United States adopting protectionist measures. To skirt this protectionism, Korea has recently implemented changes in its trade and foreign investment policies. Korean trade policies also confront another critical issue. To keep their exports thriving, its assemblers have relied heavily upon Japan to supply parts and components. The soaring Japanese yen has worsened Korea's trade structure. Apart from raising Korea's costs of production and reducing its competitiveness, the rising yen has enlarged that nation's trade deficit to a record figure.[10]

The fundamental problem of South Korea's international trade, thus, is rooted in its lopsided market structure in which all surpluses draw from the United States and all deficits come from trade with Japan.[11] To deal with this structural problem, Koreans are seeking other export markets. Recently, South Korea's government announced a policy to reduce its dependence on imported capital goods. Increasing domestic production of machinery and industrial components is Korea's top priority in response to the strong yen and its persistent trade deficit with Japan. The plan includes attracting Japanese manufacturers of capital goods to invest in

Korea by offering low rents for land and relaxing restrictions on the import of machinery. South Korea's government is also encouraging the development of a local industrial equipment industry by allowing purchasers of Korean machinery access to foreign currency loans, which are cheaper than domestic ones.[12]

ENHANCING THE NATION'S COMPETITIVENESS THROUGH ECONOMIC ALIGNMENT

Many nations gain benefits from economic blocs. These blocs allow the nation's companies to access greatly enlarged markets with reduced or abolished country-by-country tariff and nontariff barriers. They also allow the factors of production (capital, technology, and labor) to flow more freely across all member states. The key features of economic blocs in creating wealth are summarized in Figure 6.4.

Today's most active economic bloc is the European Community (EC), which formed a Single Market in January 1993, a market of more than 300 million consumers. Its main purposes are to remove *physical*, *technical*, and *fiscal barriers* to economic growth. The Single Market today allows all member states to move their goods, services, capital, and labor forces freely within the EC boundaries. As a result, the market size for all member states will be greatly expanded and should enhance economies of scope and scale. Industrial efficiency will be greatly increased because each member state's companies will have to cope not only with their domestic competitors but with a flood of newcomers from their intra-EC counterparts.

Subsequently, the EC began negotiating with EFTA (European Free Trade Area) to create a European Economic Area (EEA). The Community is also negotiating association agreements with several East European countries, which, if concluded, would grant these countries preferential access to the EC market.

Across the Atlantic, the United States and Canada negotiated a North American Free Trade Agreement (NAFTA), which later extended to Mexico. There is discussion about further enlargement to include Chile and some other Latin American countries.

In Southeast Asia, the ASEAN Summit in 1992 agreed to implement an ASEAN Free Trade Area (AFTA) with a common external preferential tariff over the next fifteen years. Unlike its NAFTA or EU's counter-

FIGURE 6.4

How Economic Alignment Creates More Wealth

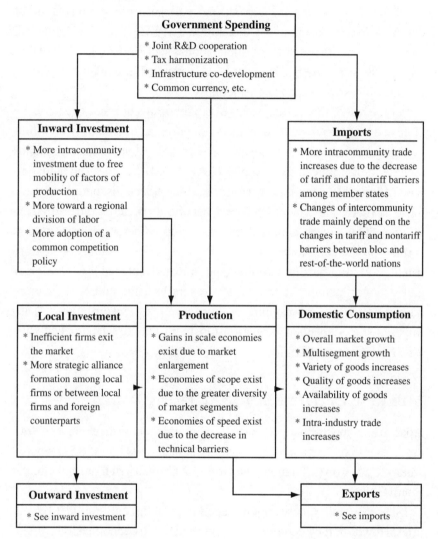

parts, however, there is a low level of interregional trade and investment among ASEAN member states. The major reasons are, first, that most ASEANs are likely to have similar economic resources and cost structures. The gains from trade, thus, are inevitably small. And second, the regional market of the AFTA is too small to reap economies of scale and scope. For ASEANs, perhaps their regional trading arrangement would not be effective unless other countries, particularly Japan, Asian NICs, and the United States, are involved. They should enlarge their markets and access to industrial countries' best practices.

One evidence of the shift toward more globalism is the formation of the Asia Pacific Economic Cooperation (APEC). This will allow all member states freely to move their goods, services, capital, and labor forces within the APEC boundary. As a result, the market size for all member states will expand considerably.

For the rest of the world, groups of neighboring countries have also established *common markets* with the main purposes of enlarging their limited internal markets and enhancing economic cooperation. Examples include the Caribbean Community (CARICOM) and the Andean Common Market. Thus far, their performances have been disappointing. Like those ASEANs just mentioned, the benefits expected from a division of labor did not exist, mainly due to their similar factor endowments and similar problems. Moreover, the smaller, weaker member states are usually afraid of becoming dominated, or disadvantaged, by their larger and stronger member states. As Professors Reitsma and Kleinpenning have pointed out, the asymmetry in power may end up with a "sub-imperialistic" dependency relationship (e.g., between landlocked Burkina Faso and Ivory Coast).[13]

THE RISE OF THE REGIONAL ECONOMIES

Apart from "macrolinkages" such as economic blocs, there are also "microlinkages" or "region-states"—geographical units like the Singapore–Johor–Riau Growth Triangle, the Northern Growth Triangle, and Greater South China.

Like economic blocs, regional economies transcend political boundaries. However, they do not involve entire national economies. The major focus of economic blocs is on trade liberalization among member states, while the focus of regional states is on economic complementarity to promote private investment. Interestingly, since they do not represent a protectionist trading bloc, regional states are more acceptable to other nonmember countries. However, both economic blocs and regional states increase a country's international competitiveness via the exploitation of economies of scale and scope.

As Professors Chia and Lee suggest, the success of regional states derives from: (1) high economic complementarity among member states; (2) close geographical proximity; (3) good investment climate; (4) sufficient infrastructure; and (5) ability to access globally.[14]

INCREASING THE INTERNATIONAL DIVISION OF LABOR

Globalization is leading to increased country links among companies in manufacturing their products. Consider the following examples:

- To develop the Boeing 767, Boeing's staff in Seattle designed the plane and manufactured the wings and cockpit. The nosetip and certain wing parts were manufactured in Italy, the rear section in Canada, the front windshields and engines in England, and the high-tech components in Japan. Altogether, twenty-nine countries participated in producing this plane.
- In Japan's semiconductor industry, the first half of the manufacturing process (chemical and exposure treatment) takes place in Japan, while the labor-intensive second stage of assembly and testing operates in Southeast Asian countries.[15]

Thus, to create national wealth in a global economy, the policymakers must realize that *specialization* is essential for competitiveness. Table 6.1 illustrates the major technological focus and industry characteristics in the Asian and Pacific region.

DEVELOPING A NATION'S MULTINATIONAL CORPORATIONS

Developing nations are increasingly expanding their own multinational corporations. By the 1980s, there were as many as 8,000 subsidiaries of firms from developing countries operating in other developing countries. To take just three examples: Brazilian firms provide engineering and construction services in Africa; the Hong Kong's Regent, Peninsular, and Park Hotel groups operate throughout Asia; and Taiwanese firms build steel mills in Nigeria and make furniture in Malaysia.[16] Most of these investments are in labor-intensive products and processes, where they have a declining comparative advantage. Some developing country MNCs

TABLE 6.1

Major Technological Focus and Industry Characteristics in the
Asian and Pacific Region

Group	Major Technological Focus	Economies	Industrial Characteristics
I	Creation of new technology based on advanced sciences	Japan	Brain-intensive (in the process of shifting toward a postindustrial society characterized by knowledge and information)
II	Improvement of imported technology and some technology generation	S. Korea Taiwan Hong Kong Singapore India	Technology-intensive (technological competence in India arising from science and technology developments for domestic markets, but in cases of other countries from export-oriented development and international competition)
III	Digestion and adaptation of imported technology and some improvement of existing technology	Indonesia Iran Malaysia Pakistan Philippines Thailand	Skill-intensive (dominance of MNCs catering to domestic markets; resource-based extractive industries, low-cost labor)
IV	Some utilization of technology	Bangladesh Fiji Nepal	Operation-intensive (early phase of and/or partial industrialization to meet domestic needs; predominance of agriculture)

Source: Economic and Social Commission for Asia and the Pacific, *Industrial Restructuring in Asia and the Pacific*, United Nations, March 1991, Box VII.2, p. 263.

have, however, shifted to the "high-technology" sector. Hong Kong firms, for example, have been shifting their foreign investment from textiles and clothing to electronics.[17]

Compared with developed country MNCs, developing country MNCs display a geographically distinctive pattern. Most of their foreign investments are concentrated in the region of the home countries. Thus Hong

Kong in 1987 was the largest foreign investor in China, the second-largest in Indonesia, and the third-largest in the Philippines, Thailand, Singapore, and Taiwan.[18]

PREPARING FOR REUNIFICATION

Countries also find opportunities when they are able to reunify several formerly partitioned areas. The reunification of East and West Germany represents the victory of geoeconomics over geopolitics. Struggles for re-unification are occurring in other regions of the world—most notably China and Korea.

In 1994, China announced a reunification formula known as "one country, two systems." China made a commitment to respect Hong Kong's current "social and economic systems," which will "remain unchanged for fifty years." China likes to use Hong Kong as a "bridge" for eventually bringing Taiwan into a bloc, forming a "common front" to compete effectively against the United States and Japan. The combination of China's abundant resources and market potential with Taiwan's growing economy and entrepreneurial dynamism would spell a powerful synergy. By the end of 1990, indirect trade (via Hong Kong) topped $4 billion. Taiwan investments in some 2,000 projects in China totaled $1.6 billion.[19]

Korean reunification is also likely by the year 2000, according to a report published by *The Economist*'s intelligence unit. The main reason is that North Korea's "Kim Il Sung-ism" will, sooner or later, collapse after the death of Kim Il Sung, and North Korea will be absorbed by the South like the German case.[20]

For the time being, however, North Korea is still resisting the tide of reforms. Unlike other former Socialist countries, it constantly tries to intensify its ideological indoctrination campaigns and inculcate the people to believe in the superiority of its form of socialism.[21]

CHANGING THE NATION'S ALLIANCES

Coupled with the formation of economic blocs, nations' alliances are also changing. India strengthened a very close economic relationship with the former Soviet Union partly because of Soviet credits and the selective potential for barter between the two countries. Undoubtedly,

India's conflicts with Pakistan and China were a major factor. The post–Cold War era has rendered such negotiated trade deals obsolete.[22] State trading is still important in India's relations with some developing nations, specifically in Africa.

In East Asia, the most dramatic change in alignments has been the establishment of diplomatic relations between the former Soviet Union and South Korea in October 1990, and between China and South Korea in 1992. This means that China turned its back on North Korea and, at the same time, South Korea cut its links with Taiwan.[23] The Korean situation challenges Japan. To prevent further isolation of North Korea, Japan has worked closely with that nation to establish diplomatic ties. Economically, North Korea needs to attract Japan's investments to restore its backward economy. Politically, it would also want to balance the recent diplomatic feats of South Korea.[24]

After the end of the Vietnam fighting, the Indochinese countries of Vietnam, Cambodia, and Laos have been moving closer to the ASEAN countries. Their "national interests" are now defined more in economic terms. Vietnam is a good example.[25] In dealing with China, one foreign ministry official argued that Vietnam now has three options:

There are three possible ways of organizing our relations with China: (1) confrontation, (2) satellite status similar to North Korea, or (3) a medium position between the two. Satellite status provides no guarantees. North Korea was sacrificed by China when it turned to South Korea. Also, even if Vietnam were to be a good satellite, China will not leave us alone. They will always pressure us and try to dominate Southeast Asia. We tried for a full year to forge a new relation with China but we failed. Take its occupation of Bay Tu Chinh [a reef in the Spratly archipelago] and the Crestone affair. Okay, we distrusted China but it was only with Bay Tu Chinh that we understood that China follows its national interest. That game is in the nature of international politics.[26]

According to Professor Carlyle Thayer, it is likely that Vietnam will intensify its bilateral ties with China, but at the same time, it will try to counterbalance this by developing strong ties with other countries.[27]

Eastern Europe countries, in post–Cold War Europe, are also shifting their alliances. There are at least three groups of alliances.

The first group can be termed the *"Free Market West."* Poland, the Czech Republic, and Hungary have all but won their battle to become democratic, market-driven economies. All these wish to join the European Union.

The second group is the *former USSR*. Russia, Ukraine, and most of the other remnants of the Soviet Union are waging a desperate struggle for survival and stability.

The last group is the *Balkan states*—a dangerous region living on the hatreds of past centuries. The old Yugoslavia has self-destructed; Romania is governed by its old Communist elite; Bulgaria is relapsing into bitter Balkan politics; and Albania remains crippled by its eerie Communist past. For this group, ethnic tensions and civil war must be solved before new economic alliances can be forged.[28]

CREATING TECHNOLOGICAL MUSCLE THROUGH COOPERATION

Opportunities are created for nations by participating in new technology development, especially in such areas as semiconductors, biotechnology, and new materials. In these areas, the United States has taken the leading position while Japan is the challenger. The European Union is unfortunately a follower, as the following evidence suggests:

- *Semiconductors*: Europe has been slipping steadily in this area, despite heavy investments over the past years. European companies now control less than 40% of their $8.5 billion home market.[29]
- *Biotechnology*: Europe's drug and chemical industries have moved slowly, and no new company has emerged as the leader as Genetech did in the United States. A new challenge: Japan has targeted biotech as a growth area for the 1990s.
- *Computers*: U.S. companies hold a 60% share of the European market. Europe is heavily dependent on U.S. and Japanese technology in such key components as disk drives and microprocessors.

Europe's lag is partly due to the fact that high-technology industries require a large economy which smaller countries cannot accommodate. One reason for forming the Single European Market in 1992 was to expand the size of member countries' internal market by eliminating trade barriers, and to create the technological muscle through member country cooperation. Five Europe-based cooperative R&D megaprojects are: (1) EUREKA— 302 joint R&D projects since 1985 developing technologies from semiconductors to mobile phones; (2) ESPRIT—an EC-sponsored program to bolster competitiveness in computers and information technology; (3) BRITE—research to develop new technology for traditional industries, mainly aeronautics and advanced materials; (4) RACE—another EC-sponsored program to develop technology for Europe-wide high-speed data telecommunications networks; and (5) COMET—an EC-sponsored program for work exchanges, scholarships, and other university-business links.[30]

FINDING TECHNOLOGICAL NICHES IN THE GLOBAL MARKET[31]

Some economists have recommended that small countries pool their resources in R&D in order to find technological niches in the global market. There are some risks in cooperation agreements, however, especially where large and small, or more and less developed countries have joined as partners. To some extent, it is possible that firms in one country develop into little more than "screwdriver factories" for the firms in other countries.

Smaller countries might find it wise to cooperate within certain R&D areas. Rather than manufacture robots, for example, a small country may buy them in order to more efficiently produce goods designed to fill market niches.

Policymakers in small industrial countries have to decide whether their companies should specialize in areas where they already have a comparative advantage or should develop a niche in a new area where the potential economic payoffs may be greater. Mediterranean countries, for example, have given priority to research in solar and wind energy and biomass, which are their current comparative advantage. However, some countries have recently changed their technology development strategy on the grounds that it is not helping them to catch up to technologically advanced countries. Spain, for one, is now strengthening its capabilities in new materials and robotics.

COPING WITH COMPARATIVE ADVANTAGE REVERSAL[32]

The recent fast pace of technological advances can provide both opportunities and threats to developing countries. There is a phenomenon termed *comparative advantage reversal*—many developed countries try to conserve on the factors of production by turning their production process to become more labor-saving (e.g., using automation and robotics) and more resource-saving (e.g., applying new materials and biotechnological methods).

It is difficult to evaluate the net impact of the recent technological advances on developing countries. On the one hand, there is some evidence showing a negative impact of biotechnology on the exports of some developing countries. In 1981, the United States replaced 1.8 million tons of sugar imports with high-fructose corn syrup. Subsequently, sugar cane exports from Latin American countries to the United States decreased drastically (from over $1.3 billion in 1981 to $568 million in 1985). The same is also true for mining, since 15 percent of U.S. copper production is now extracted from low-concentration deposits, using a specially designed bacterium. In addition, in the near future, advances in biomass technology could completely replace oil as a source of energy. This would benefit many oil-consuming countries at the expense of some oil-producing nations.

On the other hand, there is some evidence that the advances in microelectronics, biotechnology, and telecommunications could promote economic growth in developing countries. Biotechnology, for example, could help developing countries to establish more autonomous manufacturing technologies. Biotechnology is a promising area because it fosters country-specific agricultural and medical developments while requiring little scale, human capital, or financial resources. Brazil, for example, was able to replace a significant portion of its oil imports with alcohol refined from sugarcane. This may promote rural industries and reduce the income gap between the rural and urban sectors. By using genetic engineering, Mexico has also experienced progress in the production of plant hormones and in the generation of improved seeds.

Advances in telecommunications allow access to education and information even in the most remote areas of developing countries. Village telephones in India have had a major impact.[33]

Professor Herminio Blanco (1988) has suggested three strategies for developing countries to deal with advances in technology: (1) defensive measures to limit the adverse consequences that technological advances could inflict upon their productive structure; (2) tactical moves to take advantage of the opportunities offered by the rapid structural changes in global industries; and (3) a long-term commitment to invest and improve productive capabilities in selected sectors and market segments.

EXPORTING ENVIRONMENTALLY HELPFUL AND FRIENDLY PRODUCTS[34]

Due to the growing concern about global health and environment, many countries are strengthening their environmental laws. Trade in pollution control technologies is increasing significantly: the United States, European countries, and Japan exported $20 billion worth of pollution control devices worldwide in 1990.

Some renewable energy industries are also increasingly targeting the global market. In 1985, 553 megawatts' worth of wind turbines were exported, valued at $720 million; in 1992, more than half of total production ($200 million worth) of photovoltaic cells were exported. General Electric has recently entered into a joint venture with the Tungstrum Corporation to produce efficient fluorescent lightbulbs in Hungary.

International competition can also force MNCs to match the environmental innovations of their foreign counterparts. Examples include the U.S. automobile industry's response to Japan's advances in fuel efficiency; low-flow toilets, which were first developed in Sweden, and have now been replicated around the world; and some air pollution control technologies, formerly led by the United States, now overtaken by the Japanese and Germans.

SUMMARY

Opportunities come and go. Nations must take advantage of them at the right time. In the 1980s, many Latin American countries changed their trade strategies from import substitution to export promotion. Unfortunately, the international environment no longer favored export manufacturers; the Latin American countries faced fierce competition from the countries of South and Southeast Asia and performed poorly by comparison.

Each nation must read the emerging opportunities and threats arising from global forces and trends, and tease out their implications. Matching these opportunities and threats with the nation's capabilities is the foundation for policymakers formulating a nation's strategic thrust, which we examine in the next chapter.

Chapter 7

Developing the Nation's Strategic Thrust

E very nation must tailor a strategy for achieving its objectives and goals. However, each nation copes with different internal and external environments which, in turn, provide different sets of competitive/cooperative conditions, strengths/weaknesses, and opportunities/threats, as we have just examined in chapters 4, 5, and 6, respectively. These environments inevitably affect not only the nation's goals but also its strategic thrust. In this chapter, we examine how nations formulate their strategic thrusts.

THE NATION'S STRATEGIC THRUST DEVELOPMENT

A nation's goals indicate what a nation wants to achieve; a nation's strategic thrust answers how to get there. Figure 7.1 illustrates the strategic thrust development process.

Environmental Analysis

A nation must examine its *competitive* environment (global competitive structure and strategic groups of nations), as well as its *internal* environ-

FIGURE 7.1

A Nation's Strategic Thrust Development Process

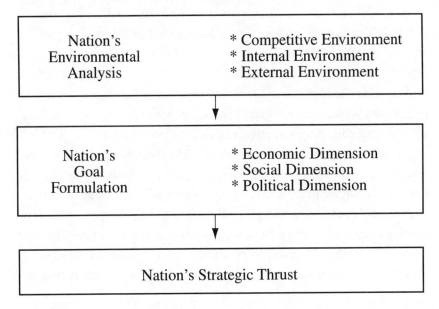

ment (nation's capabilities) and *external* environment (global forces and trends) before it can formulate objectives. Assessing the competitive environment helps policymakers to identify the competitive and cooperative patterns it has with other nations. Assessing the internal environment aids policymakers in identifying national strengths and weaknesses, while assessing the external environment enables them to identify both the nation's opportunities and its threats.

Goal Formulation

The people of all nations ultimately aspire to a good economy, a good society, and a good political process. A nation's objectives are set to meet these aspirations: raising the level of GNP per capita; improving international competitiveness; a high level of employment; stable prices; good health; good education; a good environment; security and peace; human freedom; and so forth.

Many nations have their objectives and goals. Singapore's government has expressed the view that its citizens should aspire to reach the prevailing Swiss living standards by the year 2000. South Korea is aspiring to reach advanced country status by the year 2000. In 1987, Taiwan's Council for Economic Planning and Development set out the broad parameters for government policy up to 2000.[1]

Assessing the nation's environments enables policymakers to formulate national objectives and goals. These face the challenge of being hierarchical, prioritized, quantitative, realistic, and consistent.

The nation should strive to order its objectives *hierarchically*, from higher objectives to derived objectives. Figure 7.2 illustrates an example that carries out one branch, namely, the distribution of income objectives.

A nation's objectives and goals also need to be *prioritized*. For less-developed countries, the economic objectives and goals may come first while the social and participatory objectives may follow, although it is difficult to rank these except in the specific context of each nation. By

FIGURE 7.2

Hierarchy of Nation's Objectives and Goals

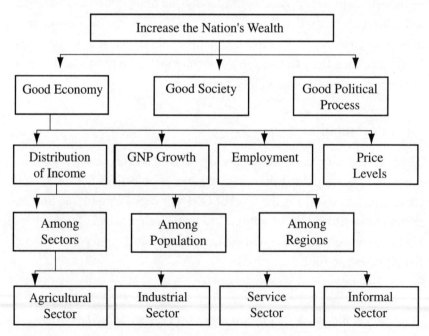

contrast, in the developed economies, all these three objectives will have an equal claim on the policymaker.

Policymakers should state the objectives *quantitatively*. The objective "increase the GNP growth" is not as satisfactory as "increase the GNP growth by 5 percent," or even better, "increase GDP per capita to $20,000 before the year 2000." Policymakers use the term *goal* to describe objectives that are specific with respect to magnitude and time. Turning a nation's objectives into measurable goals facilitates policymakers' planning, implementation, and control.

A nation should set *realistic* goals. The levels should arise from an analysis of its environments—competitive, internal, and external—not from wishful thinking.

Finally, the nation's objectives need to be *consistent*. For example, it may not be possible to maximize both "high income growth and income distribution," or "high level of employment and stable prices." These may conflict, and one or the other may have to yield, at least for now.

FORMULATING THE NATION'S STRATEGIC THRUST

Wealth creation is an ultimate goal of most nations. However, to augment national wealth, nations have to compete with one another. The higher the nation's competitiveness, the higher its wealth possibilities. The nation's strategic thrust is influenced by both its relative competitiveness and its relative wealth position. Four strategic thrusts are distinguished in Figure 7.3, along with some nations that embrace each. We shall now examine each strategic thrust in turn.

SUSTAINING STRATEGY

Countries that are strong in relative wealth position and relative competitiveness, like Japan and Germany, require strategic thrusts that will sustain their wealth and competitiveness.

Japan: Pursuit of Global Industrial Excellence

Japan's emergence as an economic superpower was aided by a strategic vision and adaptability that fit the post–World War II changing environment (see Table 7.1). Japanese companies relied heavily on licensing

FIGURE 7.3

Strategic Thrusts of Nations

		Strong	Weak
Relative Wealth Position	High	**Sustaining Strategy** ᵗʰJapan *Germany	**Revitalizing Strategy** ⁺The U.S. *Australia *Industrial Nichers
	Low	**Building Strategy** *Four Tigers *Little Tigers *India *China	**Turnaround Strategy** *Latin America *Former Socialists *Subsistent Economies

Relative Competitiveness

U.S. and European technology for product development. Product quality was improved through intensive investments in manufacturing processes aiming at garnering differential advantage over foreign competitors. During the 1950s and early 1960s, Japan manufactured low-cost imitative products, but by the late 1960s it introduced products of quality and reliability into the world market. In the 1970s, the emphasis shifted to improved product designs and productivity.[2]

In order to stem Japan's advances and trade surpluses, deficit nations like the United States adopted measures such as Voluntary Export Restraints. These pressured Japan to increase the value of its products in order to compensate for the forced decline in export volume. Japanese automobiles, which used to be of medium quality and medium price, now entered into the premium segment. Japan managed to turn a liability into an asset.

From product innovation in the 1980s, Japan moved on to a decade of creativity that is evident from its advances in the fields of optoelectronics, HDTV, memory chips, robotics, factory automation, and so forth. Moreover, Japan is making a bid for superiority in supercomputers, fine ceramics, biotechnology, aerospace, superconductors, nanomechanism technology, medical electronics, marine development, optical communi-

TABLE 7.1

The Evolution of Japanese Industries

Period	Industry Emphasis	Management Technique	Target Industries
1950–60s	Quality	Total quality control	TVs, radios, steel, chemicals
1970s	Aesthetic design	Product refinement	Cameras, audio equipment, VCRs
1980s	Product innovation	Spiral development	Laptop computers, 8mm video, facsimile machines
1990s	Creativity	Technology fusion networks	Bioceramics, neural optomechatronics, bioelectronics, video computers
2000+	Spiritual and physical well-being	Humanware engineering	Biomechatronics, biocomputing, biocommunication

Source: Sheridan M. Tatsuno, *Created in Japan, From Imitators to World-Class Innovators* (New York: Harper & Row Publishers, 1990), Table 1-1, p. 6.

cations, and automotive electronics.[3] In order to meet global industrial excellence, Japan has already targeted the technological-oriented industries for the next twenty years (see Figure 7.4).

On the demand side, Japan has already been one of the most affluent, upscale markets in the world. Private consumption has taken a major role in driving the Japanese economy. Japanese companies are now launching their new products first in their domestic markets. When a new product has been successful at home, it is then exported worldwide.[4]

Germany: Playing the Leverage[5]

The breaching of the Berlin Wall in November 1989, which led to the economic and monetary union and subsequently to the political union of the two Germanys, has enhanced Germany's relative political and economic power in Europe, and altered quite fundamentally its short-term and longer-term growth prospects.

In the short term, the cost of uplifting East Germany to West German

FIGURE 7.4

Japan's Target Industries for the Next 20 Years

1994—CAD of computer chips with more than 1 million gates

1996—New protocol technology to link communication networks

1997—Sludge removal from ocean floor; fishing site cleanup; underwater robots used to 1,000 feet

1999—Artificial Intelligence in aircraft management and control
    Nursing robots to help the elderly and handicapped
    Local disaster forecasting and preventing systems

2000—Electric data storage safe from human errors, viruses, or natural disasters

2001—Artificial organs not rejected by the human body

2002—Prevention of cancer cell spread in the body
    Quick turnaround of bug-free, complex software
    Space robots with sophisticated Artificial Intelligence

2003—International digital communication network
    High-performance materials for space travel
    Medicine and semiconductor production in space

2005—Turn cancer cells back to normal cells

2011—Room-temperature superconductors for industrial machinery

---

Source: Sheridan M. Tatsuno, *Created in Japan, From Imitators to World-Class Innovators* (New York: Harper & Row, 1990), pp. 269–270.

standards lies in a range between $300 billion and $650 billion. On social infrastructure alone, Germany has to spend more than $6 billion a year. There is also the burden of integrating the former East Germany's industry into the West. Many industrial sectors in East Germany need to be reorganized because they were grossly inefficient or grossly polluting. Between one-third and two-fifths of East Germany's industrial capacity is thought to face closure in part, if not in full. Industrial restructuring in the East will inevitably leave some 1.4 million people unemployed, most of them relatively less skilled and less disciplined.

The reconstruction of the East will absorb real product and capital from the former West Germany for many years. Even though West Germany has already gained the "unification bonus" to growth, the huge resource costs of absorbing the East resulted in high interest rates, exchange rates, and inflation. Nevertheless, Germany stands as a major economic power, as evidenced in Table 7.2.

REVITALIZING STRATEGY

Countries with a strong current wealth position but an eroded relative competitiveness, such as the United States, the European Community, Australia, and many small industrial nations, require strategic thrusts that will revitalize their competitiveness.

Reinventing America

The United States has benefited from a number of advantages, including abundant natural resources, a unified internal market, and political stability. Since the mid-1960s, however, the U.S. economic performance and competitiveness have been eroding, as indicated by trade deficits, declining world shares in most manufacturing goods, lower profitability of American firms, and reduced real earnings of American workers.[6]

Moreover, the U.S. technological investment strategy appears to have been misguided. Almost all its technological innovations still concentrate on only three main industrial sectors: defense, medicine, and agriculture. For these three sectors, the United States has built broad-based organizational capabilities to continuously develop new technologies and

TABLE 7.2

Economic Indicators of a United Germany Compared with USA, Japan, and the USSR (unit in billion $ U.S.)

	Export	Balance of Trade	Per Capita GDP	Registered Autos per 1,000 People
United Germany	354.1	73.9	13,987	376
United States	321.6	−138.0	19,340	572
Japan	264.9	77.5	14,340	235
USSR	110.6	3.3	8,850	42

Source: Compiled from *Newsweek*, Feb. 26, 1990, pp. 8–14.

upgrade the existing ones. These three sectors employ more than half of the nation's scientists and engineers and deploy 80 percent of the federal R&D funds, leaving other sectors to be less competitive in the global market.[7]

Thus, if the United States is to revitalize its economy, the central requirements are:

- *Review international commitments.* Focus trade policy on opening up foreign markets.
- *Promote business investment.* Increase public- and private-sector savings to develop a more stable macroeconomic environment, thus encouraging a stronger foundation for investment.
- *Encourage innovation.* Allocate more federal aid to new technologies and cutting-edge businesses. Speed the diffusion of new knowledge and manufacturing techniques to the small and medium business sectors.
- *Fortify the infrastructure.* Sharply boost public investment in physical and social infrastructure, resorting to user fees and privatization where possible.
- *Remake budget policy.* Reduce the federal budget deficit through big spending cuts and carefully targeted tax increases.
- *Ease regulation.* Use government regulation to foster competition.
- *Invest in human capital.* Spend more on training and encourage increased spending on R&D by business. Shift welfare funding and recipients into jobs programs. Expand access to health care while getting costs under control.[8]

Australia: Reshaping the Industrial Strategy[9]

In contrast to Japan in 1946 or Korea in 1970, Australia has potentially many advantages: a high standard of living, technical and research skills, a good physical infrastructure, a good standard of health and education, and a small but strong entrepreneurial sector. However, Australia has not put out continuous efforts to sustain its competitive position, while its competitors spent their efforts creating new competitive advantages to offset their initial disadvantages. For some decades, Australia's terms of trade have been weakening. Its industrial strategy, which is mainly based on commodity exporting with little added value, is inappropriate for the prevailing international environment.

Professor R. B. Mckern (1989) suggests that Australia should shift its industrial strategy. He proposes three options:

1. *Await a Resurgence in Commodity Prices.* A low-cost position is a critical factor for producers of commodity goods. Along the value chain, some steps should be taken toward cutting costs, acquiring downstream businesses to strengthen control in foreign markets, differentiating the products (e.g., in steel), and offering other extended benefits (e.g., delivery, quality, specifications, technical service). For some commodities, new technologies (such as CRA's new steel process) may provide an edge. However, the long-term market conditions of the commodity sector are not encouraging, so this may not be a promising long-term strategy.

2. *Strengthen the Services Sector.* This is a more promising long-term strategy. A range of services is possible, including tourism and inward travel, consultancy services, software, entertainment media exports, and educational services. Even though there is stiff international competition in each area, economies of scale are not required, and hence the "focus" strategy is viable. These services are promising areas for differentiation, where costs of skilled labor could give Australia a competitive edge. Success in these services depends, to a great extent, on demand arising from contact with a viable manufacturing sector. Australia's lack of a fully diversified advanced manufacturing industry is thus an inhibiting factor.

3. *Manufacture for Export.* To be competitive, Australian companies should avoid entering global industries (e.g., motor vehicles, semiconductors, consumer electronics, heavy petrochemicals, and aircraft) in which most segments of the business are operated at global scale. They will need instead to focus on segments where they can either differentiate successfully or gain a cost advantage by dedicated specialization. While the markets may be global for Australia, its products should not depend on a globally coordinated manufacturing base.

A few companies, with affiliations to foreign parents that form part of an integrated global industry, will export successfully whenever Australian costs provide an advantage. An example is GMH's exports of engines to Europe, the United States, and Korea. In addition, there will be opportunities in foreign industries that depend on components and sub-assemblies that can be supplied via subcontractors.

BUILDING STRATEGY

Countries that are weak in relative wealth positions, yet strong in relative competitiveness, like the Four Tigers, the "little tigers," India, and China, require strategic thrusts that will build up their positions of wealth.

South Korea: Pursuit of an Innovation-Driven Economy

Many East Asian NICs have already been successful in achieving factor-driven development.[10] Relatively abundant and cheap labor from the ASEAN countries and China and India, however, diminishes their current comparative advantage. Each country presently faces the common problem of managing the shift from a low-wage economy to a high value-adding economy.

The transition to an innovation-driven economy requires a virtual reconstruction of the ideology of development. The Asian NICs need to:

1. rediscover the entrepreneurial spirit;
2. respond promptly and effectively to environmental changes and challenges;
3. develop a long-term orientation and commitment;
4. plan more systematically;
5. improve the development and use of human resources; and
6. develop more productive government-business relationships.[11]

Take the case of South Korea. In its private sector, South Korea could consider embracing the changes shown in Table 7.3. The Korean management style has been traditionally characterized by autocratic leadership and top-down decision making. The need for a change to a new management style has been widely recognized by many Korean enterprises.[12]

Singapore: Strategic Direction for the 1990s

Singapore aims to improve its standard of living so as to move from a developing to an industrial nation. Given its small size, Singapore wisely

TABLE 7.3

Changes in Korean Management Styles

Characteristic	From	To
Management Control	ownership	professional management
Corporate Strategy	random and diversification	strategic and incremental development
Human Resource Management	people-oriented	people and efficiency
Labor Relations	seniority and authoritarian	seniority and merit cooperation

Source: Richard M. Steers, Yookeun Shin, and Gerardo R. Ungson, *The Chaebol, Korea's New Industrial Might* (New York: Harper & Row, 1989), Exhibit 8.3 p. 140.

formulates most of its aspirations in terms of *quality* rather than *quantity*. It seeks to be the technologically advanced and best managed nation.[13] The report of Singapore's Economic Development Board clearly articulated the nation's economic mission:

> *Singapore must catch up with the industrial nations in maturity and level of development of our economy. By the 1990s, we must aim to become a developed nation. We must aspire to be as good as any developed nation in terms of education and skill level, range and sophistication of our economic activities, capital invested per worker and productivity per worker.*[14]

Here is Singapore's philosophy: "If it cannot be the final destination of goods, Singapore can still be a place to send them on their way. Even if it cannot absorb much more large industry within its own borders, it can facilitate and help manage industrial operations in a nearby location."[15]

To create such an environment, Singapore's government has concentrated on four main themes:

> *First, competitiveness, differentiation, as opposed to low cost, is pursued. Singapore cannot be as cheap as other up-and-coming*

*developing countries. What Singapore can do is to provide supe-
rior and technical skills. Businesses will derive maximum value
by operating from Singapore.*

*Second, Singapore considers the nation as part of a chain of
value adding activities. It will look at the total value chain, seeking to optimize every part of it. This means close coordination of
infrastructure development, manpower training, development of
industrial estates and business parks, education policies, and
labor policies.*

*Third, at the corporate level the same value chain analysis
will also be applied by positioning itself to be highly competitive
in certain parts of the value chain. Other parts of the value chain
can be established in other countries. It will not only support the
establishment of such activities, either according to vertical or
horizontal division of labor, but will also actively network the
Singapore operation and related ones in other countries.*

*Finally, it will monitor its overall competitive position closely
so that any signs of the economy losing its competitiveness will
be dealt with quickly.*[16]

Based on its top-quality human capital and strong government leadership, Singapore plans to be an innovator and a real marketer. It has
presently made the "Singapore model" (see Chapter 3) a product—
"mini-Singapore"—and commercialized it internationally.

Strategic Intent of India by the Year 2005[17]

For policymakers, the globalization effort must start with a clear formulation of long-term goals. Professor C. K. Prahalad had outlined a framework for India to create its potential in the world economy by the year
2005. It is based on two critical factors:

- *The size of the domestic market.* India is among a very few countries
  that command a world-scale domestic market (others include China,
  Indonesia, Brazil, and Mexico).
- *The home of world-class competitors.* Countries with small domestic
  markets like Switzerland, The Netherlands, Sweden, and Finland are

FIGURE 7.5

Views of World Trade, 1993 and 2005

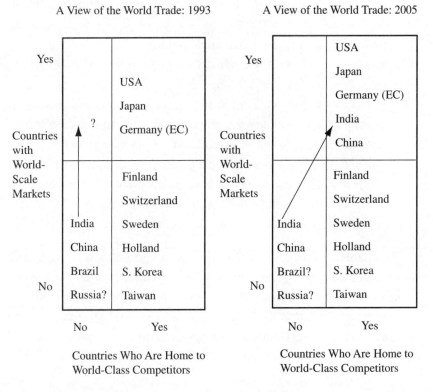

Source: C. K. Prahalad, *Globalization: Pitfalls, Pain and Potential,* Rajiv Gandhi Institute for Contemporary Studies (n.d.), Exhibit 1, p. 3.

the home of world-class competitors. Only a select few have the unique advantage of both these points, as shown in Figure 7.5.

From Figure 7.5, India's strategic intent is clearly to join a select group of leading nations in the world economy. India's current approach to liberalization, however, will not be sufficient to meet that goal. Professor Prahalad suggests that visionary leadership, political will, and a shared national agenda are the major ingredients of this strategic intent. He further argues that "India's potential is not constrained by opportunity or resources but by imagination and will." He proposes the following strategy for India to meet the goal:

1. *Building a world-scale domestic market by opening its economy to new products and services.* The expansion of product and service availability in India will create new jobs. Restructuring the Indian market can result in access to new technologies and attracting greater investment from industrial countries.
2. *Building world-class competitors by enabling the economy to upgrade itself.* India needs to upgrade its competence base to ensure that it catches up with the industrial nations in terms of research and development, quality, manufacturing, and marketing. Indian MNCs have currently invested in manufacturing minicomputers in Singapore and precision tools and sophisticated carbon black in Thailand. The goal here is constantly to develop its strong MNCs. However, during the transition, India has to depend on foreign MNCs for technology and know-how transfers, as well as access to markets.

The challenge for India, during the next decade, is how to shift from its inward focus for two generations on self-sufficiency to an outward focus in the global economy. For government leaders, the emphasis has to shift from regulation to development. Businesses will have to shift from lobbying in New Delhi and selling in a shortage economy to selling in the competitive world economy.

TURNAROUND STRATEGY

Countries that are weak in both relative wealth positions and relative competitiveness, such as the former Socialists, the Latin Americans, and subsistence economies, require strategic thrusts that will turn around their wealth position and competitiveness.

Eastern Europe: The Economic Transformation

Economic transformation in Eastern Europe requires two main steps: (1) economic reforms; and (2) subsequent economic restructuring.[18]

Economic Reform. The major objective of economic reform is to improve the standards of living by increasing outputs of consumer goods, improving industrial efficiency, enhancing productivity, encouraging innovation, and becoming competitive internationally. The reforms themselves can and should be introduced quickly, in three to five years. The elements of reform can be broadly grouped into four broad categories:

1. *Macroeconomic stabilization*: monetary reform to ensure control of the money supply and credit; fiscal control to ensure budgetary balance and to limit monetization of a budget deficit if one occurs.
2. *Price and market reform*: price and wage deregulation to link prices and wages to costs and productivity, respectively; liberalizing trade; currency convertibility to link the transforming economy to the world and to competition in international markets.
3. *Enterprise reform*: privatization, private-sector development, establishing and clarifying property rights, facilitating entry and exit of firms to provide for competition; worker and management incentives that reflect changes in relative market prices.
4. *Institutional reform*: redefining the role of the state; legal and regulatory reform; social safety net; reform of government institutions (tax administration, budget and expenditure control, monetary control).[19]

Clearly, most elements of reform are closely intertwined. Professor Lawrence Summers suggests that macroeconomic stabilization and price and trade reform should be pursued at the first stage of the reform process, followed by tax reform, social safety net development, and entrepreneurial development. Privatization and legal and institutional framework reforms can be addressed early in the reform process. Full convertibility of capital, as well as financial and wage liberalization, should be pursued afterwards in the reform sequence.[20]

Economic Restructuring.[21] Economic reforms will set the stage for a sustained process of economic restructuring. The restructuring process will take a decade or more since it needs time for start-ups in many new sectors of the economy to come in line with the newly introduced market signals. Consider the case of Poland. Under the Communist regime, its economy was heavily skewed toward manufacturing and away from services. Once market forces were unleashed, a significant portion of resources moved from the overextended manufacturing sector into previously neglected sectors. New private businesses have substantially emerged in trade, services, and residential construction, while manufacturing employment fell sharply.

A restructuring within the manufacturing sector—from resource- and energy-intensive heavy industry to more labor- and skill-intensive industries—can also be expected. However, due to the lack of clarity in property rights, and the political instability of Poland's reforms, foreign direct investment is still modest. If the reforms are sustained, foreign direct investment should increase markedly in the coming years.

In addition to the manufacturing and services sectors, agriculture is another ripe area for major restructuring. Under the Communist regime, many small farms were sustained by large subsidies to keep social peace in the countryside. The recent sharp cuts in agricultural subsidies led many small farming households to sell their farms. Farmlands will be consolidated into a much smaller number of larger farms. Agricultural efficiency will increase, while many agricultural workers will migrate to urban centers.

Latin America: Reoriented Toward a Free Market Economy

Latin America is undergoing a process of profound economic and social change. The past import substitution strategy failed to raise Latin American economies to international productivity levels. The attempt of a "catch-up industrialization," in isolation from the rest of the world economy, resulted in economic stagnation, social crisis, and serious environmental degradation. By contrast, Latin America presently is strengthening its market and global focus. It is directed by the concept of a *free market economy*. Latin America is becoming increasingly attractive as a market for foreign investment and exports.[22] For the former, MNCs are currently reorganizing their subsidiaries in Latin America to achieve better implementation of global strategies. For the latter, as trade barriers have been removed, the companies experiencing the most growth are those contributing to world-market-oriented specialization (e.g., in mining, agriculture, and natural resource-intensive industries). Most have increased their productivity significantly.[23]

The reorientation of economic policy is also producing radical effects in local Latin American industries. A large number of local capital goods producers have closed down. To become internationally competitive,

Latin American companies have adopted technologies and machinery from abroad. The aim now is to expand certain production chains (e.g.), the footwear industry in Brazil), a requirement being that all the links in the chain are competitive. Large industrial complexes have begun organizational and technical modernization programs. Examples include those in the steel and petrochemical industries of Brazil, Mexico, Argentina, and Venezuela. Furthermore, large local private firms are emerging. After an initial period of consolidation and specialization, some of these firms will be able to compete strongly in world market segments.

In summary, free market policies are helping to eliminate inefficient economic units. However, they do not automatically create improvements in equity and environmental conditions. For many Latin American countries, the challenge in the late 1990s will be to improve international competitiveness as well as create more equitable and better social conditions.[24]

SUBSISTENCE ECONOMIES: BREAKING THE VICIOUS CIRCLE

For subsistence economies, the problems and dilemmas are many and varied. External shocks and natural disasters are not predictable, but their harsh consequences can be mitigated by more adaptive economic institutions and better management (flexible exchange rates, flexible labor contracts, reducing the scope of inefficient state-owned enterprises, etc.). Rapid population growth, the highest in the world, also undermines the growth of these nations' economies.[25]

To create wealth for economies in this group, one industrial strategy has been proposed by Irma Adelman (1984). The strategy is based on the basic assumption that a domestic mass market will develop as a result of increased agricultural productivity. But instead of moving to large-scale agriculture (as recommended for Poland), Adelman argues that small- and medium-scale agriculture is most appropriate for subsistent economies. The strategy is known as *agricultural-demand-led industrialization (ADLI).*[26]

The ADLI strategy consists of building a domestic mass-consumption market by improving the productivity of small- and

medium-scale agriculture . . . small- and medium-scale agricul-
ture has larger linkage effects with domestic industry than does
large-scale agriculture while having at least as high a productiv-
ity level. Smaller farms are labor intensive and use domestic im-
plements and machinery . . . small farmers have a larger
marginal propensity to consume, and a larger marginal share of
their consumption is devoted to locally produced textiles, cloth-
ing, footwear and simple consumer durables such as refrigera-
tors, bicycles, sewing machines and simple electronics. Also,
they tend to invest heavily in the buildup of human capital, de-
voting a large share of their incremental income to education.[27]

The ADLI strategy seems appropriate for poorer countries like sub-Saharan Africa, which have limited potential for export growth in manufactures. The rationales of ADLI strategy are twofold. First, for countries with food shortages, static agricultural output, and rapid population growth, boosting agricultural productivity would be the correct policy. Second, agricultural-led growth could give birth to small-scale manufacturing enterprises that may be able to take more significant leaps into international markets. In order to increase agricultural productivity, price and investment incentives should be established for small farmers, along with institutional and structural reforms designed to improve the marketing and distribution of agricultural produce.[28]

Most subsistent economies are trapped, as Professors Reitsma and Kleinpenning argue, in a complex web of interlocking vicious circles (see Figure 7.6). Without assistance from the outside world, it is believed that these countries will not be able to free themselves from the vicious circles. From Figure 7.6, low productivity is one of the major bottlenecks holding back economic development.[29]

Improving productivity requires improving the "Eight M's": *management* (government leadership); *manpower* (human capital); *machines* (production system and equipment); *money* (capital); *materials* (natural resources); *methods* (appropriate technology); *message* (gathering critical information); and *market* (accessing the world market). For subsistent economies, foreign aid (financial, technical, and managerial) would allow these countries to increase their productivity. Then earnings would rise, the domestic market would expand, and agricultural and industrial

FIGURE 7.6

Four Interlocking Vicious Circles

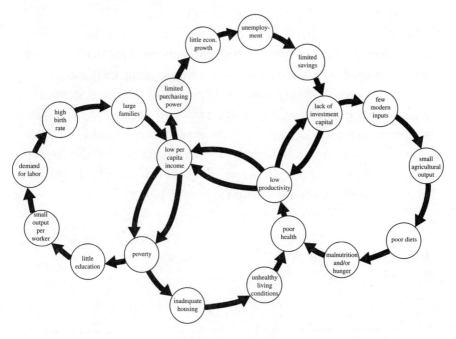

Source: H. A. Reitsma and J. M. G. Kleinpenning. *The Third World in Perspective* (Totowa, NJ: Rowman & Allanheld, 1985), Figure 16, p. 214.

producers could sell more, make more profit, and be able to make investments to raise productivity and output further. In this way, the countries would break out of their vicious circles and become sufficiently dynamic.[30]

SUMMARY

A nation needs to set a strategic thrust in order to fulfill its goals. Conceptually, the nation's strategic thrust is the nation's grand strategy, in which both its *strategic vision*—what is the nation going to do?—and its *strategic posture*—how is the nation going to do it?—are incorporated.

Differences in initial positions in wealth and competitiveness result in different nations' strategic thrusts. Countries that command a leading position have the mission of sustaining their current positions. Countries that lose their competitiveness have the mission of revitalizing their competitiveness. Countries whose current wealth and competitiveness are strong have the mission of extending their competitiveness to further build their nation's capabilities. Countries whose current wealth and competitiveness are weak face a turnaround mission.

Once a country charts its strategic thrust, strategies must be developed and implemented to achieve that mission. Policymakers must maintain strategic control, or else countries with strong current wealth and competitiveness may gradually lose their competitiveness and position of wealth. Conceptually, the wealth and competitiveness of a nation can head either upward or downward. Nations must monitor and adapt to the changes in global forces and trends (Chapter 6), the competitive intensities both within and among strategic groups of nations (Chapter 4), and the nation's own capabilities (Chapter 5).

Part III

DEVELOPING
THE NATION'S
STRATEGIC POSTURES

Chapter 8

Developing the Nation's Investment Policies

S ince World War II, international economic activity has expanded in
almost every region of the world. International competitiveness has
become critically important for every country, since a nation's wealth depends mainly on its ability to expand export earnings. To build its competitiveness, a nation must adopt clear and coherent policies toward
foreign direct investment, industry, and trade.

Governments ideally want to see their own firms compete effectively
in the global economy. This might be sought by encouraging collaboration with foreign firms, as well as inviting them to enter their economy.
Such a policy could bring in several benefits, by stimulating competition,
by encouraging higher quality in local supplies, by transferring new
skills and knowledge to the host country's workforce, and so forth.
Therefore, it is not surprising that some developing countries that previously discouraged foreign firms have now begun to compete for their investment. Industrial nations are not an exception. They are also trying to
attract foreign investment, mainly for the purpose of job creation.

In this chapter, we describe a nation's investment policies, and in the
next three chapters its industry and trade policies. Here we will examine
how nations formulate and implement their foreign investment attraction

strategies. First we describe the linkages between international trade, industry, and foreign investment. Then we discuss foreign direct investment policies. Finally, we will examine a nation's foreign direct investment strategies in detail.

INTERNATIONAL INVESTMENT, INDUSTRY, AND TRADE LINKAGES

In the current growth wave in world trade and investment, five major trends can be discerned:

1. *The globalization process is continuing on both the demand and supply sides.* However, the process has organized itself around three regional centers, the so-called *triad*—the industrial countries of North America, Western Europe, and East Asia (Japan and the Four Tigers). The linkages among these economies have created the "borderless world" described by Kenichi Ohmae (1990). Interlinkage within the triad, and between triad countries and others, requires the development of institutionalized systems of international trade and finance.

2. *There is a growing dysnychronizing of economic cycles in the triad.* Professors Schwab and Smadja argue that each region of the triad is becoming less vulnerable to fluctuations that may occur within the others. East Asia, for example, has been growing despite the deep recession in the Japanese economy. Meanwhile, the United States has avoided a recession while Europe has still been stuck in one of the most prolonged recessions in recent times.[1]

3. *There is a continuous emergence of "new economic actors" in the global marketplace.* The members of OPEC, for example, had influenced the world economy during the 1970s. In the 1980s, Japan emerged as a major world economic power, followed by the Four Tigers of the Pacific Rim (Hong Kong, Singapore, South Korea, and Taiwan). The recent economic transition of Eastern Europe and the former Soviet Union has brought new players onto the scene, not to mention the recent high growth rates of Chile and Argentina. The emergence of new economic competitors requires new agreements and structures that reflect diverse, but mutually interdependent interests.[2]

4. *There is an emergence of "global industries" that operates in many parts of the world.* The growth of global industries creates new conditions for the "international division of labor."

5. *The freedom of action of national governments is being constantly eroded.* The exercise of state power is constrained by international institutions (like international financial and capital markets, MNCs) and supragovernmental bodies (like the European Union Commission and WTO).[3] The very concept of "money" is expanded and diluted to include many instruments of liquidity beyond the reach of the U.S. Federal Reserve. Monetary policy is no longer a simple matter of targeting commercial bank reserves, high-powered money, or monetary aggregates.

FOREIGN DIRECT INVESTMENT POLICIES

The globalization of production and consumer lifestyles, coupled with rapid technological change, has fundamentally altered the rules of global competition. "Classical trade theory" emphasized competition between countries where each specialized in the production of a set of goods based on comparative advantage. Classical trade theory assumed that the basic unit of analysis should be the country.[4]

Under the new theory of "strategic trade policies," the analysis shifts to emphasize that monopolistic competition, monopoly pricing, economies of scale, and government intervention may actually improve national welfare. Yet the basic unit of analysis remains a country.[5]

Today, foreign direct investment weakens the arguments of both classical trade theory and strategic trade policies. It blurs the distinction between MNCs and indigenous firms. Both inward and outward linkages among economies are interwoven so that it is very difficult to assess the real gains and losses from any particular policy. The differences between the MNC's nationality and the international location of its various operations undermine the effectiveness of policies that attempt to control foreign firms. Professor Phedon Nicolaides points out two main reasons for this.

First, from the MNC perspective, the mode of investment is, to a great extent, dependent on the MNC's global objectives, the prevailing government policies of the host country, and the nature of its technology. The investment alternatives range from being the sole owner of a foreign-built factory to establishing a joint venture, having a local firm manufacture its products under its supervision, or manufacturing under a local brand name. Therefore, if the host country's policies change, MNCs would accordingly change their optimum investment mode.

Second, suppose a government requires an MNC to meet a specific requirement for its product manufactured locally. Why should it not extend the same requirement to the products of national firms with overseas operations.[6]

The important criterion in trade issues has changed from "nationality of the product" to "where and to whom it provides jobs." As Schwab and Smadja point out:

A new order of priorities set by the (Clinton) administration put U.S. corporations located in the United States first in line for protection, foreign corporations located in the United States second and U.S. corporations operating outside the country a mere third. The clear emphasis on job protection for U.S. workers is being echoed in Europe with assertions of a similar order of priority.[7]

Competition for Foreign Direct Investment[8]

The inflows of foreign direct investment (FDI) into developing countries have increased from $31 billion in 1990 to $80 billion in 1993, with almost 60 percent going to Asia. The inflows of FDI into developed economies, however, is still larger (see Figure 8.1). Almost all FDI was undertaken by just seven industrial countries: the United States, Britain, Japan, Germany, The Netherlands, France, and Canada.

Incentives to shift factories to developing countries due to their cheap labor costs have been currently diminishing for a number of reasons.

1. Wages are no longer the critical factor in deciding investment location. As R&D and marketing increase in importance, the competitive advantage of low wages is diminished. According to one recent study,[9] the share of low-skilled labor in many industries has fallen from 25 percent two decades ago to only 5–10 percent of total production costs in indus-

FIGURE 8.1

Inflows of Foreign Direct Investment

A Movable Feast

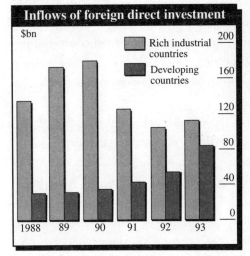

Recipients of FDI	
Ten largest developing countries 1988-92, $bn	
China	25.6
Singapore	21.7
Mexico	18.4
Malaysia	13.2
Argentina	10.6
Thailand	9.5
Hong Kong	7.9
Brazil	7.6
Taiwan	6.0
Indonesia	5.6

Source: "Survey of the Global Economy," *The Economist,* Oct. 1, 1994, Figure 12, p. 23.

trial countries. Direct labor costs account for only 3 percent of total costs in semiconductors, 5 percent in the manufacture of color TVs, and 10–15 percent of costs in the automobile industry. Labor costs, however, still play a major role in clothing and footwear, accounting for about one third of total production costs.

2. Lower unit-labor costs may easily be offset by other disadvantages such as an inferior infrastructure or poor-quality labor.

3. Advance technology and production methods have stricter requirements for quality and reliability. These new production methods are more vulnerable to bottlenecks, and so it becomes more important to have such infrastructure strengths as reliable electricity supply and good transport links. The attractiveness of producing in developing countries is reduced, due to their infrastructure constraints.

4. Educational standards in developing countries still lag far behind industrial countries. The lack of skilled labor limits the shift of complex technological operations to these countries.

Yet there will be a continued shifting of some investment from the developed world to developing countries. The skill gap is narrower or closing in some cases. Although Soviet bloc countries did not run their countries well in the past, they produced educated citizens—particularly a high number of engineers and scientists. There is a higher proportion of South Korean twenty- to twenty-four-year-olds in formal education programs than in most European countries. The belief that developing countries will focus only on producing low-tech, labor-intensive goods is no longer correct.

Recent business relocation to the developing countries has not been limited to manufacturing. It is increasingly occurring in the service sector.

Swissair has transferred all of its revenue accounting to Bombay. With a large number of skilled, English-speaking engineers and scientists, India has also become a center of computer software programming. Most American computer firms now subcontract labor-intensive programming to Bangalore. This has depressed software development charges in America. Around the world, workers in developing countries are processing data for western companies on hospital patients' records, consumer credit reports, insurance claims and magazine subscription renewals.[10]

Thus not only unskilled but also skilled workers in the developed countries will face competition from developing countries as a result of business relocation in the coming years. In the world economic perspective, this will lead to a more efficient international division of labor.

Given the phenomenon of increasing supply and demand for FDI, coupled with the limited prospects for receiving finance from the international banking institutions, it is not surprising to see stiff competition among countries to attract FDI.

FOREIGN DIRECT INVESTMENT STRATEGIES

The reason for foreign inward investment differs between outward-oriented and inward-oriented economies. The major attractiveness of investing in inward-oriented economies is related to the retention of import barriers—the MNC wants to have a presence in a protected market and therefore establishes a plant there. By contrast, the major attractiveness of investing in outward-oriented economies is related to the advantages of production in existing exporting sectors or industries with high export potential. This type of investment results in plants running on a world-wide scale.[11]

According to Robin Gaster, if a nation accepts FDI as beneficial in principle, its FDI policies should meet at least two fundamental objectives. First, in the short run, a sound FDI strategy should seek to *attract foreign investment*, thus adding capital inflow into the nation. Second, it should *direct those investment flows* in such a way as to maximize the long-term benefit of the host nation's economy.[12]

Attracting FDI

Governments seeking to develop competitive strategies for FDI marketing activities can, to some extent, manipulate three elements in their overall marketing programs:

1. *Product*: the intrinsic advantages and disadvantages of investing in the country, ranging from the country's general attractiveness to a specific investment site's attractiveness.
2. *Price*: this usually means tax incentives, grants, tariff protection, and similar price mechanisms.
3. *Promotion*: activities that disseminate information about, or attempt to create a favorable image of, the investment site.[13]

The Country's Investment Attractiveness. Foreign investors pay attention to at least four attributes of a country's investment attractiveness: its comparative and competitive advantages; its domestic economic and political stability; property rights protection; and foreign trade zones.

1. *Comparative and Competitive Advantages.* According to Michael Porter (1990), a nation's attractiveness for investment in a particular industry lies in four broad attributes:

   • *Factor conditions.* A nation's investment attractiveness is greater, the better its natural resources, location, skilled and unskilled labor, and basic infrastructure.

- *Demand conditions.* A nation's investment attractiveness is greater, the greater the sophistication of its home demand for the industry's product and service.
- *Related and supporting industries.* A nation's investment attractiveness is greater, the greater the presence within the nation of related and supporting industries that are internationally competitive.
- *Firm strategy, structure, and rivalry.* A nation's investment attractiveness is greater, the greater the intensity of domestic rivalry.[14]

Porter has used these conditions to explain why certain regions in the world are strong in certain industries, such as the clothing industry in Italy, the printing industry in Germany, and the cheese industry in Holland.

2. *Domestic Economic and Political Stability.* The daily news is so filled with reports of unstable governments and faltering economies that business firms are hesitant to invest in other countries. If seemingly secure governments like the Shah's regime in Iran and Marcos's regime in the Philippines could topple, can any country be depended on? Since 1960, over 1,500 companies have been expropriated in 511 separate actions by 76 nations. Even short of expropriation, a company could lose the value of its investment because of strikes, currency devaluation, blocked currency, and so on.

Economic and political stability has been the key to East Asia's success in attracting FDI. On the other hand, Brazil's failure to maintain macroeconomic stability has been a major factor in the decline of FDI in that country in the 1980s.

Analysts distinguish between two types of country risk. The first is *asset protection/investment recovery risk*, which arises from direct action taken by the government or people that results in destroying, expropriating, or limiting transfer of invested resources. The second is *operational profitability/cash-flow risk*, which arises from economic downturns, currency depreciation, strikes, and so on. Some analysts think of the former risk as political risk and the latter risk as economic risk, but both types often intermingle.

3. *Property Rights Protection.* The legal and institutional framework governing FDI should be open, predictable, and stable. Free access to

foreign exchange for profit remittances and to procure imported inputs should be pursued. Prospective foreign investors are often afraid of pressure to indigenize ownership, or of outright nationalization (see more details in Chapter 14).[15]

4. *Foreign Trade Zones.* One way to attract FDI is to build a *foreign trade zone (FTZ)* in which exporting-only enterprises can be set up free of most local legislation. The MNC is allowed to operate, import, manufacture, and even wholly own a business inside the FTZ. As long as the MNC does not sell its imported goods inside the host country, it has no effect on the local market. The host country benefits from job creation, improved skills in its labor force, technology transfer, and rising income for its citizens.[16]

FTZs have been established not only in developing countries but also in developed countries. Some countries (such as Hungary) designate a factory or a warehouse where goods can be stored or assembled as an FTZ, while others designate an entire area instead. There is also a version of FTZ termed *Special Economic Zones (SEZs)*, which encompasses entire regions. The Chinese SEZs are the prototype. This involves a mix of policies, allowing for favorable terms for foreign investment, access to credit, transshipment of goods, and so forth.[17]

Pricing Investment. The provision of tax holidays, R&D incentives, capital grants, training grants, and so on has been a common feature of many countries' foreign direct investment policies.

Ireland's industrial-development schemes are among the most elaborate offered anywhere in the world. Ireland will provide capital grants that can reach 40–60% of the total capital cost for plant and equipment for a new facility. It will also provide grants for research and development and for training. Through tax-based leasing and interest subsidies, the Irish government will provide favorable financing for working capital, and often for the portion of fixed-asset investment that a company makes itself. The government normally imposes a 10% tax on corporate prof-

its, but this can, in effect, be easily reduced to zero through various depreciation and tax-credit schemes.

These incentives, plus Ireland's membership in the EC and the excellent marketing efforts of the Industrial Development Authority of Ireland, have resulted in hundreds of U.S. companies building plants in Ireland.[18]

As a general rule, however, incentives per se are usually not sufficient to attract and retain most MNCs. In fact, public policies that create a good climate for investment in general are likely to be superior to special incentives to attract foreign direct investment, such as tax holidays. The latter may attract footloose companies that exit when the tax holiday is over. However, special incentives work better if they are supported by good infrastructure, such as investment in education, roads, ports, airports, and so on.[19]

The Singapore government has a number of tax incentives designed to encourage companies to do research and development in Singapore. Companies that undertake R&D can have "pioneer status" (tax holidays) for longer-than-average periods of time; an investment allowance of up to 50% in addition to normal capital allowances for R&D-associated fixed investments is possible; R&D operating costs including manpower, materials, and utility costs can receive a double deduction; and companies can set aside 20% of income as an R&D reserve to be spent tax free within three years.

In addition, a number of grant programs are available. For example, companies with at least 30% local ownership can receive a dollar-for-dollar grant to assist with the direct manpower, materials, prototyping, consulting fees, and equipment required to develop new products. There is also a research-and-development assistance scheme that contributes to R&D efforts associated with the Science Park. . . . While many of these have been for local Singapore utilities and agencies, foreign companies are increasingly taking advantage of the funds. Seagate Technology received a grant to work with the Department of Electrical Engineering and the Department of Mechanical and Production Engineering of the National University of Singapore on a fast random-access compact-optical-disc storage device, for example.[20]

Investment Promotion.[21] Investment promotion is generally designed to accomplish three objectives:

• *To promote a country's image within the investment community as a favorable location for investment.* Image building is the appropriate strategy aimed to attract investors who are in the early stages of investment decision making. The promotion techniques include advertising in general financial media; participating in investment and trade exhibitions; advertising in industry- or sector-specific media; conducting general investment missions from source country to host country or from host country to source country; and conducting general information seminars on investment opportunities.

• *To generate specific investments.* The emphasis shifts to specific investment opportunities when prospective investors are in the later stages of investment decision making. Here promotion techniques include engaging in direct-mail or telemarketing campaigns; conducting industry- or sector-specific investment missions from source country to host country or vice versa; conducting industry- or sector-specific information seminars; and engaging in firm-specific research followed by "sales" presentations. In shifting from image building to direct investment generation, government agencies increase their reliance on personal contact with companies.

• *To provide services to prospective and current investors.* Here promotion techniques include providing investment counseling services; expediting the processing of applications and permits; and providing postinvestment services.

MAXIMIZING THE NATION'S LONG-TERM BENEFITS FROM FDI: TECHNOLOGY TRANSFER

As discussed in Chapter 2, FDI is a way of filling in five major gaps: (1) resource gap; (2) foreign exchange gap; (3) efficiency gap; (4) budgetary gap; and (5) technical and management know-how gap. The first four can enhance a nation's competitiveness in the short to medium run, whereas the last can sustain the nation's long-term competitiveness.

Malaysia's FTZ is a case in point. Though the net gains to Malaysia's balance of payments and employment have been valuable, the hoped-for transfers of technology to local suppliers have been disappointing. Some technological capabilities have been enhanced, but the main benefits have been restricted to the simpler parts of the industry.[22]

Technological development in many developing countries basically depends on the nation's technology policies and on technology transfer from MNCs to these countries. National technology policies vary considerably with the country's factor endowments and current level of technological development. The rate of technology transfer varies with the different modes, ranging from foreign direct investment by MNCs through their subsidiaries or through joint ventures; nonaffiliate technology licensing; contractual arrangements for the supply of technology know-how and services; franchises for use of foreign names; and provision of special expertise for certain products and services.[23]

Technology transfer, however, is not as simple as the purchase of capital goods. Substantial efforts are required to assimilate, modify, and improve upon the original technology before disseminating it to other firms or industries. The existence of complementary assets, particularly administrative and organizational capabilities, is also a necessary precondition for assimilating the foreign technology successfully.[24]

Government-Mandated Technology Transfer

A prominent feature of Japan and Asian NICs' technology policies during their "catch-up" period has been a set of policies to induce technology transfers from MNCs. These policies reflect the interdependence of trade and technology policy instruments and goals. Since the government was involved in the diffusion of technology from foreign sources to domestic firms, they were named *adoption-oriented* policies.[25]

During the 1950s and 1960s, the Japanese government made extensive use of these technology transfer policies by restricting access to domestic markets or investment opportunities by MNCs. They demanded MNCs to license critical technologies to their indigenous firms in exchange for investing in its large and rapidly growing market.[26] Computers are a case in point.

In the late 1950s, MITI pressured IBM to give Japanese companies access to basic patents at low fees in exchange for granting IBM permission to produce in Japan. MITI also controlled the type and volume of computers that IBM produced and required the company to export a large proportion of its production.[27]

Technology transfer policies, when accompanied by policies that favor export promotion and human capital investment, may produce greater technological spillovers and economic payoffs from foreign to indigenous firms.

Brazil has come up with an export winner—aircraft—a product that NICs have had great difficulty selling internationally. The catalyst was Empresa Brasileira de Aeronautica (EMBRAER), a local joint public-private company that proved adept at exploiting market niches and utilizing foreign technology. It pursued realistic product development and sales strategies. EMBRAER specialized in producing simple, inexpensive and reliable aircraft, particularly well suited to third world conditions. This strategy provided a reliable sales base, and offered export potential. EMBRAER was also flexible in taking advantage of foreign technology and know-how through licensing arrangements and joint ventures reflecting specific needs.[28]

As Professor David Mowery has suggested, the rate of technology spillovers is highly subject to the ability of indigenous managerial and technical talent to assimilate and disseminate the transferred technology. Outward orientation and strong competition among the domestic recipients is one critical factor.[29]

Consider the case of the Japanese computer industry:

- *An important domestic component of Japanese inward technology transfer policies was MITI's diffusion of foreign-sourced technologies to numerous domestic firms. MITI used domestic licensing of foreign technologies to "level the playing field" among domestic firms and enforce intense domestic competition in the application of these technologies.*[30]

- *From 1961 to 1981, the Japanese government put some $6 billion into the computer industry for R&D, new equipment, and working capital. Subsidized R&D was tied to performance. If a company failed to commercialize a project's results or became uncompetitive, it could expect to be excluded from the next stage. And the government pushed companies to do risky research they would otherwise have avoided (e.g., the VLSI project). Thus the Japanese government helped the companies advance in this area but left them to compete in commercializing R&D and going to market. For every company there is a time to compete and a time to cooperate. That is a lesson worth learning.*[31]

Strong competition among MNCs is another critical factor. In Brazil, many foreign aircraft firms were seeking to gain access rights to its general aviation and commuter aircraft market. The stiff competition provided the Brazilian government a monopsonist power, resulting in a generous technology transfer agreement with the winning firm (Piper of the United States) that subsequently contributed to the growth of the Brazilian aircraft industry.[32]

Some Options Available to the Host Government

Here Professor John Dunning (1993) lists several policy choices that governments might pursue to increase inward technology transfer. It should be noted that these policy options are not mutually exclusive.

- Set entry conditions regarding technology transfer for new and/or current foreign investors.
- Specify performance requirements from MNC affiliates.

- Eliminate restrictions on the use of technology supplied by MNCs.
- Limit royalty payments to foreign firms for technology transfer.
- Improve understanding of the costs and benefits of technology and improve domestic negotiating abilities.
- Solicit competitive bids from alternative technology suppliers.
- Encourage MNCs to sell technology on a contractual basis.
- Limit duration of technology contracts.
- Encourage indigenous development of technology.
- Encourage market structures that are most conducive to an efficient inflow and diffusion of technology.
- Impose training obligations on MNCs.
- Give more incentives to MNCs to set up R&D facilities in host countries.
- Encourage development of state-owned enterprises (as in India and Brazil).
- Provide fiscal and other incentives to encourage privately financed R&D to the point where its marginal social benefits equate with its marginal costs.
- Reconsider macroeconomic policies and organization so as to remove structural distortions in cross-border technology markets.
- Support industrial restructuring and encourage development of clusters of supporting or related activities.
- Encourage interaction between universities, cooperative research associations and private firms.
- Facilitate the upgrading of indigenous human capital by general educational and other related policies.
- Liberalize technology and other markets which distort terms of technology transfer and diffusion.[33]

Appropriateness of Technology

According to Erdener Kaynak, appropriateness of technology raises four concerns:

1. *Appropriateness for goals*: Does the technology support the goal of the development policy?
2. *Appropriateness of product*: Is the product or service useful, acceptable, and affordable by the end users?

3. *Appropriateness for process*: Does the production process make productive use of resources?
4. *Cultural and environmental appropriateness*: Are the technology and its institutional arrangements compatible with the local environmental and cultural setting?[34]

A major concern of industrial countries is the application by foreign MNCs of good business practices—as defined by Peter Dicken: "the demonstration of the effectiveness of 'social' innovations regarding work organization, labor relations, relationship with suppliers, and so on." Japanese investment in Britain is a case in point. It is thought that the adoption of highly efficient Japanese business practices will reshape British industry and foster efficiency in the economy.[35]

Alternative Ways of Acquiring Technology

There are three major alternatives for acquiring technology. First, by acquiring or licensing the technology alone from the MNC. However, an MNC may be unwilling to license the technology or it may charge a very high price. Second, by forming cross-border alliances. However, it is very difficult to seek the right partners if one has nothing valuable to exchange. And third, by developing the technology domestically. This may be feasible for some of the more advanced industrial nations but rarely for developing nations.

It is worth noting that since technology is just one part of the whole package of attributes which the MNC brings to a host country, it is difficult to assess the cost incurred with each alternative way of acquiring the same technology.[36]

SUMMARY

Five major development trends have evolved with the growth in world trade and investment: increasing *interlinkages* among nations and regions; a growing *dysynchronizing of economic cycles*; continuous emergence of *new economic actors*; the growth of *"global industries"*; and the *eroding of* national governments' *freedom of action*.

Foreign direct investment multiplies both inward and outward linkages between economies. Assessment of real gains and losses from any particular policy is difficult. In addition, the differences between the firm's nationality and the location of its various operations reduces the effectiveness of policies that attempt to target foreign firms.

Unskilled and semiskilled labor are no longer the critical factor in deciding where to locate. As the costs of R&D, capital, and marketing increase, the competitive advantage of low wages diminishes. This threatens many developing countries, which usually have an abundant labor supply. The nature of modern, flexible production methods, which have stricter requirements for quality and reliability, is another factor that reduces the attractiveness of producing in developing countries with underdeveloped infrastructures. A further factor is that the educational standards of many developing countries still lag far behind industrial countries and countries like South Korea, Taiwan, and so on.

The nation's FDI policies should have two fundamental aims: In the short run, a sound FDI strategy should seek to attract foreign investment, thus adding to the inflow of capital; in the long run, it should guide those investment flows for the maximum long-term benefit of the host nation's economy.

Governments seeking to develop competitive strategies for FDI marketing activities can manipulate three elements in their overall marketing programs: (1) Product: the intrinsic advantages and disadvantages of investing in the country, ranging from general investment attractiveness to specific investment sites' attractiveness. (2) Price: tax incentives, grants, tariff protection, and similar price mechanisms. And (3) Promotion: activities that disseminate information about, or attempt to create a favorable image of, the investment site.

Technology transfer policies, when coupled with policies supporting exports and investment in human and physical capital, may produce greater technological spillovers and economic payoffs from foreign to domestic entrepreneurs and firms. However, both the appropriateness and the cost of technology transfer need to be taken into account.

Chapter 9

Building the Nation's Industrial Clusters

G lobal competition in the postwar period primarily revolved around
the three regional centers of North America, Europe, and Japan. In
the 1980s, however, a new group of international economic powers
emerged in Asia. These countries shifted from a Third World ranking to
the class of newly industrialized countries (NICs).

What determines a country's international competitiveness in today's
world economy? Professor Porter argues (1990) that the explanation can
be found in the status of industrial clusters, industries, and firms, not in
national aggregates and attributes. The competitive thrust from the new
Asian challengers, indeed, comes not from favorable factor endowments
but rather from coherent industry-building strategies. Each nation constantly mobilizes and shapes its limited but productive capabilities and
resources to achieve economic advantage.[1]

This chapter first discusses the notion of *industrial clusters*. We then
examine the *interactive effects* among industries in the cluster. The notion of industrial clusters provides policymakers with insights for developing the nation's industrial portfolio, which will be examined in the
next chapter.

BUILDING THE NATION'S INDUSTRIAL CLUSTERS

An industrial cluster is a group of industrial segments that share positive vertical and horizontal linkages. If an industry diversifies into fields that are either inputs or outputs of that industry, the direction of diversification is "vertical." There are two kinds of vertical linkages: *forward linkages* and *backward linkages*. Forward linkages are the linkages between the focal industry and its downstream industries, whereas backward linkages are the linkages between the focal industry and its upstream industries. The steel industry, for example, requires inputs from other industries: mining (coals, limestone, iron ore). These constitute backward linkages. Steel also is sold to a wide variety of customers—such as transportation, industrial machinery, construction—who constitute its forward linkages.

From the focal industry point of view, all vertically linked industries are called "supporting industries."

Under the leadership of Prime Minister Mahathir, Malaysia focused on building world-class "vertical" capabilities in just a few industries: semiconductors, automobiles, and consumer packaged goods. It did so with the full expectation that its long-term advantage—given the likely emergence of India, China and other extremely low-wage Asian nations—did not lie in its currently low labor costs but, rather, in its potential mastery of each industry's full value-added chain. Malaysia would not just assemble semiconductors; it would also learn to do wafer fabrication. It would not just assemble automobiles; it would manufacture components as well.[2]

By contrast, if an industry does not diversify through input-output relations, the direction is "horizontal." Horizontal linkages connect a focal industry with other industries that are complementary in technology and/or marketing. All such industries involved in the horizontal linkages are called "related industries." Three examples of technological related industries are illustrated in Figure 9.1.

FIGURE 9.1

Related Industries Around Biotechnology, New Materials, and Microelectronics

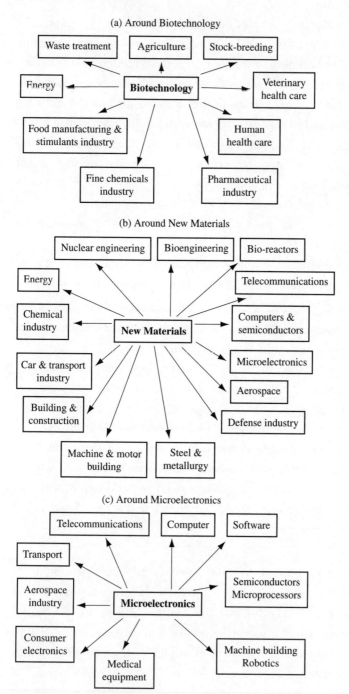

(a) Around Biotechnology

(b) Around New Materials

(c) Around Microelectronics

Source: Annemieke J. M. Roobeek, *Beyond the Technology Race: An Analysis of Technology Policy in Seven Industrial Countries* (Amsterdam: Elsevier, 1990), p. 58, Graph 3.1; p. 63, Graph 3.2; and p. 73, Graph 3.3.

The Importance of Industrial Clusters

The presence in the nation of related and supporting industries is one of the major determinants of a nation's competitiveness. Successful innovation within the industrial cluster is highly dependent on close and persistent *user-producer contacts*. The producer gains from "learning-by-doing" while the user gains from "learning-by-using." Thus, the success of a given innovation is highly determined by the extent of *learning-by-interacting* between parties connected together by flows of knowledge, skills, and services.[3] Sweden's related and supporting industries are the case in point.

Sweden has four or five distinctive industrial sectors comprising a large number of internationally competitive industries: (1) metals and fabricated metal products; (2) transportation and transportation equipment; (3) forest related industries; (4) mechanical engineering equipment; and (5) power generation. These sectors include a number of industrial clusters, formed by a network of closely related industries.

New products are developed in cooperation between firms in technologically related industries. The mere creation of a new market is one part of the clustering effect; another is the close links between the companies involved. Examples are Atlas Copco and Sandvik's co-development of the "Swedish Method" in rock drilling; Flakt's introduction of drying systems for matches produced by Swedish Match; and SPM Instrument's commercial introduction of the shock pulse method for control of anti-friction bearings with the help of SKF. Another pattern is found in the way small entrepreneurial firms are spawned from large, established firms or develop out of major research institutions. The smaller firms often find new products through impulses from the parent company. For example, the founders of the two Swedish producers of electrical trucks received their ideas from working for large Swedish firms with logistical needs that needed solutions. Firms in the Swedish industry for image processing systems are located close to the Linköping Institute of Technology, which has provided not only ideas but also personnel for the attempts to commercialize research findings.[4]

Governments can play an integral role in facilitating learning-by-interacting processes.

At the national level, a rather closed labor market and a potentially closed capital market enhance the learning-by-interacting among industrial cluster participants. There is evidence that user-producer relations are facilitated by culture, national standardization and a large set of industrial organizations. Therefore, national linkages are, among other things, helpful to learning, and thereby to industrial and technological competitiveness.[5]

Each industrial segment in the industrial cluster represents a source of capital, technology, and market demand for a variety of other industrial segments.

The Interactive Effects in Industrial Clusters

Innovations in one industrial cluster may remain concentrated there—the *clustering effect* (e.g., speed-resistant tires and disc brakes stayed in the automotive industry) or spread to other industrial clusters—the *converse effect* (e.g., pressure die casting moved to other industries). Demand-side complementaries in consumption may lead to pressure for innovations in products jointly demanded with that just innovated. Some industries may be blessed with an excessive quota of innovating entrepreneurs or research staff at a point of time.[6]

Related industries also can create interactive effects within industrial clusters. These effects derive from coordinating the network among industrial segments within the cluster structure. They share economies of scope, and economies of scale, learning, and experience, with other industrial segments in the industrial cluster. This sharing of activities possibly occurs across the board, ranging from research and development to manufacturing, distribution, marketing, and services. Some of these effects follow.

Snowball Effects: Hybrid Technologies. The combination of different technologies underlying two or more related products may snowball and yield a new composite technology. In this case, the function of each technology combined in the product remains unchanged.[7]

Since World War II, hybrid technologies have been a popular method of recycling old technologies. Consumer electronics firms are combining their television, VCR, stereo, CD, and telephone technologies to create videophones, stereo televisions, and high-definition television (see Figure 9.2). For the office equipment market, facsimile machines are combined with telephones, copiers, and printers.[8]

Substitution Effects. Technology innovations developed from related industries can confer a synergistic or an antagonistic effect on the focal and supporting industries. The latter occurs when the innovation threatens the industrial incumbents with superior substitute products and processes.

A technological discontinuity may result in: (1) the incumbents retaining their leading market position but with a significantly diminished share; or (2) the incumbents dropping far down in the rankings or even leaving the business. Incumbents lose their positions because consumers prefer newer, cheaper, or better products.[9]

Consider the case of containers and packaging. Glass bottles, which helped Owens Illinois prosper, were replaced by paper cartons (led by International Paper) and steel cans (led by Amer-

FIGURE 9.2

The Japanese Approach to Hybrid Technologies

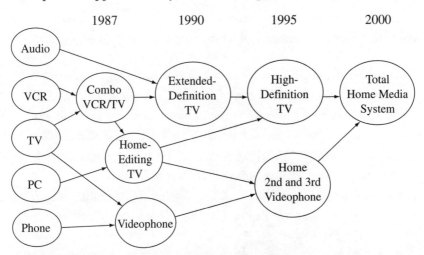

*ican Can and Continental Can). Steel cans in the beverage seg-
ment are replaced by the aluminum cans of Reynolds Metals and
Alcoa. Glass bottles for soft-drink beverages have given way to
plastic bottles, which meant new business for Eastman Kodak
and Hoechst (a German chemical company). In the convenience
stores, plastic milk jugs fill the refrigerator shelves that once
were preserved for plastic-coated paper cartons. Plastic
pouches are now replacing metal frozen food packages as "Lean
Cuisine" replaces TV dinners. Even tennis balls were not im-
mune to packaging changes as they moved from cardboard packages to metal cans, and now to clear plastic containers. In all
these cases, one technology and its backer has ousted another in
seemingly uninterrupted cycles.*[10]

Spillover Effects: Crossover Technologies. Crossover technologies refer
to technology innovations occurring in one industrial segment that can be
applied to or spill over to other industrial segments.[11]

In biotechnology industries, soybean fermentation technique gave
way to monosodium glutamate fermentation. In computing, color TV
know-how helped create high-resolution graphics terminals and engineering work stations. Robot makers are diversifying into firefighting
robots, hospital nurse robots, and underwater robots. Textile makers
are combining their dye techniques with advanced chemical processes to
diversify into industrial dyes.[12]

The spillover effect may occur not only in growth but also in mature
industries. Consider the case of textiles industries.

*From a manufacturing perspective, the spinning of thread is
quite similar to the creation of carbon fiber, a lightweight, high-
strength material critical in such areas as aircraft manufacturing. From the analytic perspective, the textile and carbon fiber
sectors overlap. Not surprisingly, the boundary between high-
technology and mature industries is blurred since the dichotomy
is an artificial contrivance. Toray, an old-line Japanese textile
firm, for example, has emerged as one of the world's leading carbon fiber producers.*[13]

Spillover Effects: Fusion Technologies. While hybrid technologies combine two ideas without changing their basic characteristics, fusion technologies affect a critical transformation of the technologies involved. In Japan, for example, many distillers are combining their fermentation know-how with new biotechnology techniques to develop new food preservatives, liquors, and medicines.[14]

Figure 9.3 illustrates the variety of state-of-the-art fusion technologies at the present time.

The machatronic industry (the merging of machine tools and electronics, such as computerized numerical control manipulators) is an example of technology fusion. Other fusion technolo-

FIGURE 9.3

Fusion Technology Occurring in Some Key Industries

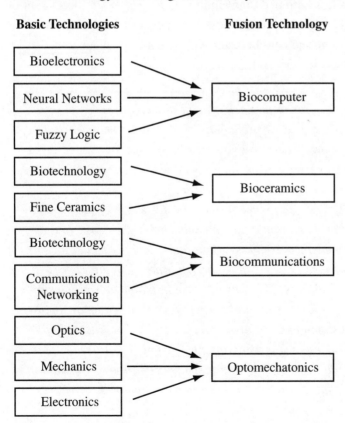

gies include optocube computing (massively parallel optical computers using Trinitron-like switching guns to transmit laser beams from one grid of the fiber-optic cables to another); opto-mechatronics (the marriage of optical, mechanical, and electronic engineering); bioceramics (biotechnology and ceramics); and biocommunications (biotechnology and communication networking).[15]

The Interactive Effects of Supporting Industries

Supporting industries provide upstream and downstream activities and added value for the industrial cluster. For many industries, industrial development progress depends on the industrial structure and technological development of their supporting industries. In the semiconductor industry, for example, continued innovation is to a large extent dependent on technological progress in semiconductor production equipment.

Members of an industrial cluster will potentially create so-called external economies toward each other.

In electronics, for example, a crucial role is played by an infrastructure of specialist producers of parts or components. The manufacturing of new products may be significantly hindered at the early stages of high-technology industrial growth by the absence of such a network of producers. In such situations, local firms will need to produce a much larger share of the product than best practice would indicate, causing higher costs and delays in complementary innovations, and placing them at a competitive disadvantage vis-à-vis foreign firms with better access to component sources. This was the case in Israel's electronics industry in the late sixties and early seventies, when local suppliers of custom-made printed circuits and other custom-made electronic components were absent. The indivisibilities in creating a capability to supply these specialized products or inputs are, prima facie, a reason for government support.[16]

Another example is the case of the Japanese steel industry in the 1950s. Because steel was an important intermediate input produced with economies of scale, policies to promote rapid expansion of high-quality domestic steel resulted in pecuniary external economies in the sense that they are reflected in lower prices and reduced cost of steel-using industries. This encouraged the expansion of these industries, which in turn fed back into further expansion of the steel industry and still lower costs. This virtuous interdependence between the steel industry and downstream users gave rise to a true externality—private increasing returns in the steel industry resulting in social increasing returns in the downstream user industries. Krugman (1987) has recently coined the phrase "linkage externalities" to apply to this type of spillover effect resulting from increasing returns in the production of inputs and their effects on the costs of downstream producers.[17]

The external economies provided by some kinds of supporting industries are sometimes termed *satellite effects*. When they occur, they take a central role in providing critical parts and components widely used in other industries. Figure 9.4 elaborates the satellite effect occurring in some key industries.

Memory chip technology provides a good example of the satellite effect. Many firms have pushed the limits of memory process technologies and are now developing specialized memory chips for high-definition TV (HDTV), telephone, message playback, laptop computer memory storage, and other new applications.

A Nation's Industrial Cluster: Some Considerations

There is much evidence showing that industry clusters support achievement of a variety of economic development goals. However, identifying industry clusters is different from "picking winners and losers."

At present, most economists agree that it is difficult to distinguish the potential winner from the potential loser. Such efforts usually turn out wrong, and governments often inappropriately subsidize industries that

FIGURE 9.4

Satellite Effects Occurring in Some Key Industries

Satellite Technology	Application
Integrated circuit	Computer and communication
	Machine tool
	Automobile
	Consumer electronics
Laser beam	Precision instruments
	Defense weapons
	Medical operations
	Laser printers
CAD/CAE	Designs of new products
	Designs of tooling
Optical fiber	Medical equipment
	Telecommunications

they expect to be winners. By contrast, identifying an industry cluster, as Professor Gary Anderson suggests, is "a process to assess the 'revealed preference' of business communities for linkages among associated industries. This process can provide guidance to industry attraction programs and in revealing areas for improvement in infrastructure and other resources needed by dominant industry clusters."[18]

Many developing countries can start their industrialization process by developing *basic industries*—producing raw material, semifinished products, or energy. These basic industries will become the supporting industries for further downstream industries. They are called basic because once they are established, they function as a basis for the development of many other industries. One unique feature of basic industry is that they have numerous forward linkages. Developing basic industry is an appropriate strategy for countries that have abundant mineral resources and sources of energy and can use these industries as a foundation for further industrialization.

A major advantage of basic industries is that they usually require a few skilled workers who can, if necessary, be acquired from abroad. Furthermore, because they have a few backward linkages, they need only a very limited number of suppliers. In political terms, basic industries make the country less dependent on imports of raw materials and semifinished products, so that in times of difficulties, such as war or serious shortages of foreign exchange, other branches of the secondary sector are less likely to be negatively affected.

Basic industries, however, have their disadvantages. They demand lumpy capital investments and create relatively little employment. Structurally, they cannot function effectively unless other downstream industries exist that require their outputs. In the case where there is not enough domestic demand, a proportion of the output must be exported; otherwise, the basic industries may operate below installed capacity. As a result of these drawbacks, many small developing countries often decide to develop only certain basic industries (e.g., cement factories and power plants). Only the more populous countries (e.g., Brazil, China, India), which already have a large number of industries producing consumer goods, have been able to develop a broad number of basic industries.[19]

In sum, the concept of industrial clusters can be used for analysis and as a guideline for strategic development in most economies. However, as Professor Anderson has suggested, there are at least two types of economies in which this approach cannot be directly used:

1. It cannot be applied where the economy is too small to support the diversification inherent in the concept of an industry cluster.
2. It cannot be applied in many underdeveloped economies.[20]

SUMMARY

An industrial cluster is defined as a group of industries that have vertical and horizontal linkages toward each other. It comprises the focal industry, related industries, and supporting industries. Vertical linkages are typically the linkages between the focal industry and the supporting industries, whereas horizontal linkages are the linkages between the focal industry and other industries that have complementarities in technology and/or in marketing with the focal industry.

Related industries are not only important in generating synergistic effects for an industrial cluster that arise from network coordination but also in generating the dynamic effects—for example, snowball effects, substitution effects, spillover effects (both the crossover and the fusion technologies)—which come from technological and marketing interactions among industrial segments.

Supporting industries, besides their added value enhancement, play an important role in generating external economies, that is, creating satellite effects in the industrial cluster.

Chapter 10

Developing the Nation's Industrial Portfolio

A nation's industrial portfolio consists of industrial clusters from many industrial sectors. One or more focal industries in the industrial cluster are surrounded by related and supporting industries. However, stiff global competition forces governments from time to time to revise their nation's industrial portfolio. They seek to attract new industries that promise higher added value and higher productivity. At the same time, they aim to revitalize existing strong but highly competitive industries and to restructure or to phase out declining or vulnerable industries.

This chapter examines the process of managing and improving a nation's industrial portfolio. The first step calls for identifying the nation's industrial development determinants. The second step involves formulating the nation's industrial vision. The final step consists in identifying the appropriate industrial support strategy.

213

STEP I: IDENTIFYING THE NATION'S INDUSTRIAL DEVELOPMENT DETERMINANTS

Strengthening the nation's industrial portfolio requires examining the two major determinants illustrated in Figure 10.1, namely, "industrial attractiveness" and a nation's "ability to compete."

Industrial Attractiveness Determinants

The attractiveness of a nation's actual or potential industries is signaled by a number of factors, among them:

1. *High Value Added per Worker.* Countries can create wealth by shifting their economic structure into high value-added activities.
2. *Linkage Industries.* There is an economic payoff to investment in "linkage" industries, such as steel and semiconductors, whose outputs are used as inputs to many downstream industries.
3. *Future Competitiveness.* Government must select industries in which a country is not currently competitive in the world market but in which it will or can be made competitive in the future.

FIGURE 10.1

Determinants of a Nation's Industrial Development

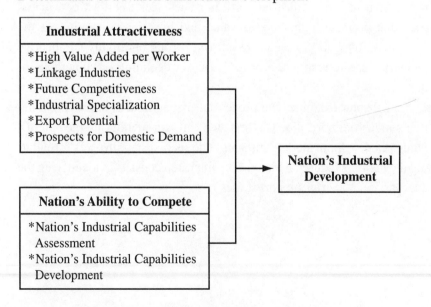

4. *Industrial Specialization.* An industry is more attractive if specializing in it is less likely to lead to a head-on collision with many other competitors.

5. *Export Potentials.* The industry's products must have a track record of export success. The world demand for the industry's products should be large and growing.

6. *Prospects for Domestic Demand.* The industry makes a significant contribution to increasing economic growth through domestic consumption. The demand characteristics of this industry's products should be highly income-elastic so that the more the country develops, the more demand there is for those products.[1]

Table 10.1 summarizes some factors contributing to a nation's industrial attractiveness.

The Ability to Compete

The next question is how well equipped is the nation to exploit the identified opportunities and avoid the threats related to that industry. Policymakers must assess a nation's ability to compete in each specific industry.

Proponents of globally oriented industrial policy have proposed actions designed to stimulate industries in certain sectors of the economy. In industrial nations, they advocate stimulating "sunrise" industries—biotechnology, artificial intelligence, precision instruments, robotics, engineering services, process control system, etc. In developing countries, they advocate stimulating the "sunset" industries found in industrial countries—steel, autos, machine tools, home appliances, etc. Industrial nations realize that their ability to compete in sunset industries is adversely impacted by the lower cost structures in developing nations. Developing nations realize that their ability to compete in high-tech markets is adversely impacted by the superior access of industrial nations to required human resources, i.e., electrical and software engineers, technicians, etc. Industrial nations can compensate for their comparative disadvantage in sunset industries by concentrating their attention on developing global markets for high-tech products. Developing nations can compensate for their comparative disadvantage in sunrise industries by concentrating their attention in increasing their global market share in sunset industries.[2]

TABLE 10.1

Factors Contributing to Industrial Attractiveness

Market Factors

- Market size
- Size of key segment
- Growth rate per year both total and segments
- Diversity of market
- Sensitivity to price, service features, and external factors
- Cyclicality and seasonality
- Bargaining power of foreign upstream suppliers
- Bargaining power of foreign downstream suppliers
- Bargaining power of foreign related industries

Competition

- Types of global competitors
- Degree of concentration
- Changes in types and mix
- Entries and exits
- Substitution by new technology
- Degree and types of integration

Financial and Economic Factors

- Added values
- Nation's contribution, such as employment, nation's security
- Global impact, such as pollution and environmental concerns
- Leverage factors, such as economies of scale and experience
- Barrier to entry or exit
- Capacity utilization

Technological Factors

- Maturity and volatility
- Complexity
- Differentiation
- Patents and copyrights
- Manufacturing process technology required

Assessing the Nation's Industrial Capabilities. A nation's existing or potential competitive advantage, as suggested by Professors Doz and Prahalad (1987), depends on: (1) its factors' competitiveness—relative strengths of its productive factors, which include its physical resources, human resources, and technology; and (2) its firms' competitiveness—relative strengths of the nation's domestic business enterprises.

When a nation's factor competitiveness is high and its domestic firms are competitive, an industry will emerge. There will be production for both domestic consumption and eventually for exports. That is how the consumer electronics industry emerged in Japan and the aerospace industry emerged in the United States.

On the other hand, when the two above-mentioned factors are weak, an industry will not emerge. Instead, the nation will import the products for local consumption. Examples are airplanes imported by developing countries and raw materials and energy-related products imported by Japan.

If the firms' competitiveness is high, but the factor competitiveness is low, there will be a pressure for *outward investment*, i.e., investing in foreign countries with high-factor competitiveness. An example would be some downstream industries of the U.S. electronic industries that arrange manufacturing or assembly in Southeast Asia where labor costs are lower.

Finally, if firms' competitiveness is low but factor competitiveness is high, there will be *inward investment* in these industries. For example, Asian countries have their electronic industries, and the Arabian Gulf states have their oil exploration, under the management of foreign firms (see Figure 10.2)[3].

FIGURE 10.2

Nation's Industrial Capabilities Assessment

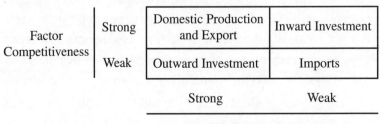

		Domestic Production and Export	Inward Investment
Factor Competitiveness	Strong	Domestic Production and Export	Inward Investment
	Weak	Outward Investment	Imports
		Strong	Weak

Firm's Competitiveness

Developing the Nation's Industrial Capabilities. After assessing the nation's industrial capabilities, policymakers have to develop a plan to improve those capabilities for both the short and the long term. Cooperation between the government and the private sector is critical to strengthen the nation's industries. Generally, the government takes the major role in building *factor competitiveness* via the development of infrastructure and the establishment of different pro-competitive public policies to encourage investment in the nation.

Through several decades of investment in infrastructure and education, Taiwan has established a very favorable environment for the diffusion of innovation and cultivated a strong base of high quality manpower to carry out technological limitation and improvement.[4]

By contrast, business enterprises play the major role in building *firm competitiveness* through entrepreneurial development, technological capabilities, and capital accumulation.

Taiwan's machinery industry consists of a large number of diligent, experienced entrepreneurs and workers, many of whom do not even possess modern equipment and advanced knowledge. Through them, many promising technologies will probably be copied and diffused rapidly and widely using similar or smaller production scales and/or with equivalent or lower product quality. The machinery industry in turn supports many other Taiwanese industries.[5]

Effective business enterprises include not only those in the private corporate sector but also the vast and growing number of less formally organized small and energetic entrepreneurs. For example, self-employed rural entrepreneurs in Taiwan have been highly active in diffusing technology to rural areas. But the activities occurring in the informal sector typically are underrepresented in official government statistical data.

In the short run, the success of building firm competitiveness in each industry does not only come from "internal development." It can also come from what the nation can acquire from abroad in the form of technology transfer and cooperative arrangements such as technical and financial cooperation at the governmental level, or a direct investment and strategic alliance between domestic firms and foreign counterparts in the forms of joint ventures, technological licensing, and upstream and downstream subcontracting. In Japan's history of industrialization, technology imports from advanced countries were among the highest priority.

In sum, policymakers should try to identify the necessary basic factors that can promote internal development for each industry, and what factors need to be acquired to strengthen company competitiveness further.

Both industrial attractiveness and the nation's ability to compete must be taken into account to assess the competitive positions of current and potential industries. In this way, it is possible to rationalize the nation's industrial portfolio (see Figure 10.3).

Consider European industries as an illustrative example. The competitiveness of European industries with regard to their competitive position in the global triad—Europe, the United States, and Japan—is evident in Figures 10.4 and 10.5. The findings reveal that the EC is most strongly represented in such areas as pharmaceuticals, machine tools, steel, food and clothing (see the bottom right-hand corner of Figure 10.4). Many of these "cash cow" industries are under attack from foreign competition and (as indicated in Figure 10.5) are at best only expected to hold their

FIGURE 10.3

Nation's Industrial Portfolio Analysis

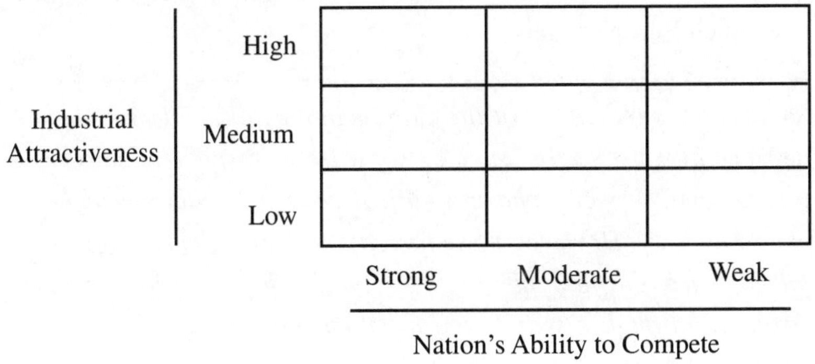

		Strong	Moderate	Weak
Industrial Attractiveness	High			
	Medium			
	Low			

Nation's Ability to Compete

FIGURE 10.4

The European Industrial Portfolio

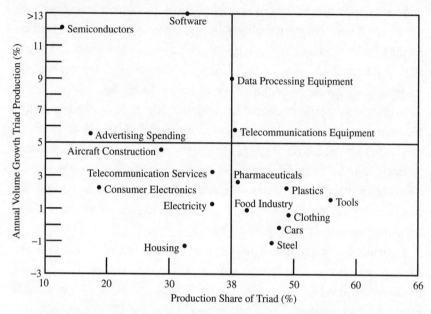

Source: Philip F. Banks and Liam Fahey, "The Changing Face of European Industries: Identifying and Assessing Business Opportunities," in Liam Fahey, ed., *Winning in the New Europe: Taking Advantage of the Single Market* (Englewood Cliffs, NJ: Prentice Hall, 1992), Figure 7.1, p. 93.

Note: Comparing Figure 10.4 here with Figure 10.3, the production share of triad (%) dimension is equivalent to the nation's ability to compete dimension, while the annual volume growth triad production (%) dimension is equivalent to the industrial attractiveness dimension.

position. Conversely, Europe is underrepresented in such areas as consumer electronics and semiconductors—two industries much more indicative of the new technological world than the formerly mentioned areas in which Europe excels.

> *Some studies indicate that the European position will probably improve in some sectors such as software, aerospace engineering, telecom services, pharmaceuticals, plastics, and consumer electronics. . . . However, these forecasts are only likely to be realized when the new moves to revitalize the EC's industrial structure through research and development programs take effect.[6]*

FIGURE 10.5

European Outlook by Sector

Sectors	Triad Growth Rate, 1987–1993	European Share
Software	15.0%	◁
Semiconductors	12.3	△
Data processing equipment	9.0	▷
Telecommunications equipment	5.3	▷
Advertising spending (TV)	5.1	◁
Aircraft construction	4.6	◁
Pharmaceuticals	3.7	◁
Telecommunications services	3.7	◁
Plastics	3.0	▷
Consumer electronics	2.8	◁
Machine tools	2.6	▷
Electricity (Twh)	2.3	▷
Food industry	1.6	▷
Textiles clothing	1.0	▷
Automotive (number of cars)	0.6	▷
Raw steel (millions of tons)	−1.2	△
Housing (number of new housing starts)	−2.4	△

Source: Ibid., Figure 7.2, p. 94.

The matrix in Figure 10.3 provides a rational basis for prioritizing four types of investing: (1) investing to penetrate; (2) investing to rebuild; (3) selective investment; and (4) reduced investment (see Figure 10.6).

1. Investing to Penetrate. This strategy aims to achieve a leading global position by strengthening the nation's ability to compete. It requires sufficient investment so as to move the industry to the left of the chart. Such a strategy is usually undertaken during the early development or growth phase of a global industry. Korea's electronic industry provides a relatively good example:

> *By the mid-1980s, Korea was emerging as a potent competitor in the commodity chip businesses. Korean firms gained access to*

FIGURE 10.6

Investment Strategies

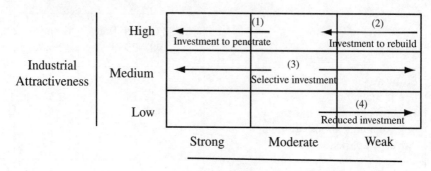

Nation's Ability to Compete

state-of-the-art design and technology by reverse engineering and by gaining licenses from U.S. and Japanese firms. In 1987, Korea had 6–7% of world semiconductor production capacity but only 2–3% world market share. In 1986, Korea launched a Semiconductor Cooperative Research Project, funded by the government, aiming to produce 4-megabit DRAMs and entering into the logic markets, especially microprocessors and ASICs. Observers believed that Korea had some of the most modern labs in the world and could capture 10% of the world market by 1990.[7]

Investing to Rebuild. This strategy aims to restore a nation's industrial strength that was lost in an industry whose attractiveness is still high. Such revitalization may require considerable investment. The German machine-tool industry provides an example:

Machine tools comprise a highly competitive global industry. Germany's share of global machine-tool exports has slipped from nearly a third to less than a quarter, even though the size of the market has grown from $3 billion in 1970 to $22 billion in 1990. The major competitor, Japan, first concentrated on mass-producing standard machine tools such as lathes, leaving German firms to produce expensive, tailor-made, and high precision models. But now, some Japanese firms are moving to producing *higher-end machines by employing computer technology advances. In waging a counterattack, German machine-tool makers made several strategic mistakes. First, most of them resumed mass-producing standard machine tools to compete with the Japanese, but at higher prices. Second, some companies overstretched their resources and incurred high debt. Lastly, German machine-tool makers are highly dependent on sales to the relatively mature West European markets, neglecting other fast-growing ones.*[8]

Selective Investment. Selective investment involves strengthening specific niches within weakening industrial segments where the benefits of selective rebuilding exceed the costs, and reducing or eliminating investment in less attractive niches. The Swiss textile and watch industries provide good examples of industries requiring more selective investments:

Under the fierce competition in the world textile market, Swiss textile companies have been losing out to Asian low-labor-cost nations. Meanwhile, the Swiss watch industry has suffered major export declines because the industry overlooked the importance of electronic and digital watches, and underestimated aggressive moves by Japanese manufacturers. The Swiss watch share of the world market fell from 30% in the early 1970s to 9% by early 1983. Swiss watch makers had lost the quantity sector of the market to low-cost products from Hong Kong while its quality sector is being threatened by Japanese manufacturers—Seiko and Citizen—who are producing high quality products carrying lower prices than the Swiss counterparts.[9]

Reduced Investment. For industries with declining potential, reducing the investment and *harvesting* the industry makes the most sense. Harvesting may be implemented over a fairly long period. In the short run, selective investment should be used to support subsectors where high-production volume is still possible.

Low investment is appropriate when a nation's capabilities have eroded in a highly competitive industry. Japan's planned retrenchment of its heavy industries (e.g., steel, aluminum, shipbuilding industries) provides an example.

Heavy industries were leading industries during Japan's high growth period (1955–1970). Japan achieved economies of scale and lower costs and thereby acquired international competitiveness. However, the price increases of oil and raw materials (the Japanese iron producers, for example, relied entirely on imported materials) decreased Japan's competitive edge, while slower economic growth after the oil shocks forced a lower utilization rate of existing capacity. Interest payments on the underutilized capacity added financial burdens to the firms, and as a result, many opted to reduce their existing capacity.

A sharp reduction of capacity and personnel similarly occurred in other Japanese heavy industries: aluminium, ship building, chemical fertilizers, and petrochemicals. As was the case in iron production, the competitiveness of these industries had deteriorated due to the increased costs of raw materials and fuels, and very low operation rates under stagnant demand.[10]

STEP II: FORMULATING THE NATION'S INDUSTRIAL VISION

From the analysis of a nation's industrial development determinants, each industrial sector can be tracked as an industrial strategic unit in the industrial portfolio, as shown in a nation's industry planning map (see Figure 10.7).

The three dimensions of an industry's planning map provide a useful starting point for envisioning an industry's future. It consists of: (1) an investment strategy for each of the nation's current and prospective industries; (2) a market boundary for each industry, depending on the competitive intensity and the nation's ability to compete in each industry; and (3) the factor intensity of the industry, which has to meet lower-cost factor substitution from other nations. This map enables policymakers to consider a strategic investment level for each specific industry, expanding

FIGURE 10.7

A Nation's Industry Planning Map

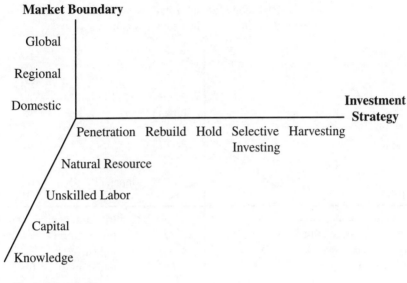

Market Boundary

Global

Regional

Domestic

Investment Strategy

Penetration Rebuild Hold Selective Harvesting
                                Investing

Natural Resource

Unskilled Labor

Capital

Knowledge

Factor Intensity

its geographic coverage or shifting factor intensity to meet the pace of competition. Moreover, the map allows policymakers to analyze current and prospective competitors in this industry on their current strategy and expected strategic moves.[11]

Japan's industrial evolution provides a clear example of industrial policy planning. Japan started with low-skilled, labor-intensive industries, but with the strategic intent of moving, first, to medium-skilled, medium-capital-using industries; second, to skilled-labor, raw material-intensive industries; and third, to knowledge-intensive industries (see Figure 10.8). The shifting industrial pattern would increase the value of existing resources. Many nations also seek to make a similar transition across sectors. But Japan has been more successful than others in integrating this sectoral restructuring pattern with the nation's industry-building strategy and the capabilities of its business enterprises.[12]

More specifically, Japan focused, in the early 1950s, on labor-intensive industries like cutlery, textiles, and toys. In the 1960s, it began to build competence in heavy industries—chemicals, coals, shipbuilding,

FIGURE 10.8

Evolution of the Japanese Industrial Structure

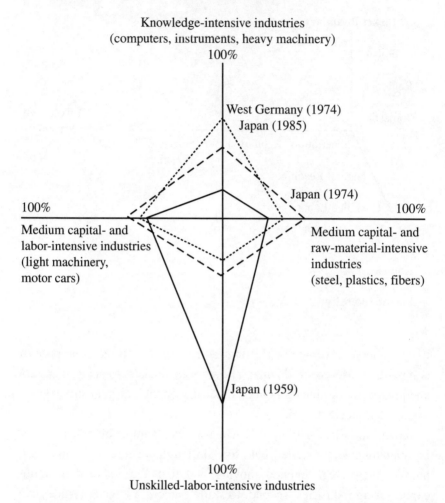

Source: Michael Best, *The New Competition: Institutions of Industrial Restructuring* (Cambridge, MA: Harvard University Press, 1990), Figure 3, p. 190.

and steel—in order to develop the key building blocks for the modern industrial infrastructure and for mass-producing simple consumer goods. By the 1970s, the Japanese achieved startling capabilities in precision instrumentation, such as cameras and machine tools, and in complex consumer products like automobiles, electronics, and pharmaceuticals. By the 1980s, their target moved to developing world-class leadership posi-

FIGURE 10.9

The Dynamism of the Japanese Industrial Portfolio

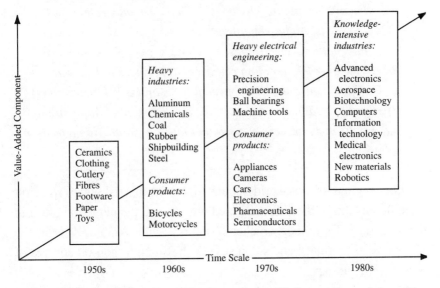

Source: Barrie G. James, *Trojan Horse: The Ultimate Japanese Challenge to Western Industry* (New York: Mercury Books, 1990), Figure 1.1, p. 6.

tions in many knowledge-intensive industries such as advanced electronics, computers, aerospace, and biotechnology (see Figure 10.9).[13]

The same pattern may be seen among later entrants to the ranks of the NICs in East Asia.

In 1973, Korea introduced a new phase of industrialization which shifted the emphasis to the development of heavy and chemical industries. During the 1970s, these industries grew at an accelerated rate. At the same time, the growth of textiles and apparel slowed down substantially. Subsequently, the emphasis shifted to consumer electronics and automobiles. In particular, there has also been a substantial shift within the electronic sector itself towards more sophisticated segments, such as industrial electronic equipment.

A similar trend can also be observed in Taiwan. The emergence of fabricated metal products, machinery and equipment as

> *the leading industrial group by 1975 indicate that Taiwan's man-*
> *ufacturing sector has shifted towards more complex and sophis-*
> *ticated activities. In line with the shift in industrial strategy in the*
> *1980s towards high technology and skill-intensive activities*
> *(e.g., information, electronics, machinery and biotechnology),*
> *the electrical machinery and electrical appliances industry grew*
> *by 19.4 per cent annually between 1982 and 1984. There has*
> *also been substantial progress in the development of automation*
> *and precision machinery, especially tools and shuttle loom tech-*
> *nology.*[14]

Other regions of the world sought to spread the risk away from oil price fluctuation in the short and medium run and the depletion of oil in the long run. "Commodity nichers" such as Saudi Arabia, Kuwait, the United Arab Emirates, and so on started shifting into non-oil sources of earnings, including:

• Related industries that depend on refinery industry by-products. The numerous by-products of the refining industry can be collected to support significant industries in the fields of petrochemicals and chemicals.

• Downstream supporting industries in the petroleum and petrochemical sectors. These industries can draw on relatively cheap basic products as well as cheap intermediate and finished products, including those processable on an export basis. They also enjoy a major comparative advantage available in the region, namely, the abundant and low cost sources of energy, such as gas and hydrocarbon fuels in general.

• Industries based on mineral resources. These include iron ore, potash, copper, phosphate, gold, limestone, etc. These industries are characterized as being capital and energy intensive. Developing such mineral-based primary industries normally creates external economies and forward linkages that render investment in derived secondary product industries more profitable.

• Industries that serve the oil industry. This is by far the largest industry in the region and its needs and requirements are numerous during the different stages of oil production (exploration, extraction, transportation, and refining). Since its beginning, this industry has been contributing to the development of a large associated business sector, and many industrial projects could emerge to serve this industry.[15]

STEP III: IDENTIFYING APPROPRIATE INDUSTRIAL SUPPORT STRATEGIES

Different governments have adopted different approaches to developing technology and stimulating industry development (see Tables 10.2 and 10.3). Consider how the three governments of Singapore, Japan, and India differed in their policies toward computer industry development.

The Singapore government pursued an open-door policy with regard to multinational computer firms. The government sought to boost employment and exports and raise the people's standard of living. While Singapore managed to satisfy the short-term needs of boosting employment and export earnings, the nation's long-term goal of absorbing the latest technology and achieving self-reliance has not been achieved. Rising Singapore wage levels and external events such as recessions led the multinational firms to move their manufacturing and assembly operations to other countries. Local firms faced a shortage of capital and technology and were unable to absorb the latest technologies and become internationally competitive.

In comparison, the Japanese government used a three-pronged approach to establishing their computer industry and achieving rapid technology absorption. First, Japanese companies obtained basic computer patents from IBM [see Chapter 13]. Then Japanese computer companies concluded licensing agreements for specific product technologies from established U.S. computer firms. Finally, a series of government subsidies augmented the research-and-development efforts of Japanese computer companies. This Japanese approach worked, and the technology gap has narrowed considerably.

The Indian government, by contrast, opted in favor of achieving the long-term goal of self-sufficiency through participating in the ownership and control of the operations of foreign computer firms in India. Wholly-owned Indian computer firms were

TABLE 10.2

Typology of Industrial Policy Characteristics of Seven OECD Countries

Policy aspects	USA	Japan	FR Germany
Relative importance of post-war policy choices	big; TNCs formed the base for expansion abroad	big; MITI acted as visionary force	big; consensus on renewed industry as base for expansion
Policy response to post-war internationalisation	export expansion direction Western Europe	export with closed national boundaries	free trade in favour of the large enterprises
Implication of post-war internationalisation on national industry	strengthening of TNCs and weakening of domestic industries	challenge of technical-advanced industry	strengthening of large companies and upgrading smaller companies
Wider context of decision making on industrial policy	hegemonial policy formulated by politicized administration	MITI-apparatus still acted as 'Ministry of War'; war economy	corporatism based on national cohesion
Influence of social and political context on industrial policy	strong management culture and varying influence of trade unions	vision development by top management; top-down consensus building	cooperation social partners; room for open discussion
Learning curves and patterns of industrial policy	from free trade to protectionism and bi-lateral trade agreements	from free trade to forced opening of the domestic market	free trade in combination with open domestic market
Characterization of post-war industrial policy	uncoordinated, covert industrial policy	very coherent industrial policy	coherent social and industrial policy

Source: Annemieke J. M. Roobeek, *Beyond the Technology Race: An Analysis of Technology Policy in Seven Industrial Countries* (Amsterdam: Elsevier, 1990), Table 7.1, p. 218.

to satisfy the majority of India's computer needs, while foreign computer firms were to supply only very large computer systems using very advanced technology. Access to and participation in the manufacture of the most advanced computer systems were sought by India's government. While progress has been

France	UK	Sweden	Netherlands
big; establishment of national industrial base	small; continuation of pre-war aspirations	big; expansion of state intervention in industry and social welfare	big; large scale industrialization was pushed strongly.
state intervention and limited expansion	free trade, but also oncoming protection	free trade and strong domestic competition	free trade in favour of TNCs
building up of advanced industrial industries for protected markets	further weakening of industry and low growth	expansion of export and strong domestic demand	expansion of shipbuilding, agriculture and chemical industry
'L'état developpeur'; elitist, central state	strong institutions, but weak in directing industry	small, central government with many intermediary links	strong expansion of government competence in various fields
limited influence of social organizations outside elites	stress on protection of existing employment	open discussion context; combination technology and humanization	limited influence trade unions; dominance of commercial spirit
openness of domestic market is politically negotiable	from free trade to protection, to open, deregulated market	international openness	international openness
political dirigism	politically capricious industrial policy	constructive socio-industrial policy	stable, moderate interventionist policy

achieved, international competitiveness and self-sufficiency are still distant goals.[16]

In practice, Professors Freeman and Lundvall (1988) suggest three general approaches for a government to support one or more of a nation's

TABLE 10.3

International Comparison of the Intensity of Industrial Policy Aspects

	USA	Japan	FR Germany	France	UK	Sweden	Netherlands
Strategies aimed at blurring boundaries between sectors	•	•••	•••	•••	•••	•	•••
Integration of policy instruments	•	•••	•••	•••	•••	•••	•••
Institutional continuity	••	•••	•••	•••	••	•••	•••
Size of the state sector	•	•••	•••	•••	•	•••	•
Intensity of generic policy	•••	••	•••	•••	•••	•••	•••
Intensity of sectoral policy	•••	•	••	•••	••	•	•
Intensity of demand policy	•••	••	•	•••	•	•••	•••
Role of defense in government demand	•••	•	•	•••	•••	•	•
Stimulation of high technologies	•••	•••	•••	•••	••	•••	•
Protection of older industries	••	••	••	•••	••	•••	•
Relative success of high technology industries	•••	•••	•••	•••	••	••	•••
Relative success of older industries	••	••	••	••	•	••	•
Competition policy/monopoly and fusion control policies	•••	•	•••	••	••	•	••
Tendency to strengthen private initiative	•••	•••	•••	•••	•••	••	•••
Regional dimension of industrial policy	••	••	•••	•••	•••	••	••
Environmental/ecological dimension of industrial policy	••	•	•••	••	•	•••	•••
Measure of societal consensus	•	•••	••	•••	••	•••	••
Export stimulation policy	•••	•••	••	•••	••	•••	••
Import restriction as main target for national policies	••	•••	•	••	••	•••	•
Import restriction as reaction to international competition	•••	•	•	•	•	•	•

••• strong
•• moderate
• weak

Table derived from DIW study and accomplished with own estimates for FR Germany and the Netherlands. Deutsches Institut für Wirtschaftsforschung, *Beiträge zur Strukturforschung*, vol. 92/1 (1987), p. 50.

Source: Ibid., Table 7.2, p. 220.

industries, ranging from free market competition at one extreme to selective government intervention at the other extreme. The three approaches can be termed *market stimulation*; *neutrality and natural selection*; and *the selective strategy*.

Market Stimulation

This approach aims to reinforce the workings of the market in the particular policy area. It involves: (1) provision of infrastructure-type services to the economy as a whole; (2) the development of market-responsive mechanisms; and (3) the stimulation and fostering of new specialized firms that work as market agents.[17]

Neutrality and Natural Selection

Neutrality involves support for particular activities (such as R&D subsidies and technology diffusion) without any explicit preference for particular industrial sectors or technologies.[18]

Israel's industrial R&D subsidy, for example, is extended at a uniform 50% rate to any project satisfying a minimum set of requirements (bona fide R&D, technical feasibility and elementary market to search).[19]

In this sense, neutrality does not interfere with market forces. It initiates a process of natural selection at both firm and industry levels. A firm's survival is mainly determined by its competitive success in the market. "Natural selection" is superior to other selective mechanisms in circumstances where there is no basis or information as to which areas will be "winners" or will create valuable spin-offs or positive externalities. The lack of a basis typifies the early stages of especially high technology industries.[20]

Two points are worth mentioning about the feasibility and efficiency of natural selection among firms and industries:

1. Natural selection will be more efficient in enhancing a firm's competitiveness when that firm possesses a pool of scientifically and

technologically trained persons, a high-quality level of education, and substantial financial support for research and development.

2. The natural selection of entrepreneurial firms may be possible in areas with *divisible* technologies (i.e., in areas where small firms are capable of acquiring technical and economic efficiency), but it may not be possible in areas where *indivisible* technologies usually require lumpy investment.[21]

A Selective Strategic Approach

The debate on competitiveness often makes reference to the concept of *strategic industries*. There are at least three definitions of a strategic industry. Briefly:

- An industry that has military significance (e.g., semiconductors and machine tools).
- An industry that is research-intensive (e.g., drugs and aircraft).
- An industry that has considerable technological and market-demand spillovers into other industries (e.g., steel, computers).[22]

The need to make large, indivisible (i.e., lumpy) investments often calls for a selective strategic approach. When investments are lumpy, the cost of acquiring information and know-how through natural selection is prohibitive. "Lumpiness" is generally a characteristic of many basic industries—for example, steel and other basic metals, cement, chemicals and petrochemicals, and some machinery and metalworking industries. Due to the substantial risks involved, the scope of investment in these industries is very limited for many small developing countries.[23]

A selective strategic approach may also be warranted to avoid coordination failures in supporting and related industries associated with *pecuniary external economies*.

In the 1950s and 1960s Japanese steel and shipbuilding were promoted because they were believed to provide substantial spillover benefits in the form of infrastructure for other industries. Proponents of this view argue that Japanese success in other industries, such as autos and machine tools, stemmed in part from access to cheaper, higher quality steel and on cheaper imported raw materials.

The spillover effects provided by the steel and shipbuilding industries are "pecuniary" in the sense that they are reflected in lower input prices to their downstream users. Because pecuniary externalities are reflected in market prices, economists often argue that there is no need for policy-makers to determine the optimal amount of investment and production. This condition holds, however, only as long as there are no "imperfections" in product markets and no "distortions" in capital markets. These would reflect difficulties in raising significant amounts of private capital to finance large, irreversible, non-marginal projects whose returns are ex ante unknowable, given the existing economic structure, and recoverable only over the long run. Once these real world conditions are recognized as facts of economic life, the Japanese rationale for targeting critical input industries appears more compelling.[24]

Yet the selective approach involves several dangers: the criteria for selection may be weak; lobbying and political corruption may influence the selection; and it may be hard to undo the subsidies once established. The result often is to create protected industries and an elite labor force who enjoy rents exceeding their productivity.[25]

We would conclude that a nation's industrial support policies should represent a combination of these three approaches. On balance, market stimulation is preferred over the other two approaches. When the possibility for implementing market stimulation does not exist, neutrality and natural selection should be applied. Only in the last resort should a selective strategic mechanism be pursued. In the late 1990s, industrial policy in many countries will vacillate among these three approaches depending on their industry portfolio vision and the ability of their policymakers to formulate effective strategies.

While government policies are influential in both the U.S. and Japan, it is no longer the Japanese government alone that pursues an aggressive industrial policy. Indeed, the Ministry of International Trade and Industry (MITI) has steadily reduced the level of its industrial intervention, while the U.S. government has largely abandoned its laissez-faire stance and now seeks a means to revitalize the civilian industrial base. Variations in corporate performance from firm to firm substantially exceed systematic differences between most industries in the two nations.[26]

SUMMARY

The first step in developing the nation's industry portfolio is to analyze its industrial development determinants—specifically industrial attractiveness and the nation's ability to compete. The second step is to formulate the nation's industrial vision. In this step, three main dimensions are taken into account: *what*—the factor intensity; *where*—the scope of market boundaries; and *how*—the investment strategies, of each industry. The final step is to identify three industrial support strategies: market simulation; neutrality and natural selection; and a selective strategic approach.

Chapter 11

Developing the Nation's Trade Policies

A round $3.5 trillion worth of trade flows across international borders each year. About 75 percent of this amount is concentrated in the industrial nations. Trade between industrial and developing countries, however, is dramatically increasing from the previous decade. The *transition economies* of former Socialist countries still face numerous challenges as they try to participate in the world market economy.[1]

This chapter will examine, first, the relative advantages of inward-oriented versus outward-oriented policies, and their respective effects on economic growth; and second, the merits of export promotion strategies. Finally, we will examine today's major international trade issues.

INWARD, OUTWARD, AND MIXED TRADE STRATEGIES

Nations can attempt to build their economies either with an inward-oriented or an outward-oriented strategy. In the *inward-oriented strategy*, the investment, industrial, and trade incentives are biased in favor of production for domestic consumption over exports. Imports are strongly discouraged in consumption, intermediate, and capital goods, depending on

237

the scope of the import substitution strategy pursued. By contrast, in the *outward-oriented strategy*, the nation does not discriminate between production for domestic consumption and for exports, nor between purchases of domestic goods and imports. Inward investment from abroad and outward investment to other countries are equally welcome.[2]

The Inward-Oriented Development Regimes

Inward-oriented development policies promote self-reliance and encourage producers to exploit the benefits of "learning by doing," and to develop indigenous technologies appropriate to a country's resource endowments. Under high-tariff protection, these countries initially substitute domestic production for previously imported simple consumer goods (first-stage import substitution), and subsequently for more sophisticated manufactured goods (second-stage import substitution).[3]

The policy instruments geared to import substitution commonly include: (1) high import tariffs and numerous nontariff barriers; (2) low interest rates and inflationary government guarantees as protection against inflation and exchange rate risks; (3) low direct taxes and numerous tax exemptions; and (4) high subsidies and generous government procurement.[4]

The import substitution policies, however, incur costs on both demand and supply sides—a departure from market-based allocation of resources resulting in higher costs of production and lower consumer welfare. Such policies often create a divergence of domestic and world market prices, rationing of scarce inputs, and rent seeking.

For the sake of employment, the former New Zealand's government required television sets to be assembled locally. One industrialist, Alan Gibbs, went to Japan to haggle over the price of components. He was greeted with disbelief. Japanese firms could supply them only by having workers unscrew complete TVs. The New Zealand firm had to pay 5% more for the parts than for the complete TV. When shipped to New Zealand and assembled, the sets were then sold for twice the world price.[5]

Despite widespread import controls, inward-oriented economies usually set lower import restrictions for capital goods that are used in domestic production. Meanwhile, their overvalued currency retards export expansion, particularly reducing revenue receipts for agricultural exports. Inward-oriented regimes, thus, often end up with balance-of-payments difficulties. The increasing trade deficits and subsequent shortages of foreign exchange make intervention in foreign exchange markets inevitable. This often induces black market transactions, smuggling, lobbying activities, faking of trade invoices, and building plants with excess capacity in order to get import licenses. The costs of foreign exchange controls and nontariff barriers tend to be high, since they involve discretionary rather than efficient resource allocation. The excessive administrative regulations give rise to a slow and arbitrary bureaucracy, corruption, lengthy regulatory procedures, and a general uncertainty. The aggregate resource cost for the economy can be considerable.[6]

Inward-oriented policies may also cause an underutilization of labor. The combined effect of overvalued exchange rates, low import restrictions for capital goods, and subsidized financing conditions promotes expansion of capital-intensive industries and thereby boosts productivity at the expense of creating sufficient employment opportunities to absorb a rapidly growing labor force. Inward-oriented industrialization, thus, may paradoxically attract capital-intensive plants within countries characterized by abundant and low-skilled labor.[7]

Inward orientation also leads to societal introspection. The major focus is on external causes that might explain dependence and underdevelopment rather than on policies and practices that might advance productivity and social development.[8]

The costs of a protectionist regime become most visible when a country experiences severe external shocks. These economies are usually unable to adjust production in line with changes in the world price structure. When such countries were faced with the declining terms-of-trade problem in the past decade, many were not able to boost their exports rapidly. In addition, there was little room for them to continue their current import substitution efficiently.[9]

The Outward-Oriented Development Regimes

Outward-oriented trade policies foster an economy's allocative efficiency through its exposure to international competition. Outward-oriented economies benefit from several positive effects: (1) The country's economic and industrial structures are brought into line with its comparative advantage; (2) the country can achieve economies of scale through exports; (3) the country's export earnings are stabilized through diversification into manufactured goods; and (4) the country can easily obtain technological innovations and know-how from abroad.[10]

There is much evidence that progressive reductions in protection do not result in long-term unemployment. Outward-oriented economies have maintained a better employment record than inward-oriented ones.[11] Of course, an outward orientation does not necessarily mean the adoption of free trade and nonintervention. In some markets, economic policies need to be reformed so that the price mechanism can function more efficiently. In such circumstances, government interventions to overcome market failures are justified—provided that such market imperfections really exist and are not derived from excessive encroachment of public authorities on the market process.[12]

The Mixed Strategies

In practice, most countries have pursued both inward and outward strategies at one time or another. The Asian NICs' path of national wealth building, for example, moved through three stages: import substitution; inward investment and export promotion; and outward investment and import liberalization (see Figure 11.1).[13]

From Table 11.1, it can be seen that during the 1950s and 1960s, trade policies in the populous Latin America and Asia (Chile, Argentina, India, Pakistan, the Philippines, and Bangladesh) were heavily inward-oriented. By the end of the 1960s, some key sub-Saharan African countries and smaller Latin American and Asian countries began to pursue this strategy. However, since the mid-1960s, export promotion strategy has been primarily adopted by South Korea, Taiwan, Singapore, and Hong Kong, followed rapidly by Brazil, Chile, Thailand, and Turkey, which switched away from an earlier import-substituting strategy.[14]

Thailand's industrialization began in the 1960s, under the highly protectionist import substitution strategy of the First and Second Economic Plan (1961–71). Under this regime, average annual growth rates of value added in manufacturing reached 11% in the 1960s, while the share of primary-process manufacturing de-

FIGURE 11.1
Asian NICs' Three-Stage Path of National Wealth Building

Stage I: Import Substituting-Oriented

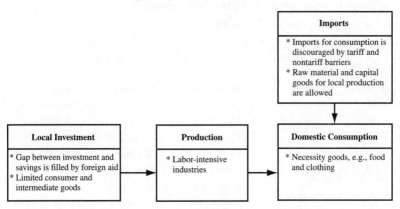

Stage II: Inward Investment/Export Promotion-Oriented

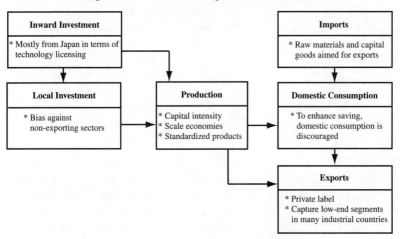

Stage III: Outward Investment/Import Liberalization-Oriented

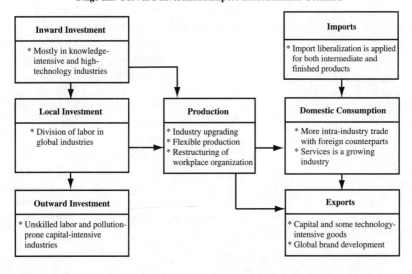

TABLE 11.1

World Bank Classification of Forty-One Developing Economies by
Trade Orientation, 1963–73 and 1973–85

	Outward-oriented		Inward-oriented	
Period	Strongly	Moderately	Moderately	Strongly
1963–1973	Hong Kong	Brazil	Bolivia	Argentina
	Singapore	Cameroon	El Salvador	Bangladesh
	South Korea	Colombia	Honduras	Burundi
	Taiwan*	Costa Rica	Kenya	Chile
		Guatemala	Madagascar	Dominican
		Indonesia	Mexico	Republic
		Israel	Nicaragua	Ethiopia
		Ivory Coast	Nigeria	Ghana
		Malaysia	Philippines	India
		Thailand	Senegal	Pakistan
			Tanzania	Peru
			Tunisia	Sri Lanka
			Turkey	Sudan
			Uruguay	
			Yugoslavia	
			Zambia	
1973–1985	Hong Kong	Brazil	Cameroon	Argentina
	Singapore	Chile	Colombia	Bangladesh
	South Korea	Israel	Costa Rica	Bolivia
	Taiwan*	Malaysia	El Salvador	Burundi
		Thailand	Guatemala	Dominican
		Tunisia	Honduras	Republic
		Turkey	Indonesia	Ethiopia
		Uruguay	Ivory Coast	Ghana
			Kenya	India
			Mexico	Madagascar
			Nicaragua	Nigeria
			Pakistan	Peru
			Philippines	Sudan
			Senegal	Tanzania
			Sri Lanka	Zambia
			Yugoslavia	

*Omitted from World Bank table.

Source: Robert N. Gwynne, *New Horizons?: Third World Industrialization in an International
Framework* (Hong Kong: Longmans Scientific & Technical, 1990), Table 6.1, p. 72 (based on World
Bank, *World Development Report, 1987*).

*clined from 60% to 40%. Consumer goods, petroleum products,
and some producer goods industries were established. The Third
Plan (1972–76) inaugurated an active phase of export promotion. A strategy of growth through the export of manufactured
goods was at the core of this success. In 1965, just 4% of Thailand's exports were manufactured goods, but by 1990 this figure
had reached 64% and a substantial diversification of manufactures exports had taken place. Since 1986, merchandise exports
grew at an annual rate of 25%.*[15]

In fact, neither inward-oriented nor outward-oriented industrialization
strategies are economic panaceas. Both are subject to systematic constraints or external shocks such as chronic inflation, recurring balance-
of-payments problems, and sharp increases in international interest rates
and the disruption of key trading partners.[16] And both require complementary efforts for effectiveness. The Latin American and Asian NICs'
industrialization are the case in point, as Professors Gereffi and Wyman's
book shows:

*The contrast often drawn between the Latin American and East
Asian NICs as representing inward- and outward-oriented development strategies, respectively, is oversimplified. While this distinction is appropriate for some periods, a historical perspective
shows that each of these NICs has pursued both inward- and
outward-oriented approaches.*

*Rather than being mutually exclusive alternatives, the import
substituting industrialization and export promoting industrialization development paths in fact have been complementary
and interactive. Each of the NICs subsequently has combined
both advanced import substituting industrialization and different
types of export oriented industrialization in order to avoid the inherent limitations of an exclusive reliance on domestic or external markets and also to facilitate the industrial diversification
and upgrading that are required for these nations to remain competitive in the world economy.*

*The early phase of industrialization—commodity exports and
primary import substituting industrialization—were common to
all of the Latin American and East Asian NICs. The subsequent di-*

vergence in the regional sequences stems from the ways in which each country responded to the basic problems associated with the continuation of primary import substituting industrialization. These problems included balance of payments pressures, rapidly rising inflation, high levels of dependence on intermediate and capital goods imports, and low levels of manufactured exports.[17]

PURSUING EXPORT PROMOTION STRATEGIES

With the advent of the global marketplace, exports have become a major determinant of national economic success. Consider the following account of India's move toward liberalizing the economy, which would favor expanded imports and exports:

For many decades, India maintained a pervasive system of industrial licensing, which enabled the bureaucracy to control much of the country's production and which also created a multitude of opportunities for corruption. Today, licensing has been abolished for all but 18 industries. Similarly, export subsidies and export controls have been abolished. A company now can use up to 60% of its export earnings for imports. Moreover, most controls on imports were to be removed by April 1992.[18]

And compare the U.S. moves toward an export strategy:

After a long period of controlling high technology exports, the U.S. government has now eased the constraints. Some specific actions included: (1) developing a commercial strategic plan for each key U.S. export market; (2) developing a national export strategy to better tap the estimated $275–$300 billion world market for environmental technologies; (3) increasing the federal government participation in standards and certification activities, including promotion of U.S. standards in foreign countries, acceptance of U.S. certification and accreditation, dissemination of information about ISO 9000 standards, and conversion of the U.S. to the metric system.[19]

Export Promotion Programs

Trade promotion and assistance by governments play an increasingly important role in today's growing international trade. Professors Seringhaus and Rosson have classified two approaches governments use to promote exports—*direct* and *indirect* programs. Direct programs concentrate on the demand side while indirect programs focus on the supply side. These two approaches are not mutually exclusive. Indeed, at the company level, they are highly complementary and interactive.[20]

Direct Programs. Direct export promotion measures aim to enhance the firm's export competitiveness. Examples include an array of programs and services that are designed to help local companies pass smoothly through several stages of internationalization.[21]

Seringhaus and Rosson distinguish five types of company situations in relation to exporting:

1. *Non-exporters*—companies that have no exporting experience and are currently not considering exporting;
2. *Failed exporters*—companies that have some experience in foreign marketing but have decided to withdraw from these activities;
3. *First-time exporters*—companies that decide to export in the near future;
4. *Expanding exporters*—companies that plan to penetrate their products into one or more new foreign markets; and
5. *Continuing exporters*—companies that plan no major changes but want to fine-tune their present export operations.[22]

Government-led export promotion programs raise some interesting questions:

What types of firms should be targeted for export stimulation and promotion? Seringhaus and Rosson propose four major types of government initiative:

- Encouraging *non-exporters* with strong competitive products to consider first-time exporting.
- Helping *first-time exporters* through the early, difficult phases of international marketing.
- Promoting the idea of renewed exporting to *failed exporters* who might succeed in the next try.

FIGURE 11.2

The Company's Need and Relevant Government Promotion Assistance

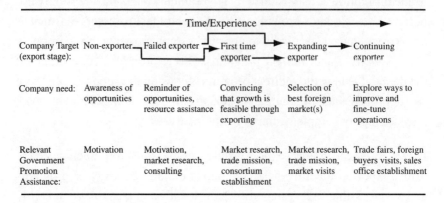

Source: F. H. Rolf Seringhaus and Philip J. Rosson, *Government Export Promotion: A Global Perspective* (New York: Routledge, 1990), Figure 5.4, p. 171.

- Supporting *continuing exporters* as they attempt to improve their performance.[23]

Figure 11.2 depicts the relevant government assistance for each type of exporting firm.

What types of programs would be most appropriate to reach and serve the particular needs of firms? Non-exporting firms may require motivational programs. These can be done by providing information on the benefits of exporting or case histories of successful exporters. First-time exporters need extensive information on "how" and "where" to export. Expanding exporters may need specific sales and representation leads for their products, as well as assistance in making successful bids for export contracts. Finally, continuing exporters may need help to publicize, advertise, and exhibit their products abroad and for meeting directly with foreign buyers.[24]

Indirect Programs. Indirect programs aim to improve the exporter's competitiveness and performance through structural and process changes. They include *productivity, research and development, technology and innovation, manpower planning, regional and sectoral development*, and *fiscal measures* such as tax and investment incentive policies, at both the industry and firm levels.[25]

In Hungary, the Institute for the Coordination of Computer Techniques (SZKI), a major government R&D facility, plays a catalytic role in developing Hungary's software programs and facilitating exports by overcoming many obstacles. Hungary's solid technological base enables SZKI to adapt foreign technology for domestic and, eventually, international use. Hungary's export success in software is noteworthy, given its late start in computers, its ban on imports of hardware from the west, and its weak image.[26]

Export Promotion Strategies: Some Considerations

To ensure efficient and effective export promotion, at least two linkages should be considered: the linkage between export promotion and import penetration; and the linkage between export diversification and specialization.

The Linkage Between Export Promotion and Import Penetration. To help exporters become more competitive internationally, governments should enable them to get quick access to imported inputs free of customs duties and indirect taxes. Otherwise, exporters will have some competitive disadvantages, since they have to pay more than their foreign counterparts for the same inputs or to use inferior domestic inputs. One way to solve this problem is to remove protection.[27]

In practice, however, many governments hesitate to remove protection. The question, then, is how to design a scheme in which export sales are being distinguished from domestic sales, and in which rebates or exemption of tariffs go into exports.[28]

Since 1955 in Taiwan, the support for exports has included rebates of import duties and other indirect taxes on inputs used directly or indirectly to produce manufactured exports. A firm that is a major, regular, law-abiding manufacturer-exporter is allowed to put its duty liabilities "on account," to be canceled against evidence of subsequent exports. Firms must furnish a

> *bank guarantee that the duty plus penalties will be paid if the exports are not produced within eighteen months.*[29]

Even though this scheme does not eliminate all the anti-export effects of protection, it removes a major part of them. Duty rebate schemes, however, are just one government instrument for effecting an inward-outward linkage.

> *Japan gave a rebate for machinery imports rather than for imports of raw materials and intermediates. However, imported raw materials paid very low duty, if any. And although duty on intermediates was typically high, exporters received a range of other subsidies (such as tax incentives, and preferential allocation of import licenses in excess of their own requirements to permit them to subsidize exports with super profits from the sale of these imported items on the protected domestic market). These extra subsidies presumably offset their competitive disadvantage in having to pay relatively high tariffs on imports of intermediates. At the same time, these rules helped to channel exporters' demand towards domestically produced intermediates, helping domestic producers to reach economies of scale and therefore get their prices close to international levels.*[30]

Other instruments include countertrade policies as used by Indonesia, and offset arrangements used by Western countries in the area of military/government purchases. Australia uses a partnership scheme that the federal government introduced in 1987.[31]

The Linkage Between Export Diversification and Specialization. In developing their export promotion policy, countries have to seek a balance between export *diversification* and export *specialization*. On the one hand, specialization may improve the likelihood of successful exporting—as with Korean and Taiwanese containerships, or banking in Hong Kong. But the risks from new entrants and from constantly changing technology and demand volatility will also be greater.

> *Korea's choice of shipbuilding shortly before shipbuilding and especially the tanker market virtually collapsed in the mid-1970s could have been disastrous.*

> *In textiles, Kenya's experience shows that cheap and plentiful
> labor was insufficient to overcome increased foreign import quo-
> tas and pressures for Voluntary Export Restraints (VERs), or
> competition from new, still cheaper competitors.*[32]

Both specialization and diversification can be taken to extremes and become counterproductive. Continued specialization in one set of products or industries over a long period of time seems not to be the right strategy in the global marketplace. Chile, for example, has consistently been overspecialized in a narrow range of products related to the processing of primary goods. The results are evident: Chile's market share has fallen from 5 percent in 1970 to 0.1 percent in the early 1990s. On the other hand, too much diversification is also not desirable. India's exports have been among the most diversified across product groups. It exports a little of many different products. This dilution effect leads to a generally declining trend in India's share of world trade.

Malaysia is a good example of balance between diversification and specialization. The Malaysia export structure was initially very similar to that of Chile. By the early 1990s, however, Malaysian exports were dominated by electrical products, constituting over half the country's exports. Further, there is an increasing trend in machinery exports, which have risen from zero to about 8 percent of Malaysian exports. Malaysia is thus an example of diversification (away from manufactures based on primary products) to specialization (in electrical products) and now a new diversification (into machinery). This mixture of strategies has helped Malaysia increase its world exports from 0.2 percent in 1970 to 0.75 percent of world-manufactured exports in the early 1990s.[33]

DEALING WITH INTERNATIONAL TRADE ISSUES

Here we will examine four current issues related to international trade: (1) economic alignments; (2) the general agreement on trade in services; (3) basic labor standards and trade; and (4) environmental policies and trade.

Economic Alignments[34]

Strong regional trade blocs—EC, NAFTA, and so on—have been emerging in recent years. An ideal trade bloc consists of countries with the most diverse range of comparative advantages generating the greatest possibility for trade creation and the least possibility for trade diversion.

Improved infrastructure and factor movement will support the expansion of both interregional and intraregional trade. Regional cooperation among member countries will also increase their leverage in negotiating with nonmember countries. ASEAN members have successfully used their association in this way.

Successful economic blocs usually exhibit four basic characteristics:

- similar levels of national income
- geographic proximity
- similar or compatible trading regimes
- political commitment to regional organization

Blocs with wide economic disparities among member states generally face difficulties since producers in the richer members see themselves as subsidizing the development of the poorer members while losing employment to them. As Paul Wonnacott and Mark Lutz have observed, "the division of gains is a major economic and political problem of almost any association that includes developing countries, whether these countries join with other developing nations or with developed nations."[35]

Geographic proximity is also another important factor for the success of economic alignments. Mexico, for example, sells more than 80 percent of its total exports to the United States and Canada. But the potential benefits from expanded trade among neighboring developing countries may also be quite limited. Asian countries export more than 50 percent of their goods outside the region because the major markets are elsewhere. In Africa, this proportion is as high as 95 percent. This is because neighboring countries tend to have similar factor endowments and cost structures, resulting in small gains from trade. Such gains are further limited by poor physical and social infrastructures among member countries.[36]

Furthermore, the expanded trade among neighboring countries also creates some social problems and conflicts.

In the early 1990s Venezuela found that its open border with Colombia brought in large transshipments of cocaine bound for the United States. China found that its new openness to foreign trade also exposed it to the AIDS epidemic in Asia. Germany and Western Europe found that accepting foreign refugees meant living with more domestic ethnic conflict.[37]

The third and fourth factors deal with the sustainability of the trading relationships among member states. Compatible trading regimes share similar, if not common, trade-related laws and institutional frameworks. Also, a supranational organization is required to maintain the plurilateral trade relationship and to mediate disputes. The presence of strong political commitment among member states will encourage such a regional body to work efficiently.

The General Agreement on Trade in Services

Services have currently become an important driving force in the global trading system, accounting for the largest share of gross domestic product in almost all countries (see Table 11.2). The service sector also is increasingly gaining the larger share of world foreign direct investment.

TABLE 11.2

The Contribution of the Service Sector to Gross Domestic Product in Developed and Developing Economies (percentage of GDP)

	Services		Industry		Agriculture	
Country group	1965	1987	1965	1987	1965	1987
Developing countries						
Low income	30	32	27	37	43	31
Lower-middle income	50	46	28	36	22	15
Upper-middle income	42	50	39	40	18	10
Developed market economies	54	61	40	35	5	3

Source: Peter Dicken, *Global Shift: The Internationalization of Economic Activity* (New York: The Guilford Press, 1992), Table 2.12, p. 41 (based on World Bank, *World Development Report, 1989*).

Services are increasingly the major source of employment in both developed and developing countries. The services sector has now been the primary engine of growth in many developing countries.[38]

As such, services have become not merely an economic but a major political issue within the protracted international trade negotiations of the Uruguay Round of the GATT. The General Agreement on Trade in Services (GATS) is set up to stimulate global trade in services by creating international standards and limiting national protectionist measures. Some critical issues for GATS are:

1. When a country's export mix shifts toward high-technology and intellectual property, two issues ensue: differences in the level and method of intellectual property protection, and the weakness of intellectual property protection in developing countries. The international community needs to formulate common rules for the protection of intellectual property and technology.

2. Foreign affiliates are usually affected by various local measures such as demand for local content, balanced exports and imports, local sales, and import restrictions. There is an attempt to reduce these trade restraints by treating them as violations of GATT.

3. Many foreign companies, particularly in the field of financial services, transportation, electricity, and communication, are pressing for reciprocal MFN (Most Favored Nation) status and reduced regulations limiting market access.[39]

The new global services economy shifts comparative advantage more in favor of human resources than natural resources. Developing countries still only have a small share of global trade in services, despite accounting for the majority of the world's population. The rapid expansion of trade in skill-intensive services certainly offers a great opportunity to developing countries—if they can substantially upgrade and invest in their human capital.[40]

Basic Labor Standards and Trade[41]

The most common fear among industrial countries over the rapid growth in the developing countries concerns jobs and the environment. Both labor standards and environmental issues are now playing an increasing role in international trade disputes.

In Shenzhen, China, some workers earn as little as one yuan (12 American cents) an hour for working 12–13 hours a day, seven days a week. In India millions of children, some as young as seven, work in carpet and textile factories. In Pakistan and Peru, children are sometimes sold into slavery. Trade union leaders are often jailed or even murdered. Hundreds of workers in the Third World die in factory fires every year. In manufacturing, the risk of being killed in a factory accident is six times higher in South Korea than in America, and fifteen times higher in Pakistan.[42]

These accounts are highlighted, as in this case, in the Western media because they pose the threat of unfair competition and violation of basic human rights.

Poor working conditions in many developing countries create an unfair trade advantage. Industrial countries cannot compete against cheap labor; if such competition is allowed, it will create pressure to reduce workers' rights in industrial countries.

It is thought to be the duty of industrial countries to foster basic human rights. To most people in the industrial nations, child labor and slave labor are repugnant. Imposing sanctions might be justified, except for the possibility that they might hurt the children and their families more than they would help them.

Developing countries are, however, warning that imposing sanctions would deny them access to world markets by preventing them from deploying the only competitive advantage they have: abundant labor. Studies by the International Labor Organization (ILO) show that earnings from child labor may be the only legal source of family income. Thus, when developing countries' governments have banned child labor in response to external pressure, children have been forced into begging, prostitution, or starvation. In addition, if these countries' imports are banned, it will keep these countries poorer for longer, and hurt rather than advance workers' incomes. Thus it is not clear whether a ban will help or hurt the developing economy and whether it is motivated by altruism or is an excuse to protect jobs in the home market.

Environmental Policies and Trade[43]

International trade necessarily creates environmental impacts. Economic growth deriving from trade may result in more ecological degradation and faster depletion of scarce natural resources, and consequent pollution and waste generation. In some circumstances, free trade goals are not congruent with environmental protection policies. Restrictions on the entry of products that do not meet domestic environmental, health, and safety laws, for example, would reduce the free flow of trade.

> *Automobile manufacturers aiming at the U.S. market must make cars that meet U.S. emissions standards. Farmers growing produce for export must ensure that pesticide residues are within the allowable limits of the importing country. Beverage companies selling abroad must make sure that their bottles are refillable, if that is the national law.[44]*

The use of environment-related trade measures must be carefully pursued to minimize disrupting the trading system. Under GATT, countries have the right to impose on foreign producers certain rules for products sold in their markets, so long as the same rules apply to domestic producers. There is always the danger that environment-related trade measures may be abused for narrow protectionist purposes.

> *The U.S. has long maintained that a ban in the European Community on beef produced using bovine growth hormone is really an attempt to protect EC cattle producers from U.S. competition.[45]*

In practice, it is difficult to distinguish a legitimate environmental measure from a disguised protectionist measure. Adverse effects on international trade would be minimized if many countries would harmonize their environmental rules (see Chapter 14, which discusses legislation for harmonization and competition). However, harmonizing environment-related penalties on manufacturing processes may go too far. If one country's chemical producers face unusually tough standards for water discharges, is it right to penalize imports of chemicals from other countries that impose weaker standards? In other words, different standards may be environmentally appropriate. For this reason, the Uruguay Round of GATT would subject some laws to a scientific test— the standards designed to protect human, plant, or animal health, such as pesticide residue limits, should be based on "scientific principles" as well as on "risk assessment, as appropriate to the circumstances."[46]

Understanding the Environmental Effects of Trade. There are several areas where common interests exist between improving the environment and furthering economic development. For example:

- Many competitive nations and companies tend to employ advanced technology and methods in processing their inputs. Policies that would help shift to a knowledge-based—rather than a resource-based—economy are likely to help preserve the environment.[47]
- Environmental regulations may in some cases stimulate the development of technologies that provide a competitive edge.

Consider how the Dutch flower industry has responded to its environmental problems. Intense cultivation of flowers in small areas was contaminating the soil and groundwater with pesticides, herbicides, and fertilizers. Facing increasingly strict regulation on the release of chemicals, the Dutch understood that the only effective way to address the problem would be to develop a closed-loop system. In advanced Dutch greenhouses, flowers now grow in water and rock wool, not in soil. This lowers the risk of infestation, reducing the need for fertilizers and pesticides which are delivered in water that circulates and is reused.

The tightly monitored closed-loop system also reduces variation in growing conditions, thus improving product quality. Handling costs have gone down because the flowers are cultivated on specially designed platforms. In addressing the environmental problem, then, the Dutch have innovated in ways that have raised the productivity with which they use many of the resources involved in growing flowers. The net result is not only dramatically lower environmental impact but also lower cost, better product quality, and enhanced global competitiveness.[48]

Understanding the Trade Effects of Environment. There is some evidence that openness to trade and foreign investment can help prevent or reduce the creation of pollution havens.

> *One World Bank study found the dirty industries developed faster in relatively closed economies such as Latin America than in open ones. Another World Bank study looked at the rates at which 60 different countries around the world adopted a cleaner pulping technology. They concluded that the new technology made its way to countries open to trade and foreign investment far more rapidly than to those closed to them.*[49]

These trends can be explained. First, closed economies protect capital- and pollution-intensive industries more than do opened ones. Second, industries trying to sell their goods to industrial countries need to be sensitive to the growing number of "green" consumers there. Finally, the equipment used by MNCs tends to be newer, more efficient, and hence cleaner than that employed by local firms.[50]

The Way Out for the Labor Standards and Environmental Issues. As world economic interdependence progresses, the demand for the harmonization of rules and regulation intensifies. However, conflicts usually arise in many domains of national policy.

> *In the EC, social issues such as the improvement and unification of working conditions, workers' participation in management and the use of mother tongues were fully discussed, but no easy conclusions were reached. Despite continuous debate, no line could be drawn between those matters which should be decided by international rule and those matters which concern national values or cultures, and which are the sole concern of individual countries.*[51]

There is an objection against the argument that lower standards are giving developing countries an unfair advantage. Since countries differ in factor endowments, goals, and priorities, as Professor Krugman (1995) argues, competition among firms in different countries can never be "fair" in the same way as competition between firms in the same country.

The benefits of international trade come from allowing these developing countries to exploit their comparative advantages—their abundant cheap labor and greater tolerance of pollution—not from imposing identical conditions on them.

We are not talking about narrow economic issues. If the West throws up barriers to imports out of a misguided belief that they will protect Western living standards, the effect could be to destroy the most promising aspect of today's world economy: the beginning of widespread economic development, of hopes for a decent living standard for hundreds of millions, even billions of human beings. Economic growth in the Third World is an opportunity, not a threat; it is our fear of Third World success, not that success itself, that is the real danger to the world economy.[52]

Instead of using trade restrictions to force these countries to improve the environmental standards, perhaps a more appropriate approach would be to encourage them to adopt cleaner methods of production and to invest in their human capital.

SUMMARY

A nation's trade policy determines whether that nation is inward-oriented or outward-oriented. In practice, most countries have employed both strategies with different degrees of emphasis at one time or another. Almost all countries passed through an initial stage of import substitution industrialization in which protection was extended to incipient manufacturing industries producing for domestic markets. Neither inward- nor outward-oriented development strategies are economic panaceas. Both are susceptible to systematic constraints or vulnerabilities, such as recurring balance-of-payments problems, chronic inflation, and the disruption of key trading relationships.

Government trade promotion and assistance play an increasingly important role in today's growing international competition. There are two broad categories of approach used by governments to promote exports—*direct* and *indirect* programs. The direct programs concentrate on the demand side, while the indirect programs focus on the supply side. These two approaches are not mutually exclusive. Indeed, they are highly complementary and interactive.

To ensure that a nation's export promotion strategies are effective, two linkages should be taken into consideration: the linkage between export promotion and import penetration; and the linkage between export diversification and specialization. The former deals with short-term export efficiency, while the latter deals with long-term export effectiveness.

Four critical issues relate to international trade: (1) the general agreement on trade services; (2) economic alignment and GATT; (3) basic labor standards and trade; and (4) environmental policies and trade. These critical issues reflect new relationships among governments and enterprises, both domestic and international. They raise the question of the appropriate balance between collaboration and cooperation, on the one hand, and competition and conflict, on the other, within the world economy.

Chapter 12

Developing the Nation's Macroeconomic Policies

Any nation's competitiveness is really a composite way of referring to the productivity of its multitudinous business enterprises and work environments. Their performance, in turn, depends to a great extent on the nature of the macroeconomic policies that surround them.

The main objectives of a nation's macroeconomic policies are to enhance its economic stability, growth, and welfare. A nation develops macroeconomic policies to deal with the following six challenges, which we examine below.

1. Coping with Inflation
2. Stimulating Capital Investment
3. Managing Foreign Exchange Rates
4. Managing Fiscal Policy
5. Dealing with Unemployment
6. Coping with External Shocks

COPING WITH INFLATION

A nation must pursue policies that avoid the occurrence of high inflation. According to Professors Dornbusch and Reynoso, inflation generally results from the interaction of four factors:

- Deficit finance (which governs the growth of the money supply);
- Financial institutions (which determine the demand for money);
- Shocks to the government budget; and
- The nation's ability to react to shocks by corrective fiscal measures.[1]

The combination of these four factors may lead to mild inflation or hyperinflation.

Brazil is a good example. Its inflation was 2,968% in 1990. The basic causes have been large public deficits at the federal and state levels and deficits incurred by state-owned enterprises.[2]

A high and unstable inflation environment distorts economic decision making, reduces the resources available for development, and shortens the capital market horizons. Gains and losses are more associated with the changes of inflation than with productive effort. One major objective of macroeconomic policies, then, is to coordinate the fiscal and monetary policies geared to enhancing price stability.[3]

However, most governments act as if some low-level inflation is a price they will need to pay for sustained growth (see Box 12.1).

The relationship between the level of inflation and economic growth is not clear. Because they have plenty of room to catch up, countries with lower income per capita can experience higher growth in their "productive potential" when the inflation rate is high than those with higher income per capita. On the other hand, the relationship between inflation and unemployment is somewhat clearer. During 1974–91, countries with low inflation had the lowest unemployment rates. In some countries, the process of reducing inflation pushed unemployment temporarily higher. This does not imply that low inflation was achieved through high unemployment; it favored job creation instead.[4]

To fight inflation, pursuing tight monetary and fiscal policies is not sufficient. Governments should reduce the resulting short-term costs of disinflation by weaning firms and workers off their inflationary habits

BOX 12.1

Zero Inflation

During the past few years, inflation has tumbled throughout the industrial world. In most nations, inflation is back at its 1960s level of about 3%. Some policymakers want to eliminate inflation completely, believing that price stability will lay the best foundation for faster growth. Yet many economists argue that the main problem is not inflation but recession, and that some low rate of inflation may be needed to reduce real debt burdens.

Larry Summers, for example, argues that 2–3% inflation is best. This holds open the possibility of negative real interest rates, which could help to pull an economy out of depression. With zero inflation, real rates cannot be negative: lenders would be paying borrowers to borrow. Moreover, moderate inflation may serve as a lubricant, helping relative prices and wages to adjust more efficiently. Trade unions in declining industries may resist a cut in nominal pay, yet be prepared to allow inflation to erode their real wages. With zero inflation this safety valve would be blocked, resulting in job losses and possibly greater labor unrest.

A counter-argument to this is that, while inflation keeps ticking, the inevitability of annual (or, at best, triennial) pay-bargaining rounds strengthens the position of trade unions. Were prices stable, wage increases would be justified only by a rise in productivity or by individual performance. So unions would play a weaker role, making industrial unrest less likely. There is evidence that high-inflation countries are more strike-prone, that is, the higher the inflation rate, the more frequent wage negotiations must take place, thus increasing the risk of strikes.

Quoted from "Zero Inflation," *The Economist*, Nov. 7–13, 1992, pp. 23–26, with minor changes.

and tackling the institutional rigidities that keep inflation going. The first priority is to remove the temptation to give the economy a short-term stimulus, by making the central bank more independent. Thus the greater independence won by central banks in New Zealand and Canada in recent years, combined with explicit inflation targets, has resulted in decreased inflationary expectations and wage demands. Both countries have reduced inflation to around 1 percent, albeit at the cost of deep recessions. New Zealand is at last starting to enjoy the rewards: output has increased and growth is expected to increase dramatically over the next few years.[5]

Reducing inflation usually involves adjustment costs, because of wrong price- and wage-setting decisions. New Zealand did not manage to escape them. The most serious setback was the wage round of 1985–86 when the trade unions pushed for high wage increases at a time when inflation was starting to come down. The resulting real wage increases produced a spurt in unemployment in the following two years. But now the fight against inflation has been won. The task now is simply to keep prices stable. Few would argue that the gains from eliminating inflation should be thrown away.[6]

STIMULATING CAPITAL INVESTMENT

Capital is one of the most important factors in the growth process. A country aiming at a given increase in income needs to secure a given increase in aggregate capital input.[7] Some studies indicate that technical progress and capital formation are also strongly related. In the United States, 70 percent of the growth in total output during 1964–85 was due to the synergistic effects of technical progress and capital formation. In other words, the economic payoff to technological innovation is enhanced by high rates of capital formation.[8]

The Determinants of Investment

According to Michael Porter, the determinants of investment can be classified into three major categories: the conditions surrounding specific investment projects; the macroeconomic environment; and the allocation mechanisms by which capital flows from its holders to investment projects. Some investment projects may yield higher returns than others, depending upon the industry characteristics, the firm's competitive position, and the specific location (country or region) of that investment.[9]

Each country formulates its macroeconomic policies with different goals in mind. U.S. economic policies, for example, focus first on stimulating domestic demand through management of fiscal and monetary policies. Stimulating economic growth through international trade and investment is the second priority. Thus, international competitiveness was never a primary concern for U.S. policymakers. East Asian countries, in contrast, pursue a different set of objectives. Production capacity in these countries is geared primarily to penetrating foreign markets and meeting foreign demand with lower prices. Domestic consumption was generally ignored in these economies. The primary thrust of the economy was to save, not to consume as in the United States.[10]

The primary function of the capital market is to "mobilize" and "allocate" capital among competing uses. For this to be possible, the economy must avoid high and unstable inflation. Furthermore, a vigorous system of property rights must be enforced. Without well-functioning contracts, investors will not have any incentive to put their money into this type of economic system.[11]

The formation of capital markets is a critical factor for the future economic development of a nation. A trend in the last decade has been the establishment of the capital markets in Asia, with Tokyo at the center, Hong Kong and Singapore as secondary but well-functioning markets, and emerging ones in Taiwan, Korea, Thailand, and Malaysia. By contrast, with the exceptions of Chile and Mexico, Latin America currently has no capital market.[12]

Savings and a Nation's Competitiveness

In general, the wealth which domestic citizens own is greatly determined by their level of savings. Economically, low savings tend to reduce investment and inhibit growth. Socially, individuals with low savings are less likely to cope with economic setbacks such as job loss, divorce, or illness. In addition, if individuals have few savings, the state inevitably has the burden of supporting them through old age at the expense of the next generation of workers.

In East Asian countries, high individual savings created a large pool of low-cost capital. This low-cost capital has mainly flowed to export-oriented industries, permitting these industries to exhibit high levels of capital intensity and lower levels of return on assets than found in the West. Japan is a good example. Its low-cost capital provided the main competitive advantage for companies in the early target industries: steel and automobiles. Due to their high levels of capital intensity, these two industries received one-third of all Japanese industrial capital investments between 1945 and 1985. On balance, a nation with low-cost capital tends to succeed in high capital-intensive industries.[13]

By contrast, the French capital market is underdeveloped. Poor return on investment makes the French capital market unattractive. Furthermore, compared to other industrial nations, investment demand in France is very low. Privately managed pension funds are almost nonexistent. The centralization of retirement schemes by only one organization, UNEDIC, has absorbed almost all cash available in the market.[14]

The combination of low returns and a high cost of capital created in 1982 the worst financial squeeze for French industry. Costs of borrowed funds by French corporations rose sharply. In 1983, the government declared a "moratorium" for debt borrowed at rates over 12 percent. Subsequently, profitability has improved and nominal rates are down, while real interest rates remain high. French companies are not able to be financed at a cost exceeding the rate of return on investment. Fundamental changes are under way aiming to restructure market mechanisms in the allocation of capital and to enhance France's competitiveness.[15]

MANAGING FOREIGN EXCHANGE RATES

Balance of Payments

There is a constant flow of money into and out of a country over a period of time. The system of accounts that records this flow is termed the *balance of payments*. This economic measure is used by central banks to maintain external and internal economic stability.

In general, the balance of payments includes three counts:

1. The *current account*—a record of all merchandise exports, imports, and services plus unilateral transfers of funds.
2. The *capital account*—a record of direct investment, portfolio investment, and short-term capital movements to and from countries.
3. The *official reserves account*—a record of exports and imports of gold, increases or decreases in foreign exchange, and increases or decreases in liabilities to foreign central banks.[16]

The Importance of Exchange Rates

Exchange rates are one of the key linkages between a country and the rest of the world, both in goods/services and financial/capital markets. A country's return on investment is subject to its cost of dollars in relation to world prices. Poor exchange rate policy may lead to lost opportunities and misallocated resources. For example:

• The U.S. policy of continual but uncertain dollar devaluation in the floating exchange rate era of the 1970s and 1980s was associated with higher domestic inflation, and with higher and less stable domestic interest rates. Higher nominal interest rates raised the cost of capital and increased the amount of borrowing needed for financing investment in relatively long-lived assets. The short-term horizons of U.S. managers that many observers criticize are in part a rational response to this increasingly uncertain, unstable, and costly financial environment that results from the U.S. international monetary policy.[17]

• An exchange rate that is kept competitive to gain access to cheap imports (financed by borrowing abroad) may be reasonable in a period of high and productive investment, but it is certainly an abused strategy when used to support a consumption boom. In fact, as the experience of Latin America in the 1970s shows, once the financing stops, a policy of overborrowing invariably ends in a foreign exchange crisis and a massive devaluation. The crisis, in turn, risks igniting inflationary pressures, and massive devaluation represents a cut in the standard of living that brings difficult political consequences.[18]

The lesson from the first example is that greater foreign exchange rate stability may be associated with greater domestic financial stability, thereby supporting more rapid technology development, investment, and trade. The second example emphasizes that exchange rate policy must maintain a competitive, stable real exchange rate.

Alternative Exchange Rate Regimes[19]

Foreign exchange markets can be either *restricted* or *unrestricted* by the central bank. Restricted would mean that foreign exchange is made available for specific eligible transactions and recipients of foreign exchange have to turn it in to the central bank at a specific price.

The foreign exchange market can also be *unified* or *segmented.* In the former, there is only one foreign exchange rate for all transactions, while in the latter, different exchange rates occur with different kinds of transactions. Professors Dornbusch and Kuenzler (1993) suggest that the combination of these two dimensions results in four possible policy options, shown in Table 12.1.

Most developing countries pursued a unified unrestricted regime (case I).* In such a system, the central bank has more policy options. Examples include: allowing a flexible exchange rate clearing demand and supply; fixing the exchange rate; or buying and selling foreign exchange in order to adjust the equilibrium exchange rate level. Typically, under this regime, there will be no difference in the treatment of trade transactions and financial transactions.

In most developing countries, by contrast, exchange rate regimes are likely to fall into the other boxes. The most common is a unified but rationed exchange regime (case III). The foreign exchange has to be rationed because, given a specified price, the foreign exchange is in short supply. Thus, this regime is a reflection of an overvalued currency. This system can be used to equalize income distribution, but at the expense of resource misallocation. To some extent, goods that are not in the import list cannot be obtained; and if the list is not well prepared, it may exclude not only dispensable luxury items but also essential intermediate inputs.

Since foreign exchange is not available for unauthorized transactions, black markets, associated smuggling, and faking of trade invoices often spring up in the regime. Dornbusch and Kuenzler suggest that the government can deal with this problem with various policy options. Examples include: (1) moving to a case I regime; (2) having multiple exchange

---

* In practice, case II does not exist as a system.

TABLE 12.1

Alternative Exchange Rate Regimes

Foreign Exchange Supply	Foreign Exchange Market	
	Unified	Segmented
Unrestricted	I	II
Rational/Requisitioned	III	IV

Source: Rudiger Dornbusch and Luis Tellez Kuenzler, "Exchange Rate Policy: Options and Issues," in Rudiger Dornbusch, ed., *Policymaking in the Open Economy: Concepts and Case Studies in Economic Performance* (New York: Oxford University Press, 1993), Table 5.1, p. 95.

rates for commercial transactions and maintaining the rationing of foreign exchange (case IV); or (3) adopting a uniform rate for specified commercial transactions and another for capital account transactions and all those commercial transactions not taking place at the commercial rate (case IV).

The difference between these policy options concerns the question of whether the policymakers manage each of the rates or whether they manage some and allow the exchange rate to find the equilibrium level in remaining markets.

Overvaluation versus Devaluation

Overvalued exchange rates are often pursued by inward-oriented economies. The rationale is to encourage the operation of local capital-intensive industries (because the price of imported capital goods is artificially lowered). However, one adverse effect of pursuing this strategy is that it penalizes the traditional primary-product export sector by artificially raising the price of exports in terms of foreign currencies.

On the other hand, there is a mistaken belief that countries should devalue their currency in order to improve their trade balance by gaining a cost advantage over foreign counterparts. U.S. policymakers, for example, have had a strong belief that by devaluating its overvalued dollars, U.S. competitiveness, especially in relation to Japan, would be restored. Unfortunately, while the yen appreciated about 50 percent over the last twenty years, the Japanese have become more rather than less competitive, and the U.S. trade balance worsened rather than improved.

The yen's appreciation relative to the dollar reflects the fact that Japan has become more productive and more competitive. In this case, the devaluation of the U.S. currency did not solve the United States' competitiveness problems.[20] In addition, Michael Porter argues that devaluation is detrimental to the upgrading process. It encourages dependence upon price competition, and focuses upon price-sensitive industries and segments while discouraging investment in innovation and automation.[21]

The alternative to a currency devaluation would be to allow foreign exchange rates to fluctuate freely in accordance with changing international market conditions. Among the major advantages for truly fluctuating rates, as some economists suggested, are: simplicity; reduced need for international reserves; independent domestic policies; and continuous adjustment. In practice, however, freely fluctuating or flexible exchange rates were not thought to be desirable. They are extremely unpredictable, subject to wide and uncontrollable fluctuations, conducive to price inflation, and susceptible to foreign and domestic currency speculation. Such destabilizing activity may create business uncertainty, weaken international competitiveness, and hence reduce the level of world trade.[22]

The present international system of floating exchange rates represents a compromise between a fixed (artificially "pegged") and a fully flexible exchange rate system. Under this regime, countries select *target exchange rates* and intervene when necessary to support them. Target exchange rates are chosen to reflect long-term economic forces that underlie exchange rate movements.[23]

Most small developing countries have decided to peg their currencies to those of developed countries or their trading partners. By doing so, fluctuations in the prices of imports and exports can be reduced, resulting in a greater stability of output and employment in the exporting and importing sectors.

Pegging to a *single currency* is generally pursued by small countries whose trade and financial relationships are concentrated with a single trading partner (for example, Ivory Coast pegs the value of its currency to the French franc). Small countries with diversified major trading partners often peg the value of their currencies to a group or *basket* of currencies of their major partners. This basket of currencies enables a country to neutralize fluctuations in export or import prices caused by the changes in its currency relative to that of its trading partners.[24]

Different Countries' Experiences

The Chilean Experience.[25] In theory, a country must continually allow devaluating of its currency when the domestic inflation rate exceeds the inflation rate of its main trading partners. Chile disregarded this rule between 1979 and 1982 when its inflation was considerably higher than the U.S. inflation. As a result, Chile experienced a drastic economic crisis during 1981–84 and seven years passed before it regained the export levels of 1980 (see Chapter 3: The Chilean Model).

The lesson from Chile is that the greater the overvalued exchange rate and the price distortions, the greater the difficulty in achieving domestic and external economic equilibrium. Although there may be considerable medium- and long-term benefits from an outward-oriented approach, the government must continuously monitor the country's real exchange rate, otherwise there will be increased potential for disaster.

The East Asian Experience.[26] Many Asian countries (e.g., Japan, Korea, and Taiwan) have experienced a favorable foreign exchange rate in addition to a lower cost of capital. They have successfully developed a system that separates its international trade and payments activity from the foreign exchange rate movements.

Exporters or banks in these countries are not allowed freely to convert foreign currencies into local currency. They have to transmit the dollars to the central bank and receive local currency in exchange. The central bank then holds the dollars in the form of foreign exchange reserves. A significant proportion of this amount is invested in U.S. government bonds.

By these means, the dollars have never been circulated in the foreign exchange market, enabling these nations to run substantial trade surpluses without any adverse effect from considerable appreciation in their currencies. The resulting undervaluation of their currencies enhances the international competitiveness of their national industries. But it should be noted that the cost of pursuing this policy is primarily borne by domestic consumers. They have to pay more for all imported goods and services.

MANAGING FISCAL POLICY

The Function of Fiscal Policy[27]

"Fiscal policy" describes the fiscal measures that governments use to influence the working of the economy. There are at least three functions of fiscal policy in the capitalist economy: (1) the *allocation function* (smoothing out the distribution of resources); (2) the *distribution function* (smoothing out the distribution of income); and (3) the *stabilization function* (smoothing out economic cycles).

Of these three functions, the *allocation* function is a major government responsibility. In capitalist economies, there are some situations when market mechanisms fail to do the job completely. Government tries to remedy these failures by allocating needed resources in a more efficient manner, first by providing public goods—goods and services that are important to society but are not supplied by the market—and quasi-public goods—goods and services that are only partially supplied by the market; and second by eliminating "bads" (as opposed to "goods") that are undesirable from a social standpoint but are oversupplied by the market (such as environmental pollution).

Income redistribution has also become an important responsibility of government. Professor Vito Tanzi (1991) points out three major objectives of income redistribution: to keep people above the poverty level; to equalize distribution of income or wealth (by using policy instruments such as progressive income taxes); and to encourage minimum levels of insurance against illness and accident, as well as pensions for the elderly (by providing subsidies).

The *stabilization* function did not play a vital role until the Great Depression of the thirties. To maintain or improve the nation's wealth, governments have tried to maintain stable prices and high rates of employment. Public spending, accompanied by regulation of the money supply and interest rates, is the tool used in the stabilization function.

Those who believe in fiscal policy, alone or with the help of other policy instruments, hold that fiscal policy can foster growth in several ways. According to Professor Tanzi, it can:

- increase the rate of savings of the country and channel these savings into more socially productive uses
- generate the means to create physical and social infrastructure

- discourage nonproductive and extravagant consumption and investment
- reduce inefficiency throughout the economy and particularly in the public sector
- maintain a climate of economic stability
- remove bottlenecks of various kinds
- reduce, if not eliminate, growth-retarding distortions introduced by the tax system and other public policies
- reduce, if not eliminate, distortions in the relative prices of factors of production[28]

Fiscal Prudence

Professor Richard E. Wagner has proposed "the law of increasing state activity" to explain the tendency of public finance to expand as economies develop:[29]

The size of the public sector in industrial nations is enormous, ranging in 1992 from 26.2% of GDP in Japan to 59.1% in Sweden. Sweden is exceptional, but all the European nations tend to have higher ratios—typically around 40 to 45%—than either the U.S. or Japan.[30]

Excessive public expenditure and high debt levels hamper longer-term prospects for sustainable growth in incomes and employment for two reasons.

First, without price competition, government agencies (e.g., state-owned enterprises) do not have enough incentives to provide what consumers want, to innovate or to minimize costs of production.

Second, the cost of debt service crowds out other public and private spending.[31]

Cost-benefit analysis should be used to determine the effects of public finance. The government must first estimate the size of the budget deficit and decide how to finance it—through domestic debt, foreign debt, money creation, or a combination. As is known, excessive borrowing may lead to complete credit rationing. Printing money is another alternative, but beyond a certain level, money creation becomes inflationary. The trouble is that many policymakers do not recognize the problem until they have used up all available credit and are unable to print more money.[32]

According to Willem Buiter and T. N. Srinivasan, countries get into debt-servicing problems as a result either of bad luck or bad management. Bad luck includes external shocks such as the rise in international real interest rates, adverse shifts in the terms of trade, and natural disaster. Bad management includes a failure to adjust to world prices, increasingly large public-sector deficits, and exchange rate overvaluation. All these policies induce capital flight or flight into importables.[33]

Professor Todaro points out: "It is estimated that between $6 and $10 billion is fleeing Brazil each year. At least $30 billion is believed to be held outside the country."[34]

Taxation

Social and economic development, particularly in the developing countries, depends largely on a government's ability to generate sufficient revenue to finance an expanding program of public services and economic and social infrastructure development.

Since people alter their behavior in response to taxes, excessive taxes will prove detrimental to output and incomes by discouraging work effort, investment, and the willingness to bear risk.[35] A sound tax system is the cornerstone for growth and stability. A productive and efficient tax system can also provide both incentive effects and equity considerations. And it eliminates the need for inflationary money creation. Tax concessions as well as fiscal incentives are usually used as a means to attract foreign direct investment.[36]

Tax Policies and International Competitiveness. One way a country can enhance its international competitiveness is by fostering high levels of savings and investing. Tax and financial systems in East Asian countries actively encourage and even enforce high levels of personal savings. In these countries, interest earned is tax-exempted while interest expense cannot be tax-deductible. In addition, governments have used consumption taxes as a major source of their revenue. This structure encourages high rates of personal saving and discourages private consumption. In the United States, by contrast, consumer credit is readily available to the average citizen. Furthermore, consumer interest expense is fully tax-deductible in the United States, encouraging borrowing to finance consumption activity.[37]

For capital investment, taxation arrangements affect capital outflows in both source and haven countries. When the effective rate of taxation on investment return or wealth is higher on assets held domestically than on those held abroad, capital outflow occurs. On the haven-country side, low taxation of investment income is perhaps the most effective policy to attract capital from the source countries. Most developed countries have now abandoned taxation of most nonresident investment income. One underlying reason is the international competition for capital. For example, nonresidents in the United States have long been exempted from taxation interest on their bank deposits: the country does not even impose a refundable withholding tax. Since 1984, interest on Treasury securities held by nonresidents has also been exempted from withholding as well. Thus, withholding tax is now applied only for nonresident income from sources such as dividends, interest on corporate securities, real estate, and royalties.[38]

Some tax policies—value-added tax (VAT), for example—play a critical role in the international context by creating a direct, price-competitive impact. Depending on the home country cost structure and the relative level of its currency exchange rate, lower VATs in a country may enable its indigenous firms to obtain a price advantage.[39]

In an interdependent global economy, policymakers should apply any tax policy carefully because sometimes it may produce unexpected and negative repercussions. The United States under the Reagan administration is a case in point:

The Reagan administration's policies were based on the supply-side argument that large tax cuts would so energize the American economy that the budget could be balanced by the end of 1983 or 1984, even as defense spending was greatly increased. The Reagan policy demonstrated the reduced effectiveness of budget stimulus by a single country in an increasingly open global system. The tax cuts stimulated domestic consumption, but by greatly widening the budget deficit, they significantly raised real-interest and exchange rates. Rising interest rates contributed considerably to the debt crisis in the developing countries, especially in Latin America. The debt crisis, in turn, contributed to Latin America's economic stagnation during the 1980s, which reduced American exports to the region and further exacerbated the U.S. trade deficit.[40]

DEALING WITH UNEMPLOYMENT

Drastic population increases without commensurate economic development can cause many difficulties. The economy must create jobs as fast as the people entering the job market. About one billion jobs must be created by the end of the century.[41]

In general, the dynamics of employment and unemployment depend on the rate of job separation and job finding. If these rates are constant, then the economy tends to a natural rate of unemployment. Movements in and out of the labor force also influence the natural unemployment rate.[42] The key to reducing unemployment is to allow productivity, wages, and working conditions to adjust. If this adjustment does not occur, the result is unemployment.[43]

Yet one of the serious problems many governments currently face is the "jobless" growth phenomenon—as employment growth has consistently lagged behind economic growth.

Economic growth alone does not necessarily lead to jobs, as the contrasting experience of the U.S. and Japan, on the one hand, and the European economies, on the other, clearly shows. Over the last 30 years the economies of all these countries doubled or, in the case of Japan, more than trebled in size. Yet employment in France, Germany and the UK is today actually less than it was in 1960, where as in the U.S. and Japan it is well over 50% and 100% higher respectively.[44]

Why the difference between these two groups of countries? The explanation is straightforward. The productivity gains that have driven output expansion has been shared in different ways. In Europe, they have been taken out mainly in the form of higher wages for those with jobs, at the expense of "outsiders" who have found it more difficult to get work. By contrast, due to the weak unionized labor markets and less extensive job protection, the labor markets in the United States and Japan have been much more flexible and the return of higher productivity has spread out in the form of employment growth. Thus, it appears that increased productivity and economic growth contribute to higher living standards while labor market flexibility contributes to higher levels of employment.[45]

At present, many governments are searching for strategies that combine a high GDP growth rate with more job opportunities. The United Nations Development Programme suggests several measures that can contribute to an increase in labor market flexibility. They are:

- Invest generously in social infrastructure such as basic education, relevant skills, and worker retraining.
- Liberalize private enterprise and make markets more accessible to everyone.
- Support small- and medium-scale enterprises and informal sector employment, mainly through reform of the credit system, fiscal incentives, training, real services, and proper legal framework.
- Create an efficient service economy by investing in the new skills required and removing international barriers.
- Encourage labor-intensive technologies, especially through tax breaks.
- Extend employment safety nets through labor-intensive public works programs in periods of major economic distress.[46]

We will discuss these measures in detail in later chapters.

High-Performance Systems versus Low Wages

With growing globalization, there are three ways for firms to compete: by reducing wages; by increasing productivity; and by upgrading product quality. Reducing wages is an inferior solution. Continuously improving productivity and product quality hold far more hope in the long run.[47]

To pursue the high-performance strategy, policymakers must develop national consensus. National policies should then encourage companies to invest and operate in high value-adding activities, discouraging the low-wage alternative as the Singapore government did to shift from a labor-intensive economy to a skilled and high-technology-intensive economy.

COPING WITH EXTERNAL SHOCKS

During the past decades, many countries have had to deal with various external shocks. These include:

Changes in Export Earnings. Booms and recessions in the global economy have generated positive or negative shocks, particularly for many developing countries that rely heavily on the export of one or a few commodities for their foreign exchange earnings. Such shocks are usually derived from unexpected changes in commodity demand and prices.[48]

> *New Zealand's past problems were partly external. Agricultural exports, the source of most overseas earnings, were affected by the closing of the EC market, the dumping of EC surplus, and the decline in wool's competitive position vis-à-vis synthetics.*[49]

Changes in Major Import Prices. The oil shocks of 1973–74 and 1979–80 were detrimental to the terms of trade for oil-importing countries while substantially improving the terms of trade for major oil exporters.

> *The immediate problem created by the oil price shocks concerned the income reductions required to pay for higher priced imported oil. Because of their more highly coordinated policies and flexible production systems, the Japanese absorbed these shocks pretty well, keeping unemployment relatively low and real wage growth relatively high. Since the U.S. had no consensus-based mechanism to negotiate ways of absorbing the shock, it allowed inflation to reduce real incomes.*[50]

Changes in the Cost of Foreign Borrowing. A change in the interest rate in international capital markets can generate negative shock for many developing countries that are heavy borrowers. By the same token, a change in the perceived risk associated with lending to the country could increase that country's cost of international borrowing.

Changes in the Availability of Foreign Credit. During past decades, the international financial system was in an overliquid position, mainly due to the huge trade surpluses of the OPEC economies and an excessive dollar creation by the United States to finance its own deficits in the 1970s. In the 1980s, however, there was a drastic shift from overliquidity to underliquidity—mainly as a result of the steady decrease of OPEC investment in the international banking system and the tight monetary policies pursued by the United States from the end of 1979.

After the end of the Cold War, one major concern of Third World countries is that they will be crowded out of the world capital market, chiefly because of socialist economic reforms which require huge amounts of international financial capital and because of the decrease in the amount of available capital as a result of the slowing of economic growth of industrial countries like Japan, Germany, and the United States. This crowding-out phenomenon will perpetuate high interest rates and, hence, the cost of debt service. New loans will be less available to many countries, thus reducing their ability to finance their current public expenditure levels.[51]

Changes in the Level of Foreign Grants. Sudden changes in the availability of foreign grants or of concessionary loans when those grants are no longer available may force countries that have relied on these sources to reduce their spending.[52]

Apart from these external shocks, there are also *domestic shocks* to be coped with. "Acts of God" such as drought and earthquakes are a common source of economic crisis. Moreover, shocks may also be associated with changes in foreign direct investment, changes in foreign workers' remittances, changes in the level of capital flight by nationals, and so on. In many cases, these changes are not truly exogenous; they are attributed to the governments' wrong policies.[53]

Adjustment to adverse external shocks can occur in two major ways: autonomous or self-correcting adjustment; and policy-induced adjustment.

For the former, the decline in the terms of trade, for example, reduces income and hence expenditure. The reduced expenditure cuts imports and stimulates exports, which, in turn, closes the "resource" gap. There are also indirect monetary effects. The increased deficit in the current account means a loss of foreign reserves. If the country is not following a fully flexible exchange rate system, this will reduce the monetary base and hence the money supply. The reduction in money supply raises interest rates and reinforces the contractionary impact of the terms of trade effect on income and expenditure.

As for policy-induced adjustments, there are at least two means. The first is external borrowing. Adjustment through external borrowing, however, can be very short-lived unless it goes into investment to enhance a country's productive capacity to eventually pay off the loans.

The second means involves restructuring the economy towards the tradable sector, especially in accordance with the changing pattern of comparative advantage.[54]

SUMMARY

The nation's macroeconomic policies should be a coordinated set of fiscal and monetary policies aimed at enhancing the efficiency of resource allocation, the equalization of wealth, and price stability. We examined six fundamental elements of a nation's macroeconomic policies—(1) coping with inflation, (2) managing capital investment, (3) managing the foreign exchange rate, (4) managing fiscal prudence, (5) dealing with unemployment, and (6) coping with external shocks.

If a nation desires to improve its international competitiveness, it is vital that programs be developed to systematically eliminate macroeconomic policy disadvantages. Since different countries have different sets of opportunities, constraints, and competitive conditions, they therefore have different goals and options in choosing macroeconomic policies.

Chapter 13

Developing the Nation's Infrastructure

Infrastructures are needed to enable a nation's wealth-building strategy to be implemented efficiently. There is broad agreement among economists that governments must invest heavily in providing and improving infrastructure, particularly in the early phase of industrialization. In this chapter, we will discuss physical infrastructure, technology infrastructure, human capital infrastructure, and a development infrastructure suited especially to the needs of small business.

DEVELOPING A PHYSICAL INFRASTRUCTURE

Investments in *physical infrastructure* can promote economic development in several ways:

1. Physical infrastructure improvements enable business to be conducted more efficiently and reliably. The resulting decrease in transaction costs will lead to an increase in productivity.
2. Physical infrastructure investments create more construction jobs. It is estimated that each $1 billion spent on physical infrastructure translates into an estimated 40,000 to 50,000 additional public and

private jobs.[1] These construction jobs, however, provide only a temporary stimulus to the economy.

3. Physical infrastructure investments enhance social welfare through their indirect effects on health, safety, convenience, and the general ambiance of a community.

4. Many physical infrastructure investments may boost community morale and create a climate that encourages other investments.[2]

Singapore provides a good example of clear and effective infrastructure development policies that support its business and industrial development.

Singapore has continuously developed and upgraded its ports, airports, and telecommunications facilities. It is the world's busiest port in terms of shipping tonnage. Forty-eight international airlines fly to Singapore, linking Singapore with 100 cities in 52 countries. The turnaround time for a jumbo jet is 1.5 hours. The turnaround time for a container ship is 8 hours, which will be reduced to 6 hours when a newly developed expert system is installed. Its sea-air cargo link enables goods to be transferred from sea to air efficiently. Telecommunications reach 208 overseas destinations, 168 on a direct dial basis. International telephone and telex rates are among the lowest in the world. Some 194 banks operate in Singapore. Another 46 foreign banks have representative offices. Crime rates are low and the environment is clean and orderly. Living conditions are comparable to those in developed countries.[3]

As the cheap labor advantage begins to diminish in other East Asian countries, they too see infrastructure as a key competitive tool. Table 13.1 shows Asian countries' spending on physical infrastructure. China, Asian NICs, and the five nations of Southeast Asia will spend $1.9 trillion by the year 2000, primarily on energy, telecommunications, and transportation.[4]

In other parts of the world, Germany aims to rebuild its Eastern infrastructure. The main issue here is cost: Just to maintain the current level of East German transportation infrastructure over the next ten years will require $61 billion, and an additional $152 billion to bring it up to current Western standards.[5]

TABLE 13.1

Physical Infrastructure Expenditure in Asia (in billions of dollars)

	Transportation	Power	Telecommunications	Other
ASEAN	$ 74.1	$64.1	$21.0	$ 63.3
China	968.4	54.0	25.2	n.a.
Hong Kong	23.2	12.8	1.2	29.6
South Korea	132.3	46.2	32.3	145.7
Taiwan	124.3	28.5	9.6	84.1

Source: Business Week, Nov. 28, 1994, p. 62.

The Transportation System

Ample transportation facilities are critical to economic development, enabling access to resources, goods, and markets. When the transportation infrastructure lags behind an expanding population and economy, the country will begin to fall behind in economic development. For example:

> *Zimbabwe expanded the agricultural sector of its economy to the point that it had excess agricultural products for export. However, of the 1.5 million tons of maize available for export, only a third could be moved to ports because the rolling stock for railroads was so inadequate.*[6]

This problem is not unique to developing countries; even Asian NICs must struggle with inadequate support services:

> *Among the four tigers, Singapore, Hong Kong, and South Korea seem to be pulling ahead of Taiwan. Taiwan still boasts loads of cash and technology, but it is attracting a shrinking volume of foreign investment because of poor infrastructure. Its manufacturers fear that power outages, lack of clean water, and chronic traffic tie-ups will gnaw away at Taiwan's competitiveness.*[7]

The general issue of transportation investment as an economic driver has many elements of complexity: various modes of transportation (such as highways and roads, public transportation, rail, water, and aviation) are involved; services may be provided by either public or private sectors, or a combination of the two; different levels of government with diverse objectives are involved; and both people and goods are transported.[8]

Highways are one of the most essential modes of transportation. Investment in highway programs is a prudent strategy in instances where roads can be built largely with local materials. Roads can also generally be constructed in rough terrain more economically than railroads. Highways foster the development of small truck and bus operations. They can be viewed as an intermediate good used in the production of final goods. Lower transportation costs may lead to lower prices for consumers, higher wages for workers, or higher profits for investors. People thus may benefit from a highway without personally using it. Highway transportation also enhances interregional trade among countries. Unfortunately, however, highway construction in some areas continues to be impeded by "political barriers" established by officials in feuding countries (see Box 13.1).[9]

The Communications System[10]

The communications infrastructure (i.e., telecommunications) means "the facilities necessary for networks that switch and transport voice, data, text or video information among users" (USDA). Communications investment will be required to build the "electronic highways" that are the critical infrastructure for a healthy information-driven economy.

Interestingly, the overall quality of Singapore's telecommunications infrastructure received a score of 96.67 out of 100, followed by the United States and Japan. In addition, 12 out of every 100 Singaporean citizens have pagers, the highest percentage in the world.[11]

The communications network infrastructure of primary concern is the *telephone network*. At present, video services are of lesser importance to economic development than voice and data services, but their significance is gradually increasing as more business and educational video applications are developed. Other modes of communication infrastructure—including coaxial cable and microwave—can also transport voice, data, text, and video, but optical fiber has become the medium of choice in most new high-capacity applications.

Telecommunications investments will probably be effective in fostering economic development in two circumstances. First, where there is reasonable likelihood that the private sector will use the telecommunications to create economic benefits; and second, where the telecommunication infrastructure is planned as a critical complement to other infrastructure or economic development programs.

The Energy System

Economic stability and security require certain and safe supplies of energy. Unfortunately, at least for the next decades, oil will remain the most important source of energy, and the Middle East will remain the main source of oil supply.

Domestically, many developing countries are suffering from an acute power crisis. Even though some countries have a significant proportion of hydroelectric generation, it is highly susceptible to seasonal variations, mainly due to the reduced flows of water and lower reservoir levels. Power generation fluctuates between 30 percent and 100 percent of capacity. Thermal generation is subject to substantial derating and outages for about half the year, due to the lack of maintenance reserves. Thus, a country can be faced with a shortage of power for about six months of every year.[12]

In some countries, electricity is not necessarily a main source of power. In India, for example, in the aggregate, power provided by animals exceeds the power provided by electricity (see Box 13.2).

But for specific uses, in manufacturing, long-distance transport, highways, and other major construction, hydroelectric power is essential. This is why India is expanding this capacity in a big way. Its investments in nuclear sources of energy are also considerable, despite their great cost. The pressing need for oil has led to considerable drilling and oil rigs as far away as Bombay High, a thousand miles into the Indian Ocean.

An effective energy policy should be based on market signals as well as

BOX 13.1

Transportation System: Administrative Problems

Numerous problems occur in planning and managing transportation systems in developing nations:

• *Lack of Integrated Planning.* A common problem in developing areas is the absence of integration between the nation's general economic plan and its transportation plan. In some instances, a transportation program is a nation's only planned project because international lenders are often more willing to provide funds for transportation development than for other sectors of the economy. There is often a tendency to overinvest in sometimes marginal transportation facilities in order to spend available loan monies. Administrators must recognize that transportation is not an end in itself but rather a means toward achieving the general economic goals of their nation.

• *Lack of Model Coordination.* All too often, transport programs in developing countries are designed on a single project basis with intermodal and intramodal considerations being overlooked. This mistake is most frequently made when an atmosphere of hostility exists between modes, i.e., between rail and highway or rail and water proponents.

• *Imbalance in Existing Facility Capacity.* Overcrowded port facilities are, for example, a serious problem in many areas. It is common to see long lines of trucks waiting in streets adjacent to wharves and docking areas. Solutions to relieving congestion at ports include implementing modern material handling procedures and wider use of warehouse fees charged on goods in the port.

At the same time, overcapacity can produce a system imbalance. This happens most frequently when a new road is built or upgraded that is parallel to an existing railway. The probable result is the diversion of freight and passengers from rail to road, which is also wasteful.

• *Inadequate Maintenance.* Failure to maintain a transport system after it is built is tantamount to negative investment. On the other hand, excessive maintenance should also be avoided. At some point, facilities should no longer be maintained and substitute facilities should be constructed.

• *Improper Pricing.* Frequently, administrators do not properly match supply and demand relationships with appropriate price levels. Transportation rates significantly influence both the scope and quality of economic development as well as the use of particular modes of transportation.

• *Too Much Paperwork.* An excess of transportation documents such as routing permits, clearances, and other administrative requirements impedes the effective development and use of transport systems in many developing countries, especially at international border points. Steps must be taken to develop uniform international shipping documents such as waybills, insurance forms, and bills of lading, which will reduce and expedite transportation paperwork, resulting in better service to customers and more profit for carriers.

• *Inadequate Statistical Information.* The problem is not so much the lack of available statistical information but rather its quality. Quality problems include data timeliness, accuracy, comparability, and relevance. The administrators face a serious handicap if they are expected to make sound decisions without appropriate data.

Quoted from Henry W. Wanderleest, "Transportation and Economic Development: Some Conceptual and Practical Considerations," in Erdogan Kumcu, et al., eds, *The Role of Marketing in Development* (Muncie, IN: Ball State University, 1986), pp. 105–107, with minor changes.

BOX 13.2

Bullock Manure

Because the slaughter of cattle is banned in almost all states in the country, India has the highest cattle population in the world—perhaps as many as 360 million. Bullocks are used for plowing fields, turning waterwheels, working crushers and trashers, and above all for hauling carts. The number of bullock carts has doubled to 15 million since India's independence in 1947. Bullocks haul more tonnage than the entire railway system (though over a much shorter distance); in many parts of rural India they are the only practical means of moving things about.

As a bonus, India's cattle produces enormous quantities of dung, which is used both as farmyard manure and when dried in cakes as household fuel. Some studies suggest that these forms of energy are the equivalent of another 10,000 MW.

Quoted from Philip R. Cateora, *International Marketing*, 8th edn (Homewood, IL: Irwin, 1993), p. 216.

---

government-initiated responses. Economic cost-benefit analysis should be conducted to evaluate and select energy-conserving and -producing options. In addition, over the long run, the government should consider the development of renewable energy in order to sustain the economic growth.[13]

DEVELOPING A TECHNOLOGY INFRASTRUCTURE

A country's *technology infrastructure* consists of science, engineering, and technical knowledge available to the nation's industries. Such knowledge can be embodied in human, institutional, and facility forms. More specifically, technology infrastructure can be disseminated directly (in "raw" form through, say, publications) or codified in standards, organized in "programs" (quality assurance techniques), and so on. A unique feature of technology infrastructure is that it requires substantial effort and long lead times to acquire and maintain, but it depreciates slowly.[14]

The government plays a vital part in fostering the proper conditions and supportive environment within which industries can successfully select and accommodate commercial technology. Examples include:

- Building the science and technology community.
- Developing an information base for diagnosing and monitoring the technological competitiveness of various industries.
- Increasing the financial attractiveness of innovation efforts by individual firms, e.g., reducing certain risks to the realization of expected innovation benefits.
- Increasing the array of promising innovation opportunities.
- Attracting foreign scientists and permitting them to remain.
- Encouraging the entry of more scientists and engineers into neglected industrial sectors.
- Ensuring that export control laws and regulations do not disrupt the interchange of scientific and technical information.
- Strengthening government capabilities for evaluating technological improvement needs and progress.
- Supporting universities in their efforts in general research and encouraging increases in basic research.
- Supporting the training and retraining of employees.[15]

Different nations have different approaches toward developing a technology infrastructure. The policy emphasis in the United States and the United Kingdom is on fostering a climate conducive to private firms' investment and innovation. In Japan and France, almost all policies reflect state intervention and industry targeting under the umbrella of "indicative planning."[16]

The main issues related to technology infrastructure development are: (1) the university-industry relationship; (2) tax and subsidy schemes for industrial R&D support; and (3) intellectual property rights protection.

The University-Industry Relationship

The closer relations between higher education, public research institutions, and industry are important in enhancing the technological development of nations.

The shorter life cycle of products indicates that both basic and applied research should be linked more closely in developing new products or processes. Some current basic research in universities may be directly applicable, or applied with some minor changes by industry, and yield economic payoffs. The skills of university scientists and engineers may be enhanced by closer links with industry. In addition, these links with industry may influence university scientists and engineers to shift their focus to new problems or issues of greater concern to industry.[17]

In many Western countries, government policies are striving to link components of their research infrastructure more closely with private firms' objectives and research activities. They provide opportunities for coordinated public-private programs that involve publicly funded research institutions.[18]

The Japanese government, by contrast, has attempted to strengthen support for basic research largely by bypassing the university system. Under the provisions of the *Key Technology Program*, new public laboratories that include substantial industrial participants and financing have been established. Their mission is to create long-term research of interest to industry.[19]

In Taiwan and South Korea, many government research institutes have worked closely with industry to "reverse engineer" products manufactured abroad, as well as to develop advanced technologies that could not be acquired from abroad.[20]

Tax and Subsidy Schemes for Industrial R&D Support[21]

Broad tax incentives and subsidies are usually employed to foster private R&D investment in both industrial and developing countries. In Japan, subsidies and favorable tax treatment for the adoption of advanced manufacturing process equipment are integral parts of its technology policy. In South Korea, almost all industrially funded R&D in 1987 came from low-interest "R&D loans" from state-controlled banks and other sources of public funds. In Europe, many governments have recently provided "targeted" R&D grants to firms for R&D in selected areas (e.g., microelectronics). These government programs augment private-sector venture capital by financing the early stages of innovation through direct intervention. They are also reinforced by preferential tax treatment for R&D expenditures aimed at stimulating private investment.

Another common instrument are government-sponsored institutions designed to improve foreign credit arrangements. Korea's Export-Import Bank, for example, provides long-term credit for foreign purchase of Korean plants and turnkey projects. It has been developed to serve the special needs of domestic industry.

All these policies are designed to overcome market failures in private firms' R&D investment decisions, aiming to reduce any gap between the private and social returns to R&D investments. R&D tax credits and subsidies relieve policymakers of the need to make choices among technologies and markets. According to David Mowery, "many such policies, particularly tax expenditures, do not appear in budget documents as outlays of public funds and thus may be preferred because of their lower political visibility."[22]

Intellectual Property Rights Protection[23]

Entrepreneurs with good commercial ideas often fail to open up markets successfully when they are operating in a poor environment where others can piggyback on their know-how and deprive them of returns on their risk and investment. Such an environment hurts not only their ability to appropriate the economic benefits but also technology development in the economy as a whole.

The two most important factors are the *efficacy of legal protection mechanisms* and the *nature of their technology*.

Legal Protection. The know-how and skills developed by an innovating firm can legally be protected if they are identified as one or another of the various kinds of intellectual property—patents, copyrights, trade secrets, and trademarks (see Table 13.2).

In practice, even when intellectual property protection exists, it does not guarantee protection. Some patents provide little protection, due to the substantial legal and financial requirements for upholding their validity or proving their infringement. Some patents can be "invented around" at modest cost. In addition, copyright protects the expression of ideas but not the ideas themselves.

There are also differences among nations regarding legal protection. Consider the case of patent systems:

TABLE 13.2

Some Comparative Characteristics of Four Types of
Intellectual Property (United States Only)

	Patent	Copyright	Trade Secret	Trademark
Term	17 years from date of grant	Life of the author plus 50 years from date of creation of a work, or in the case of a "Work for Hire," 75 years from date of creation	Perpetuity	Perpetuity so long as the mark does not become generic
Matter that is protected	Invention or discovery must be a new and useful process, machine, manufacture or composition of matter or a new and useful improvement thereof	Original works of authorship fixed in any tangible medium from which the work can be perceived, reproduced or otherwise communicated either directly or with the aid of a machine or device	Information used in one's business that supports a competitive position	Words or symbols
Condition for protection	The invention must not (1) have been known or used by others in the U.S., (2) have been patented or described in a printed publication in the U.S. or any foreign country, (3) have been in public use or on sale in the U.S. for more than one year prior to the date of application, or (4) have been abandoned	The work must be original	Confidentiality	Registration

Source: David J. Teece, "Strategies for Capturing the Financial Benefits from Technological Innovation," in Nathan Rosenberg, Ralph Landau, and David C. Mowery, eds., *Technology and the Wealth of Nations* (Stanford, CA: Stanford University Press, 1992), Table 7.1, p. 178.

The goal of Western patent systems is to protect and reward individual entrepreneurs and innovative businesses, to encourage invention, and to advance practical knowledge. The intent of the Japanese patent system is to share technology, not to protect it. In fact, it serves a larger, national goal: the rapid spread of technological know-how among competitors in a manner that avoids litigation, encourages broad-scale cooperation, and promotes Japanese industry as a whole.[24]

The Nature of the Technology. The efficiency of intellectual property protection is partly determined by the degree to which knowledge about an innovation is tacit rather than codified. Tacit knowledge is difficult to articulate and is therefore less vulnerable to industrial espionage. Codified knowledge is easier to transmit and easy to imitate.

Taking both legal protection and the nature of technology into account, we can classify appropriability regimes into those that are *weak*—innovations are easy to imitate due to their codified knowledge and there is ineffective protection of intellectual property—and those that are *strong*—innovations are difficult to imitate due to their tacit knowledge and there is effective protection of intellectual property.

On the one hand, wide-open international trade seems to increase the pressure on governments to strengthen intellectual property protection, because ownership of such property becomes more important in accessing foreign markets and in blocking non-complying imports. On the other hand, wide openness gives foreign counterparts more opportunities to acquire and copy technologies, designs, and other protected intellectual property. In theory, free trade probably enhances the effectiveness of intellectual property protection, but in practice this conclusion is uncertain.[25]

DEVELOPING HUMAN CAPITAL INFRASTRUCTURE

Economists such as Theodore W. Schultz (1961, 1971) and Gary Becker (1975) have developed the concept of *human capital*, treating education and training as a form of investment generating future benefits (higher income, less delinquency and crime, etc.). Maureen Woodhall discusses how the concept of human capital can be extended from education and training to any activity that increases the quality and productivity of the labor force.[26]

Singapore has produced one of the most substantial changes in its worker-profile. In the 1960s, a high proportion of workforce was unskilled and had little education. Over the last 25 years, the government has invested heavily in education and training. For instance, between 1980 and 1987, total student enrollment at tertiary institutions increased from 22,500 to 45,000. Singapore's first degree engineering graduate output per 100,000 population is 38, which is more than West Germany (13), the UK (19), France (23), and the U.S. (32).

The Singapore government runs specialized training institutes which train craftsmen and technicians in state-of-the-art technologies.

Singapore has training centers in robotics, CAD/CAM design and flexible manufacturing systems. There are programs for the intensive post-graduate training of automation engineers. For skills in short supply, the government has provided generous grants for overseas training. As a result, Singapore's workforce has been rated as the best in the world in each of the last ten years.[27]

The main institutional mechanism for building up human capital is the *formal educational system.* Fundamentally, as George Psacharopoulos and Maureen Woodhall suggest, formal education fulfills a basic human need for knowledge and provides a means of helping to meet other basic needs.[28] Its contributions to social and economic activities are pervasive. Education facilitates the process of industrialization by improving the quality of the labor force. Research by the World Bank (1987:64) reveals that the lack of education is a greater obstacle to industrialization than the lack of physical assets. In addition, education also acts as a change agent in disseminating modern values and aspirations.[29]

It is interesting to point out that Korea's 11% annual growth in manufacturing between the mid-1970s and the mid-1980s was

> *founded on a 1975 educational profile in which 48% of its labor*
> *force had completed secondary education and another 36% had*
> *at least some primary education.*[30]

Even though educational investment by itself does not equalize incomes and employment opportunities across different groups of people, it can help to raise the incomes of the poor if the emphasis is on equalizing the social and regional distribution of education investment.[31] Furthermore, education provides some indirect economic payoffs by improving health, fertility, and life expectancy, and by enhancing the return from other forms of social and physical investment.[32]

To invest in human capital, however, requires paying attention to the distinctive features of human capital:[33]

1. To invest in human capital, an individual must do it in person. This individual's stock of human capital, unlike his or her stock of physical capital, cannot be separated from its owner. It is not tradable, nor can it be transferred to someone else.

> *Most Third World states seek to build up their own educated elite*
> *with knowledge and skills to run the national economy. One way*
> *to do so is to send students to industrial countries for higher ed-*
> *ucation. This entails some risks, however. Students may enjoy*
> *life in the North and fail to return home. In most third-world*
> *countries, every student talented enough to study abroad repre-*
> *sents a national resource and usually a long investment (in pri-*
> *mary and secondary education), which is lost if the student*
> *emigrates and does not return. The same applies to professionals*
> *(for example, doctors or architects) who emigrate later in their*
> *careers. The problem of losing skilled workers to richer coun-*
> *tries is called the brain drain. It has impeded economic devel-*
> *opment in such states as India, Pakistan, Sri Lanka, the*
> *Philippines, and China.*[34]

2. The value of an individual's human capital cannot be sustained beyond his or her life span. It is therefore wise to invest in an individual's

human capital during the period of youth, since there will be more years to exploit the benefit from the acquired human capital.

3. Like physical capital, human capital depreciates over time. Some forms become rapidly obsolete because of new knowledge; other forms may be invariable even as circumstances change. It is thus very important to distinguish between these two kinds of human capital investments.

4. The return on human capital investments will be diminished in the absence of a well-functioning social and economic environment.

Any policies designed to make education more relevant for development must operate simultaneously to achieve two objectives: (1) external effectiveness; and (2) internal efficiency and equity.[35]

The *external effectiveness* of educational investment is usually judged by: the extent to which educational or training institutions supply the needed skills for the smooth running of the economy; the extent to which graduates are employed and are able to use their skills and capabilities at the earning levels they expect; and the return on education investment as measured by the higher productivity of educated workers.

The policymakers can foster education's *internal efficiency and equity* by improving the quality of the school inputs (e.g., course content and teacher quality); revamping structures of public versus private financing; changing methods of selection and promotion; and so forth.

Recycling the Nation's Labor Force[36]

Apart from formal education systems, the government should formulate action programs aimed to make the education system more responsive to the need to recycle the nation's labor force. These action programs include the following options:

Establishing a Committee for Education and Labor Market Forecasts. This committee would focus on labor market gaps, and forecast labor supply and demand.

Retraining for Employed and Unemployed People. Investment should be set aside for the retraining of both kinds of labor. Almost all retraining of employed people can be left to big business enterprises, but the government should focus its support on retraining for labor in small and medium-scale enterprises and on vocational training of unemployed people. Here is one example:

> *As part of a strategy to develop the metals manufacturing indus-*
> *try, Singapore's government established a board in the 1970s to*
> *administer a range of incentive programs designed to attract for-*
> *eign investment in new manufacturing. Training was provided*
> *to enable workers to shift from low-skill employment in other*
> *industries to higher-skill jobs in metals manufacturing. After*
> *several years, the strategy paid off; the industry had grown sub-*
> *stantially, and the board was phased out.*[37]

Professional Upgrading in New Technologies. A program should be organized for the training of vocational secondary school teachers in new science and technology areas.

Schemes to Stimulate the Transfer of Knowledge. The objective is to foster the transfer of knowledge from research institutes to the private sector and to facilitate collaboration among universities.

Importing Skilled Labor and Management Talents

Many developing countries are coping with a shortage of skilled labor and management talent. Under such circumstances, importing skilled people from abroad represents a sound solution. Venezuela provides a good example:

> *Until recently, Venezuela's major employment problem was a*
> *shortage of skilled workers and managers to operate what has*
> *been a burgeoning and increasingly technological economy. To*
> *fill the gap, Venezuela recruited many skilled foreign techni-*
> *cians, expanded its technical education facilities, and sent*
> *Venezuelans abroad for training. With Venezuela's economic de-*
> *cline of the past decade, however, rising unemployment has be-*
> *come the primary manpower concern, though the lack of*
> *technically qualified personnel remains a significant factor.*[38]

DEVELOPING ENTREPRENEURIAL AND SMALL BUSINESS ENTERPRISES

Governments have recognized the value of creating and promoting *an entrepreneurial environment* that fosters the emergence and growth of small businesses. These small businesses implant related and supporting industries into a nation's industrial cluster.

Entrepreneurial Development

Entrepreneurs emerge for various reasons. Certain characteristics that contribute to entrepreneurial success are either innate (e.g., people whose parents owned a business have a higher propensity to start their own business than those whose parents were salaried employees), or culturally determined (e.g., different propensities for risk taking). Yet government policy can play a vital part for two reasons: first, other aspects of entrepreneurship such as managerial skills can be learned or improved; and second, the effectiveness of entrepreneurial talent depends partly on the availability of other complementary resources in an economy.[39]

Medium to Small Enterprises Development

Almost all the members of an industry cluster, particularly the supporting industries, are medium to small-scale business enterprises. These medium to small businesses: (1) create employment opportunities; (2) lead to specialized technological capabilities; (3) foster systematic and balanced industrial development; and (4) expedite technological transfer and the diffusion of technology.

A study by David Birch revealed that 52 percent of all new jobs in the United States were created by firms with twenty or fewer employees. A Small Business Administration study concluded that firms of that size generate about 63 percent of new jobs in rural areas.[40]

Entrepreneurial and Small Enterprise Development Strategies

The development of new businesses requires two ingredients: a favorable economic context and individuals skilled in operating a business. Therefore, to enhance the nation's entrepreneurial and small business development, at least three elements are needed: (1) provision of credit; (2) provision of training; and (3) provision of services.[41]

The Provision of Credit. Of all the measures governments can take to encourage entrepreneurs, probably none is more important than ensuring ready access to capital. A 1989 survey found that almost 90 percent of the enterprises perceived the lack of credit as a serious constraint to new business development. In general, the financial market is very unfriendly to the small entrepreneur—partly because new entrepreneurs cannot offer acceptable collateral and partly because the amount they require is often too small to be profitable. And even if they obtain credit, smaller firms tend to have a cost of fund around one-third higher than larger ones. With difficult access to formal credit, one common mechanism in many countries is a *"five-six"* arrangement, in which a borrower receives five pesos in the morning and repays six pesos in the evening—20 percent interest a day. As a result, small enterprises report that up to 50 percent of the small business capacity is idle because of a shortage of working capital.[42]

To make funds more available to small and medium-size enterprises, a better distribution of assets (such as land) would increase their ability to offer collateral. Moreover, the government can encourage informal credit schemes, such as local rotating savings, credit associations, and group lending schemes.[43] Today these informal credit schemes have partially replaced the moneylender and the pawnbroker.[44]

In local rotating savings and credit associations, a leader of a group of individuals collects a certain amount of savings from each member. The leader then allocates this fund as an interest-free loan to each member on a rotating basis.[45]

In group lending schemes, a group of individuals forms an association to borrow funds from a financial institution. The loan is then allocated to the individual members. By this means, the association is responsible for repayment of the loan to the financial institution while the individual member is responsible to the association.[46] An example of a group lending program is the Grameen Rural Bank in Bangladesh:

The program is designed to help the rural landless obtain credit.
The bank's customers are organized into five-person groups of

the very poor. Each group must demonstrate a weekly pattern of saving before seeking a loan. Loans are first allocated to two members, who must make regular weekly payments before any other members become eligible for loans. The program has been a great success. The Grameen Bank now operates more than 300 branches in over 54,000 villages catering to 250,000 people in Bangladesh. Records show that 97% of all Grameen loans are repaid within one year and 99% within two years.[47]

Apart from informal finance programs, another way to support medium and small-scale enterprises is to combine improved credit availability with measures aimed at enhancing competitiveness.

In Western Guatemala, the weavers of Momostenango use almost 40% of the country's wool to weave ponchos, blankets and other products. But the quality of the wool had been low, and the weavers lacked credit to expand production. In 1986, a foundation with technical and financial support from the government and international donors was set up. A year later, 14 technical assistance centers were organized to help increase wool quantity and quality. Funds of up to $20,000 were available to offer credit to weavers to increase production. As a result of these and other measures, export volumes have increased substantially.[48]

The Provision of Training. A key form of assistance to small enterprises is training—not only vocational training but also the development of management skills. One of the best known training programs aimed at developing entrepreneurial talent in small-scale business activities is the Entrepreneurship Development Program (EDP) in the Gujarat State of India.

The EDP model assumes that not everybody is meant to be an entrepreneur. Selection is made by a combination of screening, testing, and interviewing. Successful candidates then undertake a ninety-day evening program if they have work experience or a six-week, full-time, residential course if they do not. These courses cover such topics as achievement, motivation, market environ-

ment, financing, product selection, marketing, skill development,
management, production, procurement, personnel, legal systems,
and letter writing. Trainees prepare project reports, go on field
trips to selected industries, receive any necessary technical train-
ing in a local industry, and receive intensive one-to-one counsel-
ing. A trainer-motivator assists graduates in applying for loans,
obtaining land and facilities, and marketing their products.[49]

Over this EDP's fourteen years of operation, 3,000 new small business
enterprises, each employing three to five people, have been established,
and nearly 8,000 new entrepreneurs have been trained. Over fifty agencies in more than twenty states in India now run EDPs.[50]

Another promising program is Italy's new Agency for Youth Entrepreneurship. This program provides training and financial assistance for
young would-be entrepreneurs. It is conducted in southern Italy for many
projects, such as the production of agriculture, craft, or industrial goods,
or the complementary services to agriculture, industry, and tourism. Project proposals are assessed by agency experts for their business feasibility
before they are granted public support.[51]

A third model is the Malawian Enterprise Development Institute,
aimed primarily at educated but unemployed youths in Malawi. Vocational training as well as training in business management and entrepreneurship are offered by this program. At the end of the course, instead of
giving the graduates a certificate which might encourage them simply to
go into the job market, they are rewarded with a tool set and loans.[52]

There is also a need for a working system of enterprises with large and
medium-size firms feeding off the smaller ones. In Europe, large companies such as Philips, General Electric, and Olivetti have all established
broad-based technological cooperation networks for manufacturing new
technologies available to smaller companies.[53] In the former USSR, the
state sector enterprises often helped small businesses by lending a hand
in establishing the basis of an infrastructure.

The Provision of Services. Consider the following case:

The manager of a factory in Jiangsu, China, that made shirts for
export had no idea of the export price for his shirts, no idea of

> *how such a price would compare with the price of a similar shirt*
> *made in a factory in Korea or Taiwan, no idea of where they were*
> *sold, or of their reputation for style or quality. He is typical of*
> *small-to-medium exporting companies in China that are asked*
> *by an import-export corporation to supply a particular number*
> *of products by a certain date, and are paid in local currency for*
> *the work. Whether the goods are being sold at a loss, or whether*
> *the factory is missing out on a share of substantial profits in for-*
> *eign exchange is an issue that passes him by.*[54]

For small to medium firms, provision of services is critically important. Examples include the translation of tenders advertised in foreign countries; the provision of information about the technical standards enforced by law in various foreign countries for a set of products; or the provision of quality-testing facilities for raw material used in manufacturing. These real services have rarely been provided by the public sector itself, mainly due to the lack of expertise and finance.[55]

SUMMARY

The government provision of adequate infrastructures in the early phase of industrialization is critically important for economic development. In this chapter, development of four main areas of infrastructure—physical, technology, human capital, and entrepreneurs and small business enterprises—was examined.

For physical infrastructure: (1) ample transportation facilities are vital to economic development because they enable access to resources, goods, and markets; (2) communications investments are essential to build up a healthy information services economy; (3) reliable and safe supplies of energy are needed for sustaining economic growth and security; and (4) well-organized and coordinated distributive systems can facilitate economic development by easing access to goods and services, which implies higher consumption and hence higher investment.

Governments play a vital part in creating the proper conditions and supportive environment within which industries can successfully select and develop commercial technology. Some of these are: (1) enhancing the university-industry relationship; (2) applying tax and subsidy schemes for industrial R&D support; and (3) adopting the protection of intellectual property rights.

The major element in the nation's human capital development is the formal education system. To employ education policies successfully, two main features should be incorporated: external effectiveness and internal efficiency. Apart from the formal education system, recycling the nation's labor forces should be implemented to make labor more responsive to changes in technology and sectoral shifts. In addition, importing skilled labor and management talent might be warranted.

In order to develop entrepreneurs and small to medium-sized business enterprises, at least three basic supports are required, namely, credit, training, and real services. These supports should be applied not only to the formal sector but also to the informal sector, with the objective of promoting the transition from the informal to the formal sector.

Chapter 14

Developing the Nation's Institutional Framework

B usiness in developing countries usually suffers from a wide range of problems, including outdated laws, price controls, unpredictable enforcement of contracts and property rights, unsettled procedures of conflict resolution, and so forth. Yet the growth of global interdependence and the international division of labor demands a predictable and equitable institutional framework. The more predictable the institutional framework, the greater the possibilities for trade, investment, and growth.[1]

The institutional framework environment consists of: (1) basic laws and regulations related to the operations of business, governing such matters as property rights protection, contract enforcement, and laws concerning business transactions; (2) industrial laws governing such matters as antitrust, privatization, prices, wages, and employment; and (3) the protection of consumer and human welfare. In the last case, governments need to establish standards for safety and product guarantees, for weights and measures, and for food and drugs, clean air, and safety in the workplace.[2]

This chapter will examine the following seven major elements of an institutional framework: property rights protection; industrial regulation and deregulation; privatization; industrial relations policies; redistributive development policies; improving women's opportunities; and social cohesion policies.

PROPERTY RIGHTS PROTECTION

Exchange consists not only in the transfer of goods and services but also in the transfer of property rights. Property rights include: (1) the right to the income generated by property; (2) the right to control or manage productive resources; (3) the right to transfer and dispose of assets (by sale, lease, bequest, etc.); (4) the right to trade in (buy and sell) these rights; and (5) the right to acquire or assemble assets and devote them to organized productive activity, including the formation of new firms.[3]

Here are two examples:

The value of a license to operate a radio station would be greater if the owner had a right to sell that license at a competitive price.

It costs more to play golf at a country club than to use a municipal golf course. Privacy is a valuable good that can be purchased at an additional cost.[4]

Property rights reduce the costs and risks of transactions, by providing specific and predictable effects to decision makers.[5] "Knowing clearly who owns what and how goods and services can be used, bought, and sold reduces uncertainty and provides the basis for the specialization and investment essential to industrialization."[6]

To a certain extent, we can distinguish between the function of controlling and managing an asset from the ownership of the asset and control over asset use from rights to receive earnings from asset. These *unbundlings* of ownership rights can be achieved by means of contracts.[7] One form of such unbundling is *leasing*, in which "the owner of land may give up control over its use to someone else, retaining only the right to claim the income from it, through a lease or other tenure and income-dividing arrangements such as sharecropping."[8] Another form is *stockholding*, where "the stockholder-owners of a firm may borrow from other sources of finance (such as bankers or bondholders) under a contract that does not give the lenders any say in the management of the property, but does give them an unconditional claim against the income from the property in the form of interest payments."[9] These forms of unbundling allow agents to specialize in the various functions and responsibilities of ownership, resulting in increasing economic efficiency along the total value chain (from production to distribution).[10]

Different economies can be defined by their structure of property rights.[11] Changing the structure of property rights will lead to a different structure of incentives for management and hence to modifications in both organizational behavior and corporate performance.[12] The question is what kinds of property rights lead to economic efficiency.[13] In the former Socialist countries, public ownership and central planning—in which everybody was in the abstract an owner—failed to provide incentives for economic efficiency. Many governments have recently chosen the path of *privatization*, which replaces public rights with private ones.[14]

INDUSTRIAL REGULATION AND DEREGULATION

For the sake of "public interest," governments usually exercise some influence or control over the price, output, and product quality decisions of private firms. Nations differ in their degree of industrial regulation. In the United Kingdom and Japan, the state refrains from detailed regulation. At the other extreme, in Germany and Sweden, the state lays down far-reaching regulations.[15]

Reasons for Regulation

Free enterprise capitalism generally assumes the norm of an unregulated marketplace. Regulation is then justified primarily to overcome market failures that might otherwise prevent purely free markets from serving the public interest. The market "failures" that usually lead to a demand for regulation are: (1) the need to control monopoly power; (2) the need to correct for spillover costs; (3) the need to control windfall profits; and (4) other justifications.[16]

The Need to Control Monopoly Power. Market power can undermine allocative efficiency by the incentive of dominant firms to set prices over marginal costs. In addition, the lack of competitive pressure further discourages incentives for dynamic and productive efficiency. On the other hand, despite its general advantages, competition is not always for the best. In some industries such as electricity generation or local telephone service, minimum economies of scale are so great as to make it inefficient for more than one firm to be running in that industry. That firm—namely, a *natural monopolist*—can earn supernormal profits by restricting output and charging above competitive prices. Regulation thus aims at improving the "allocative efficiency" of such industries by holding prices down closer to costs.[17]

Coupled with the issue of the desirability of competition, there is also the issue of whether it is feasible (in the absence of government intervention). Professors Kay and Vickers (1990) have distinguished these two questions, as shown in Figure 14.1.

Figure 14.1 reveals three kinds of market failure to consider. First is severe natural monopoly—the case in which competition is neither feasible nor desirable. Antitrust regulation is then the only check on the firm's behavior.[18]

Second is cream-skimming—the case where competition is not desirable even if it is feasible. The issue is whether the competition will reduce the social welfare by either colluding or engaging in predatory practices. One way to overcome this problem is to set up a regulated natural monopoly and prohibit new entrants into the market.[19]

The third is where a dominant incumbent(s) prevents entry—the case

FIGURE 14.1

Desirability and Feasibility of Competition

		Yes	No
Is Competition Feasible?	Yes	Typical Case	Cream-Skimming
	No	Dominant Incumbent(s) Prevents Entry	Severe Natural Monopoly

Is Competition Desirable?

Source: John Kay and John Vickers, "Regulatory Reform: An Appraisal," in Giandomenico Majone, ed., *Deregulation or Re-Regulation? Regulatory Reform in Europe and the United States* (New York: Pinter Publishers, 1990), Figure 12.1, p. 227.

in which competition is desirable but is thwarted by predatory behavior by the incumbent firm(s).[20]

The "price and entry" regulation of airlines, trucking, and ocean shipping was often justified by the asserted need to control "excessive" competition—competition that allegedly would lead to unreasonably low prices, bankruptcies, and the survival of one or two firms, which would then set unreasonably high prices. . . . The argument sometimes amounted to a fear of "predatory" pricing. A dominant firm might set prices below its variable costs, with the object of driving its rivals out of business, later raising its prices and recouping lost profits before new firms, enticed by the higher prices, enter the industry. Most economists doubt that firms can readily set predatory prices in the transportation industries.[21]

In this case, many regulatory measures aim at checking anticompetitive behavior by dominant firms.

In sum, these three kinds of market failure require three different types of regulation: (1) to contain monopolistic behavior; (2) to limit competition; and (3) to promote competition, respectively.[22]

The Need to Correct for Spillover Costs. Sometimes a product's price does not reflect the real costs that its production imposes on society. The prices of automobiles, for example, do not incorporate the "spillover costs" of generating air pollution. Demand for automobiles is therefore higher than in the case where buyers would have to pay for these spillover costs. Regulation, particularly environmental regulation, is a way to correct for the presence of such negative externalities.[23]

By the same token, one important kind of externality in the financial market deals with capital adequacy requirements. For example, if a large number of bank customers attempted to withdraw their money at the same time, the bank would not have sufficient funds to honor their claims. The imposition of capital adequacy requirements creates customer confidence and hence minimizes the chance of a bank run. Capital adequacy requirements are also imposed on financial institutions in connection with contracts for future delivery, including options and insurance contracts.[24]

The Need to Control Windfall Profits. Windfall profits are a form of "economic rent." Regulation is not necessary if windfall profits exist temporarily in a highly competitive industry. In cases where windfall profits are irregularly large and do not reflect any particular talent or skill, regulation may be proposed to transfer what appear to be huge and undeserved profits from producers to consumers.[25]

Other Justifications. Competitive markets need adequate information to function efficiently. Three conditions call for government action aimed at minimizing the costs of obtaining adequate information:

1. Failure in markets for information;
2. Problems deriving from imperfect price information; and
3. Asymmetric information regarding product quality.[26]

There are numerous ways to try to overcome these three kinds of information problems without government intervention. Companies can distribute comparative information; third parties can enter the business of publishing information; and so on. Yet these alternatives are neither perfect nor costless.[27]

Another occasion for regulation is during sudden or drastic price increases or supply failures (such as an oil boycott), which can undermine allocative efficiency in an unregulated marketplace. In these circumstances, regulation is used to allocate goods that are in short supply.[28]

Yet another occasion for regulation is inequality in bargaining power. The aim is to protect small firms, employees, or customers from the power of large firms, employers, or sellers. Labor unions, for example, are exempted from antitrust laws, permitting them to have some bargaining power vis-à-vis employers.[29]

The International Context of Regulation

National regulations can be used as nontariff barriers to protect national industries. Health or safety risks, for example, are often used to exclude foreign products. However, some national regulation only reflects internal needs and is innocently motivated.[30]

Rapid technological change often causes these protective measures to become counterproductive. They suppress technological development by domestic firms and so reduce their long-term international competitiveness. Apart from keeping away foreign competitors from the national market, they impede domestic firms from expanding internationally. State activities to support national industrial development should favor open rather than closed markets.[31]

Professors Kay and Vickers suggest two basic approaches to reconcile international differences in regulation. The first is to harmonize the regulations across different jurisdictions; the second is to permit competition between rules and between regulators.[32] The choice between these two approaches—*harmonization* and *competition*—rests on the following underlying economic circumstances:

1. Where regulation is based on *externalities*, the appropriate geographic scope of regulation is the geographic scope of externalities. If aerosol propellants, for example, damage the ozone layer, this is a global problem that should be handled by international negotiation; competition would be an inappropriate answer. This also applies in the case of audit requirements, rules to maintain confidence in the financial system, and safety rules.[33]
2. In the case of *natural monopoly*, the proper scope of regulation is the scope of the monopoly. If a true natural monopoly exists, then the state has no need to support the statutory entry barriers. By contrast, if there is viable entry, then there is no natural monopoly. The government should seek to remove entry barriers defended on natural monopoly grounds.[34]
3. Where regulation is justified by *information asymmetry*, the competition between rules will be appropriate. Such competition will drive out those rules, which offer protection that consumers do not in fact require.[35]

Antitrust and Deregulation

The role of national antitrust law has been sharply diminished as a result of the globalization process. To some extent, the presence of global competitors makes indigenous monopolies less effective in exercising market power. The increase in global competitive intensity has put more pressure for greater efficiency, mergers and acquisitions, and other actions that result in economies of scale and scope. In addition, the emergence of global industries (e.g., automobiles, steel, and chemicals) makes a high-concentrated industry in one country a part of an unconcentrated and much larger group of worldwide competitors.[36] Thus, restrictions on mergers and interfirm cooperation imposed by antitrust legislation are increasingly regarded as obstacles to enhancing the competitiveness of national firms.[37]

Recent technological developments have blurred the boundaries between different industrial sectors. Firms from adjacent sectors that have experience in the same basic technologies become at least potential competitors in other sectors as well. In addition, it becomes increasingly difficult to delineate relevant markets. Competition in many areas seems, therefore, to have increased rather than decreased.[38]

The more the national markets become globalized, the less the relevance of citing domestic market shares as the basis for antitrust regulations. Antitrust laws and enforcement need to be updated to conform more closely to the new realities of the global economy.[39]

The Linkage Between Deregulation and Less Government Subsidy. Relaxed antitrust legislation has also reduced the need for government subsidies in two ways.

1. Subsidies are one of the instruments a government uses to enhance the nation's international competitiveness. However, subsidizing the same projects in different firms will make an uneconomic use of scarce resources. Yet if the government exclusively subsidized only one firm, it could be accused of discriminating against the firm's competitors. The policy implication of this dilemma is to let the firms cooperate. This cooperation is expected to make the national firms more competitive.

2. Larger and more integrated firms are expected to need less government support in the future, hence relaxing pressure on the government budget in the medium run.[40]

However, an obvious negative consequence of relaxing antitrust legislation is that structural economic rigidities may result in the long run. Consider the French efforts to create national champions by stimulating concentration:

> *The number of suppliers in French telecommunications equipment, integrated circuits, robotics, etc., has been reduced within a decade. In the case of telecommunications, this has been strongly opposed by the French PTT which prefers to deal with more than one supplier to make sure that the most advanced technology remains available and that prices are competitive. This preference resulted in a—still limited—opening of the market to a foreign supplier. The very policy that aimed at mobilizing and concentrating all national resources in order to remain independent thus ironically finally implies an opening to foreign suppliers.[41]*

Controlled Deregulation. Government policies that allow for a higher degree of concentration should be complemented by deregulation measures to ensure continuing competition.[42] If industry deregulation enhances economic efficiency through increased reliance on competition, consumers would enjoy these benefits in the forms of cheaper prices, higher quality, greater choices, and so forth. In the United States in recent years strong industrial deregulation has taken place in securities brokers, airlines, and telecommunications equipment businesses. There has also been partial deregulation in trucking, railroads, financial services, and long-distance telecommunications services.[43]

Some economists advocate that all markets should be free. Yet Professor Kohn (1992) has pointed out that the claimed advantages of deregulation have often proven illusory or short-lived or selective. Here are a few examples:

> *The recent deregulation of the U.S. airline industry has led to lower fares on busy routes, but service to less heavily traveled cities is either much more expensive or no longer available. Precisely the same thing happened when bus companies were able to compete without regulation: they "cut out less-profitable routes, and the cheap service that the young, the elderly and the poor have historically depended on [was] less available."*

> *Increased competition for large depositors has led banks to offer high-interest accounts. But how do banks pay for this? They have either had to make riskier, high-interest loans or jack up fees and minimum requirements on small accounts, thus penalizing poorer people. States compete fiercely for business investment by lowering their taxes. The corporations benefit, but citizens lose critical services when the tax base declines.*[44]

According to Jan Tinbergen, there are two types of markets, "stable" and "unstable," and only the former should be free.[45]

Unstable markets do not necessarily lead automatically to a satisfactory price and quantity level. Because of their instability, agricultural product markets are regulated in many countries. At the world level, the United Nations Commission for Trade and Development (UNCTAD) encourages the negotiation of commodity agreements, as part of an international system of prices acceptable to both producers and consumers.

An instability of prices also occurs in high-fixed-cost industries, where under free competition, producers will continue to produce at prices that are too low. Such producers will prefer collusion or price leadership, but this is illegal in many countries. One way to eliminate heavy losses is to use two-part pricing—a fixed amount independent of the quantity bought, plus an amount variable with that quantity. Using this procedure requires regulation, either private or public. Another way of dealing with these losses is to let public enterprises produce these goods and services. In Europe, both energy and transport are offered by city or state enterprises.

In conclusion, the relaxation of antitrust regulation to reduce competition (as in agriculture) and general deregulation to encourage competition are not necessarily contradictory steps, but might complement each other.

PRIVATIZATION

Privatization is defined as "the transfer of a function, activity, or organization from the public to the private sector," ranging from the sale of the equity to management contracts or leasing agreements with private firms.

Privatization may also involve a degree of market deregulation. The main objectives of privatization are to foster economic efficiency and to increase the extent to which the national economy can truly become a part of the world economy.[46]

Privatization became an integral part of national economic policy in the United Kingdom, which undertook two of the largest privatizations ever to take place—British Gas and British Telecommunications.[47] Privatization efforts have since then spread widely throughout the world. Between 1980 and 1991, nearly 7,000 state enterprises were privatized, mostly in the eastern part of Germany (4,500) and other countries with formerly centrally planned economies. Around 1,400 were privatized in developing countries; 59 percent were in Latin America, 28 percent in Africa, 9 percent in Asia, and 4 percent in the Arab States.[48]

Constraints on Privatization

A number of factors constrain the process and speed of privatization. They can be grouped under the categories of institutional, infrastructure, information, politics, and social questions.

Institutional Factors. In many developing countries, the institutional frameworks are still in transition. The underdeveloped institutional framework places a serious constraint on privatization. These governments need to offer strong evidence to potential investors that institutional reform is high on their agenda.

In general, the more sophisticated the country's capital markets, the easier privatization will be. Divestitures are difficult in countries with underdeveloped capital markets, since prospective local investment is inadequate. Then a disproportionate interest in attracting foreign capital arises. For privatization to be successful, the financial climate in which the privatization is taking place must be taken into account.[49]

Infrastructure. Privatization is seriously constrained in a country whose physical infrastructure (e.g., transport, telephone, electricity, water, and communications) is weak. It is of special importance when foreign capital is expected to be the integral part of privatization. Foreign capital can freely flow and it certainly prefers to flow to the countries with a well-developed infrastructure.

Information. Potential investors need general information about privatization policies and programs as well as reliable financial information on the enterprises themselves. According to the UN Center on Transnational Corporations:

> *Very often accounting information is so deficient in some enterprises that it is impossible to draw up commercial balance sheets and income statements for interested buyers. More important there is often little relationship among the book value of the assets, the value of the enterprise as a going concern, and its sale price.*[50]

Political Factors. A government usually assumes a political risk when it decides to privatize state-owned enterprises (SOEs). This risk ranges from alienating a few high-level supporters to creating popular and widespread discontent. If the government fails to handle questions of pension rights and labor code reforms, strong labor opposition to privatization can thwart the divestment of large labor-intensive SOEs.[51] It is better to consult with the SOE's employees in advance about the possibilities of worker ownership and retraining schemes, as well as the inevitable job losses.[52]

> *Trade unions often oppose privatizations since they frequently lead to job losses. Colombia, for example, was paralyzed for a week in 1992 by a strike of telecommunications workers protesting privatization. Elsewhere, the process has been smoother: in Mexico, telecommunications workers were given credits of $325 million to help them purchase shares in the privatized company.*[53]

A strong political commitment is also important. This exists, for example under military rule in Nigeria, while on the other hand there is no "political consensus" in its favor in India, Tobago, and Trinidad.[54] For privatization to be successful, a government should try to build a broad consensus and to use democratic parliamentary procedures to minimize strong opposition.[55] The government should make sure that the benefits from privatizing will be obtained within a reasonable period in the forms of available and cheaper goods or increasing income.[56]

Social Factors. Social perception regarding privatization may not be sufficiently enthusiastic in countries where the government has long played the central role in economic activity.[57]

A recent Gallup poll, commissioned by the European Community, on the attitudes to political and economic changes in ten former socialist countries found "high levels of satisfaction with post-communist life and gloom," though they believed in a free market economy. Surveys conducted in Poland, Czechoslovakia, Hungary and the former Soviet Union suggested "a strong resistance to wide salary differences and to performance-related pay." Such thinking is not limited to former centrally planned economies. It applied to some others too—e.g., Ghana, Uganda and Tanzania.[58]

For governments that pursue wealth redistribution policy as part of their social program, the presence of a capital market will help to create greater public acceptance of a sale by stock offering. Shares selling through a unit trust or mutual fund can be viewed as a form of saving and thus foster the growth of the economy as a whole.[59]

Privatization: Some Considerations[60]

There are so many cases, as a 1993 UNDP report points out, where privatization has taken place for the wrong rationales, under the wrong conditions, and in the wrong direction. Some divestitures have been undertaken to maximize short-term revenue rather than build a long-term competitive environment. For example, the sale of a company as a monopoly would probably fetch a better price for the government. Creating private monopolies without an effective system of monitoring and control, however, usually results in long-term losses for consumer welfare and in industrial efficiency.

The whole process of privatization should be kept open to outside scrutiny. It should start with a publicity campaign explaining the rationale for the privatization selling procedure, and then proceed through competitive bidding, preferably through the stock exchange.

Governments should not limit their options by selling shares only to foreign investors. A widespread distribution of shares to nationals and foreigners should be pursued—with the objective of maximizing revenue as well as protecting national interests.

INDUSTRIAL RELATIONS POLICIES

A close working relationship between management and labor is a prerequisite for maintaining industrial harmony and increasing productivity. This means that the rights of both parties must be mutually respected.

According to John Wanna, industrial relations can be viewed from different perspectives. The first view focuses on the institutionalization of custom and practice, predictability, procedural mechanisms, and acceptable terms governing conditions of employment. This view is more concerned with the form and means of dispute resolution. The second view focuses on power relations, the generation and distribution of economic surplus, and how industrial relations processes foster or limit the accomplishment of economic goals. This view is more concerned with ends, and the linkages between means and ends. The third view of industrial relations focuses on change. This regards processes of bargaining and negotiation, removing obstacles to change and improving communication procedure. Its consultative nature results in better practice. It is worth noting that these three approaches are not mutually exclusive.[61]

Industrial countries differ in their levels of providing social welfare. Among developed countries, the Japanese social services system is not well developed: employees are increasingly dependent on their company as they grow older. In the United States, the government provides a small amount of social relief, leaving employees highly dependent on their company for Social Security. On the other hand, in many European countries (such as the United Kingdom, The Netherlands, West Germany, and Sweden), employees enjoy an extensive system of social services.[62]

In many developing countries, by contrast, the governments usually limit the rights of workers and suppress the union movement so as to control labor costs. In the early stages of development in East and Southeast

Asian countries, labor unions were given very little freedom. As Professor Prahalad has argued, "authoritarian political systems (e.g., South Korea, China) or 'discipline' (e.g., Singapore) enabled them to marketize the idea of cheap labor and no disruption to work. China may have a very inefficient system but it can guarantee 'no strikes.'"[63]

Consider the case of South Korea:

In the 1960s and 1970s, under the Korean government policy of growth first and distribution later, workers were deprived of their rights. Even though there were basic labor laws such as the Labor Union Acts, the Labor-Management Conference Act, and the Labor Standard Act, which were designed to protect the workers' rights to organize, negotiate, and strike, these rights were not vigorously enforced. In order to weaken the rights of labor, the government enacted the Special Law for National Security in 1971, which made organizing unions very difficult. To further weaken labor rights, the government in 1980 banned national unions and reorganized them into enterprise unions around individual companies. As a result of these suppressive legislations, union membership has declined from 20% of the total labor force in 1979 to about 16% in 1982.[64]

Job Security

The labor codes in many countries generally contain job security measures that set up legal conditions and procedures under which companies can lay off one worker or groups of workers. Even though these procedures can be lengthy, costly, and troublesome for the employers, the cost of layoffs can encourage them to invest in workers' skill development. The assurance of employment can also keep workers with a sense of loyalty. Increased productivity may follow, too, since workers no longer fear that they will be displaced by new technology.[65]

From the workers' perspective, these procedures provide important protection from arbitrary firing or dismissals.[66] However, job security can provide an adverse effect on employment. In the United States, an increase in severance pay from zero to three months leads to an increase of unemployment since employers are more careful about hiring workers. It also leads to an increase in the number of part-time and temporary employees since these workers tend to be exempt from severance pay rules.[67]

A major trend today in both the industrial and developing worlds is that companies are likely to reduce their reliance on a permanent labor force, hiring instead a highly skilled core group of workers augmented by a contingent of temporary workers.[68]

In the UK by the early 1990s, almost 40% of jobs were not regular full-time employment. Others among these workers may be self-employed individuals working from home. But a large number will be engaged through subcontractors. Medium-size and large firms in South and South-East Asia—particularly in garments, footwear and woodworking—are subcontracting a growing proportion of their production to smaller firms.[69]

The substitution of part-time and temporary workers for full-time and permanent workers reduces the need for training because of anticipated worker turnover. A mobile labor force also leads firms to shift their production base to more capital-intensive activities.[70]

Employment Safety Nets

Different nations pursue different policies to deal with unemployment. For example, the Japanese government pursues three employment policies: (1) increasing opportunities for employment; (2) improving the standard of living of the unemployed; and (3) helping the jobless find employment.[71]

For many years, Sweden has run a sophisticated national employment service to match demand and supply for workers. About 50 percent of new job openings are filled by this service.

About 130,000 people, or 3% of the Swedish work force, receive some sort of training paid for by the government each year. The labor market board (AMS) also provides incentives to stimulate the demand for labor where and when it is necessary. This program is most often used for teenagers, who are guaranteed at least a four-hour-a-day job, and for disabled persons. About

> *75% of the funds go for disabled workers to create employment alternatives instead of early retirement and other social programs. The incentives make their work economic for a company, give society the benefit of the productive capabilities they do have, and allow the people to live productive lives.*[72]

In some developing countries, governments have designed employment guarantee schemes through public works programs—doing hard work in exchange for low pay or for small amounts of food.

> *In Bangladesh during the 1980s, 90% of the participants in the Food for Work Program were below the poverty line. In Botswana and Cape Verde, public works programs in the 1980s are estimated to have saved the lives of 60,000 to 90,000 people in each country. In Chile and Peru, such programs helped soften the impact of recession during the 1980s, and in Egypt, the productive Families Program is benefiting one million people.*[73]

In the future, employment guarantee schemes could be expanded beyond public works programs, covering many environmental tasks and the provision of social services. They could also include doing a national service in exchange for a guaranteed education, as was recently proposed by the U.S. administration.[74]

Trade Unions

Trade unions, like many other capitalist institutions, pool the interests of different people to pursue a common goal. When trade unions are aligned with the national goals, they can contribute to economic growth.[75]

There is evidence that potential democratization often leads to more trade union power. In Korea, the political reform in 1987 removed government intervention in labor management practices. With their new-found freedom, workers demanded higher wages and improved working conditions, and undertook collective actions when these demands were not met. As Korea moves toward more democracy, the number of employees joining unions is likely to increase, and their demand for higher wages will be vigorously pursued.[76]

The five countries with the highest percentages of union membership are Sweden (85%), Iceland (78%), Finland (71%), and Norway (55%). Scandinavian countries have combined high living standards with the highest percentages of trade union membership in the OECD (Organization for Economic Cooperation and Development). Also, due to the powerful labor unions, German workers have enjoyed almost the highest wages and shortest working hours in the OECD countries.[77]

Recently, however, trade union membership has been declining in most industrial countries. In The Netherlands, union membership fell from 39 percent in 1978 to 24 percent in 1991. The United States has seen a drastic decrease in union membership, from 30 percent to about 15 percent within three decades. Trade unions in many nations are currently coping with threats from various directions. First, industrial relocations to other regions of the world are likely to weaken trade unions: among other things, capital investment and business development have moved from countries with powerful trade unions to low-wage, nonunionized countries. Second, many governments, particularly in developing countries, have often passed tougher legislation or repressed their workers' organizations in order to attract foreign direct investment. Third, unemployment has reduced the number of workers and strengthened the bargaining power of employers.[78]

Nevertheless, a more fundamental problem is the fragmenting of the labor force. The growing numbers of part-time workers, or those adopting flexible working patterns and the shift to service sectors, make it difficult for workers to form and organize unions.[79] Workers today tend to be more individually oriented. The diversity of jobs makes for less solidarity. As the International Labor Organization's *World Labor Report* pointed out:

> *Working life today is very different from that in the old smoke-stack industries where trade union solidarity was originally forged. Today's workers in manufacturing are more likely to be operating complex equipment, often using computers and robots and developing skills which blur the traditional dividing lines between blue-collar and white.*[80]

Workers performing different jobs feel much less solidarity, their aspirations change, and they tend to be more individually oriented. If trade unions are to be effective in the years ahead, they clearly have to reinvent themselves to represent a new generation of workers.[81]

REDISTRIBUTIVE DEVELOPMENT POLICIES

That economic growth may have a higher priority than equity does not mean that a very uneven distribution of income is good for growth. A more even distribution of income would mean a larger market for products produced by the local industry, which would be particularly desirable if the larger market leads to a greater utilization of industrial capacity and employment. If those with relatively high incomes have a greater propensity to import, then some income redistribution could contribute positively to the balance of payments. In other cases, an increase in consumption by the lower income classes might increase their productivity and incentives. Consequently, the consumption increase might be viewed as an investment since it would accelerate the growth. In addition, an improvement in income distribution might increase total private saving rather than decrease it.[82]

Economists have begun to seek ways to improve distribution without slowing growth. Professor Michael Todaro suggests that the relative price of labor (particularly the wage rate) may be higher than that determined by free market mechanisms. This is mainly due to institutional constraints (e.g., trade unions) and faulty policies. On the other hand, the price of capital equipment is "institutionally" set at artificially low levels by various policy instruments such as investment incentives and tax allowances. If these investment privileges and subsidies were removed and the prices of labor relative to capital were adjusted, producers would have an incentive to increase their use of labor and lower their deployment of scarce capital.[83]

To create employment, Professor Todaro suggests that tax incentives should be designed to affect areas that use labor intensively and where unemployment is high and rising. Construction and the repair and maintenance of buildings is a prime example. For households, tax deductions might be given for home repairs. For firms, tax deductions might be given for certain labor-intensive investments. Infrastructure investment is another area for producing higher employment.[84]

The removal of factor-price distortions and the favoring of labor intensive investments can lead to more growth, higher employment, and less poverty. However, these policies are not sufficient to eliminate widespread poverty or to reduce income inequalities effectively where asset ownership and education are still very unequally distributed.[85]

Redistribution policies, thus, should be used to overcome the wealth concentration problem. One of the most effective instruments is *land reform*. The basic concept of land reform is to transform tenant cultivators into small farm holders, who will then have an incentive to raise production, improve productivity, and increase their incomes.[86]

Under the guidance of the Allied Occupation forces, Japan instituted large-scale land reforms. Land owned by absentee landlords was distributed (with nominal compensation) among the tenant farmers who worked the soil. Thus, there has been a rapid increase in the percentage of farmers who own their own farms. The average size of a farm is about 1 hectare (2.5 acres). This area is quite small compared to farms in other countries. Because of the small size, the farmers have concentrated on increasing productivity through labor-saving devices and through the use of agricultural chemicals and pesticides.[87]

In South Korea between 1952 and 1954, the proportion of cultivators who were owners rather than tenants increased from about 50% to 94%. As a result, between 1954 and 1968, the labor used per hectare increased by 4.7% a year.

Land reform also had a very positive impact on employment in Taiwan. After the reform, the number of people involved in agriculture increased rapidly—from 400,000 to about two million between 1952 and 1968. There was a substantial increase in output, too, particularly from adding new crops. Using multiple-cropping techniques, accompanied by irrigation facilities and improved water management, the farmers were also able to grow fruits, pulses and vegetables. These opened up more job opportunities after harvesting since they required more processing—whether drying, pickling, canning, freezing, or dehydrating. In Taiwan in the 1960s, the number of workers in food processing rose from 11,000 to 144,000. Such increases

*in employment led to enhanced income and purchasing power
for the people.*[88]

To make land reform effective, other institutional barriers and price distortions that thwart small farm holders from accessing critical inputs (such as fertilizers, seeds, credit, marketing facilities, and agricultural knowledge) should be removed. By the same token, similar reforms can be applied in urban areas. One effective instrument is the *microloan*—the provision of financial credit at market rates—to small and medium business, so that they can expand their business and create more jobs for local workers (see Chapter 13).[89]

Improved income distribution also requires more investment in education and skill building, especially creating wider access to educational opportunities. At the same time, the nation must provide more productive employment opportunities for the educated. The return from educational investment will not materialize if the educated workforce cannot find jobs.[90]

Direct and progressive taxation on both income and wealth can assist in improving the living standards of the poor. Government can also raise the income of the poor by increasing public expenditures toward lower income groups. Examples include public employment, public health projects in rural villages and urban fringe areas, school lunches and preschool nutritional supplementation programs, and the provision of clean water and electrification to remote rural areas. Such public policies raise the real income levels of the poor above their actual market-determined personal income levels.[91]

However, one problem with these instruments is identifying the truly poor. In many cases, the main beneficiaries have mostly been individuals from higher deciles of the income distribution.[92]

IMPROVING WOMEN'S OPPORTUNITIES

During the past two decades, striking progress toward gender equality has occurred in many developing countries—particularly in terms of adult literacy and school enrollment. The school gap between men and women was halved between 1970 and 1990; maternal mortality rates also have been almost halved. Among the 900 million illiterate people in poor countries, however, women still outnumber men by two to one; 60 percent of the 130 million children with no access to primary school are girls; and women's wages are typically only 60–70 percent those of men.

Narrowing this gap would not only make for a fairer society but also significantly foster economic growth. A study by the World Bank examined the links between economic performance and gender inequality. The evidence is strongest in the case of education. Interestingly, women's education provide additional growth-promoting benefits. Educating women reduces fertility. Lower fertility implies more capital accumulation per worker—and this raises growth rates per capita. Furthermore, educated women are more likely to raise better-fed and healthier children—who will themselves be better educated. Another interesting finding is that women who are given access to credit generate more economic gain than when men receive loans.[93]

SOCIAL COHESION POLICIES[94]

A plurality of ethnic groups need not impede the nation's wealth creation process if these ethnic groups are mutually respected, and brought into active power sharing. When mutual respect is eroded, the state is less viable, as in the case of the suppression of the Tamils in Sri Lanka.

In these countries, "consociational" democracy seems to be more appropriate than "majority rule" democracy. Power sharing and divisions of jurisdiction are two main features of the consociational model. It rests upon the segmentation of society into vertical groups. Only the representatives of the different groups interact, on the basis of overarching consensus.

Switzerland is often referred to as the prototype of this model. The Swiss Confederation comprises 23 sovereign cantons of which three are divided into six half-cantons, with four official languages. . . . The level of negotiation required to make the federation work, village by village and canton by canton, is very high. . . . Equality of economic status has been a continuing issue, and one which has been dealt with more or less successfully through regional specialization.[95]

As an independent country since 1830, Belgium has struggled for a century with ethnic separatism, stemming from Flemish economic deprivation compared to the more affluent French-speaking Walloons. Three cultural community regions have been created through constitutional engineering, altering profoundly the institutions, jurisdictions, and responsibilities of the state. Each citizen must be a member of a Dutch, French, or minority German-speaking community; and regional governments function in Flanders, Wallonia, and Brussels. Current ethnic power-sharing agreements require constant negotiation, bilingual Dutch-French conduct of all government activities, and a mutual respect for each identity group's needs.

For these countries, good negotiating skills, accompanied by luck, have been very important in turning potential ethnic violence into relative ethnic peace and political stability.

SUMMARY

This chapter discussed seven main elements of institutional frameworks: property rights protection, industrial regulation and deregulation, privatization, industrial relations policies, redistributive development policies, improving women's opportunities, and social cohesion policies.

The growth of specialization, the interdependence of various economic agents, and the complexity of their relationships lead to an increasing demand for legal and institutional frameworks: (1) basic laws and regulations relating to the operations of business enterprises; (2) macroeconomic laws; and (3) the protection of consumer welfare.

Property rights provide for the ownership and transfer of factors of production and goods. The main purpose is to reduce the cost and risk of transactions.

Industrial regulation refers to governmental efforts to control individual price, output, or product quality decisions of private firms, in order to prevent purely private decision making that would fail to take adequate account of the "public interest." The market "failures" that usually lead to a demand for regulation are: monopoly power; spillover costs; adequate information; windfall profits; and so forth.

International differences in regulation may be reconciled in two ways. The first is to harmonize regulations across different jurisdictions. The second is to permit competition between rules and between regulators.

National antitrust law has increasingly come under pressure as a result of certain globalization processes: (1) the globalization of production; (2) the increased cross-border flows of capital, technology, and information; and (3) the resultant rise of the MNCs. The more national markets become globalized, the less it seems justified to take domestic market shares as the basis for antitrust regulations.

There is a conception that all markets should be free. According to Tinbergen, however, there are two types of markets, "stable" and "unstable," and only the former should be free.

Privatization may be defined as the transfer of a function, activity, or organization from the public to the private sector. The intention of privatization is to increase economic efficiency and to increase the degree to which the country can become a part of the global economy. Yet privatization is constrained by institutional, infrastructure, information, political, and social factors.

In capitalist societies, a satisfactory relationship between labor and management is a prerequisite to maintaining industrial harmony and increasing productivity. This means that the rights of both employees and employers must be respected and protected.

In many countries, the labor codes frequently contain job security measures that establish legal procedures and conditions under which employers can lay off individuals or groups of workers.

Different nations pursue different policies to deal with unemployment. Many governments have policies to improve the conditions of the unemployed. Some developing country governments have designed employment guarantee schemes through public works programs.

Trade unions arise to promote and protect the interests of workers vis-à-vis employers. When trade unions are closely in tune with their members and also with the national needs, they can help foster industrial progress. However, trade union membership has been recently falling in many countries mainly as a result of the shift to service sectors, the growing numbers of part-time workers, and the adoption of flexible working patterns.

Economists have considered ways to improve income distribution without slowing growth. Todaro identified four broad areas of possible government policy intervention: (1) altering the functional distribution of income between labor and capital; (2) increasing income at the lower levels through land reform and other measures; (3) reducing the size distribution; and (4) increasing public expenditures at the lower income levels.

Social cohesion policies are also needed. A plurality of ethnic groups need not impede the formation of a stable nation-state if these ethnic groups are recognized, respected, and brought into active power sharing. When mutual respect is eroded or when negotiating arrangements to achieve an appropriate constitutional order cannot be maintained, the state is not viable. Needed is a "consociational" democracy, in which power sharing and divisions of jurisdiction are two key characteristics.

Part IV

SUPPORTING
COMPANY GROWTH
AND PROSPERITY

Chapter 15

Bridging Corporate Strategy with the Nation's Wealth-Building Strategy

A nation's wealth is largely influenced by the activities and scope of its business sector. In a market economy, businesses generate wealth by increasing global value added (which will then be distributed in higher wages for employees, higher dividends for shareholders, higher reinvestment for the firm, and higher tax revenue for the state), and creating work for the businesses in related and supporting industries. This wealth creation process is inherent in any market economy and the role of business enterprises is to exploit the nation's opportunities.

The nation's wealth-building strategy, especially its macroeconomic policies, industrial portfolio, trade and investment strategies, and infrastructure and institutional framework, will affect different industrial sectors differently. The nation's strategy will provide opportunities for some industries and threats to others. Hence, management's responsibility is to formulate a corporate strategy that aligns with the nation's wealth-building strategy.

We see this challenge as consisting of three steps:

1. Assessing the company's business portfolio
2. Identifying the company's goals
3. Redefining the company's business domain

STEP I: ASSESSING THE COMPANY'S BUSINESS PORTFOLIO

Government policies can affect the industrial portfolio of an individual firm positively and negatively, directly and indirectly. This depends on whether the industries in the firms' portfolio are government-supported or government-not-supported industries (see Figure 15.1).

Government-Supported Existing Business

Government can support the nation's businesses in numerous ways. Consider the following two examples:

> *One of the most explicit illustrations of government-supported existing business is the deregulation of the financial services sector. Increasingly, banks can act as securities houses, securities houses can act as banks, and both can offer a bewildering array of financial services. One of the leading UK banks' current portfolio of offerings now includes clearing banking, corporate finance, insurance, brokering, commercial lending, life insurance, mortgages, unit trusts, travelers' cheques, treasury services, credit cards, stockbroking, fund management, development capital, personal pensions and merchant banking.*[1]
>
> *Another example is the Japanese supercomputer project. In 1980, MITI announced the Supercomputer Project whose goal was to develop by 1989 an ultrafast machine capable of ten gigaflops. In 1981, six of Japan's top computer makers—Fujitsu, Hitachi, Mitsubishi, NEC, Oki Electric, and Toshiba—formed the Scientific Computer Research Association to work with MITI on the project. The project conducts joint research at MITI's Electrotechnical Laboratory, but most of the research occurs in the corporate laboratories. The nine-year project was budgeted at $150 million, of which half comes from MITI and half from the six companies.*[2]

When the firm's existing business is primarily in a government-supported industry, the investment decision rests on the firm's relative

FIGURE 15.1

The Corporate Industrial Boundary

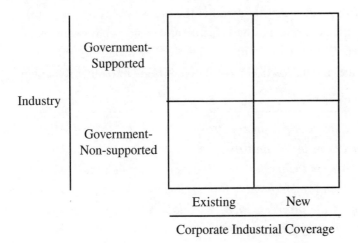

strength and whether the aim is to lessen or promote competition (see Figure 15.2).

If the firm's business involves the government promoting competition (e.g., by reducing trade barriers, pursuing openness policies, encouraging development of new technologies that can replace the old one), the policy will provide threats toward the firm's existing business. If the government policy is to enhance protection or encourage cooperation (e.g., by limiting the number of firms, creating trade barriers, subsidizing R&D), these policies certainly provide opportunities for the firm.

FIGURE 15.2

Investment Decisions in Government-Supported Existing Business

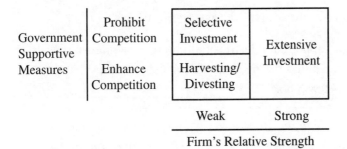

Government supportive measures, combined with the firm's relative strength, determine the firm's investment decisions. When the firm's business is strong, regardless of whether the industry is supported or not supported by the government, the investment decision is to invest extensively in its current business. This can be done by broadening its scope through forward and backward links, or diversifying into other related industries.

The U.S. automobile industry provides a good example. After some relaxation in the antitrust law, the "big three"—General Motors, Ford and Chrysler—got together to launch the United States Council for Automotive Research (USCAR) to coordinate their joint R&D projects, such as collaborating on computer-aided design, recycling, and advanced batteries. Some of these projects' budgets, staffs, and facilities are largely sponsored by the government.[3]

On the other hand, if the firm's business has weak relative strength but the government has a policy to lessen competition, the investment decision is to redefine its current business. Then management should pursue selective investment in the focal industry, supporting industries, or related industries. For example, if the firm is a product specialist, it should seek to capture a profitable segment. It can choose a technology that can produce products differentiated from the competitors or a technology that can produce products at a lower cost for that segment.

If the firm's business has a weak relative strength and the government aims to enhance competition, management should make a harvesting or divesting decision. Management should consider a diversification strategy and search for new business in other potential industries.

Government-Not-Supported Existing Business

Government-not-supported industries fall into two categories: industries in which government has no special policies; and industries that the government declines to support.

A good example of the latter is the Japanese shipbuilding industry which accounted for 40% of the world annual production.

> *The Japanese government is about to end the officially sanc-*
> *tioned cartel which has stopped its shipbuilders from sinking*
> *each other in the midst of a prolonged downturn in world ship-*
> *building. Under the supervision of the official body regulating*
> *the industry, they have reduced the combined capacity of their*
> *yards from 9.8 million gross tons in 1980 to 4.6 million gross*
> *tons today. This allowed the remaining shipbuilders to expand*
> *their capacity to compete aggressively with their Korean, Tai-*
> *wanese, and European counterparts in order to catch up with the*
> *presently increasing demand for ships.*[4]

If the firm's business is not in a government-supported industry, it does not mean that the industry is not attractive. There are two distinctive determinants for the case: (1) the potential of that industry (without any government support); and (2) the firm's relative strength. Considering both factors will enable management to form an appropriate investment decision (see Figure 15.3).

On the one hand, if the existing business has quite a high potential and the firm has a strong relative business strength, management should pursue extensive investment to sustain its competitive position. On the other hand, if the industry potential is high but the firm's business has weak relative strength, management should pursue selective investments, which fit with its corporate competencies.

If the industry has a low potential, regardless of whether the firm's

FIGURE 15.3

Investment Decisions in Government-Not-Supported Existing Business

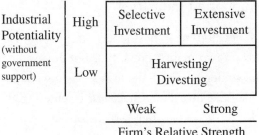

business has a strong or weak relative strength, management should harvest or divest that business and search for a new business which is more attractive. The steel and the aluminum industries are cases in point.

Until 1974, the world's steel industry operated at over 90 percent of effective capacity. Later, utilization rates sank to less than 60 percent. In the United States, after the government refused to install strong forms of import restraint,[5] some U.S. steelmakers began to diversify into other unrelated industries such as oil refining, chemicals, and so on. By contrast, the Japanese steelmakers remained in the industry by specializing in "high-strength" steels, which compete with aluminum in the manufacture of automobiles, containers, and other mass-produced items. Since around 1985–86, however, Japan's five largest steelmakers have diversified into information and electronics businesses.[6]

In the case of aluminum, after the first oil crisis (1974), aluminum smelting has been moving to countries where raw materials—particularly energy—are cheap. In North America, the aluminum industry has shrunk by 12% since 1974; Japan's has been all but eradicated; and with a third of the world capacity, the aluminum industry in Europe has also run into trouble. Regarding the cost structure, it costs only 47 cents a pound to produce aluminum in Venezuela, where energy and bauxite are abundant. In Italy, operating costs are 76 cents a pound and in Spain 72 cents. Even in Germany, where the latest technology is operating, making aluminum costs an average of 65 cents a pound. Moreover, the strict environmental law in Europe will put the European smelters at a greater disadvantage.[7]

Entering Government-Supported Industries

Management's decision to develop new businesses in government-supported industries depends on two main factors: types of government supportive measures; and the strategic fit with the firm's existing competencies. Figure 15.4 illustrates the investment decision in entering the new government-supported industry when the two factors are put together.

FIGURE 15.4

Investment Decisions in Government-Supported New Business

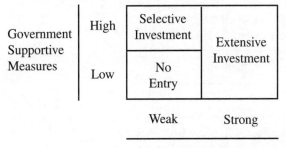

Fit with the Firm's Existing Competencies

If the business fits with the firm's existing competencies, the investment decision is to pursue extensive investment in that industry regardless of government policy.

If, however, the business has a low strategic fit with the firm's existing competencies, and the industry falls in the lessen competition category, which will give the firm the chance to obtain monopolistic power, the investment decision is to pursue selective investment by choosing the product, market, and technology that best fit the corporate competencies.

Finally, if the business has a low strategic fit with the firm's existing competencies, and the government wants to encourage competition, then the investment decision is not to enter that industry.

Entering Government-Not-Supported Industries

If management decides to enter a government-not-supported industry, it has to consider the industrial potential along with the strategic fit with the firm's existing competencies (see Figure 15.5).

If the industry has a high potential and fits the current corporate competencies, the investment decision is to pursue extensive investment.

If the industry has a high potential but there is a low fit with current corporate competencies, the management should pursue selective investment.

For the low potential industry, no matter how high the strategic fit, the firm should not step into that industry.

FIGURE 15.5

Investment Decisions in Government-Not-Supported New Business

Industrial Potentiality (without government support)	High	Selective Investment	Extensive Investment
	Low	No Entry	
		Weak	Strong

Fit with the Firm's Existing Competencies

It is worth noting that sometimes policies toward businesses and industries come not directly from the government itself, but from bilateral or multilateral agreements among nations (e.g., EC, NAFTA). Consider the case of the European Community:

The strategic impact of Europe 1992 hinged on the competitive barriers that would be affected by 1992, and those that would remain despite 1992. Barriers that would disappear included import duties, country-specific product standards, and border documentation. The impact upon a particular industry is then a function of the strength of impact of these barrier reductions. Barriers remaining unaffected by 1992 would include, among others, the need for local language interaction, local preferences for local products, and products where cross-border transportation would be too costly or inconvenient.

Figure 15.6 is a useful way to consider these barriers in tandem. An industry in the top left-hand corner had high barriers to cross-border business which would largely be removed by 1992. However, it has very few other barriers to international trade, and hence it can expect a major impact from 1992. Telecommunication equipment (especially customer premises equipment) falls into the first category as customers are unconcerned about nationally differing technical standards (affected by 1992) that do not affect their perceptions of the equipment's functionality. Where 1992-impacted barriers are already low, but remaining

FIGURE 15.6

Industry Structure: Assessing the Impact of 1992

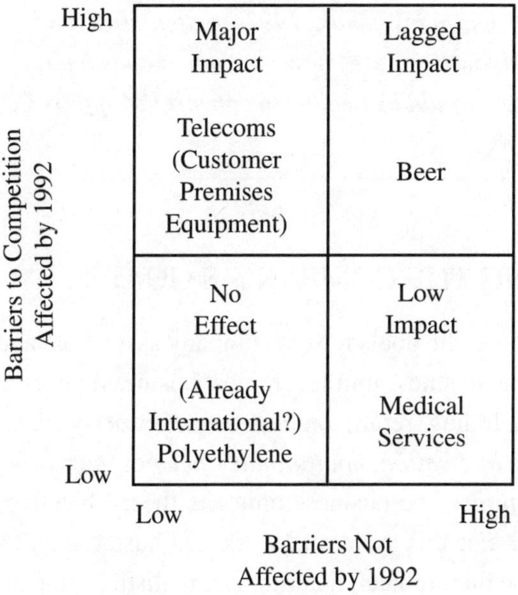

Source: H. William Ebeling, "Positioning Strategies in the New Europe," in Liam Fahey, ed., *Winning in the New Europe: Taking Advantage of the Single Market* (Englewood Cliff, NJ: Prentice Hall, 1992), Figure 9.1, p. 126.

barriers are high (bottom, right-hand corner), 1992 would have little impact. The services provided by local medical practitioners are unlikely to be affected at all by 1992 (bottom right-hand corner). In the bottom left-hand corner, a business like polyethylene manufacture would be relatively unaffected, having a starting point of relatively low barriers—essentially "selling a molecule"—and with few international impediments to trade.

At the top right-hand corner of the figure, "lagged impact" is of special interest because it poses unique strategic challenges. Early on, Germany attempted to ban imports of beer manufactured to non-German technical standards (levels of preservatives, and so on). This attempt was overruled in the European Court of Justice, and beer manufacturers based elsewhere in Europe (EC) are now able to export their beer to Germany. In order to be commercially successful, however, these exporters would have to convince German consumers that they would enjoy the experience of drinking "foreign" beers. This may not be straightforward, given the prevalence of strong local tastes and preferences for beer in Germany. Thus, 1992 created strategic opportunities technically in this case; however, much consumer advertising and "selling" would be needed to convert the opportunity into a profitable one.[8]

STEP II: IDENTIFYING THE COMPANY'S GOALS

The next step is to develop specific goals for the company as a whole and for each business unit. At the business unit level, most businesses pursue an array of objectives, including return *on investment, stockholders' gain, market share, product innovation, operational efficiency, corporate image,* and *working conditions.* The business unit sets these objectives and *manages by objectives.* For this system to work, the business unit's various objectives should be hierarchical, quantitative, realistic, and consistent. Moreover, these objectives have to be coherent with the company's overall goals.

The importance of different objectives not only varies across industries but also across nations. A comparative study of the organizational goals in three countries—the United States, Japan, and Korea—by Professors Chung and Lee (1989) provides interesting findings. Among the three nations, American managers ranked return on investment (ROI) and economic gains for stockholders as the two most important goals; market share, product portfolio, and operational efficiency as moderately important goals; and product innovation as somewhat important (see Table 15.1).

Korean Japanese managers rated market share, ROI, and product innovation as their most important goals. Unlike American managers, they place a high value on product innovation but place lower importance on shareholder's gains. ROI is an important goal for all firms, but they pursue it for different purposes. Americans do it to maximize shareholder value and their performance rating, whereas Japanese and Koreans do it for further market expansion.[9]

TABLE 15.1

Comparison of Corporate Goals

Items	America	Japan	Korea
Return on investment	2.43 (1)*	1.24 (2)	1.23 (3)
Stockholders' gains	1.14 (2)	0.02 (9)	0.14 (8)
Market share	0.73 (3)	1.43 (1)	1.55 (1)
Product portfolio	0.50 (4)	0.68 (5)	0.19 (6)
Operational efficiency	0.46 (5)	0.71 (4)	0.47 (5)
Financial structure	0.38 (6)	0.59 (6)	0.82 (4)
Product innovation	0.21 (7)	1.06 (3)	1.24 (2)
Corporate image	0.05 (8)	0.20 (7)	0.12 (9)
Working conditions	0.04 (9)	0.09 (8)	0.15 (7)

* The scores range from 0 (lowest) to 3 (highest). The numbers in parentheses are the ranking.

Source: Kae H. Chung and Hak Chong Lee, "National Differences in Managerial Practice," in Kae H. Chung and Hak Chong Lee, eds., *Korean Managerial Dynamics* (New York: Praeger, 1989), Table 12.2, p. 172.

STEP III: REDEFINING THE COMPANY'S BUSINESS DOMAIN

After assessing the company business portfolio, which links to the nation's wealth-building strategy and setting up the company's goals, the third step is to redefine the company's business domains by:

1. Maintaining the business in the focal industry by strengthening its existing corporate value chain.
2. Entering a supporting industry by anchoring in the corporate surplus chain.
3. Entering a related industry by engaging in the corporate complements chain.
4. Pursuing unrelated diversification.

Before examining these different objectives, it should be pointed out that there is a major difference across countries in their corporate portfolio mixes (see Table 15.2). The proportion of stars and cash cows is

TABLE 15.2

Comparative Business Portfolio Matrix

STARS		WILDCATS	
America	30.7%	America	18.2%
Japan	23.6	Japan	19.5
Korea	26.7	Korea	26.4
CASH COWS		DOGS	
America	36.2%	America	14.9%
Japan	34.1	Japan	22.9
Korea	36.5	Korea	10.4

Source:Ibid., Table 12.3, p. 174.

higher in the United States than in Japan. Conversely, the proportion of dogs is higher in Japan than in the United States. The proportion of wildcats is much higher in Korea than in the United States and Japan, reflecting the characteristics of a newly developing economy.

Strengthening the Existing Corporate Value Chain

There are two situations in which the strengthening of the existing corporate value chain makes sense. First, diversification is not necessary if the firm's value chain has a strong competitive position in an attractive industry. Second, where the firm possesses a few unique strengths but operates in a medium attractive industry, it may make sense to develop existing skills and improve its competitive position before considering any diversification.[10]

Anchoring in the Corporate Surplus Chain

The strategy of *anchoring* is to consider diversifying into upstream and/or downstream supporting industrial businesses in order to capture more of the surplus value and improve functional linkages. This strategy can be applied in a variety of situations.

First, where the firm is in a highly attractive industry but possesses only average or even below-average competencies, supportive industrial diversification can improve that firm's overall competitive position by enhancing its functional competencies.

More and more Japanese chip manufacturers, for example, are producing a variety of office machines because these machines are now electronic rather than mechanical products. Many Japanese camera manufacturers have also become active in office automation by extending their competence in lens manufacturing into business areas that are related to image-processing technology.[11]

The firm can improve its competitive position through supportive industrial diversification, even where the firm is a weak competitor in a medium attractive industry.[12]

Engaging in the Corporate Complements Chain

One way to strengthen the existing corporate value chain is to diversify into related *complementary* businesses. Potential benefits are expected from several dynamic effects that derive from interactions between the focal and related industrial activities (e.g., economies of scale, economies of scope, snowball effect, fusion effect, etc.—see Chapter 9 for more details). This strategy is undertaken in various circumstances.

First, where the firm has a strong competitive position but operates in an industry of only moderate or low attractiveness, there is the obvious potential to increase growth rates and profitability by applying existing competencies to new, more attractive markets or related industrial businesses.

Matsushita, the biggest Japanese consumer electronics producer, provides a good example. The world market for consumer electronics products is growing at 2% a year, compared with 5% for electronic components and 7% for industrial electronic products. So Matsushita decided to expand its businesses into seven major related business areas—office automation, factory automation, new audio-visual products, semiconductors, housing-related products, car electronics and air-conditioning—to sustain their future growth.[13]

Second, where the firm qualifies as only an average competitor in a specific industry or market which has become relatively unattractive, there are potential benefits to using existing competencies and resources to enter more attractive, related industrial product markets.[14]

Unrelated Diversification

This strategy is to *diversify* out of the current industrial domain by searching for newer and more attractive industries. Balancing the portfolio this way will presumably improve the overall rates of growth and the firm's profitability. However, almost all unrelated diversification inevitably detracts from focus, commitment, and sustained investment in the focal industries. Their disadvantages include: (1) a lack of synergy among the industry and the firm's business units and competencies; (2) unrelated diversification, particularly through acquisition, makes less contribution to innovation.

America and Britain are the two nations in which unrelated diversification has been the most popular and acquisitions are the easiest to make.

By the late 1960s in the United States, mergers and acquisitions had become almost mania. The number rose from just over 2,000 in 1965 to over 6,000 in 1969. From 1963 to 1972, close to three-fourths of the assets acquired were for product diversification, and one-half of these were in unrelated product lines. From 1973 to 1977, one-half of all assets acquired through merger and acquisition came from unrelated industries.[15]

In both countries, such unrelated diversification often led to competitive problems. In the United States, diversification resulted in the separation of top management from running the operating divisions. In the first place, top managers often had little specific knowledge of or experience with the technological processes and markets of the acquired businesses. The second reason was simply that the large number of acquired businesses created an extraordinary overload in decision making at the corporate office.

By the early 1970s, divestitures had become widespread. By the mid-1970s, restructuring has become commonplace. Continuing stiff competition provided the rationale for top managements to reshape and rationalize their business in order to maintain or regain competitive position.[16]

In Continental Europe and Japan, by contrast, many of the strongest MNCs are diversifying into closely related businesses, often through internal development.

In the case of Korea, diversification strategies have been pursued as a part of national economic policy, striving for the creation of world-class big businesses. With governmental support, conglomerations of big business groups (*chaebol*) such as Samsung, Hyundai, Lucky-Goldstar, and Daewoo were able to pursue an "octopus arms" diversification. In early 1991, however, the Korean government forced *chaebol* to specialize more in an effort to improve efficiency.[17]

SUMMARY

In a market economy, companies generate national wealth by increasing global value added and creating work for businesses in related and supporting industries. This wealth creation process is inherent in any market economy and the role of the business enterprises is to exploit these opportunities.

The first step in formulating corporate strategy is to assess the firm's current industrial portfolio. Government policies can affect a firm's business portfolio positively or negatively, directly and indirectly. This depends in part on: (1) whether the kinds of industries the firm operates in or plans to enter are government-supported or government-not-supported industries; (2) in the case of the firm's current business, it depends on the firm's competitive position with respect to its competitors, while in the case of potential businesses, it depends on how well the new business fits with the firm's corporate competencies.

The second step is to identify company business goals. Most business units pursue a mix of objectives, including *return on investment, stockholders' gain, market share, product portfolio, operational efficiency, financial structure, product innovation, corporate image,* and *working conditions.* The business unit sets these objectives and *manages by objectives.*

The third step in company strategy is to redefine the company's business domains: (1) maintaining the business in the focal industry by strengthening its existing corporate value chain; (2) entering supporting industries by anchoring the corporate surplus chain; (3) entering related industries by engaging in the corporate complements chain; and (4) pursuing unrelated diversification. Choosing a single or combined strategic option depends on the industry's attractiveness, the firm's internal capabilities, and the expansion potential of the specific industry. The strategic fit which occurs from the formulated strategy will enable the firm to survive and compete with both domestic and foreign counterparts in the global arena.

Chapter 16

Nourishing Company Growth

S uccessful companies do not only react to changes in the external environment, but also actively seek to create new, internal sources of advantage around their core competencies. In 1990, Professors Hamel and Prahalad wrote an insightful article pointing out that the Japanese have outsmarted U.S. companies by leveraging their core competencies while U.S. companies have been systematically abandoning their core competencies. They define a *core competence* as one that provides a potential access to a wide variety of markets, makes a significant contribution to the perceived customer benefits of the end product, and is difficult for competitors to imitate.

Chrysler, for example, no longer makes its own engines, preferring to outsource them from Mitsubishi. How can an automobile company compete in the long run when it no longer commands the core skills to make something as basic to a car as its engine? Many other U.S. companies no longer even make the end products on which they put their name: Apple's laptop computer, Magnavox's video recorder, and RCA's fax machine are simply U.S. company names put on outsourced products made by

345

Japanese, South Korean, and other Far Eastern companies. All of this portends a "hollowing out" of U.S. technology and manufacturing skills.

In contrast, Japan's Honda has nurtured its major core competence, namely, making engines. Its skill at designing and improving engines has been the basis of its move into such end products as motorcycles, automobiles, lawnmowers, snowmobiles, power tillers, and outboard motors. Similarly, Canon's skills in fine optics, precision mechanics and microelectronics are the basis for its success with such products as copy machines, video cameras, printers, and fax machines.[1]

CREATING THE CORPORATE CORE COMPETENCIES

As Professors Hamel and Prahalad argued, core competence is not merely about harmonizing streams of technology; it is also about the organization of work and the delivery of value. By these means, patterns of diversification and market entry are determined by the core competencies. It is not just the bridge that connects existing businesses, but also the engine for new product and business development.

In dreaming up business as diverse as "Post-it" notes, magnetic tape, photographic film, pressure-sensitive tapes, and coated abrasives, 3M has brought to bear widely shared competencies in substrates, coating, and abrasives and devised various ways to combine them. Indeed, 3M has invested constantly in them. What seems to be an extremely diversified portfolio of businesses belies a few shared core competencies.[2]

The force of core competencies is felt in both manufacturing and services. For many manufacturers, the goal of the core competencies is to build world leadership in the design and development of a particular class of product functionality—be it compact data storage and retrieval, as with Philips' optical-media competence, or compactness and ease of use, as with Sony's micromotors and microprocessor controls. In the services sector such as banking and insurance, increasing competition is generating new demands for marketing personnel able to identify new markets, develop new systems, and sell new financial services (e.g., swaps, futures, etc.).[3]

FROM CORE COMPETENCIES TO CORE PRODUCTS

Prahalad and Hamel dramatize contrasting strategies by offering the metaphor of a tree in which the roots are *core competencies* (basic skills in making engines), the trunk is *core products* (such as engines), the branches are *business units* (cars, motorcycles, and so on), and the leaves are *end products* (Accord, Civic, and so on). Companies that only work at the business unit and/or end product levels will increasingly be at the mercy of those who work at the roots and trunk level of the tree.

A dominant position in core products allows a company to shape the evolution of applications and end markets.[4] In general, core products are developed by two major innovation processes: "ladder" or "technology-driven" innovation process; and "cyclical" or "production and design-driven" innovation process.

The *ladder* innovation process is a linear, step-by-step strategy of technology substitution: the semiconductor replaced the vacuum tube, the CD replaced the vinyl record. The *cyclical* innovation process, by contrast, blends incremental technical improvements from several previously separate fields of technology to create products that revolutionize markets.[5]

Two examples of the cyclical innovation process are:

- Combining optics and electronics created optoelectronics, which gave birth to fiber-optics communications systems;
- Fusing mechanical and electronics technologies produced the mechatronics revolution, which has transformed the machine-tool industry.

In comparison to Japanese firms, Western firms have demonstrated considerable weakness in their management of the "cyclical" innovation process. Culturally, many Western creativity approaches are breakthrough, spontaneous, fission, Cartesian logic, and unifunctional-oriented, whereas the Japanese and many Oriental creativity approaches are followthrough, cultivated, fusion, "fuzzy logic," and multifunctional-oriented. Structurally, America's scientific strength is heavily concentrated in the universities. This, in turn, helps much in the process of idea generation. By contrast, the Japanese technical strength is in entities that are tied to industry or actually in industry. Japan's industries, thus, function extremely well in the process of appropriating new ideas.[6]

In today's competitive world, relying on breakthrough innovations alone may fail because it is risky, time-consuming, focuses on too narrow R&D areas, and ignores the possibilities of combining technologies. To strengthen competitive advantage, companies need to build up both the breakthrough and the cyclical innovation processes in their portfolio of core competencies.

COMMERCIALIZATION OF END PRODUCTS

In formulating its marketing strategy, a company should ask in what specific ways it can obtain a competitive advantage. The number of differentiation opportunities varies with the type of industry. There are industries that present numerous opportunities for differentiation and those that present few opportunities. The Boston Consulting Group distinguished four types of industries based on the number of available competitive advantages and their size (see Figure 16.1):

• *Volume Industry*: A volume industry is one in which companies can gain only a few, but rather large, advantages. An example is the construction equipment industry, where a company can strive for the low-cost po-

FIGURE 16.1

The Boston Consulting Group

		Number of Approaches to Achieve Advantage	
		Few	Many
Size of the Advantage	Large	Volume	Specialized
	Small	Stalemated	Fragmented

Source: Philip Kotler, *Marketing Management: Analysis, Planning, Implementation and Control*, 9th edn (Upper Saddle River, NJ: Prentice Hall, 1997), Figure 10.1, p. 282.

sition or the highly differentiated position and win "big" on either basis. Here profitability is correlated with company size and market share.

• *Stalemated Industry*: A stalemated industry is one in which there are few potential advantages and each is small. An example is the steel industry, where it is difficult to differentiate the product or lower its manufacturing cost. The company can try to hire better salespeople, entertain more lavishly, and the like, but these are small advantages. Here profitability is less related to company market share.

• *Fragmented Industry*: A fragmented industry is one in which companies face many opportunities for differentiation, but each opportunity is small. A restaurant, for example, can differentiate in many ways but end up not gaining a large market share. Profitability is not related to scale—both small and large restaurants can be profitable or unprofitable.

• *Specialized Industry*: A specialized industry is one in which companies face many differentiation opportunities, and each differentiation can have a high payoff. An example would be companies making specialized machinery for selected market segments. Some small companies can be as profitable as some large companies; Germany's *Mittelstand* companies are an example of small global-niching companies enjoying high profits.

Thus, not every company faces a plethora of cost-reducing or benefit-building opportunities for gaining competitive advantage. Some companies will find many minor advantages available, but all are highly imitable and therefore perishable. One solution for these companies is continually to identify new potential advantages and introduce them one by one to keep the competitors off balance. These companies need to "routinize" the innovation process, expecting not so much to achieve a major sustainable advantage but rather to gain market share by introducing many small differences over time.

Here are four differentiation strategies the firm can pursue to enhance its competitive advantage.

1. Changing the Terms of Engagement

A company can enhance its competitive advantage by refusing to accept the conventional definition of industry and segment boundaries, or what

Professors Hamel and Prahalad called "changing the terms of engagement." Canon's entry into the copier business illustrates this approach:

*During the 1970s, both Kodak and IBM tried to match Xerox's
business system in terms of segmentation, products, distribution,
service, and pricing. As a result, Xerox had no trouble decoding
the new entrants' inventions and developing countermoves. IBM
eventually withdrew from the copier business, while Kodak remains a distant second in the large copier market that Xerox still
dominates.*

*Canon, by contrast, changed the terms of competitive engage-
ment. While Xerox built a wide range of copiers, Canon standardized machines and components to reduce costs. Canon
chose to distribute through office-product dealers rather than try
to match Xerox's huge direct sales force. It also avoided the need
to create a national service network by designing reliability and
serviceability into its product and then delegating service responsibility to the dealers. Canon copiers were sold rather than
leased, freeing Canon from the burden of financing the lease
base. Finally, instead of selling to the heads of corporate dupli-
cating departments, Canon appealed to secretaries and department managers who wanted distributed copying. At each stage,
Canon neatly sidestepped a potential barrier to entry.*

*Canon's experience suggests that there is an important dis-
tinction between barriers to entry and barriers to imitation.
Competitors that tried to match Xerox's business system had to
pay the same entry costs—the barriers to imitation were high.
But Canon dramatically reduced the barriers to entry by changing the rules of the game.*

*Changing the rules also short-circuited Xerox's ability to re-
taliate quickly against its new rival. Confronted with the need to
rethink its business strategy and organization, Xerox was para-
lyzed for a time. Xerox managers realized that the faster they
downsized the product line, developed new channels, and improved reliability, the faster they would erode the company's traditional profit base. What might have been seen as critical
success factors—Xerox's national sales force and service net-*

*work, its large installed base of leased machines and its reliance
on service revenues—instead became barriers to retaliation. In
this sense, competitive innovation happens not by matching the
leader's capabilities but by developing contrasting capabilities
of one's own.*[7]

2. Building Quality and Innovation into Product

Michael Treacy and Fred Wiersema (1993) recently distinguished three
strategies that lead to successful differentiation and market leadership.[8]

- *Operational excellence*: providing customers with reliable products or
  services at competitive prices and easy availability. Examples: Dell
  Computer, Wal-Mart, American Airlines, Federal Express.
- *Customer intimacy*: knowing customers intimately and being able to
  respond quickly to their specific and special needs. Examples: Home
  Depot, Staples, Ciba-Geigy, Kraft.
- *Product leadership*: offering customers innovative products and services that enhance the customer's utility and outperform competitors'
  products. Examples: Nike, Apple, and Sony.

*With the rising wage scale and high yen, the Japanese are no
longer capable of being the low cost producer. They look beyond
low cost by building some combination of operational excellence, customer intimacy, and product leadership into their
products.*

*Consider Japan's strategy in the U.S. automobile market,
where the two fastest growing segments are sporty cars and luxury automobiles. These burgeoning segments are dominated by
European car manufacturers. Japanese auto companies introduced Lexus, Infinity, Acura, and Miata into the market, providing European luxury styling and power at affordable prices.
They pay great attention to detail in basic design.*

*Mazda, for example, exhaustively used the concept of kansei
engineering in designing the Miata. Mazda tested over 150 potential tunings for the Miata's exhaust system. This was done to
match the sound of the Miata to the consumer's perceived idea of*

what a roadster should sound like. Would any American automobile manufacturer be this meticulous? Not likely. The sound of an exhaust system is presumably a trivial and unimportant detail. But this is exactly why Japanese new products excel. They provide consumers with unexpected touches of quality that go beyond the obvious.[9]

3. Skillful Positioning

Positioning is the act of designing the company's offer and image so that it occupies a distinct and valued place in the target customers' minds. The word "positioning" was popularized by two advertising executives, Al Ries and Jack Trout. They see positioning as a creative exercise done with an existing brand; they argue that well-known brands generally have a position in the minds of consumers. "Hertz is thought of as the world's largest auto-rental agency, Coca-Cola as the world's largest soft-drink company, Porsche as one of the world's best sport cars, and so on."[10]

These brands own those positions and it would be difficult for a competitor to steal these positions. A competitor has only three strategy options.

One strategy is for a brand to strengthen its own current position in the mind of consumers. Thus Avis took its second position in the auto rental business and made a strong point about it: "We're number two. We try harder." This is believable to the consumer. And 7-Up capitalized on the fact that it was not a cola soft drink by advertising itself as the Uncola.

The second strategy is to search for a new unoccupied position that is valued by enough consumers and to grab it. Ries and Trout call it *cherchez creneau*, or "look for the hole." Find the hole in the market and fill it. Thus Milky Way candy wanted to strengthen its market share against Hershey. Its marketers noticed that most candy bars were eaten within a minute once they were opened, but Milky Way lasted longer. So they went after the position "last longer," which no competitor owned.

The third strategy is to position or reposition the competition. Most U.S. buyers of dinnerware thought that Lenox china and Royal Doulton both came from England. Royal Doulton put out ads showing that Lenox china was made in New Jersey, but theirs came from England.

The fourth strategy, not mentioned by Ries and Trout, can be called "the exclusive club strategy." It can be developed by a company when a number-one position along some meaningful attribute cannot be achieved. A company can promote the idea that it is one of the Big Three, Big Eight, and so on. The Big Three idea was invented by the third-largest auto firm, Chrysler, and the Big Eight idea was invented by the eighth-largest accounting firm (the market leader never invents this concept). The implication is that those in the club are the "best."

4. Cost Containment

Apart from differentiation, cost reduction is another strategy designed to create a competitive advantage for the firm. In the Japanese product development process (see Figure 16.2), the price at which the product is most likely to appeal to potential buyers will first be determined. After deducting the desired profit margin from this price level, design and marketing elements that make up the product's costs will then be estimated. Each element is further broken down to estimate the cost of each component that goes into the finished product. Intense negotiations are then conducted between the company and its suppliers, and among departments. At the end, compromises and trade-offs by product designers, process engineers, and marketing specialists generally produce a projected cost that falls within close range of the original target price.

This is significantly different from standard practice in many Western companies. The latter designs a product by passing it from one department to another—from engineering, to manufacturing, to marketing, and so on. At the end of the design phase, the accountants announce what the cost will be. Then the manufacturer adds a markup to arrive at the price. Too often, the price is higher than the target market would pay.[11]

PENETRATING THE GLOBAL MARKET

The Japanese achieved global market leadership in industries thought by others to be "mature" and dominated by impregnable giants: autos, motorcycles, watches, cameras, optical instruments, steel shipbuilding, musical instruments, zippers, radios, television, VCRs, hand calculators, and so on. Japanese firms are currently moving into the number-two

FIGURE 16.2

Product Development Process—United States and Japan

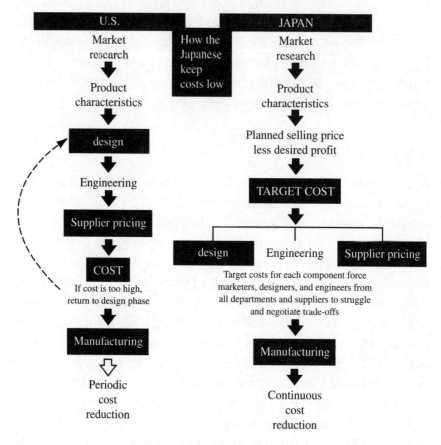

Source: Ford S. Worthy, "Japan's Smart Secret Weapon," *Fortune,* Aug. 12, 1991, p. 73.

position in computers and construction equipment, and making strong inroads into the chemical, rubber tire, pharmaceutical, and machine-tool industries. They are building a stronger position in designer clothing and cosmetics and slowly moving into aircraft manufacture.

One of the main keys to Japan's performance is its skill in marketing strategy formulation and implementation.[12] The Japanese came to the United States to study marketing and went home understanding its principles better than many U.S. companies did. The Japanese know how to (1) *select a market*; (2) *enter it*; (3) *build their market share*; and (4) *protect their leadership position* against competitors' attacks.

Selecting Markets

The Japanese government and companies work hard to identify attractive global markets. They favor global industries that are capital-intensive and knowledge-intensive but that require only small quantities of natural resources. Candidates include consumer electronics, cameras, watches, motorcycles, and pharmaceuticals. They prefer product markets that are in a state of technological evolution. They also identify product markets where consumers are dissatisfied and the market leaders are complacent or underfinanced. They adopt a strategic intent to dominate these industries and reduce or destroy competition.

Entering Markets

The Japanese send study teams into the target country to spend several weeks or months evaluating the market and figuring out a strategy. They study and license existing technology from abroad. They manufacture first in Japan and build their base, discouraging foreign competitors from selling in Japan through a variety of tariff and nontariff barriers. They often enter a foreign market by selling their products to a private brander, such as an American department store or manufacturer. Later, they will introduce their own brand—a low-price, stripped-down product, or a product as good as the competitors' but priced lower, or a product exhibiting higher quality or new features or designs.

The Japanese proceed to line up good distribution in order to provide reliable service to their customers. They rely on advertising to bring their products to the public's attention. A key characteristic of their entry strategy is to build market share rather than early profits. The Japanese are patient capitalists who will wait even a decade before realizing their profits.

Building Market Share

Once Japanese firms gain a market foothold, they direct their energies toward expanding their market share. They rely on product and market development strategies. They pour money into product improvement, product upgrading, and product proliferation, so that they can offer more and better things than the competition. They spot new opportunities through market segmentation and sequence market development across a number of countries, with the aim of building a network of world markets and production locations. They gain further volume through an aggressive program of buying up competitors or joint-venturing with them.

Protecting Leadership Positions

Once the Japanese achieve market domination, they find themselves in the role of defenders rather than attackers. The Japanese defense strategy is a good offense through continuous product development and refined market segmentation. Japanese firms use two market-oriented principles to maintain their leadership. The first is known as "zero-customer-feedback time," whereby they survey recent customers to find out how they like the product and what improvements they would want. The second is "zero-product-improvement time," whereby they add worthwhile product improvements continuously, so that the product remains the leader.[13]

To penetrate the global market today is more difficult than when Japanese firms made their moves starting in the 1960s. Management now has to face many obstacles from countries pursuing either free trade or protectionist policies. In protected markets, companies have to face several market barriers, both short- and long-term ones. The firm will have to face tariff and nontariff barriers, as well as economic blocs. In the case of protected markets, firms within the member states face no tariff or nontariff barriers (in principle), while outside firms still have to contend with the barriers. In the free trade situation, of course, firms will have to face other competitors.

To penetrate the global market, five marketing strategies are worth considering: (1) entering Third World markets; (2) using megamarketing to break into blocked markets; (3) utilizing the country image; (4) establishing owned brands; and (5) noncash pricing when necessary.

Entering Third World Markets

Some trade strategists have argued that it is not worthwhile to sell in the Third World; the lucrative markets are in North America, Western Europe, and the Far East. Kenichi Ohmae argued this view in his *Triad Power* (1985). He notes that

Opportunities are great in booming states such as California, which is bigger than Brazil (in economic terms), and Texas, where gross state product is bigger than the combined GNP of the Association of Southeast Asian Nations.

He goes on to say:

The "triad" of Japan, Europe, and the United States represents not only the major and fastest growth market for most products but also an increasingly homogeneous one. Gucci bags, Sony Walkmans, and McDonald's hamburgers are seen on the streets of Tokyo, Paris, and New York.

Kenichi Ohmae also thinks multinationals make a mistake in rushing to Third World countries to produce components just because the wages are lower. Lower wages do not necessarily spell lower costs if the labor is inefficient or redundant, or product quality is poor. With growing automation, labor costs are becoming a smaller percentage of total costs.

Ohmae also criticizes multinationals for taking too much time to introduce their new products into foreign markets. Swift competitors copy their products and launch them in foreign markets before the pioneer gets there. His solution: A multinational should establish strategic alliances with companies that operate in each triad market, so that the multinational could introduce its new products in all triad markets simultaneously and capture leadership. This strategy would provide a sufficient-size market to justify larger initial plant investment and lower unit costs. In addition, the multinational need not worry about being kept out by trade barriers, since its partners would be "insiders" in the foreign markets.

While Ohmae's position makes short-run sense—that is, profits are likely to be higher in the triad regions—it can spell a disastrous policy for the world economy in the long run. The triad markets are rich but mature; companies have to strain their creativity to find growth opportunities in these markets. In contrast, while each individual Third World market may be too small to be a target market, with most of them quite poor, their combined wealth is impressive due to the large number of Third World countries.[14]

The Third World constitutes huge potential markets for food, clothing, shelter, consumer electronics, appliances, and other goods. About 42 percent of America's exports, 20 percent of Western Europe's (47 percent if intra-European Union trade is excluded), and 48 percent of Japan's presently go to the Third World. Interestingly, Western Europe exports twice as much to the Third World as it does to North America and Japan together. Likewise, America exports more to Third World countries than to Western Europe and Japan.[15] Unless purchasing power is somehow put into the Third World, the industrial world will remain saddled with excess capacity and a very slow growth rate.[16]

On the supply side, rising productivity in the Third World will reduce the cost of goods exported to the industrial world, giving consumers a boost in real income. In addition, more competition from Third World producers should stimulate a more economical use of resources which, in turn, encourages more investment in human and physical capital, thus speeding up growth in the industrial world.[17]

Finding paths to link these two worlds dynamically and synergistically in a mutually beneficial relationship is thus a challenging task for both governments and multinationals (see Box 16.1).

Using Megamarketing to Break into Blocked Markets

A company's market entry plan can be thwarted when it confronts *blocked* markets. The problem of entering blocked markets calls for a megamarketing approach, defined as the strategic coordination of economic, psychological, political, and public relations skills to gain the cooperation of a number of parties in order to enter and/or operate in a given market. Commenting on Porter's (1980) three generic strategies, Professor J. Boddewyn argues that "if a firm cannot be a cost, differentiation or focus leader, it may still beat the competition on another ground, namely the non-market [political] environment." Pepsi-Cola faced this problem in seeking to enter the Indian market.

After Coca-Cola was asked to leave India, Pepsi began to lay plans to enter this huge market. Pepsi worked with an Indian business group to seek government approval for its entry over the objections of both domestic soft-drink companies and anti-multinational legislators. Pepsi saw the solution to lie in making an offer that the Indian government would find hard to refuse.

BOX 16.1

Doing Business in the Third World—Unilever's Approach

Unilever operates in forty Third-World countries. Turnovers in Africa, Asia, and Latin America contributed more than a fifth of Unilever's $20 billion sales. Its core products are soaps, detergents, margarine, and other inexpensive edible oils that are bought frequently and in small amounts.

Unilever has targeted rural consumers as a prime constituency. As these consumers enter the cash economy, among the first items they want are the soaps, cooking oils, and simple packaged foods that Unilever sells. The market is huge. In India, for example, agricultural workers account for 75% of total consumption of manufactured consumer goods.

Unilever carefully scrutinizes how consumers use their products. For example, when executives noticed that women in India and the Far East traditionally relied on soap to wash clothing, the company developed a detergent bar that could be used by hand. In Africa and Asia, Unilever subsidiaries are actively engaged in business ventures to create durable infrastructures in agricultural regions. The aim is to raise the overall standard of living, thus stimulating demand for company products. Although the perspective is long-term, the payoff can be immediate. Unilever's Indian subsidiary preserved an important part of its business by launching a campaign to improve animal husbandry methods and revive a flagging dairy industry near the company's milk-processing plant.

Local raw materials are used when possible to reduce overhead and stimulate local industry and thus local markets. One Kenyan subsidiary slashed the cost of importing chemicals from Europe by altering its detergent formula to make use of abundant nearby stocks of soda ash. To overcome a costly local shortage of palm oil, company scientists adapted a number of previously neglected indigenous oils for use in soap manufacture. This eliminated the need for imports, lowered the cost of manufacturing, and helped to support the local economy and Unilever's markets.

Quoted from Philip R. Cateora, *International Marketing* (Homewood, IL: Irwin, 1993), p. 218.

> *Pepsi offered to help India export some of its agricultural prod-*
> *ucts in a volume that would more than cover the cost of import-*
> *ing soft-drink concentrate. Pepsi also promised to focus*
> *considerable selling effort on rural areas to help in their eco-*
> *nomic development. Pepsi further offered to transfer food-pro-*
> *cessing, packaging, and water-treatment technology to India.*
> *Clearly, Pepsi's strategy was to bundle a set of benefits that*
> *would win the support of various interest groups in India.*[18]

Thus Pepsi's marketing problem went beyond the normal four Ps (product, price, place, and promotion) of operating effectively in a market. To enter India, Pepsi faced a six-P marketing problem, with politics and public opinion constituting the two additional Ps. Winning over the Indian government and public to gain admission is a much tougher challenge than just offering a good product.

Once in, a multinational must be on its best behavior, since it is under great scrutiny, and critics abound. This task calls for well-thought-out civic positioning by the multinational. Olivetti, for example, enters new markets by building housing for workers, generously supporting local arts and charities, and hiring and training indigenous managers. In this way, it hopes to realize long-run profits by accepting high short-run costs.[19]

The second kind of megamarketing is the using of agents of influence. Japanese companies provide a good example. To protect their huge market in the United States, the Japanese have spent more than $100 million each year to hire well-connected U.S. lobbyists, lawyers, former high-ranked public officials, public relations specialists, and political advisers. They also have spent $300 million each year to build a nationwide grassroots political network to influence public opinion and an additional $400 million per year in political campaigns to advance Japan's economic interests, influence U.S. trade policy, and gain market share in the United States for its target industries.

By knowing about decisions ahead of competition, by using their network of well-connected insiders and lobbyists in Washington, D.C., by activating their broad-based network in local communities across the country, by shaping American journalists' coverage of economic issues, and by promoting their opinion leaders in universities and think tanks, Japanese companies and the Japanese government are able to use political strategy as a critical element of global marketing strategy.[20]

The third kind of megamarketing is the forming of cultural ties. When culture—in the form of religion, language, or ethnic roots—spreads across political boundaries, its bonds can provide a new mechanism for conducting regional and global businesses. The network among the Chinese-based economies is the case in point.

Countries with Chinese-based economies are usually defined as the small, industrial "dragons" of South Korea, Taiwan, Hong Kong, and Singapore or the monolithic but underdeveloped People's Republic of China. Yet for generations, emigrant Chinese entrepreneurs have operated comfortably in a network of family and clan across many national borders.[21]

Professor John Kao (1993) calls this global network the *Chinese commonwealth*. This commonwealth is basically an interconnected but open system of entrepreneurial relationships, which are accessing local resources of raw materials, low labor costs, information, and business connections in a variety of business environments.

A close understanding of cultural distinctions also provides valuable insights into why particular trade and investment patterns occur. For example, Iran, despite its Muslim religion, has a closer relation with Israel than any other Middle Eastern nations. This is mainly because it is not an Arabic-speaking nation and its population are Shiite Muslims as opposed to the Sunni Muslims in other countries of the region. These factors resulted in the transshipment of American arms to Iran via Israel.

Sometimes it is a common second or a third language, not a common dominant language, that facilitates international business ties. For example, the relatively heavy trade between West Germany and several Eastern European countries is in part attributed to the fact that the German language was spoken during the German occupation of Eastern Europe (during two world wars). The common language facilitates the transfer of technology and training to these countries.[22]

Utilizing the Country Image

Buyers draw distinct evaluations of brands based on their "country of origin." A product's country of origin can have a positive, neutral, or negative effect on prospective buyers. For example, most buyers in the world are favorably disposed to apparel bearing the label: "Made in Italy." They would also expect high quality and reliability from automobiles and consumer electronics made in Japan. At the other extreme, a car or stereo set produced in Ghana would be viewed negatively. In between are those products—often raw materials and natural resources such as oil from Nigeria or timber from Canada—whose image is not much affected by knowing its country of origin.

Consumers form their preference based on their personal background, experience, and national stereotypes about different nations' quality, reliability, and service. Several country-of-origin studies have identified the following points:

- The impact of country of origin varies with the type of product. Consumers would want to know where a car was made but not where the lubricating oil came from.
- Consumers in highly industrial countries tend to rate their domestic goods highly, whereas consumers in the developing world tend to rate foreign goods more favorably.
- Campaigns to persuade people to favor domestic products rarely succeed when these products are perceived to be inferior to foreign products. Furthermore, a "Buy American" campaign may end up favoring foreign jobs, as when a town board voted to buy a John Deere excavator that turned out to be made in Japan instead of a Komatsu excavator built in the United States.
- Certain countries enjoy a strong reputation for certain goods: Japan for automobiles and consumer electronics; United States for high-tech innovations, soft drinks, toys, cigarettes, and jeans; and France for wine, perfumes, and luxury goods.
- The more favorable a country's image, the more prominently the "Made in" label should be displayed in promoting the brand.
- Attitudes toward country of origin can change over time. Note how Japan has greatly improved its quality image in comparison to pre–World War II days.

Implications for Less-Known Country Brands. A company whose products are competitively equal or superior but whose "place of origin" turns off consumers can consider five strategies:

1. *Pursuing co-production* with a foreign company that has a better name. Thus South Korea makes a fine leather jacket which it sends to Italy for finishing. The final jacket is then exported with a "Made in Italy" label and commands a much higher price.
2. *Acquiring country-of-origin firms.* The perfume industry, for decades, has been greatly affected by the "Made in France" phenomenon. To overcome the "Made in Paris" effect, many foreign companies have acquired French cosmetic firms. Foreign firms are presently controlling about 25% of the French perfume market.[23]
3. *Using anchoring strategy.* In the U.S. market, Heineken is the leading beer exporter. The French beer—Kronenbourg—attempted to take on Heineken by claiming that "Europeans like Heineken, but they love Kronenbourg." Since the brand name sounded German to most U.S. consumers, the company decided to anchor its brand name on the positive image of German beers in general.[24]
4. *Redefining the product.* Shiseido, the leading Japanese cosmetics firm, avoided a direct attack on the top French firms by primarily emphasizing skin products. When it entered the German market, the company conveyed the message that Japanese women had used skin care for generations. Shiseido thus positioned itself as an expert in skin care products rather than in fragrance and makeup.[25]
5. *Using local celebrity to endorse the product.* When Mazda was less known in the United States, Mazda hired the American actor James Garner to tout the Mazda in U.S. commercials. And Nike used America's best known professional basketball star, Michael Jordan, to promote its footwear in Europe.

Implications for Well-Known Country Brands. Well-known brands from countries with a strong positive image make good use of their image advantage. For example, the German beer Beck was touted in the United States as "the German beer that is number one in Germany." The idea was to capitalize on the image of German beer drinkers as being the most discriminating.[26]

Multinational corporations with a strong global brand image can generate more profit by sourcing product from, or manufacturing in, low-wage countries. The success of this multicountry sourcing strategy is based on the assumption that the new country of origin will not hurt the original country-of-origin image.

But multinational firms that produce in or source from unfavorable countries of origin should proceed with caution. A Sony made in Indonesia is perceived to be not the same as a Sony made in Japan. Consumers may still have doubts as to whether Sony can maintain its product quality when produced in the developing countries. A study by David Tse and Gerald Gorn (1993) indicated that a strong global brand (e.g., Sony) made in an unfavorable country of origin (e.g., Indonesia) received the same evaluation rating as a less known brand (e.g., GIW) made in a favorable country of origin (e.g., Japan). Thus less well known competitive brands made in a country with a strong image may be able to compete with a well-known brand made in a weaker country of origin. This "country extension" strategy may have another advantage. It may be easier for consumers to develop a positive brand image toward a neutral new brand (e.g., GIW) than to turn an originally negative country-of-origin image (e.g., Indonesia) into a positive one.[27]

Establishing Owned Brands

One basic component in designing an effective global marketing strategy is the strength of a company's brand in the international marketplace. A global brand provides a distinctive image, permitting the company to command a higher price for the same level of quality. By this strong image, the company can also manufacture the product countercyclically and counterseasonally in different countries, thus smoothing its revenue and cost flows.[28]

Many Asian manufacturers—often the anonymous producers behind some of the world's most famous labels—are attempting to gain a competitive edge by launching their own brands as well. One Taiwanese company, Kennex, made its reputation in the United States selling mid-range tennis racket and sport equipment under its Pro Kennex label, though it had some higher priced models as well. When the company decided to make a plunge in the Japanese market, it sold only the top-of-the-line rackets.

Some Hong Kong electronics makers are trying to reduce their reliance on subcontracting work by establishing their own brands. Gold Peak Industries has been a producer of car radios and other audio products for European manufacturers such as Blaupunkt. In 1991, Gold Peak introduced its own line of audio products, dubbed GP Audio, which plans to sell first in Hong Kong, then in Southeast Asia.[29]

Different strategies are used by Asian producers seeking a brand name niche. Hong Kong watchmakers, for example, have bought established Swiss and French names. The more difficult, but potentially more rewarding, approach is for a manufacturer to nurture its own name. Some governments, particularly Taiwan and Hong Kong, are encouraging their companies to develop and promote their own brands. Taiwan has launched a "Made in Taiwan" promotional campaign in Western markets. The idea is to give its goods a cachet they often lack and counter the notion of Taiwan as a counterfeiting producer. Moreover, in 1989, Taiwan established a state-backed group called the Brand International Promotion Association, with a board comprising the chief executives of Taiwan's leading companies. In 1991, the government provided U.S.$10 million worth of guaranteed loans at preferential rates to support this effort. Companies use the funds for marketing and other activities aimed at spreading brand name sales.[30]

Noncash Pricing

A *countertrade* is used when a prospective customer may not be able to pay in hard currency. Due to the scarcity of foreign exchange, countertrade was and is still presently used among former Socialist countries, and between them and Western countries. It is not limited only to government-sponsored foreign trade organizations. Countertrade is now popular in many private and privatized companies.

Kotva, Czechoslovakia's leading department store, could not get access to sufficient Western goods even after liberalization in late 1989. The store traded Czech paper for Lego toys and Czech cheese for Italian vermouth.[31]

To respond to this challenge, international marketers have developed several forms of countertrade (see Figure 16.3).

FIGURE 16.3

Forms of Countertrade

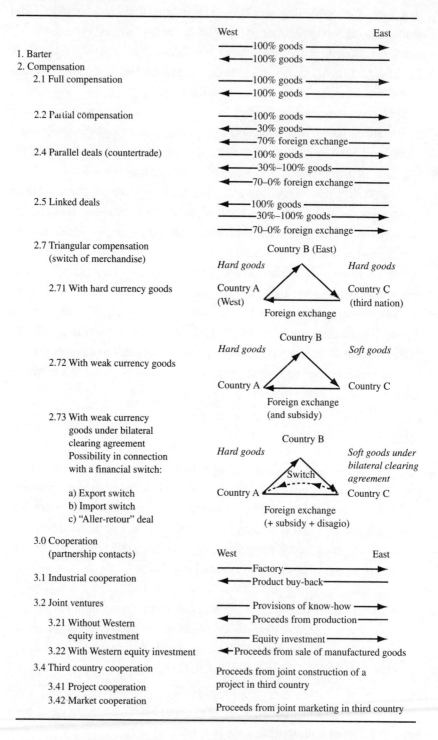

Source: Jean-Pierre Jeannet and Hubert D. Hennessey, *Global Marketing Strategies* (Boston: Houghton Mifflin, 1992), Figure 13.4, p. 459 (based on *Barter, Compensation and Cooperation*. Credit Suisse, Zurich, vol. 47. no. 4 (1978), pp. 8–9.

Sometimes, countertrade leads to very convoluted transactions. Consider the following proposal, which combines direct and third-country trade:

A Japanese trading company proposed to buy used, surplus refrigerated railroad cars in Japan cheap, and sell them to the Trans-Siberian Railroad, which has a shortage of such cars. The cars would be used to haul fish from Soviet Pacific fisheries to China via Mongolia. The Chinese would process the fish and sell it in the United States. The cars would be used to haul cheap Mongolian pork for shipment to Japan from Chinese or Soviet Far East ports. The Siberian railroad would not need cash to pay for the cars; it would pay the trading company by shipping the fish and pork free until the cars are paid for in transportation charges. Everybody wins: The Japanese make a profit on used, refrigerated railroad cars and get a source of cheap pork; the Russians and Chinese get products to market and a new source of hard currency.[32]

SUMMARY

Successful firms do not merely react to changes in the external environment; many concentrate their business portfolio around the company's core competencies and actively seek to create new, internal sources of advantage.

Core competencies are not only about harmonizing streams of technology; they are also about the organization of work and the delivery of value. Patterns of diversification and market entry are influenced by the core competencies. They are the glue that binds existing businesses, and also the engine for new product and business development.

Control over core products is critical. A dominant position in core products allows a company to shape the evolution of applications and end markets. As a company multiplies the number of application arenas for its core products, it can consistently reduce cost, time, and risk in new product development by means of economies of scale and scope. Core products are generally developed by two major innovation processes:

(1) "ladder" or "technology-driven" innovation process; and (2) "cyclical" or "production and design-driven" innovation process. Conventional wisdom suggests that technology is the key to new product success. But most marketers realize that it is not that simple.

In developing its marketing strategy, a company must ask in what specific ways it can obtain a competitive advantage. The number of differentiation opportunities varies with the type of industry. Thus not every company faces a plethora of cost-reducing or benefit-building opportunities for gaining competitive advantage. Some differentiation strategies discussed in this chapter include: (1) changing the terms of engagement; (2) building quality and innovation into the product; (3) skillful positioning; and (4) cost containment.

To penetrate the global market, five related marketing strategies are discussed: entering Third World markets; using megamarketing to break into blocked markets; utilizing the country image; establishing owned brands; and noncash pricing when necessary.

Chapter 17

Strategic Development Through Cooperative Strategies

Every relation between two business enterprises has some degree of both competition and cooperation. On the one hand—horizontally—competitive rivalry in the same markets can be reduced by membership in the same business association (e.g., acting together against some threatening government regulations). On the other hand—vertically—many buyer-seller relationships are characterized by intensive and long-term cooperation. Examples include joint product development processes, shared logistics, and common quality goals.[1]

In this chapter we start by discussing the substantial growth of strategic alliances. We next illustrate the driving forces behind forming a network of strategic alliances. Then major aspects of strategic alliances—strategic alliances across industries; strategic alliances along the technological life cycle; and cross-border alliances—are examined. Finally, we examine some additional aspects of strategic alliances.

THE GROWTH OF STRATEGIC ALLIANCES

Professors Johanson and Mattsson have defined strategic alliance as "a particular mode of inter-organizational relationship in which the partners

369

FIGURE 17.1

Various Forms of Strategic Alliances

————Increasing Formality and Indivisibility of Collaborative Effort————▶

     * Exclusive supplier agreement (TRW-Chrysler)
      * Assistance agreement (raw sharing by competitors)
      * Joint bidding agreement (offshore drilling consortium)
       * Cooperative agreement (Cetus, Inc.)
        * Licensing agreement (Fokker–McDonald Douglas)
        * Franchise agreement (McDonald's)
         * Cross-distribution agreement (AT&T-Olivetti)
          * Cross-licensing agreement (Eli Lilly–Genentech)
          * R&D partnership agreement (MCC)
           * Buyback agreement (Siemens-Philips)
            * Production swap agreement (steel/chemical industries)
             * Operating joint venture (Intel-Siemens)
              * "Spiders Web" joint venture (Bell&Howell/Ojawa/Mamiya)

Source: J. Quincy Hunsicker, "Strategies for European Survival," *The McKinsey Quarterly* (Summer 1989), Exhibit III: Spectrum of Alliances.

make substantial investment in developing a long-term collaborative effort, and common orientation."[2] Figure 17.1 illustrates different kinds of strategic alliances according to the level of formality and indivisibility of collaborative effort.

Conceptually, strategic alliances allow a firm to focus on its value chain activities, permitting it to reap all the benefits of specialization. Meanwhile, all the firms in the network gain added flexibility by not having to perform activities that can be performed better by others. Alliances thus are an expedient way to penetrate new markets; to gain skills, technology, or products; and to share fixed costs and resources.[3]

The Limits to Internal Growth

The rapid changes in technological and market conditions in an industry induce firms to search for a new equilibrium between static and dynamic efficiency.[4] But only a few companies can change their resource base, and shift skills fast enough, to adjust to new conditions on the basis of internal growth alone.[5] A more flexible structure and new forms of organization jointly based on internal growth and the establishment of an external network are needed to establish optimal trade-offs between production and transaction costs, and between these and the costs of change and adaptation.[6]

Limits on Forming Mergers and Acquisitions

On the other hand, various circumstances limit resorting to mergers and acquisitions. Targeted firms may be privately owned or protected by elaborate ownership schemes that exclude takeovers and mergers. Public policy restrictions may be another reason as governments attempt to protect certain industries from foreign takeover. In some cases, genuine antitrust, antimonopoly concerns have blocked mergers. In still other cases, it is very difficult to put a price on the targeted firms—this is especially true in high-tech intensive start-ups, where their values highly depend on one's assumption about future research results, market growth, and continued commitment of key technical staff and managers.[7]

DRIVING FACTORS BEHIND FORMING A NETWORK OF STRATEGIC ALLIANCES

The benefits of strategic alliances are compelling since they may overcome the obstacles faced by mergers and acquisitions, as well as provide a shortcut to growth that internal growth alone would not provide.

Probably the greatest stimulus to forming alliances has been the emergence of global competitors on the one hand, and the need to compete globally on the other. The rapid pace of technological development, shorter product life cycles, and the high cost of the associated research and development are other factors stimulating alliance formation.

The Philips-Sony alliance for the joint product development of audio visual compact discs, the Olivetti-Canon arrangement to develop copiers and image processors, and the recent announcement by AT&T that it was taking a 20% stake in Sun Microsystems are characteristic. These trends are not endemic to the electronics industries. The American Cyanamid-Celltech collaboration arrangement centered on the latter's leading edge biotechnology development capability for "engineering" agents

> *to attack cancer cells and the former's distribution and market-*
> *ing capability.*[8]

In addition, strategic alliances can be effective ways to diffuse new technologies rapidly, to enter a new market, to bypass governmental restrictions, or to learn quickly from the leading firms in a given field.

> *Many early U.S. joint ventures in Japan can be characterized in*
> *terms of having been driven by several of these rationales (e.g.,*
> *CPC International and Ajinomoto within the food industry in*
> *1963 and Hewlett-Packard and Yokogawa Electric within the*
> *electronics industry in 1971). These ventures allowed U.S. firms*
> *to disseminate new products rapidly into the otherwise exceed-*
> *ingly demanding Japanese market.*[9]

Governments have also been responsible for encouraging collaboration between companies. The most notable are the highly successful Airbus program and the publicized European Strategic Program in Information Technologies (ESPRIT).

Fashion and fear motives should also be included as driving factors in alliance formation.

> *Mitsubishi Motors (Japan) allied with Hyundai Motors (South*
> *Korea) to manufacture and distribute a line of low price cars;*
> *this step pre-empted any potential alliance between Hyundai and*
> *one of Mitsubishi's Japanese competitors.*[10]

STRATEGIC ALLIANCES ACROSS INDUSTRIES

Alliances have been more common in such industries as automobiles, computers, and commercial aircraft, whereas they have been rare in industrial commodities like cement and basic chemicals, and in capital goods like industrial machinery and the food-processing industry. Professor Jain (1987) suggests that two factors determining the relevance of a strategic alliance across industries: (1) *the importance of seeking cost advantage through scale operation and/or joint R&D*; and (2) *market access perspectives.* Combining these two factors provides four types of strategic options (see Figure 17.2).

1. Industries where strategic alliances are most desirable. Here they provide market access and cost advantage, either through scale operations or joint R&D operations. Examples include aircraft construction, computers, bioengineering, and automobile industries.
2. Industries in which market access is critical, but economies of scale in manufacturing and/or R&D are required. Examples include pharmaceuticals, fine chemicals, and medical equipment.
3. Industries in which major economies of scale are not critical and market access is not a problem. Examples include processing foods, cement, steel, and synthetic fibers.
4. Industries in which blocked areas are a problem. Examples include local telephone networks, distribution sectors, and certain types of armament industries.[11]

FIGURE 17.2

Determining Strategic Alliance/Separation Trade-Off

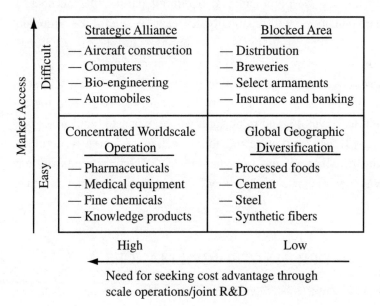

Source: Subhash C. Jain, "Perspective on International Strategic Alliances," in S. Tamer Cavusgil, ed., *Advances in International Marketing* (Greenwich, CT: JAI Press, 1987), Vol. 2, Exhibit 2, p. 108.

STRATEGIC ALLIANCES ALONG THE TECHNOLOGICAL LIFE CYCLE[12]

A propensity toward cooperation will be naturally high in the introductory stage of the technological life cycle. When the participating members bring complementary skills and resources to the emerging industry, they may speed up its development by ensuring that these skills and resources are combined early and at a low transaction cost.

The propensity toward cooperation reaches its maximum value in the early development phase, owing mainly to nonequity marketing and production agreements that allow firms to gain rapid access to specialized assets that are complementary to innovations and critical for their commercial success.

During maturity, the markets are already established, the technologies are better known, and learning needs are fewer on both the demand and supply side. Nonequity collaborative ventures will be pursued in order to revitalize the technological trajectories and stabilize market structure. There is also an attempt by the firms to reap residual oligopolistic rents by transferring technology to other parts of the world market (see Figure 17.3).

During the full development and declining phases, the number of agreements concluded will drastically decrease. In the full development stage, the reduced appropriateness of technology and the growing competitive pressure—particularly from the threat of substitutes—will induce firms to internalize the control of specialized complementary assets by means of internal growth, mergers, and acquisitions. During the declining phase, technological opportunities are exhausted and firms will resort to divestments and write-offs to rationalize the market structure.

In industries that are not only mature but declining, alliances may offer a way toward capacity adjustment and rationalization that enhances the industry's stability.

CROSS-BORDER STRATEGIC ALLIANCES

Collaborative ventures between firms across national boundaries have a long history. In the past, firms from developed countries formed alliances

FIGURE 17.3

Average Propensity Toward Agreements During the Phases of the
Technological Life Cycle

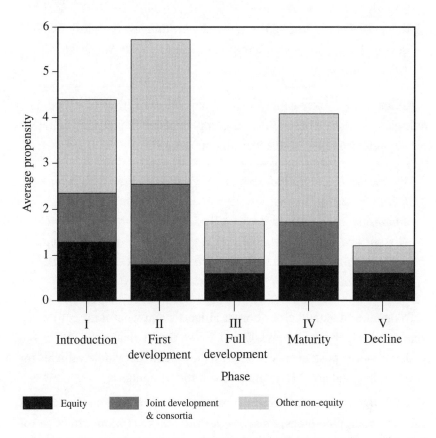

Source: G. C. Cainarca, M. G. Colombo, and S. Mariotti, "Agreements Between Firms and the Technological Life Cycle Model: Evidence from Information Technologies," Research Policy, 21 (1992),
Figure 2, p. 56.

with firms in lesser developed countries to gain market access. More and
more alliances today involve firms from developed countries who team
up to serve whole regions or the whole world market.

*In the pharmaceutical industry, networking has enabled Glaxo
to become one of the world's most successful companies and an
industry leader. The success of ranitidine, an H_2 blocker used in*

the treatment of ulcers, marketed internationally under the brand name Zantac, is largely responsible for this. Launched in Europe in 1981, the product's sales accounted for 829 million pounds in 1987, representing 48% of the Group's sales. This was achieved mainly through a network of alliances, the most successful being the co-marketing arrangement with Roche in the United States.[13]

Alliances also increasingly extend beyond marketing to encompass multiple activities. These alliances complement each partner's competitive strengths and give both a learning opportunity.

Within the U.S. auto industry, each of the Big Three U.S. manufacturers has an extensive series of supply alliances with their Japanese counterparts (e.g., GM-Isuzu, Ford-Mazda, Ford-Nissan, and Chrysler-Mitsubishi) that involve co-designing and co-producing small cars under such labels as GM's Geo and Sprint, Ford's Escort line, and Chrysler's Dodge Colt.[14]

To better understand cross-border alliances and what it takes to make them work, Joel Bleeke and David Ernst found that although cross-border alliances pose many challenges, they are in fact viable vehicles for international strategy.[15] Here are a few of their findings:

1. While *cross-border acquisitions* work well for core businesses and existing geographic areas, *cross-border alliances* are more effective for diversifying into related businesses or new geographic markets.

Corning's well-publicized joint venture with Siemens to produce fiber-optic cable is an example of a successful move into a related business. The Siecor joint venture, started in 1977, succeeded for many reasons. For one thing, the parents brought complementary skills and capabilities. Corning had developed and patented processes to manufacture high-quality optical fibers. Siemens had capital, scale, and worldwide distribution of telecommunications cable. Siemens also brought the manufacturing technology and equipment to produce cable from fiber. The alliance had distinct advantages over acquisition. It allowed the creation of an enterprise focused on commercializing fiber-optic cable, and it relieved some of the financial pressure by dividing the investment. Moreover, neither company had to recoup an acquisition premium.

Credit Suisse–First Boston, a joint venture formed in 1978 to expand both companies' position in the Eurobond market, shows the benefits of using alliances to leverage complementary geographic strengths. First Boston provided access to U.S. corporate issuers of bonds and possessed the skills for restructuring new financial vehicles like convertible Eurobonds. Credit Suisse provided the capability to place issues with investors in Europe. This combination allowed the joint venture to assume a leading role in the rapidly growing Eurobond markets in the early 1980s. (The joint venture was bought out by Credit Suisse in 1988 after First Boston began to experience financial problems, which were partly due to increasing competitiveness in the Eurobond markets.)[16]

---

2. Alliances between strong and weak companies may fail. Since they do not complement the missing skills needed for growth, they usually lead to mediocre performance.

One U.S. leading pharmaceutical company was seeking to expand its position in Japan. It partnered with the second tier company with a large sales force rather than with one of the leading Japanese pharmaceutical companies, which might have had products that competed more directly. The joint venture failed for several reasons. First, the sales force of the Japanese company was poorly managed and was unable to meet its targets for distributing the drugs of the Western partner. Second, over time, the Japanese partner was simply unable to push drugs that had been successful in other markets through Japan's development and approval process. It did not have insider contacts to guide the approval process, and it lacked the management resources and excellent products. The top-tier position of the Western partner could not compensate for its partner's shortcomings.[17]

Alliances can be effective when participating members bring complementary skills to the table—strong R&D versus well-developed manufacturing processes, innovative products versus solid and established distribution and sales capabilities. The strongest alliances exist when each partner brings both products and established market presence in different geographic regions.

The Toshiba-Motorola alliance is an example of getting the balance right: Toshiba brought expertise in DRAMs and access to Japan; Motorola brought expertise in microprocessors and access to the U.S. market. This alliance seems to have a more stable balance of power because neither partner relies solely on the other for technical expertise, products, or market entry.[18]

---

3. The ability to evolve beyond initial expectations and objectives is the sustainable hallmark of successful alliances. This requires autonomy for the venture and flexibility on the part of both partners.

GMF Robotics was set up in 1982 by GM and Fanuc to develop robotics for the auto industry. The venture has gradually broadened its focus and now sells robotics to nonautomotive customers in industries like food processing and computer manufacturing.[19]

---

4. After meeting the partners' goals, alliances often terminate with an acquisition by one of the parents. This termination is not necessarily equivalent to failure.

By 1990, when Sandoz and Sankyo agreed to dissolve their alliance, Sankyo was selling 22 Sandoz drugs, which took in ¥82 billion in revenues. Sandoz and Sankyo are continuing to cooperate with each other and are planning a phased withdrawal over four years of five key Sandoz drugs from Sankyo's sales channels. Sankyo is also helping Sandoz build its marketing force by sending personnel to Sandoz's Japan operations.[20]

There is evidence that the alliance relationships are increasingly polygamous rather than monogamous. Companies like Philips, Toshiba, AT&T, and Olivetti are at the hub of what are often *overlapping* alliance networks. As a result, it becomes more and more difficult to identify the precise boundaries between firms.[21]

STRATEGIC ALLIANCES: SOME ADDITIONAL CONSIDERATIONS

Although many alliances have been forged in a large number of industries, there is no guarantee whether these alliances will actually become successful business ventures. Strategic alliances frequently are more difficult to operate than wholly owned business ventures. The challenge lies in the creation of new types of managerial capabilities: living with ambiguity and displaying a mature attitude. There are at least three fundamental reasons for this: (1) more than one party is usually involved in the decision making, often leading to slower, more complex decision making; this is further attenuated by (2) the merging of different corporate cultures, in which (3) the parent firms may have different, even ultimately conflicting, strategic intents.[22] For future success, management must ensure that these strategic alliances are viewed in a true strategic perspective rather than as an opportunistic "quick fix."[23]

SUMMARY

Rapid changes in technology and market conditions induce firms to search for more flexible structures and new forms of organization jointly based on internal growth and the establishment of external networks. Strategic alliances provide one solution. The purpose of forming an alliance may be to achieve the size necessary to compete, to set the industrial standards, to rationalize the production processes, to exploit the benefits of economies of scale and scope, or to extend marketing efficiencies.

Strategic alliances tend to be most prevalent in industries where two factors operate: (1) importance of seeking cost advantage through scale operation and/or joint R&D; and (2) market access perspectives.

The propensity toward cooperation will be high in the introductory stage of the technological life cycle. The propensity toward cooperation reaches its maximum value in the early development phase. During maturity, the technologies are better known, the markets are already structured, and learning needs are fewer. Finally, during the declining phase, write-offs and divestments will clearly prevail.

Historically, firms from developed countries formed alliances with firms in lesser developed countries to perform marketing activities (often required to gain market access). More and more alliances today involve firms from developed countries that team up to serve whole regions or the entire world.

For an alliance to succeed, management must ensure that the strategic alliance is viewed in a true strategic perspective rather than as an opportunistic "quick fix."

Chapter 18

National Wealth-Building Strategies: From Strategic Vision to Strategic Implementation

In this last chapter, we review the main arguments about proceeding to build a nation's wealth. Nations need a framework and an approach that will help them clarify what they can realistically hope to accomplish. Ultimately, the people of all nations aspire to a good economy, a good society, and a good political process. Nations develop their wealth-building strategies to fulfill these goals. Designing effective strategies requires defining the nation's *strategic thrust*, *strategic posture*, and *strategic implementation*. We will review these three components in the sections that follow.

THE NATION'S STRATEGIC THRUST

To formulate a strategic thrust for the nation, its policymakers need to assess the nation's current competitive, internal, and external environments. They also need to set or review the nation's objectives and goals subject to these environments.

Three steps are involved in analyzing a nation's current situation: (1) analyzing the *global competitive structure*; (2) analyzing the impact of the major *global forces and trends*; and (3) analyzing the nation's *capabilities*.

381

Global Competitive Structure

In a highly interdependent global economy, a nation's wealth critically depends on its competitive position in the global marketplace. Each nation will face certain close competitors, namely, other nations pursuing the same target markets with the same or similar strategies. Therefore, we can conceptually divide countries into strategic groups of nations—where the members of each group follow the same or similar strategy in the global marketplace.

We classified nations into eight strategic groups: (1) the Industrial Giants; (2) the Rising Stars; (3) the Latin Americans; (4) the Populous Countries; (5) The Former Socialists; (6) the Industrial Nichers; (7) the Commodity Nichers; and (8) the Subsistents. Each group has a distinct competitive condition and a distinct role in the world economy. Each nation should monitor its overall competitive position closely so that any signs of weakening competitiveness can be dealt with quickly.

Global Forces and Trends

Following the end of the Cold War, nations turned their focus from military and political struggles to the economic challenges. Nations are now competing more for the means to create national wealth than for political control over other nations.

Six fundamental forces underlie this shift: (1) the increase of global interdependence; (2) the widespread protectionism and growth of regional economic blocs; (3) the transnationalization of MNCs; (4) the rapid technological advances; (5) the increasing and conflicting politics of nationalism; and (6) the growth of environmental concerns. These forces affect different nations differently. Thus, each nation must read the emerging opportunities and threats arising from global forces and trends, and tease out their implications.

The Nation's Capabilities

The degree to which each nation captures opportunities or copes with threats depends upon its capabilities. Such capabilities include: the nation's culture, attitudes, and values; its social cohesion; its factor endowments; its industrial organizations; and its government leadership. A nation's capabilities must be analyzed not just in terms of the scope and intensity of each element but also in terms of the interactive effects among these elements over time. Such an assessment helps the policymakers identify both major strengths and weaknesses.

Assessing the nation's environment aids policymakers in setting objectives and goals.

Goal Formulation

Ultimately, the people of all nations aspire to a good economy, a good society, and a good political process. The nation's objectives are set to meet these aspirations: raising the level of GNP per capita; improving the international competitiveness; achieving a high level of employment; stable price levels; good health; good education; a good environment; security and peace; human freedom; and so forth.

The nation should strive to arrange its objectives *hierarchically*, from the higher level to the lower, more derived levels. Where possible, objectives and goals should be *prioritized*. For the less developed countries, perhaps economic objectives and goals should come first. In the more developed economies, policymakers try for a greater balance of economic, social, and political objectives.

Objectives should be stated *quantitatively*. And they should be specified with respect to *magnitude* and *time*. This will facilitate policymakers' planning, implementation, and control.

A nation should set *realistic* goals. The levels should arise from an analysis of the nation's environments—competitive, internal, and external—not from wishful thinking. Finally, some objectives are in a *trade-off* relationship. Thus, policymakers should beware and avoid *inconsistency* among the nation's objectives.

Matching the nation's strengths/weaknesses, opportunities/threats, and competitive/cooperative patterns with its objectives and goals serves as the foundation for formulating the nation's strategic thrust. Differences in a nation's relative wealth and relative competitiveness result in four different formulations for that strategic thrust:

1. Countries that command a leading position, like Japan and Germany, have the mission of *sustaining* their current positions.

2. Countries that are losing some competitiveness, like the United States and Australia, have the mission of *revitalizing* their competitiveness.
3. Countries whose current wealth position is low but whose competitiveness is strong, like the Four Tigers and the "little tigers," have the mission of extending their competitiveness to *build* further their national wealth.
4. Countries whose current wealth and competitiveness are weak, like Latin American countries, former Socialists, and subsistent economies, face a *turnaround* mission.

There are a multitude of economic routes that countries can take in their pursuit of wealth creation. These include: (1) the Korean selectivist model; (2) the Hong Kong fundamentalist model; (3) the Singapore model of high technology and service development; (4) the Chilean model of free market development; (5) the China model of primary-sector development; (6) the former Soviet model of heavy industries development; (7) the Hungarian model of gradualism; and (8) the Polish model of shock therapy. Each model has its own merits and drawbacks.

There is no one best pathway to development. Each nation is subject to a unique set of opportunities, constraints, and competitive conditions. By assessing the advantages and drawbacks of each pathway, subject to a nation's unique set of opportunities, constraints, and competitive conditions, the economic development policymakers than can select or develop the optimal pathway for that nation.

THE NATION'S STRATEGIC POSTURE

The nation's strategic thrust must be translated into pragmatic and concrete guidelines for identifying specific public policies to improve competitiveness.

Hugh Mosley and Gunter Schmid (1993) suggest that a nation's competitiveness comprises both its microcompetitiveness and its international competitiveness. *Microcompetitiveness* (competitive advantage) is the ability of domestic firms to sell their products in the global marketplace, based on their relative price and quality attractiveness in comparison with their foreign competitors. Enterprises in countries with low costs, including cheap labor and abundant natural resources, may enjoy a competitive advantage because they can be more price-competitive.

A nation's *international competitiveness* (comparative advantage), on the other hand, refers to its ability to achieve high-factor incomes in the global economy. If the nation competes only on a cheap labor advantage, it has to maintain its wages and working conditions permanently low for its labor force. Therefore the goal is not merely to engage in international trade but to do so at high wage levels on the basis of superior productivity, service, quality, and innovation. Public policies may play an integral role here.[1]

Two main types of public policy are needed to enhance competitiveness: government primary policies and government support policies.

Government Primary Policies

To improve the nation's competitiveness, policymakers must formulate their primary policies for competing and cooperating with other countries. The three primary policies involve investment, industry-building strategies, and trade.

Investment. Governments now realize that it is hard to "bootstrap" economic growth relying primarily on their own domestic firms. Most governments compete today to attract foreign firms to invest in their economy. Foreign investment brings several benefits. It improves the economy's efficiency by spurring competition, by demanding improvements in the quality of supplied components and labor, and so forth. The global growth in foreign investment has increased the interlinkage and interdependence among nations.

A nation's foreign direct investment (FDI) policies should have two fundamental aims. (1) In the short run, a sound FDI strategy should seek to attract foreign investment, thus augmenting the stock of capital available to the nation. Policymakers should view the nation as a link in the international chain of value-adding activities. They should seek to position the nation to be highly competitive in specific parts of the value chain. (2) In the long run, the nation should leverage investment flows to provide the maximum long-term benefit. National policies should encourage foreign companies to assist in exports, to invest in human and physical capital, and to provide technology transfer.

Industry-Building Strategies. A nation's economic strength depends on the choices and health of its industrial clusters, industries, and firms. An *industrial cluster* is a group of industrial segments—the focal industry, related industries, and supporting industries—that have vertical and horizontal linkages with each other. Related industries generate synergistic effects for an industrial cluster. These include *snowball* effects, *substitution* effects, and *spillover* effects (both crossover and fusion technologies). By the same token, supporting industries, besides their added value enhancement, play an important role in generating external economies, i.e., creating *satellite* effects in the industrial cluster.

A nation's industrial portfolio comprises industrial clusters from many industrial sectors. Stiff global competition forces governments to review and revise their nation's industrial portfolio from time to time. Government aim to develop attractive new industries that promise higher added value and higher productivity. At the same time, governments seek to revitalize existing strong but highly competitive industries, and finally to restructure or to phase out declining or vulnerable industries.

The first step in developing the nation's industry portfolio is to analyze its industrial development determinants, specifically industrial attractiveness and the nation's ability to compete. The second step is to formulate the nation's industrial vision. In this step, three main dimensions are taken into account: *what*—the factor intensity; *where*—the scope of market boundaries; and *how*—the investment strategies, of each industry. The final step is to identify industrial support strategies: neutrality; market stimulation; and selective-strategic approach.

Trade. Government export promotion and assistance play an increasingly important role in today's growing international competition. Two broad categories of approach are used by governments to promote exports—direct and indirect programs. *Direct* programs concentrate on the demand side, while *indirect* programs focus on the supply side. These two approaches are not mutually exclusive. Indeed, they are highly complementary and interactive.

To ensure that a nation's export promotion strategies are effective, two linkages need to be taken into consideration: the link between export promotion and import penetration; and the link between export diversification and specialization. The former deals with short-term export efficiency, while the latter deals with long-term export effectiveness.

Government Support Policies

Some support policies are needed to enable the government's primary policies to work efficiently. These include macroeconomic policies, the nation's infrastructure development, and the development of the institutional framework.

The nation's macroeconomic policies are a coordinated set of mostly fiscal and monetary policies geared to enhancing economic stability and continuity, and to a lesser extent, prosperity and equity. A nation develops macroeconomic policies to deal with the following challenges: (1) coping with inflation; (2) managing capital investment; (3) managing foreign exchange rates; (4) managing fiscal prudence; (5) dealing with unemployment; and (6) coping with external shock.

Infrastructure development, particularly in the early phase of industrialization, is critically important for economic development. The major infrastructure developments include: (1) physical infrastructure development; (2) technology infrastructure development; (3) human capital development; and (4) entrepreneurs and small business enterprise development.

The growth of specialization, the interdependence of various economic agents, and the complexity of their relationships leads to an increasing need for the state to define a clear legal and institutional framework. Such a framework will include (1) property rights protection; (2) industrial regulation and deregulation; (3) privatization; (4) industrial relation policies; (5) redistributive development policies; and (6) social cohesion policies. Without this institutional framework, the predictability of economic outcomes—and hence the economy's effectiveness—will be drastically diminished.

THE NATION'S STRATEGIC IMPLEMENTATION

All six public policies just mentioned are critical for enhancing a nation's competitiveness. These policies indicate which functions the state should perform. Professors Stephen Bell and John Wanna (1992) classify the state's functions as follows:

1. The State as a Wealth Initiator. This is related to state activities that promote economic development by providing infrastructure, using various policy instruments to enhance private investment, creating the platform for building the industry clusters, acting as a joint venturer, and providing other forms of hybrid public-private development.

2. The State as Protector and Upholder. This entails state expenditures for defense and also the state's support of various interest groups, such as ethnic groups or the socially disadvantaged. It also involves the maintenance of the legal and institutional framework.

3. The State as Regulator. This involves the state establishing standards and regulations over a wide range of social and economic activities. Examples include product standards, competitive behavior, pollution controls, and measures regarding industrial and labor market regulations.

4. The State as Arbitrator and Distributor. This involves state action designed to adjudicate or settle disputes, to guarantee income, or to provide minimum wages for workers.

5. The State as Organizer. The state may influence the organization of social interests and groups by deliberately sponsoring interest groups or recognizing some interest groups but not others.

Four elements are critical for implementing the nation's wealth-building strategies:

- assessing the state's strengths and weaknesses;
- recognizing dilemmas and trade-offs among policy options;
- building a healthy business-government relationship; and
- enhancing government-government cooperation.[2]

These are described in the sections that follow.

Assessing the State's Strengths and Weaknesses

Since the states can often make things worse, market failure does not always justify government intervention. On the other hand, unproductive rent-seeking activities can be found not only in inefficient state operations but also in poorly functioning business enterprises. The relative performance of public versus private economic activities should, therefore, be judged in the context of individual countries and specific situations.[3]

Political institutions, like many economic institutions, are not all created equal. Countries differ in the configuration of their interest groups, the voting system, the bureaucratic structure, the role of the court, and public opinion. It is hard to believe that two governments with different political institutions, trying to do exactly the same thing, should achieve the same outcomes. In addition, the relationship between the market and the state is presently being redefined all over the world. Many countries in Eastern Europe, for example, have realized that the market performs an indispensable corrective function with regard to demand, price, and productivity. At the same time, neoclassicists can no longer ignore the role of the state in shaping and reshaping the conditions within which the market does operate.[4]

Recognizing Dilemmas and Trade-offs Among Policy Options

If a nation desires to improve its competitiveness, it is vital that programs be developed systematically to eliminate public policy disadvantages, as well as managerial inadequacies.

For policymakers, one would think they could follow a simple logic to arrive at a set of feasible public policies. Starting from recognizing constraints and opportunities, they would proceed to define a broad set of wealth-building strategies. Unfortunately, along the way they would confront major dilemmas and trade-offs at every juncture. The major issues facing policymakers include: growth orientation versus income distribution orientation; sectoral balance versus sectoral imbalance; shock therapy versus gradualism; high unemployment versus high inflation; state ownership versus private ownership; large private companies versus small entrepreneurs; interventionism versus free markets; and inward investment facilitation versus bootstrapping.

The choices of policies and administrative actions are partly influenced by the nation's culture, attitudes, and values (e.g., countries with individualistic cultures are likely to choose free trade policies whereas countries with communitarian cultures are likely to choose managed trade policies); depends partly on the stage of the nation's economic development (e.g., less developed countries usually focus on growth-oriented wealth creation, while developed countries usually focus on equality-oriented wealth creation); and is partly determined by the nation's factor endowments (e.g., there is evidence that large countries, like some in Latin America, are likely to pursue import substitution protectionism whereas small countries, like the Four or Five Tigers and the little tigers, are likely to pursue export promotion strategies). Thus, when choosing policies and administrative actions, policymakers should consider not only the pros and cons of the policy choices but the specific factors in each nation's makeup that would determine success.

Building a Healthy Business-Government Relationship[5]

A nation's wealth can be viewed as the sum of wealth created by the nation's business. In a market economy, corporations generate wealth by increasing global value added, which will then be distributed in higher wages for employees, higher dividends for shareholders, higher reinvestment for the firm, and higher tax revenue for the state, and will also create work for the businesses along related and supporting industries. This wealth creation process is inherent in any market economy, and the role of business enterprises is to exploit these mechanisms.

Economic development requires *cooperation* between business and government. Traditionally, each group has viewed the other with suspicion and thus has often, unwittingly, worked at cross purposes.[6] The level of cooperation between business and government is partly influenced by the structure of the government (unitary versus federal government). Federal political structures (such as those of the United States and Australia) tend to involve structured forms of conflict between different levels of government. Such governmental structures tend to encourage decentralized or fragmented interests, and patterns of representation from outside groups, such as business. On the other hand, centralized and unified governmental structures and attempts to coordinate policymaking within the context of federalism tend to encourage more unity and concerted approaches from external interests.

The type and quality of leadership within the business and government sectors can also affect the character of business-government relations. Strong and charismatic leadership among the top echelons of government or business often sets the tone for how communication is maintained and what topics are placed on the policy agenda.

Business-government relations are influenced, too, by the relative power of the two sectors. Businesses may be able to develop cooperative relations with government when their relative credibility is high. If the government is responsive, capable, and electorally secure, with the opposition divided, then business needs to foster closer relations as an ongoing political investment. Alternatively, when government is not secure, or when short-term election cycles and strong party competition render political outcomes uncertain, then business tends to assume its natural caution in its day-to-day dealings with government. By the same token, business too can be divided or lack public credibility. In recent decades, for example, business has been criticized for being out of step with mounting community concern about the environment. Critiques of reckless "entrepreneurialism" in the 1980s have also exposed business to community disapproval and in some aspects weakened its position in the broader political environment.

Enhancing Government-Government Cooperation

Henry Kissinger argues that the international system of the twenty-first century will be marked by a seeming contradiction: on the one hand, fragmentation; on the other hand, growing globalization. He also suggests that, on the level of relations among states, the new order will be more like the European state system of the eighteenth and nineteenth centuries than the rigid patterns of the Cold War. The new order will consist of at least six major powers—the United States, Europe, China, Japan, Russia, and India—as well as a wide range of medium-sized and small countries. At the same time, international relations have become truly global for the first time. A whole set of issues has surfaced that can only be dealt with on a global basis, among them environment deterioration, the population explosion, and economic interdependence.[7]

After the Cold War, the century-long focus of geopolitics has shifted toward a focus on geoeconomics. States are becoming more and more interdependent, in that the well-being of states depends on each other's competition and cooperation. Consider a global system of free trade. In the absence of a world government, the benefits of trade depend on international cooperation—to enforce contracts, harmonize rules and regulations, and diminish protectionism. If any states break the rules of free trade, the benefits of free trade exchange slip away from all parties involved.

Reciprocity is one of the important principles that help international cooperation to emerge. Through reciprocity, norms and rules are enforced. On the one hand, states reciprocate each other's cooperation in opening markets. On the other hand, they punish each other's refusal to let in foreign products.[8]

Professors Schwab and Smadja (1995) suggest that if the current worldwide economic revolution is to lead to a new phase of widespread and steady growth, two major issues should be emphasized:

1. New international institutions will need to be established and existing ones revamped in order to sustain, monitor, and supervise the new global economic order. The creation of the World Trade Organization (WTO), for example, is one important step. Another is the ongoing debate about the role of the World Bank and the IMF in view of the entry of so many new countries into the world market.

2. International trade among regions and between regions remains of central importance in the world economy. The whole modus operandi of the international economy will have to be reviewed in light of the new strategic parity among regions. The key element will be support for whatever policies and initiatives sustain and expand the notion of open regionalization.[9]

Finally, as the trend toward regionalization gains momentum, WTO governance should, as Professor Jagdish Bhagwati (1991) has suggested, be reconsidered. Four suggestions follow:

• A forceful statement must be made by the major players that regionalism and the WTO are not incompatible and that the WTO remain the central institution supervising issues of world trade policy, despite regional blocs.

• A strict interpretation of Article XXIV [of the GATT] in regard to all newly emerging and prospective free trade areas must be insisted upon so that less demanding preferential and discriminatory arrangements do not multiply in the present proregionalism climate.

• For free trade areas, the rule should be that the "duties and other regulations of commerce" are not to be "higher or more restrictive" than those previously in effect.

• Equally important, it is necessary to build a commitment into Article XXIV to look favorably at accepting new members into a union (or free trade area, if not ruled out by the adoption of the immediately preceding proposal), so that these arrangements more readily serve as building blocks of, rather than stumbling blocks to, WTO-wide free trade.[10]

NOTES

Chapter 1: Challenges to Building a Nation's Wealth

1. "In South Korea, A Different Kind of Dread," *BusinessWeek,* July 25, 1994, pp. 42–43.
2. Michael P. Todaro, *Economic Development in the Third World,* 5th edn (White Plains, NY: Longmans, 1994), p. 39.
3. Ibid., p. 41.
4. Quoted from ibid., pp. 41–42, with minor changes.
5. Ibid., p. 45.
6. UNDP, *Human Development Report 1993* (New York: Oxford University Press, 1993), p. 12.
7. Todaro, op. cit., p. 43.
8. Ibid., p. 45.
9. Ibid., p. 46.
10. Ibid.
11. Member of Working Group on Energy Technology Cooperation, "The Policy Paper," in Donald L. Guertin, John E. Gray, and Henri-Claude Bailly, eds., *Energy Technology Cooperation for Sustainable Economic Development* (Lanham, MD: University Press of America, 1993), p. 8.
12. UNDP, op. cit.; Box 3.2, p. 33.
13. David H. Geddes, "Economic Development in the 1990s: Toward a Sustainable Future," *Economic Development Review* (Summer 1993), p. 71. See also William T. Ziemba and Sandra L. Schwartz, *Power Japan* (Chicago: Probus Publishing Company, 1992), p. 347.
14. Quoted from "Be Fruitful and Multiply," *Europe* (January–February 1984), p. 4, with minor changes.
15. Quoted from UNDP, op. cit., pp. 35–37, with minor changes.
16. Todaro, op. cit., p. 47.
17. Quoted from Azizur Rahman Khan and Mahabub Horrsain, *The Strategy of Development in Bangladesh* (New York: Macmillan, 1989), p. 6, with minor changes.

18. See "Politics and Markets: Russia and Brazil Compared: Jeffrey Sachs in Conversation with Norman Gall," *World Affairs* (Winter 1994), pp. 147–155.
19. Quoted from "The Case of Central Planning," *The Economist,* Sept. 12, 1992, pp. 14–14, with minor changes.
20. Ibid.
21. See John Stopford and Susan Strange, with John S. Henley, *Rival States, Rival Firms: Competition for World Market Shares* (New York: Cambridge University Press, 1991), pp. 19–23. See also Lee. E. Preston and Duane Windsor, *The Rules of the Game in the Global Economy: Policy Regimes for International Business* (Norwell, MA: Kluwer Academic Publishers, 1992), p. 3.
22. Ibid.
23. Quoted from Klaus Schwab and Claude Smadja, "Power and Policy: The New Economic World Order," in Kenichi Ohmae, ed., *The Evolving Global Economy* (Boston: Harvard Business School Press, 1995), pp. 108–109, with minor changes.
24. See Stopford and Strange, op. cit., pp. 19–23.
25. Robert H. Girling, "Trade Conflicts of the 1980s," in Philip King, ed., *International Economics and International Economic Policy: A Reader* (New York: McGraw-Hill, 1990), p. 148.
26. See Jeffrey J. Schott, "Trading Blocs and the World Trading System," *The World Economy* (March 1991), pp. 1–4.
27. Ibid.
28. See Michael E. Porter, *The Competitive Advantage of Nations* (New York: The Free Press, 1990).
29. See Stopford and Strange, op. cit., p. 14.
30. Quoted from ibid.
31. Ibid.
32. Quoted from ibid., with minor changes.
33. Ibid., pp. 4–5.
34. Sam Pitroda, "Development, Democracy, and the Village Telephone," *Harvard Business Review* (November–December 1993), pp. 66–79.
35. Jack N. Behrman and Dennis A. Rondinelli, "The Cultural Imperatives of Globalization," *Economic Development Quarterly* (May 1992), pp. 118–119.
36. See Joshua S. Goldstein, *International Relations* (New York: HarperCollins, 1994), p. 395.
37. Quoted from ibid., p. 145, with minor changes.
38. H. A. Reitsma and J. M. G. Kleinpenning, *The Third World in Perspective* (Totoma, NJ: Rowman & Allanheld, 1985), p. 182.
39. Quoted from ibid., p. 183, with minor changes.
40. Ibid., p. 184.
41. See Michael Best, *The New Competition: Institutions of Industrial Restructuring* (Cambridge, MA: Harvard University Press, 1990), p. 277. See also Seymour H. Fine, "Global Warming: A Social Marketing Imperative," in *Marketing and Economic Re-Structuring in the Developing World,* Fourth International Conference on Marketing and Development (San Jose, Costa Rica, 1993).
42. Mark Memmott, "World Bank Special Report," *USA Today.*

43. Michael P. Todaro, *Economic Development in the Third World,* 4th edn (White Plains, NY: Longmans, 1989), p. 168.
44. Ibid.
45. Quoted from Hamish McRae, *The World in 2020* (Boston: Harvard Business School Press, 1994), pp. 35–36, with minor changes.
46. Quoted from Goldstein, op. cit., p. 120, with minor changes.
47. Quoted from Rajendra S. Sosodia, "Singapore Invests in the Nation-Corporation," in Ohmae, op. cit., pp. 77–78, with minor changes.
48. Thomas S. Axworthy, "Democracy and Development: Luxury or Necessity?" in Kenneth E. Bauzon, ed., *Development and Democratization in the Third World* (Washington, DC: Crane Russak, 1992), p. 116.
49. See the excellent review article by Subbiah Kannappan, "The Economics of Development: The Procrustean Bed of Mainstream Economics," in *Economic Development and Cultural Change* (July 1995) pp. 863–888, in which Kannappan points out the inadequacies of a strictly economic framework for analyzing and prescribing national wealth-building strategies.
50. See Robert J. Barro, *Macroeconomics* (New York: John Wiley & Sons, 1984), pp. 517–523.

Chapter 2: Major Dilemmas and Trade-Offs in Public Policy Toward Economic Development

1. Michael P. Todaro, *Economic Development in the Third World,* 4th edn (White Plains, NY: Longmans, 1989), p. 143.
2. Ibid., p. 144.
3. "Politics and Markets: Russia and Brazil Compared: Jeffrey Sachs in Conversation with Norman Gall," *World Affairs* (Winter 1994), pp. 147–155. See also UNDP, *Human Development Report 1993* (New York: Oxford University Press, 1993), pp. 21–22.
4. Todaro, op. cit., p. 144.
5. Michael P. Todaro, *Economic Development in the Third World,* 5th edn (White Plains, NY: Longmans, 1994), p. 158.
6. Ibid., p. 159.
7. UNDP, op. cit., pp. 21–22.
8. Todaro (5th edn), op. cit., p. 159.
9. Ibid.
10. Sung-Soo Koh and Zannis Res, *Capital Markets in Korea and the Far East* (London: IFR Books, n.d.), pp. 42–43.
11. See Charles K. Wilber, *The Soviet Model and Underdeveloped Countries* (Chapel Hill, NC: University of North Carolina Press, 1969), pp. 86–91.
12. Dieter Senghaas, "Catching Up on Development—A Chance?" *Universitas* (February 1992), pp. 78–79.
13. Bruce Herrick and Charles P. Kindleberger, *Economic Development,* 4th edn (New York: McGraw-Hill, 1983), p. 237.
14. UNDP, op. cit., p. 56.

15. Herrick and Kindleberger, op. cit., p. 238.
16. Ibid., p. 237.
17. Wilber, op. cit., p. 87.
18. Ibid., p. 91.
19. UNDP, op. cit., p. 46.
20. Hubert Gabrisch and Kazimierz Laski, "Transition from Command to Market Economies," in Peter Havlik, ed., *Dismantling the Command Economy in Eastern Europe* (Boulder CO: Westview Press, 1991), pp. 25–27. See also Jeffrey Sachs, "The Economic Transformation of Eastern Europe: The Case of Poland," *Economics of Planning,* 25 (1992), p. 7.
21. Gabrisch and Laski, op. cit., pp. 25–27.
22. Quoted from UNDP, op. cit., p. 62.
23. Gabrisch and Laski, op. cit., pp. 25–27.
24. Ibid.
25. Thorkil Kristensen, *Inflation and Unemployment in the Modern Society* (New York: Praeger, 1981), p. 41.
26. See ibid., pp. 41–42.
27. David W. Conklin, *Comparative Economic Systems* (New York: Cambridge University Press, 1991), p. 39.
28. L. Gray Cowan, *Privatization in the Developing World* (New York: Greenwood Press, 1990), pp. 1–2.
29. John Stopford and Susan Strange, with John S. Henley, *Rival States, Rival Firms: Competition for Market Shares* (New York: Cambridge University Press, 1991), p. 121. See also Vito Tanzi, *Public Finance in Developing Countries* (Brookfield, VT: Edward Elgar, 1991), p. 46.
30. Tanzi, op. cit., p. 46.
31. Cowan, op. cit., p. 4.
32. Ibid.
33. Quoted from Stopford and Strange, op. cit., pp. 120–121, with minor changes.
34. It should be noted that although state ownership may be desirable where severe monopoly problems or major externalities exist, technological changes have substantially reduced the prevalence of such problems. For example, Internet, facsimile machines, and cheaper telephone charges have undermined the postal monopoly.
35. Ajit Singh, "Industrial Policy in the Third World in the 1990s: Alternative Perspectives," in Keith Cowling and Roger Sugden, eds., *Current Issues in Industrial Economic Strategy* (Manchester, UK: Manchester University Press, 1992), pp. 127–130. See also Todaro (5th edn), op. cit., p. 585.
36. Singh, op. cit., pp. 127–130.
37. Michael Best, *The New Competition: Institutions of Industrial Restructuring* (Cambridge, MA: Harvard University Press, 1990), p. 263.
38. Bennett Harrison, "The Myth of Small Firms as the Predominant Job Generators," Commentary in *Economic Development Quarterly* (February 1994), pp. 3–16.
39. Ibid., pp. 3–5.
40. William L. Waugh, Jr., and Deborah McCorkle Waugh, "Economic Development Programs of State and Local Governments and the Site Selection Decisions of Smaller

Firms," in Richard J. Judd, William T. Greenwood, and Fred W. Becker, eds., *Small Business in a Regulated Economy* (New York: Quorum Books, 1988), p. 112.

41. Robert Howard, "Can Small Business Help Countries Compete?" *Harvard Business Review* (November–December 1990), p. 88.

42. Ibid., p. 94.

43. Hermann Simon, *Hidden Champions* (Boston: Harvard Business School Press, 1996). See also Roger D. Blackwell, *From the Edge of the World* (Columbus, OH: Ohio University Press, 1994), p. 51.

44. Edward Goodman, "Introduction: The Political Economy of the Small Firm in Italy," in Edward Goodman and Julia Bamford with Peter Saynor, eds., *Small Firms and Industrial Districts in Italy* (New York: Routledge, 1989), p. 1.

45. Quoted from Howard, "Can Small Business Help Countries Compete?" p. 96, with minor changes.

46. UNDP, op. cit., pp. 39–41.

47. *The Economist,* June 8–14 1991, p. 86. See also T. W. Kang, *Is Korea the Next Japan?: Understanding the Structure, Strategy and Tactics of America's Next Competitor* (New York: The Free Press, 1989), p. 30.

48. *The Economist,* op. cit., p. 86. See also Byoung-Lo Philo Kim, *Two Koreas in Development* (New Brunswick, NJ: Transaction Publishers, 1992), p. 126.

49. Kang, op. cit., p. 30.

50. Kim, op. cit., p. 182.

51. Ibid., p. 118.

52. *The Economist,* op. cit., p. 86.

53. John de la Mothe and Louis Marc Ducharme, "Science, Technology and Free Trade: Towards an Understanding of the New Competitive Agenda," in John de la Mothe and Louis Marc Ducharme, eds., *Science, Technology and Free Trade* (New York: Pinter Publishers, 1990), pp. 3–4.

54. Giovanni Dosi, John Zysman, and Laura D'Andrea Tyson, "Technology, Trade Policy and Schumpeterian Efficiencies," in de la Mothe and Ducharme, eds., op. cit., pp. 21–22.

55. See F. M. Scherer, *International High-Technology Competition* (Cambridge, MA: Harvard University Press, 1992), pp. 9–10.

56. Quoted from Joshua S. Goldstein, *International Relations* (New York: Harper-Collins, 1994), p. 314, with minor changes.

57. Paul R. Krugman, "Introduction: New Thinking About Trade Policy," in Paul R. Krugman, ed., *Strategic Trade Policy and New International Economics* (Cambridge, MA: MIT Press, 1988), p. 7.

58. Scherer, op. cit., p. 21.

59. David B. Yoffie, *International Trade and Competition* (New York: McGraw-Hill, 1990), p. 18.

60. Ibid.

61. Vinod Thomas, John Nash, and Associates, *Best Practices in Trade Policy Reform,* A World Bank Publication (New York: Oxford University Press, 1991), Box 1–2, pp. 10–11. See also Yoffie, op. cit., p. 18.

62. Professor Barbara Spencer, cited by Trevor Matthews and John Ravenhill, "Strate-

gic Trade Policy and Its Implications," in Stephen Bell and John Wanna, eds., *Business-Government Relations in Australia* (Marrickville, NSW: Harcourt Brace Jovanovich, 1992), p. 186.

63. Thomas, Nash, and Associates, op. cit., pp. 10–11.

64. Ibid.

65. Philip King, "The Multinational Corporation: Pro and Con," in Philip King, ed., *International Economics and International Economic Policy: A Review* (New York: McGraw-Hill, 1990), p. 234.

66. Todaro (5th edn), op. cit., pp. 531–533. See also Phedon Nicolaides, "Investment Policies in an Integrated World Economy," *The World Economy* (June 1991), pp. 125–127.

67. Todaro (5th edn), op. cit., p. 533.

68. Ibid., pp. 533–534.

69. Nicolaides, op. cit., p. 125.

70. Peter Dicken, *Global Shift: The Internationalization of Economic Activity,* 2nd edn (New York: The Guilford Press, 1992), p. 394.

71. Todaro (5th edn), op. cit., p. 534.

72. King, op. cit., p. 236.

73. Quoted from ibid., p. 237, with minor changes.

Chapter 3: Distinguishing Alternative Pathways to Development

1. See Roger D. Blackwell, *From the Edge of the World* (Columbus, OH: Ohio State University Press, 1994), p. 6.

2. Ryokichi Hirono, "Japan: Model for East Asian Industrialization?" in Helen Hughes, ed., *Achieving Industrialization in East Asia* (New York: Cambridge University Press, 1988), p. 241.

3. John M. Page, "The East Asian Miracle: An Introduction," *World Development,* vol. 22, no. 4 (1994), p. 618.

4. Ibid.

5. Ibid.

6. Ibid.

7. Ibid., p. 619.

8. Ibid.

9. Taewon Kwack, "Korea's Experience and Future Prospects of Economic Development," in Richard Harvey Brown and William T. Liu, eds., *Modernization in East Asia: Political, Economic, and Social Perspectives* (New York: Praeger, 1992), pp. 65–66.

10. Ibid., pp. 66–67.

11. Ibid., pp. 67–68. See also Vinod Thomas, John Nash, and Associates, *Best Practices in Trade Policy Reform,* A World Bank Publication (New York: Oxford University Press, 1991), p. 130.

12. Kwack, op. cit., p. 68.

13. Ibid., p. 69. See also Thomas, op. cit., p. 132.

14. Thomas, op. cit., p. 132.

15. Kwack, op. cit., p. 69.

16. Ibid.
17. Ibid., pp. 69–71.
18. Ibid., p. 69.
19. Marcus Noland, *Pacific Basin Developing Countries: Prospects for the Future* (Washington, DC: Institute for International Economics, 1990), p. 16.
20. Ibid.
21. B. Karin Chai, "Export-Oriented Industrialization and Political and Class Development: Hong Kong on the Eve of 1997," in Brown and Liu, eds., op. cit., p. 105.
22. Ibid., pp. 101–102.
23. Noland, op. cit., p. 16.
24. Ibid., p. 22.
25. Robert N. Gwynne, *New Horizons?: Third World Industrialization in an International Framework* (Hong Kong: Longmans Science & Technical, 1990), pp. 190–191. See also Noland, op. cit., p. 22.
26. Gwynne, op. cit., pp. 190–191.
27. Rajendra Sisodia, "Singapore Invests in the Nation-Corporation," *Harvard Business Review* (May–June 1992), p. 40.
28. Noland, op. cit., p. 23.
29. Ibid.
30. Garry Rodan, *The Political Economy of Singapore's Industrialization: National State and International Capital* (New York: Macmillan, 1990), p. 142.
31. Ibid.
32. Noland, op. cit., p. 24.
33. Rodan, op. cit., p. 142.
34. Ibid., pp. 147–148.
35. Ibid., p. 148.
36. Dwight H. Perkins, "There Are at Least Three Models of East Asian Development," *World Development,* vol. 22, no. 4 (1994), p. 660.
37. Ibid.
38. Quoted from ibid., pp. 660–661.
39. Ibid., p. 661.
40. Joshua S. Goldstein, *International Relations* (New York: HarperCollins, 1994), p. 517.
41. Gwynne, op. cit., pp. 77–78. See also Patricio Meller, "Trade Opening of the Chilean Economy: Policy Lessons," in Adolfo Canitrot and Silvia Junco, eds., *Macroeconomic Conditions and Trade Liberalization* (Washington, DC: Inter-American Development Bank, 1993), p. 123.
42. Gwynne, op. cit., p. 77.
43. Meller, op. cit., p. 153.
44. Gwynne, op. cit., p. 80.
45. Ibid., p. 79.
46. Ibid.
47. Pedro Belli, "Globalizing the Rest of the World," *Harvard Business Review* (July–August 1991), pp. 50–55.
48. Paul Kennedy, *Preparing for the Twenty-First Century* (New York: Random House, 1993), p. 175. See also Gavin Boyd, "China in the Pacific Regional Economy," in Brown and Liu, eds., op. cit., p. 147.

49. Kennedy, op. cit., p. 175.

50. Jan S. Prybyla, *Reform in China and Other Socialist Economies* (Washington, DC: AEI Press, 1990), p. 80.

51. "Survey of China," *The Economist,* Nov. 28, 1992, pp. 6–8.

52. Ibid.

53. Prybyla, op. cit., p. 81.

54. Ibid.

55. "Survey of China," *The Economist,* op. cit., pp. 6–8.

56. Ibid.

57. Ibid.

58. Adi Schnytzer, *Stalinist Economic Strategy in Practice: The Case of Albania* (New York: Oxford University Press, 1982), pp. 3–4.

59. Charles K. Wiber, *The Soviet Model and Underdeveloped Countries* (Chapel Hill, NC: University of North Carolina Press, 1969, pp. 76–77. See also Schnytzer, op. cit., pp. 3–5.

60. Martin Janicke, *State Failure: The Impotence of Politics in Industrial Society,* trans. Alan Braley (University Park, PA: Pennsylvania State University Press, 1990), pp. 118–123.

61. Ibid.

62. Kennedy, op. cit., pp. 230–232.

63. See Svetozar Pejovich, *The Economics of Property Rights: Towards a Theory of Comparative Systems* (Boston: Kluwer Academic Publishers, 1990), p. 113.

64. Kennedy, op. cit., pp. 230–232.

65. Quoted from ibid., p. 232.

66. Paul G. Hare, "Hungary," in David A. Dyker, ed., *The National Economies of Europe* (White Plains, NY: Longmans, 1992), p. 213.

67. Istvan P. Szekely and David M. G. Newbery, "Introduction," in Istvan P. Szekely and David M. G. Newbery, eds. *Hungary: An Economy in Transition* (New York: Cambridge University Press, 1993) p. 4. Reprinted with the permission of Cambridge University Press.

68. Ibid.

69. Hare, op. cit., p. 233.

70. Szekely and Newbery, "Introduction," op. cit., pp. 4–5.

71. Jeffrey Sachs, "The Economic Transformation of Eastern Europe: The Case of Poland," *Economics of Planning,* 25 (1992), p. 6.

72. Ibid.

73. Ibid., pp. 7–8.

74. UNDP, *Human Development Report 1993* (New York: Oxford University Press, 1993), p. 62.

75. Stanislaw Wellisz, Maciej Iwanek, and Marek Bednarski, "Privatization," in Henryk Kierzkowski, Marek Okolski, and Stanislaw Wellisz, eds., *Stabilization and Structural Adjustment in Poland* (New York: Routledge, 1993), pp. 179–180.

76. Ibid.

77. Ibid.

78. UNDP, op. cit., p. 62.

79. Ibid.
80. Schaffer, op. cit., pp. 274–275.

Chapter 4: Strategic Groups of Nations and the Global Competitive Structure

1. See Walt Whitman Rostow, *The Stages of Economic Growth: a Non-Communist Manifesto* (Cambridge, UK: The University Press, 1964).
2. Erdener Kaynak, *Marketing and Economic Development* (New York: Praeger, 1986), pp. 1–3.
3. Robert M. Grant, "Porter's 'Competitive Advantage of Nations': An Assessment," *Strategic Management Journal,* 12 (1991), p. 539.
4. We use GDP per capita as a measurement of a country's current wealth position. Indeed, various indicators can also be used to measure a country's degree of industrialization. As Professors Reitsma and Kleinpenning have suggested, manufacturing's contribution to the GDP or the proportion of the working population employed in manufacturing can be used to measure the degree of industrialization. Since each indicator has its disadvantage, a number of them can be combined into a *composite index.* Apart from these two indicators, energy consumption per capita and industrial output per capita can also be used to develop an index of industrialization. See H. A. Reitsma and J. M. G. Kleinpenning, *The Third World in Perspective* (Totowa, NJ: Rowman & Allanheld, 1985), p. 122.
5. "An Economy's Best Friend," *The Economist,* Nov. 16, 1991, p. 87.
6. This section draws heavily from "Survey of the Global Economy," *The Economist,* Oct. 1, 1994, pp. 37–38.
7. The main reason the Philippines is not grouped as a "rising star" is following Noland's argument that "in some respects the Philippines, with its plantation-style farming, protected manufacturing industries, large external debt, and political instability, more closely resembles a stereotypical Latin American economy than an East Asian one. And like some countries in Latin America, the Philippines today is in the midst of a comprehensive liberalization program that at least holds the promise of improving the country's economic performance." See Marcus Noland, *Pacific Basin Developing Countries: Prospects for the Future* (Washington, DC: Institute for International Economics, 1990), p. 160.
8. John M. Page, "The East Asian Miracle: An Introduction," *World Development,* vol. 22, no. 4 (1994), pp. 615–625.
9. Ibid.
10. Noland, op. cit., p. 141.
11. Ibid., pp. 141–142.
12. Colin Kirkpatrick, "Regionalisation, Regionalism and East Asian Economic Cooperation," *The World Economy* (March 1994), pp. 194–195.
13. Noland, op. cit., p. 159.
14. Joshua S. Goldstein, *International Relations* (New York: HarperCollins, 1994), p. 517.
15. Noland, op. cit., p. 161.
16. B. J. McCormick, *The World Economy* (Totowa, NJ: Philip Allan/Barnes & Noble Books, 1988), p. 253.

17. To make a success of the policy, some specific infrastructures and conditions such as a real large internal market, a large and diversified industrial base, and most importantly, independent scientific and technical capabilities are needed. See Table 2.1 of "Three Development Models: Alternatives to Status Quo," in G. S. Kindra, ed., *Marketing in Developing Countries* (London: Croom Helms, 1984), p. 15.

18. Dirk Messner, "Shaping Industrial Competitiveness in Chile: The Case of the Chilean Wood-Processing Industry," in Klaus Esser, Wolfgang Hillebrand, Dirk Messner, and Jorg Meyer-Stamer, eds., *International Competitiveness in Latin America and East Asia* (Portland, OR: Frank Cass, 1993), p. 33.

19. McCormick, op. cit., pp. 253–272.

20. Ibid., p. 244.

21. Robert N. Gwynne, *New Horizons?: Third World Industrialization in an International Framework* (Hong Kong: Longmans Science & Technical, 1990), p. 203.

22. UNDP, *Human Development Report 1993* (New York: Oxford University Press, 1993), p. 59.

23. Ibid., p. 56.

24. Michael P. Todaro, *Economic Development,* 5th edn (White Plains, NY: Longmans, 1994), p. 218.

25. See UNDP, op. cit., p. 59. See also Todaro, op. cit., p. 218.

26. Todaro, op. cit., p. 218.

27. Quoted from Hamish McRae, *The World in 2020* (Boston: Harvard Business School Press, 1994), pp. 7–8.

28. Goldstein, op. cit., p. 521.

29. Jan Winiecki, "Regional Survey," in Jan Winiecki and Andrzej Kondratowicz, eds., *The Macroeconomics of Transition: Developments in East Central Europe* (New York: Routledge, 1993), p. 5.

30. UNDP, op. cit., p. 63.

31. While the Czechs feel that forty years of Soviet rule destroyed their economy, the Slovaks had obtained many benefits from the Soviet decision to put industry in Slovakia (nearer the Soviet Union). As a result, Slovaks presently feel less hostility toward Russia and less urgency to join the European Union. See *Chicago Tribune,* Oct. 12, 1994.

32. Winiecki, op. cit., p. 5.

33. *Chicago Tribune,* Oct. 10, 1994.

34. Todaro, op. cit., pp. 645–646.

35. Otto Hieronymi, *Economic Policies for the New Hungary: Proposals for a Coherent Approach* (Columbus, OH: Battelle Press, 1990), pp. 3–4.

36. Christopher Freeman and Bengt-Ake Lundvall, eds., *Small Countries Facing the Technological Revolution* (New York: Pinter Publishers 1988), pp. 48–49.

37. Ibid., p. 40.

38. Henry T. Azzam, *The Gulf Economies in Transition* (New York: St. Martin's Press, 1988), p. 3.

39. Todaro, op. cit., pp. 642–644.

40. Ibid.

Chapter 5: Assessing the Nation's Strengths and Weaknesses

1. Hamish McRae, *The World in 2020* (Boston: Harvard Business School Press, 1994), p. 8.
2. Richard H. Franke, Geert Hofstede, and Michael H. Bond, "Cultural Roots of Economic Performance: A Research Note," *Strategic Management Journal,* 12 (1991), pp. 165–173.
3. See George C. Lodge, "Introduction: Ideology and Country Analysis," in George C Lodge and Ezra F. Vogel, eds., *Ideology and National Competitiveness: An Analysis of Nine Countries* (Cambridge, MA: Harvard University Press, 1987), pp. 9–10.
4. Lester C. Thurow, "Who Owns the Twenty-First Century?" *Sloan Management Review* (Spring 1992), p. 6.
5. See Charles Hampden-Turner, "The Boundaries of Business: The Cross-Cultural Quagmire," in Kenichi Ohmae, ed., *The Evolving Global Economy* (Boston: Harvard Business School Press, 1995), p. 86. See also Coral R. Snodgrass and Uma Sekaran, "The Cultural Components of Strategic Decision Making in the International Arena," in Anant R. Negandhi and Arun Savara, eds., *International Strategic Management* (Toronto: Lexington Books, 1989), pp. 146–147.
6. Thurow, op. cit., p. 6.
7. Ezra F. Vogel, "Conclusion," in Lodge and Vogel, eds., op. cit., pp. 322–323.
8. Paul A. Herbig, "The Rise and Fall of Great Britain's Technological Leadership: Is the United States Following in Britain's Footsteps?" *Technological Forecasting and Social Change,* 40 (1991), pp. 218–219.
9. Telesis, *Competing for Prosperity: Business Strategies and Industrial Policies in Modern France* (London: Policy Studies Institute, 1986), pp. 302–303.
10. McRae, op. cit., pp. 39–41.
11. New Zealand Business Roundtable, *The Old New Zealand and the New* (March 1994), pp. 53–54.
12. Quoted from ibid.
13. UNDP, *Human Development Report 1993* (New York: Oxford University Press, 1993), p. 10.
14. Ibid., Box 2.5, p. 26.
15. Ibid., Box 2.6, p. 27. See also Hossein Askari, "It's Time to Make Peace with Iran," *Harvard Business Review* (January–February 1994), pp. 50–63.
16. See Ministry for Planning of France, *France, Europe Xth Plan 1989–1992* (Paris: French Planning Office, 1989).
17. Angus Maddison, *Dynamic Forces in Capitalist Development: A Long-Run Comparative View* (New York: Oxford University Press, 1991), p. 57.
18. Quoted from McRae, op. cit., pp. 9–10.
19. Deborah S. DeGraff, "Population Growth and Government Policy in the Developing World: Lessons from Asia," in Kenneth E. Bauzon, ed., *Development and Democratization in the Third World* (Washington, DC: Crane Russak, 1992), pp. 155–157.
20. Ibid.
21. Maddison, op. cit., p. 64.

22. Ibid., pp. 65–66.
23. Ibid., pp. 66–67.
24. Ibid., pp. 30–35.
25. Telesis, op. cit., pp. 311–312.
26. Ibid., pp. 310–311.
27. This section draws heavily from Michael E. Porter, *The Competitive Advantage of Nations* (New York: The Free Press, 1990), pp. 76–80.
28. See Mitchell Y. Abolafia and Nicole W. Biggart, "Competition and Markets: An Institutional Perspective," in Amitai Etzioni and Paul R. Lawrence, eds., *Socio-Economics: Toward a New Synthesis* (Armonk, NY: M. E. Sharpe, 1991), p. 225. And also William H., Davidson, "Ecostructure and International Competitiveness," in Negandhi and Savara, eds., op. cit., p. 13.
29. Charles H. Ferguson, "Computers and the Coming of the U.S. Keiretsu," *Harvard Business Review* (July–August 1990), p. 58. See also *The Economist,* Jan. 5, 1991, p. 54.
30. Gary G. Hamilton and Marco Orru, "Organizational Structure of East Asian Companies," in Kae H. Chung and Hak Chong Lee, eds., *Korean Managerial Dynamics* (New York: Praeger, 1989), pp. 43–46.
31. Ku Hyun Jung, "Business-Government Relations in Korea," in Chung and Lee, eds., op. cit., pp. 21–23.
32. Hamilton, op. cit., pp. 43–46.
33. Ku Hyun Jung, "Business-Government Relations in Korea," in Chung and Lee, eds., op. cit., pp. 21–23.
34. Ibid., p. 46.
35. Hamilton, op. cit., pp. 43–46.
36. Michael Best, *The New Competition: Institutions of Industrial Restructuring* (Cambridge, MA: Harvard University Press, 1990), pp. 203–204.
37. *The Economist,* March 9–15, 1991, pp. 74–75.
38. Hubert Schmitz and Bernard Musyck, "Industrial Districts in Europe: Policy Lesson for Developing Countries?" *World Development,* vol. 22, no. 6 (1994), pp. 889–910.
39. William H. Davidson, "Ecostructure and International Competitiveness," in Negandhi and Savara, eds., op. cit., p. 14.
40. Nikhilesh Dholakia, "The Marketing of Development: An Exploration of Strategic Forms of Development," Research in Marketing, Supplement 4. *Marketing and Development: Toward Broader Dimensions* (Greenwich, CT: JAI Press, 1988, pp. 63–78.
41. Anis Chowdhury and Iyanatul Islam, *The Newly Industrialising Economies of East Asia* (New York: Routledge, 1993), p. 56.
42. Ibid., p. 48.
43. Dholakia, op. cit., p. 64.
44. Quoted from Rajendra S. Sisodia, "Singapore Invests in the Nation-Corporation," in Kenichi Ohmae, ed., *The Evolving Global Economy* (Boston: Harvard Business School Press, 1995), p. 77.
45. Quoted from Klaus Esser, "Latin America—Industrialization Without Vision," in Klaus Esser, Wolfgang Hillbrand, Dirk Messner, and Jorg Meyer-Stamer, eds., *International Competitiveness in Latin America and East Asia* (Portland, OR: Frank Cass, 1993), p. 11.

46. John Stopford and Susan Strange, with John S. Henley, *Rival States, Rival Firms:Competition for World Market Shares* (New York: Cambridge University Press, 1991), p. 10.
47. Quoted from Klaus Esser, "Latin America—Industrialization Without Vision," in Esser, et al., eds., op. cit., pp. 10–11, with minor changes.
48. Michael Beenstock, quoted in Bruce Herrick and Charles P. Kindleberger, *Economic Development*, 4th edn (New York: McGraw-Hill, 1983), pp. 274–275.
49. Ibid., p. 275.
50. Don E. Kash, *Perpetual Innovation, The New World of Competition* (New York: Basic Books, 1989).
51. Svetozar Pejovich, *The Economics of Property Rights: Towards a Theory of Comparative Systems* (Boston: Kluwer Academic Publishers, 1990), p. 129.
52. Askari, op. cit., pp. 50–63.
53. Roy Hofheinz, Jr., and Kent E. Calder, *The Eastasia Edge* (New York: Basic Books, 1982), pp. 69–71.
54. Ibid.
55. Byoung-Lo Philo Kim, *Two Koreas in Development* (New Brunswick, NJ: Transaction Publishers, 1992), pp. 133–137 and 194–195.
56. Taewon Kwack, "Development Strategy and Investment Incentives: A General Equilibrium Simulation Analysis," *Korea Development Review*, vol. 5, no. 3 (December 1983).
57. Taewon Kwack, "Korea's Experience and Future Prospects of Economic Development," in Richard Harvey Brown and William T. Liu, eds., *Modernization in East Asia: Political, Economic and Social Perspectives* (Westport, CT: Praeger, 1992), p. 75.
58. Ibid., p. 76.
59. Ibid. See also Robert N. Gwynne, *New Horizons?: Third World Industrialization in an International Framework.* (Hong Kong: Longmans Scientific & Technical, 1990), p. 185.
60. *The Economist,* June 8–14, 1991, p. 86.
61. Sung-Soo Koh and Zannis Res, *Capital Markets in Korea and the Far East* (London: IFR Books, n.d.), p. 35.
62. Quoted from Kwack, "Korea's Experience," in Brown and Liu, eds., op. cit., p. 73. See also R. Dornbusch and Y. C. Park, *Korean Growth Policy* (monograph, 1987).
63. Koh and Res, op. cit., pp. 36–37.
64. Dornbusch and Park, op. cit., and Kwack, "Korea's Experience," and Liu, eds., op. cit., pp. 71–76.

Chapter 6: Assessing the Nation's Opportunities and Threats

1. This section draws heavily from pages 133–134 of Alfred D. Chandler's, "The Enduring Logic of Industrial Success," *Harvard Business Review* (March–April 1990), pp. 130–140. Reprinted by permission.
2. Terutomo Ozawa, "Japan in a New Phase of Multinationalism and Industrial Upgrading: Functional Integration of Trade, Growth and FDI," *Journal of World Trade* (February 1991), pp. 53–55.
3. Ibid., p. 53.

4. See Barrie G. James, *Trojan Horse: The Ultimate Japanese Challenge to Western Industry* (London: Mercury Books, 1990), p. 9.

5. Ozawa, op. cit., p. 54.

6. Marcus Noland, *Pacific Basin Developing Countries: Prospects for the Future* (Washington, DC: Institute for International Economics, 1990), p. 22.

7. Anis Chowdhury and Iyanatul Islam, *The Newly Industrialising Economies of East Asia* (New York: Routledge, 1993), pp. 248–249.

8. Noland, op. cit., pp. 26–27.

9. This section draws heavily from Guiguo Wang, "China's Return to GATT: Legal and Economic Implications," *Journal of World Trade* (June 1994), pp. 57 and 64.

10. Sung-Soo Koh and Zannis Res, *Capital Markets in Korea and the Far East* (London: IFR Books, n.d.), pp. 39–40.

11. Ibid.

12. *Financial Times,* May 11, 1995, p. 6.

13. H. A. Reitsma and J. M. G. Kleinpenning, *The Third World in Perspective* (Totowa, NJ: Rowman & Allanheld, 1985), p. 140.

14. Chia Siow Yue and Lee Tsao Yuan, "Subregional Economic Zones: A New Motive Force in Asia-Pacific Development," in C. Fred Bergsten and Marcus Noland, eds., *Pacific Dynamism and the International Economic System* (Washington, DC: Institute for International Economics, 1993), pp. 225–269.

15. Jetro, *White Paper on International Trade: Japan 1992*, Tokyo, p. 103.

16. John Stopford and Susan Strange, with John S. Henry, *Rival States, Rival Firms: Competition for World Market Shares* (New York: Cambridge University Press, 1991), p. 94.

17. Peter Dicken, *Global Shift: The Internationalization of Economic Activity,* 2nd edn (New York: The Guilford Press, 1992), pp. 82–83.

18. Noland, op. cit., p. 20.

19. See James C. Hsiung, "China in the Twenty-First Century," in Cal Clark and Steven Chan, eds., *The Evolving Pacific Basin in the Global Political Economy: Domestic and International Linkages* (Boulder, CO: Lynne Rienner Publishers, 1992), pp. 76–78.

20. Huh Monn Young, "Internal and External Changes on the Korean Peninsula and Prospects for Unification," *East Asia Review* (Summer 1993), pp. 28–30.

21. Kang In Duk, "The Unification Policy of the New Government in Seoul, and the Prospects," *East Asian Review* (Autumn 1993), pp. 67–68.

22. See *The Economist,* Nov. 30, 1991, pp. 33–34, for details.

23. *The Economist,* Aug. 29, 1992, pp. 27–28.

24. See Tsuneo Akaha, "Japan's Post-Cold War Challenges and Opportunities in Asia Pacific," in Clark and Chan, eds., op. cit., p. 56.

25. Carlyle A. Thayer, "Sino-Vietnamese Relations: The Interplay of Ideology and National Interest," *Asian Survey* (June 1994), pp. 527–528.

26. Quoted from ibid., pp. 527–528.

27. Ibid.

28. *Chicago Tribune,* Oct. 9, 1994.

29. *BusinessWeek,* Oct. 9, 1989, p. 52.

30. Ibid., p. 46.

31. This section draws heavily from Vivien Walsh, "Technology and the Competitive-

ness of Small Countries: Review," in Christopher Freeman and Bengt-Ake Lundvall, eds., *Small Countries Facing the Technological Revolution* (New York: Pinter Publishers, 1988), pp. 58–60.

32. This section draws heavily from Herminio Blanco, "Global Competition and the Special Challenges of Developing Countries: The Perspective of Developing Countries," in Antonio Furino, ed., *Cooperation and Competition in the Global Economy* (Cambridge, MA: Ballinger Publishing Company, 1988), pp. 249–252.

33. Sam Pitroda, "Development, Democracy, and the Village Telephone," *Harvard Business Review* (November–December 1993), pp. 66–79.

34. This section draws on Hilary F. French, "Reconciling Trade and the Environment," in *State of the World 1993* (New York: W. W. Norton, 1993), pp. 168–169.

Chapter 7: Developing the Nation's Strategic Thrust

1. Quoted from Anis Chowdhury and Iyanatul Islam, *The Newly Industrialising Economies of East Asia* (New York: Routledge, 1993), pp. 246–247.

2. Sheridan M. Tatsuno, *Created in Japan, From Imitators to World-Class Innovators* (New York: Harper & Row, 1990), p. 5.

3. Ibid., p. 6.

4. Terutomo Ozawa, "Technical Alliances of Japanese Firms: An 'Industrial Restructuring' Account of the Latest Phase of Capitalist Development," in Jorge Niosi, ed., *New Technology Policy and Social Innovations in the Firm* (New York: Pinter Publishers, 1994), p. 156.

5. This section draws heavily from Chris Flockton, "Federal Republic of Germany," in David A. Dyker, ed., *The National Economies of Europe* (White Plains, NY: Longmans, 1992), pp. 32–67.

6. Bruce R. Scott and George C. Lodge, eds., *U.S. Competitiveness in the World Economy* (Boston: Harvard Business Press, 1985), p. 1.

7. Don E. Kash, *Perpetual Innovation, the New World of Competition* (New York: Basic Books, 1989).

8. See "Reinventing America," *BusinessWeek,* Special Issue, 1992, p. 26.

9. This section draws heavily from R. B. McKern, "Industrial Strategy and Comparative Advantage: The Case of Australia," in Erdener Kaynak and Kam-Hon Lee, eds., *Global Business: Asia-Pacific Dimensions* (New York: Routledge, 1989), pp. 136–138.

10. See Chowdhury and Islam, op. cit., pp. 251–255. According to Michael Porter, an economy's trajectory may be conceptualized as proceeding along a continuum that may be summarized as *factor-driven, investment-driven,* and *innovation-driven phases of development* (see Chapter 3).

11. Richard M. Steers, Yookeun Shin, and Gerardo R. Ungson, *The Chaebol, Korea's New Industrial Might* (New York: Harper & Row, 1989), pp. 143–146.

12. Wolfgang Hillebrand, "Technology Modernization Processes in Korean Small- and Medium-Scale Industry—A New Success Story," in Klaus Esser, Wolfgang Hillebrand, Dirk Messner, and Jorg Meyer-Stamer, eds., *International Competitiveness in Latin America and East Asia* (Portland, OR: Frank Cass, 1993), pp. 98 and 100.

13. Rajendra S. Sisodia, "Singapore Invests in the Nation-Corporation,: *Harvard Business Review* (May–June 1992), p. 50.

14. Quoted from Economic Development Board, *Global Strategies: The Singapore Partnership,* pp. 10–11, with minor changes.
15. Sisodia, op. cit., p. 50.
16. Quoted from Economic Development Board, op. cit., pp. 10–11.
17. This section heavily draws from C. K. Prahalad, *Globalization: Pitfalls, Pain and Potential,* Rajiv Gandhi Institute for Contemporary Studies, (n.d.), pp. 1–8.
18. Jeffrey Sachs, "The Economic Transformation of Eastern Europe: The Case of Poland," *Economics of Planning,* 25 (1992), p. 6. See also Lawrence Summers, "The Next Decade in Central and Eastern Europe," in Christopher Clague and Gordon C. Rausser, eds., *The Emergence of Market Economies in Eastern Europe* (Cambridge, MA: Basil Blackwell, 1992), p. 32.
19. Charles Wolf, Jr., *Markets or Governments: Choosing Between Imperfect Alternatives,* 2nd edn (Cambridge, MA: MIT Press, 1993), pp. 170–171.
20. Summers, op. cit., p. 32.
21. This section draws heavily from Sachs, op. cit., pp. 16–17.
22. W. H. Mahatoo, "Marketing and Economic Restructuring in the Developing World: The Impact of a North American Free Trade Agreement (NAFTA) on Its Members," in *Marketing and Economic Re-Structuring in the Developing World,* Fourth International Conference on Marketing and Development (San Jose, Costa Rica, 1993), pp. 111–112.
23. Klaus Esser, "Latin America—Industrialization Without Vision," in Esser, et al., eds., op. cit., p. 16.
24. Ibid., p. 16–17.
25. Michael P. Todaro, *Economic Development in the Third World,* 5th edn (White Plains, NY: Longmans, 1994), p. 644.
26. Robert N. Gwynne, *New Horizons?: Third World Industrialization in an International Framework* (Hong Kong: Longmans Science & Technical, 1990), p. 202.
27. Quoted from ibid., with minor changes.
28. Ibid. See also Todaro, op. cit., p. 644.
29. H. A. Reitsma and J. M. G. Kleinpenning, *The Third World in Perspective* (Totowa, NJ: Rowman & Allanheld, 1985), pp. 213–215.
30. Ibid.

Chapter 8: Developing the Nation's Investment Policies

1. Klaus Schwab and Claude Smadja, "Power and Policy: The New Economic World Order," *Harvard Business Review* (November–December 1994), p. 44.
2. Lee E. Preston and Duane Windsor, *The Rules of the Game in the Global Economy: Policy Regimes for International Business* (Norwell, MA: Kluwer Academic Publishers, 1992), p. 23.
3. See John M. Stopford and Susan Strange, with John S. Henley, *Rival States, Rival Firms: Competition for World Market Shares* (New York: Cambridge University Press, 1991), p. 22.
4. Robin Gaster, "Protectionism with Purpose: Guiding Foreign Investment," *Foreign Policy* (Fall 1992), pp. 91–106.

5. F. M. Scherer, *International High Technology Competition* (Boston: Harvard Business School Press, 1992), p. 21.

6. Phedon Nicolaides, "Investment Policies in an Integrated World Economy," *The World Economy* (January 1991), pp. 127–128.

7. Quoted from Schwab and Smadja, op. cit., p. 43.

8. This section draws heavily on "Survey of the Global Economy," *The Economist*, Oct. 1, 1994, pp. 23–24.

9. This study was conducted by Charles Oman, at the OECD Development Center.

10. Quoted from "Survey of the Global Economy," *The Economist*, op. cit., p. 24.

11. Robert N. Gwynne, *New Horizons?: Third World Industrialization in an International Framework* (Hong Kong: Longmans Science & Technical, 1990), pp. 76–77.

12. Gaster, op. cit., pp. 91–106.

13. Louis T. Wells, Jr., and Alvin G. Wint, *Marketing a Country: Promotion as a Tool for Attracting Foreign Investment* (Washington, D.C.: International Finance Corporation: Multilateral Investment Guarantee Agency, 1990), p. 2. See also the more extensive treatment of investment attraction from a marketing point of view in Philip Kotler, Irwin Rein, and Donald Haider, *Marketing Places: Strategies for Attracting Industry, Investment and Tourists to Cities, States, and Nations* (New York: The Free Press, 1994).

14. Michael E. Porter, *The Competitive Advantage of Nations* (New York: The Free Press, 1990), p. 71.

15. Vinod Thomas, John Nash, and Associates, *Best Practices in Trade Policy Reform*, A World Bank Publication (New York: Oxford University Press, 1991), p. 190.

16. Nadeem M. Firoz, Ugur Yucelt, and Ahmed S. Maghrabi, "Free Trade Zone: A Stimulus to the Economic Development of a Developing Country," in *Marketing and Economic Re-Structuring in the Developing World*, Fourth International Conference on Marketing and Development (San Jose, Costa Rica, 1993), pp. 106–108.

17. "Free-Trade Zones in Europe: A Boom in the East, A Burden in the West," *EuroSphere* (KPMG Peat Marwick, August–September 1991), pp. 2–3.

18. Quoted from Ira Magaziner and Mark Patinkin, *The Silent War* (New York: Vintage Books, 1989), p. 356.

19. Ibid., p. 357.

20. Quoted from ibid., p. 331.

21. This section heavily draws from Wells and Wint, op. cit., pp. 9–21.

22. Quoted from ibid., pp. 9–10, with minor changes.

23. Katherine Marton and Rana K. Singh, "Technology Crisis for Third World Countries," *The World Economy* (June 1991), p. 200.

24. N. Mohan Reddy and Liming Zhao, "International Technology Transfer: A Review," *Research Policy*, 19 (1990), p. 291. See also John H. Dunning, *Multinational Enterprises and the Global Economy* (Reading, MA: Addison-Wesley, 1993), p. 289.

25. David C. Mowery, *Science and Technology Policy in Interdependent Economics* (Boston: Kluwer Academic Publishers, 1994), pp. 37–38.

26. Marie Anchordoguy, "How Japan Built a Computer Industry," in Charles H. Ferguson, "Computer Keiretsu and the Coming of the U.S.," *Harvard Business Review* (July–August 1990), p. 65.

27. Quoted from ibid., p. 65, with minor changes.

28. Quoted from Yung Whee Rhee and Therese Belot, *Export Catalysts in Low Income Countries, A Review of Eleven Success Stories,* World Bank Discussion Paper #72, p. 46, with minor changes.

29. Mowery, op. cit., pp. 37–38.

30. Quoted from ibid., with minor changes.

31. Quoted from Anchordoguy, op. cit., p. 65, with minor changes.

32. Mowery, op. cit., p. 38.

33. John H. Dunning, *Multinational Enterprises and the Global Economy* (Reading, MA: Addison-Wesley, 1993), p. 321 (Exhibit 11.2).

34. Erdener Kaynak, *Marketing and Economic Development* (New York: Praeger, 1986), p. 56.

35. Peter Dicken, *Global Shift: The Internationalization of Economic Activity,* 2nd edn (New York: The Guilford Press, 1992), pp. 394–395.

36. Ibid., p. 395. See also Jong-Tsong Chiang, "Technology and Alliance Strategies for Follower Countries," *Technological Forecasting and Social Change,* 35 (1989), pp. 347–348.

Chapter 9: Building the Nation's Industrial Clusters

1. See Lee E. Preston and Duane Windsor, *The Rules of the Game in the Global Economy: Policy Regimes for International Business* (Norwell, MA: Kluwer Academic Publishers, 1992), p. 58.

2. Quoted from Kenichi Ohmae, *The End of the Nation State: The Rise of Regional Economies* (New York: The Free Press, 1995), pp. 120–121.

3. This section draws heavily from Esben Sloth Andersen and Bengt-Ake Lundvall, "Small National Systems of Innovation Facing Technological Revolutions: An Analytical Framework," in Christopher Freeman and Bengt-Ake Lundvall, eds., *Small Countries Facing the Technological Revolution* (New York: Pinter Publishers, 1988), pp. 11–12.

4. Quoted from Orjan Solvell and Ivo Zander, "European Myopia," in L. G. Mattsson and B. Stymne, eds., *Corporate and Industry Strategies for Europe* (New York: North Holland, 1991), pp. 361–362, with minor changes.

5. Quoted from Esben Sloth Andersen and Bengt-Ake Lundvall, "Small National Systems of Innovation Facing Technological Revolutions: An Analytical Framework," in Freeman and Lundvall, eds., op. cit., p. 12.

6. Christian Debresson, "Technological Clusters and Competitive Poles: The Case of Canadian Energy," in Jorge Niosi, ed., *Technological Competitiveness* (Montreal: McGill-Queen's University Press, 1991), p. 61.

7. Sheridan M. Tatsuno, *Created in Japan* (New York: Harper & Row, 1990), p. 63.

8. Ibid.

9. Richard N. Foster, *Innovation: The Attacker's Advantage* (New York: Pan Books, 1986), pp. 115–116.

10. Quoted from ibid.

11. Tatsuno, op. cit., p. 67.

12. Ibid., p. 68.

13. Quoted from Bruce Rubinger, "Competing Through Technology: The Success Fac-

tors," in Jerry Dermer, ed., *Competitiveness Through Technology* (Lexington, MA: Lexington Books, 1986), p. 36.

14. Tatsuno, op. cit., pp. 64–67.

15. Quoted from ibid., pp. 66–67, with minor changes.

16. Quoted from Moshe Justmen and Morris Teubal, "Innovation Policy in an Open Economy: A Normative Framework for Strategic and Tactical Issues," in Morris Teubal, ed., *Innovation Performance, Learning and Government Policy* (Madison, WI: University of Wisconsin Press, 1987), pp. 209–219.

17. Quoted from Laura D'Andrea Tyson, "Making Policy For National Competitiveness in a Changing World," in Antonio Furino, ed., *Cooperation and Competition in the Global Economy* (Cambridge, MA: Ballinger Publishing, 1988), pp. 34–35.

18. Quoted from Gary Anderson, "Industry Clustering for Economic Development," *Economic Development Review* (Spring 1994), p. 27.

19. This section heavily draws from H. A. Reitsma and J. M. G. Kleinpenning, *The Third World in Perspective* (Totowa, NJ: Rowman & Allanheld, 1985), pp. 133–134.

20. Quoted from Anderson, op. cit., p. 32, with minor changes.

Chapter 10: Developing the Nation's Industrial Portfolio

1. Paul R. Krugman, "Targeting Industrial Policies: Theory and Evidence," in Dominick Salvatore, ed., *The New Protectionist Threat to World Welfare.* (New York: North Holland, 1987), pp. 268–269. See also T. W. Kang, *Is Korea the Next Japan?: Understanding the Structure, Strategy, and Tactics of America's Next Competitor* (New York: The Free Press, 1989), pp. 86–89.

2. Quoted from Gerald M. Hampton and Erwin Buske. "The Global Marketing Perspective," in S. Tamer Cavusgil, ed., *Advances in International Marketing* (Greenwich, CT: JAI Press, 1987), p. 270.

3. See Yves L. Doz and C. K. Prahalad, *The Multinational Mission* (New York: The Free Press, 1987).

4. Quoted from Jong-Tsong Chiang, "Technology and Alliance Strategies for Follower Countries," *Technological Forecasting and Social Change,* 35 (1989), p. 346, with minor changes.

5. Quoted from ibid., with minor changes.

6. Quoted from Philip F. Banks and Liam Fahey, "The Changing Face of European Industries: Identifying and Assessing Business Opportunities," in Liam Fahey, ed., *Winning in the New Europe: Taking Advantage of the Single Market* (Englewood Cliffs, NJ: Prentice Hall, 1992), p. 94, with minor changes.

7. Quoted from David B. Yoffie, *International Trade and Competition* (New York: McGraw-Hill, 1990), pp. 398–400, with minor changes.

8. Quoted from *The Economist,* Nov. 16–22, 1991, pp. 87–88, with minor changes.

9. Quoted from Barrie G. James, *Business Wargames* (Cambridge, MA: Pan Books, 1984), with minor changes.

10. Quoted from Ippei Yamazawa, *Economic and International Trade: The Japanese Model* Honolulu: The Resource System Institute, East-West Center, 1990), pp. 205–206, with minor changes.

11. In using this analysis, each dimension of the map needs to be broken down into lower

levels: investment strategy for various product groups of the specific industry; market segmentation for specific geographic coverage; and technology variety of a specific factor intensity. At these lower-level analyses, strategic guidelines are provided not only for the nation's policymakers but also for the corporate policymakers of that specific industry as well.

12. Michael Best, *The New Competition: Institutions of Industrial Restructuring* (Cambridge, MA: Harvard University Press, 1990), p. 189.
13. Barrie G. James, *Trojan Horse: The Ultimate Japanese Challenge to Western Industry* (London: Mercury Books, 1990), p. 5.
14. Quoted from Anis Chowdhury and Iyanatul Islam, *The Newly Industrialising Economies of East Asia* (New York: Routledge, 1993), p. 93.
15. Quoted from Henry T. Azzam, *The Gulf Economies in Transition* (New York: St. Martin's Press, 1988), pp. 126, 131, and 132, with minor changes.
16. Quoted from Anant R. Negandhi and Aspy P. Palia, "Alternative Approaches to Development of Computer Technology: A Comparison of India, Japan, and Singapore," in Erdener Kaynak and Kam-Hon Lee, eds., *Global Business: Asia-Pacific Dimensions* (New York: Routledge, 1989), pp. 420–421, with minor changes.
17. Christopher Freeman and Bengt-Ake Lundvall, eds., *Small Countries Facing the Technological Revolution* (New York: Pinter Publishers, 1988), pp. 235–236.
18. Ibid., p. 235.
19. Quoted from ibid.
20. Ibid. See also Morris Teubal, "Neutrality in Science Policy: The Promotion of Sophisticated Industrial Technology in Israel," in Morris Teubal, ed., *Innovation Performance, Learning and Government Policy* (Madison, WI: University of Wisconsin Press, 1987), pp. 193–194.
21. Ibid.
22. Peter T. Jones and David J. Teece, "What We Know and What We Don't Know About Competitiveness," in Antonio Furino, ed., *Cooperation and Competition in the Global Economy* (Cambridge, MA: Ballinger Publishing, 1988), pp. 284–285.
23. Freeman and Lundvall, eds., op. cit., p. 236.
24. Quoted from Laura D'Andrea Tyson, "Making Policy for National Competitiveness in a Changing World," in Furino, ed., op. cit., pp. 34–35, with minor changes.
25. Freeman and Lundvall, eds., op. cit., p. 237.
26. Quoted from Fumio Kodama, *Emerging Patterns of Innovation: Sources of Japan's Technological Edge* (Boston: Harvard Business School Press, 1995), p. xix, with minor changes.

Chapter 11: Developing the Nation's Trade Policies

1. Joshua S. Goldstein, *International Relations* (New York: HarperCollins, 1994), pp. 311–313.
2. Robert N. Gwynne, *New Horizons?: Third World Industrialization in an International Framework* (Hong Kong: Longman Scientific & Technical, 1990), p. 71.
3. Michael P. Todaro, *Economic Development in the Third World,* 5th edn (White Plains, NY: Longmans, 1994), p 484. India is an exception to this pattern. First- and

second-stage substitutions were pursued quite early, leading to a very high cost structure and a low rate of technology growth.

4. Klaus Esser, "Latin America—Industrialization Without Vision," in Klaus Esser, Wolfgang Hillebrand, Dirk Messner, and Jorg Meyer-Stamer, eds., *International Competitiveness in Latin America and East Asia* (Portland, OR: Frank Cass, 1993), p. 8.

5. Quoted from John McMillan, "Kiwis Can Fly," *International Economic Insights* (January–February 1994), p. 40.

6. Vinod Thomas, John Nash, and Associates, *Best Practices in Trade Policy Reform,* A World Bank Publication (New York: Oxford University Press, 1991), p. 8. See also Juergen B. Donges and Ulrich Hiemenz, "Export Liberalization," in Lawrence B. Krause and Kim Kihwan, eds., *Liberalization in the Process of Economic Development* (Berkeley: University of California Press, 1991), pp. 216–219; and Gwynne, op. cit., p. 197.

7. Gwynne, op. cit., p. 197.

8. Esser, op. cit., p. 22.

9. Thomas, Nash, and Associates, op. cit., pp. 5 and 8.

10. Donges and Hiemenz, op. cit., pp. 215–216.

11. New Zealand Business Roundtable, *The Old New Zealand and the New* (March 1994), p. 135.

12. Donges and Hiemenz, op. cit., pp. 215–216.

13. Gary Gereffi and Donald L. Wyman, eds., *Manufacturing Miracles: Path of Industrialization in Latin America and East Asia* (Princeton, NJ: Princeton University Press, 1990), pp. 17–22.

14. Todaro, op. cit., p. 485.

15. Quoted from Stephen C. Smith, "Thailand and the Philippines: Trade Strategy," in Todaro, op. cit., pp. 556–558, with minor changes.

16. Gereffi and Wyman, eds., op. cit., pp. 17–22.

17. Quoted from ibid., with some changes.

18. Quoted from Barbara Rudolph, "India: A Painful Cure," *Time,* March 9, 1992, with minor changes.

19. Quoted from *Technology for Economic Growth: President's Progress Report,* (November 1993), pp. 29–30, with minor changes.

20. F. H. Rolf Seringhaus and Philip J. Rosson, *Government Export Promotion: A Global Perspective* (New York: Routledge, 1990), p. 31.

21. Ibid., p. 32.

22. Ibid., pp. 168–170.

23. Ibid., p. 170.

24. S. Tamer Cavusgil, "On the Internationalization Process of Firms," in Hans B. Thorelli and S. Tamer Cavusgil, *International Marketing Strategy* (Oxford: Pergamon Press, 1990), pp. 158–159.

25. Seringhaus and Rosson, op. cit., pp. 31–32.

26. Quoted from Yung Whee Rhee and Therese Belot, "Export Catalysts in Low Income Countries, A Review of Eleven Success Stories," *World Bank Discussion Paper* #72, p. 44, with minor changes.

27. Robert Wade, "How to Protect Exports from Protection: Taiwan's Duty Drawback Scheme," *The World Economy* (September 1991), p. 299.
28. Ibid.
29. Quoted from Thomas, Nash, and Associates, op. cit., pp. 136–137, with minor changes.
30. Quoted from Wade, op. cit., p. 308, with minor changes.
31. See Lawrence S. Welch and Raijo Luostarinen, "Inward-Outward Connections in Internationalization," *Journal of International Marketing*, 1 (1993), pp. 53–54.
32. Quoted from John M. Stopford and Susan Strange, with John S. Henley, *Rival States, Rival Firms: Competition for World Market Shares* (New York: Cambridge University Press, 1991), p. 135, with minor changes.
33. This section draws heavily from Ashoka Mody, "Reviving International Confidence Through Micro Reforms," Working Paper, June 9, 1992, pp. 10–12.
34. This section draws heavily from Jeffrey J. Schott, "Trading Blocs and the World Trading System," *The World Economy* (March 1991), pp. 1–4.
35. Paul Wonnacott and Mark Lutz," Is There a Case for Free Trade Areas?" in Jeffrey J. Schott, ed., *Free Trade Areas and U.S. Trade Policy* (Washington, DC: Washington Institute for International Economics, 1989), p. 71.
36. Thomas, Nash, and Associates, op. cit., pp. 195–197.
37. Quoted from Goldstein, op. cit., p. 395, with minor changes.
38. Saskia Sassen, "Economic Globalization: A New Geography, Composition, and Institutional Framework," In Jeremy Brecher, John Brown Childs, and Jill Cutler, eds., *Global Visions: Beyond the New World Order* (Boston: South End Press, 1993), p. 63. See also Peter Dicken, *Global Shift: The Internationalization of Economic Activity* (New York: The Guilford Press, 1992), p. 349.
39. Quoted from Jetro, *White Paper on International Trade: Japan 1992*, Tokyo, pp. 209–210, with minor changes.
40. UNDP, *Human Development Report 1993* (New York: Oxford University Press, 1993), p. 42.
41. This section draws heavily on "Survey of the Global Economy," *The Economist*, Oct. 1, 1994, pp. 34–35.
42. Ibid., p. 34, with minor changes.
43. This section draws on (1) "Should Trade Go Green?" *The Economist*, Jan. 26, 1991, pp. 13–14; (2) Hilary F. French, "Reconciling Trade and the Environment," in *State of the World 1993* (New York: W. W. Norton, 1993), pp. 168–171; (3) Candice Stevens, "The Environmental Effects of Trade," *The World Economy* (July 1993), pp 443–445; and (4) David W. Cheney, "International Competitiveness and Sustainable Development," *Economic Development Review* (Summer 1993), pp. 69–70.
44. Quoted from French, op. cit., p. 171, with minor changes.
45. Ibid.
46. Ibid.
47. Michael E. Porter and Claas van der Linde, "Green and Competitive: Ending the Stalemate," *Harvard Business Review* (September–October 1995), p. 133.
48. Quoted from ibid., pp. 120–121, with minor changes.
49. Quoted from French, op. cit., pp. 168–169.

50. Ibid.
51. Quoted from Jetro, op. cit., pp. 210–211, with minor changes.
52. Quoted from Paul Krugman, "Does Third World Growth Hurt First World Prosperity?" in Kenichi Ohmae, ed., *The Evolving Global Economy* (Boston: Harvard Business School Press, 1995), p. 126.

Chapter 12: Developing the Nation's Macroeconomic Policies

1. Rudiger Dornbusch and Alejandro Reynoso, "Financial Factors in Economic Development," in Rudiger Dornbusch, ed., *Policymaking in the Open Economy: Concepts and Case Studies in Economic Performance* (New York: Oxford University Press, 1993), p. 73.
2. Quoted from Michael P. Todaro, *Economic Development in the Third World,* 5th edn (White Plains, NY: Longmans, 1994), p. 22.
3. Dornbusch, ed., op. cit., p. 6.
4. "Zero Inflation," *The Economist,* Nov. 7–13, 1992, pp. 23–26.
5. Ibid.
6. Quoted from New Zealand Business Roundtable, *The Old New Zealand and the New* (March 1994), p. 135.
7. Vito Tanzi, *Public Finance in Developing Countries* (Brookfield, VT: Edward Elgar, 1991), p. 12.
8. Michael J. Boskin and Lawrence J. Lau, "Capital, Technology, and Economic Growth," in Nathan Rosenberg, Ralph Landau, and David C. Mowery, eds., *Technology and the Wealth of Nations* (Stanford, CA: Stanford University Press, 1992), pp. 17–55.
9. Michael Porter, "Capital Disadvantage: America's Failing Capital Investment System," *Harvard Business Review* (September–October 1992), pp. 65–82.
10. See William H. Davidson, *Ecostructure and International Competitiveness* (Lexington, MA: Lexington Books, 1989), p. 4.
11. Dornbusch, ed., op. cit., pp. 7–8.
12. Ira W. Lieberman, "The Role of Financial Institutions in Industrial Restructuring and Investment Coordination: The Implications for Certain ASEAN Developing Countries," in James A. Roumasset and Susan Barr, eds., *The Economics of Cooperation: East Asian Development and the Case of Pro-Market Intervention* (Boulder, CO: Westview Press, 1992), pp. 112–113.
13. William H. Davidson, "Ecostructure and International Competitiveness," in Anant R. Negandhi and Arun Savah, eds., *International Strategic Management* (Toronto: Lexington Books, 1989), p. 8.
14. See Telesis, *Competing for Prosperity: Business Strategies and Industrial Policies in Modern France* (London: Policy Studies Institute, 1986), pp. 199–205.
15. Ibid.
16. Philip R. Cateora, *International Marketing* (Homewood, IL: Irwin, 1993), p. 37.
17. Quoted from Ronald McKinnon and David Robinson, "Dollar Devaluation, Interest Rate Volatility, and the Duration of Investment in the United States," in Rosenberg, Landau, and Mowery, eds., op. cit., pp. 281–325.

18. Dornbusch, ed., op. cit., pp. 6–7.
19. This section draws heavily from Rudiger Dornbusch and Luis Tellez Kuenzler, "Exchange Rate Policy: Options and Issues," in Dornbusch, ed., op. cit., pp. 95–97.
20. Ezra F. Vogel, "Competition and Cooperation: Learning from Japan," in Antonio Furino, ed., *Cooperation and Competition in the Global Economy: Issues and Strategies* (Cambridge, MA: Ballinger Publishing Company, 1988), p. 52.
21. Michael E. Porter, *The Competitive Advantage of Nations* (New York: The Free Press, 1990).
22. Robert J. Carbaugh, *International Economics,* 3rd edn (Belmont, CA: Wadsworth Publishers, 1989), p. 307.
23. Todaro, op. cit., pp. 503–504.
24. Carbaugh, op. cit., p. 296.
25. This section draws from Robert N. Gwynne, *New Horizons?: Third World Industrialization in an International Framework* (White Plains, NY: Longmans, 1990), pp. 83–84.
26. Davidson, op. cit., pp. 9–10.
27. This section draws heavily from Ryuichiro Tachi, *The Contemporary Japanese Economy* (Tokyo: University of Tokyo Press, 1993), pp. 96–99.
28. Tanzi, op. cit., pp. 20–21.
29. Wagner quoted in Tachi, op. cit., pp. 96–99.
30. Quoted from Hamish McRae, *The World in 2020* (Boston: Harvard Business School Press, 1994), p. 185.
31. See New Zealand Business Roundtable, op. cit., p. 17.
32. See Dornbusch, ed., op. cit., p. 7.
33. Willem H. Buiter and T. N. Srinivasan, "Rewarding the Profligate and Punishing the Prudent and Poor: Some Recent Proposals for Debt Relief," in Philip King, ed., *International Economics and International Economic Policy: A Reader* (New York: McGraw-Hill, 1990), pp. 413–415. And see also Sung-Soo Koh and Zannis Res, *Capital Markets in Korea and the Far East* (London: IFR Books, n.d.), p. 15.
34. Todaro, op. cit., p. 23.
35. New Zealand Business Roundtable, op. cit., p. 17.
36. Todaro, op. cit., p. 611.
37. Davidson, "Ecostructure and International Competitiveness," in Negandhi and Savara, eds., op. cit., p. 6.
38. John Williamson and Donald R. Lessard, *Capital Flight: The Problem and Policy Responses* (Washington, DC: Institute for International Economics, 1987), pp. 40 and 45.
39. F. H. Rolf Seringhaus and Philip J. Rosson, *Government Export Promotion: A Global Perspective* (New York: Routledge, 1990), p. 32.
40. Quoted from *Foreign Policy* (Fall 1995), p. 57.
41. Cateora, op. cit., p. 79.
42. Robert J. Barro, *Macroeconomics* (New York: John Wiley & Sons, 1993), p. 268.
43. *Foreign Policy,* op. cit., pp. 54–55.
44. Quoted from New Zealand Business Roundtable, op. cit., pp. 135–136, with minor changes.

45. Ibid., p. 136.
46. UNDP, *Human Development Report 1993* (New York: Oxford University Press, 1993), p. 36.
47. *Foreign Policy,* op. cit., pp. 54–55. And also New Zealand Business Roundtable, op. cit., pp. 135–137.
48. Tanzi, op. cit., p. 85.
49. Quoted from John McMillan, "Kiwis Can Fly," *International Economic Insights* (January–February 1994), pp. 39–40, with minor changes.
50. Quoted from *Foreign Policy,* op. cit., pp. 56–57.
51. Todaro, op. cit., p. 646.
52. Tanzi, op. cit., pp. 85–86.
53. Ibid.
54. Quoted from Anis Chowdhury and Iyanatul Islam, *The Newly Industrialising Economies of East Asia* (New York: Routledge, 1993), pp. 193–195.

Chapter 13: Developing the Nation's Infrastructure

1. "Reinventing America: Meeting the New Challenges of a Global Economy," *BusinessWeek, Special Issue,* 1992, pp. 197–198.
2. United States Department of Agriculture, *Infrastructure Investment and Economic Development: Rural Strategies for the 1990s* (Washington, DC, 1990), pp. 4–6.
3. Quoted from Economic Development Board, *Global Strategies: The Singapore Partnership,* pp. 5–7. See also Telesis, *Competing for Prosperity: Business Strategies and Industrial Policies in Modern France* (London: Policy Studies Institute, 1986), pp. 310–311, with minor changes.
4. *BusinessWeek,* Nov. 28, 1994, p. 62.
5. Herbert Henzler, "Managing the Merger: A Strategy for the New Germany," *Harvard Business Review* (January–February 1992), pp. 26–27.
6. Quoted from Philip R. Cateora, *International Marketing* (Homewood, IL: Irwin, 1993), p. 217, with minor changes.
7. Quoted from *BusinessWeek,* Nov. 28, 1994, pp. 63–65, with minor changes.
8. See Henry W. Wanderleest, "Transportation and Economic Development: Some Conceptual and Practical Considerations," in Erdogan Kumcu, et al., eds., *The Role of Marketing in Development* (Muncie, IN: Ball State University Press, 1986).
9. Ibid., pp. 105–107. See also United States Department of Agriculture, op. cit., p. 30.
10. This section heavily draws from United States Department of Agriculture, op. cit., pp. 44–58.
11. Quoted from Rajendra S. Sisodia, "Singapore Invests in the Nation-Corporation," *Harvard Business Review* (May–June 1992), p. 42, with minor changes.
12. Daud Beg, "Privatization Initiatives in Developing Countries with Particular References to the Power Sector," in Donald L. Guertin, John E. Gray, and Henri-Claude Bailly, eds., *Energy Technology Cooperation for Sustainable Economic Development* (Lanham, MD: University Press of America, 1993), p. 78.
13. Scott Sklar, "Renewable Energy: A Key to Sustainable Development," In Guertin, Gray, and Bailly, eds., op. cit., pp. 170–171.

14. Gregory Tassey, "The Functions of Technology Infrastructure in a Competitive Economy," *Research Policies,* 20 (1991), p. 347.

15. Quoted from See Hamid Noori, *Managing the Dynamics of New Technology: Issues in Manufacturing Management* (Englewood Cliffs, NJ; Prentice Hall, 1990), p. 320, with minor changes.

16. Ibid.

17. David C. Mowery, *Science and Technology Policy in Interdependent Economies* (Norwell, MA: Kluwer Academic Publishers, 1994), p. 17. See also Rob Van Tulder and Gerd Junne, *European Multinationals in Core Technologies* (New York: John Wiley & Sons, 1988), p. 147.

18. Mowery, op. cit., pp. 16–17.

19. Ibid., pp. 16–19.

20. Ibid., pp. 18–19.

21. This section draws heavily from ibid., pp. 28–31. See also Moshe Justmen and Morris Teubal, "Innovation Policy in an Open Economy: A Normative Framework for Strategic and Tactical Issues," in Morris Teubal, ed., *Innovation Performance, Learning and Government Policy* (Madison, WI: University of Wisconsin Press, 1987), pp. 209–219.

22. Mowery, op. cit.

23. This section draws heavily from David J. Teece, "Strategies for Capturing the Financial Benefits from Technological Innovation," in Nathan Rosenberg, Ralph Landau, and David C. Mowery, eds., *Technology and the Wealth of Nations* (Stanford, CA: Stanford University Press, 1992), pp. 177–179. Reprinted by permission.

24. Quoted from Cateora, op. cit., p. 195, with minor changes.

25. Christopher T. Hill, "National Technology Strategies," in John de la Mothe and Louis Marc Ducharme, eds., *Science, Technology and Free Trade* (London: Pinter Publishers, 1990), p. 94.

26. M. Woodhall, "Economics of Education: A Review," in George Psacharopoulos, ed., *Economics of Education: Research and Studies* (Oxford: Pergamon Press, 1987), p. 1.

27. Quoted from Economic Development Board, op. cit., pp. 5–7. See also Rajendra S. Sisodia, "Singapore Invests in the Nation-Corporation," *Harvard Business Review* (May–June 1992), p. 42, with minor changes.

28. George Psacharopoulos and Maureen Woodhall, *Education for Development: An Analysis of Investment Choices,* A World Bank Publication (New York: Oxford University Press, 1985), p. 321

29. Ibid.

30. Quoted from Robert N. Gwynne, *New Horizons?: Third World Industrialization in an International Framework* (Hong Kong: Longmans Science & Technical, 1990), p. 68, with minor changes.

31. See Psacharopoulos and Woodhall, op. cit., p. 321.

32. Ibid.

33. The section that follows heavily draws from T. W. Schultz, "Education and Population Quality," in Psacharopoulos, ed., op. cit., p. 12. See also John Middleton, Adrian Ziderman, and Arvil Van Adams, *Skills for Productivity: Vocational Education and*

Training in Developing Countries, A World Bank Book (New York: Oxford University Press, 1993), p. 86.

34. Quoted from Joshua S. Goldstein, *International Relations* (New York: Harper-Collins, 1994), p. 533.

35. The section that follows draws heavily from Michael P. Todaro, *Economic Development in the Third World,* 4th edn (White Plains, NY: Longmans, 1989), pp. 354–355. See also Psacharopoulos and Woodhall, op. cit., pp. 316–320.

36. This section is modified from Jacques Bughin, "Benelux," chapter 6 in David A. Dyker, ed., *The National Economies of Europe* (Singapore: Longmans, 1992), pp. 150–151.

37. Quoted from Middleton, Ziderman, and Van Adams, op. cit., p. 216.

38. Quoted from Michael P. Todaro, *Economic Development in the Third World,* 5th edn (White Plains, NY: Longmans, 1994), p. 471.

39. Laura D'Andrea Tyson, Tea Petrin, and Halsey Rogers, "Promoting Entrepreneurship in Eastern Europe," *Small Business Economics,* 6 (1994), p. 171.

40. Both studies are described in Daryl McKee, "Targeted Industry Marketing: Strategy and Techniques," *Economic Development Review* (Spring 1994), p. 11.

41. Hubert Schmitz and Bernard Musyck, "Industrial Districts in Europe: Policy Lessons for Developing Countries?" *World Development,* vol. 22, no. 6, pp. 889–910.

42. UNDP, *Human Development Report 1993* (New York: Oxford University Press, 1993), p. 40.

43. Ibid., p. 41.

44. Todaro (5th edn), op. cit., p. 608.

45. Ibid.

46. Ibid.

47. Quoted from ibid., pp. 608–609.

48. Quoted from UNDP, op. cit., pp. 39–41.

49. Quoted from Middleton, Ziderman, and Van Adams, op. cit., p. 239.

50. Ibid.

51. Tyson, Petrin, and Rogers, op. cit., pp. 165–184.

52. UNDP, op. cit., pp. 39–41.

53. Ibid.

54. Quoted from D. Dodwell, "Industry: A Labyrinth of Obstacles to Market Forces," *Financial Times China Survey,* Dec. 18, 1987, p. 8.

55. Schmitz and Musyck, op. cit., pp. 889–910.

Chapter 14: Developing the Nation's Institutional Framework

1. Robert N. Gwynne, *New Horizons?: Third World Industrialization in an International Framework* (Hong Kong: Longmans Scientific and Technical, 1990), p. 68. See also Martin Janike, *State Failure: The Impotence of Politics in Industrial Society* (University Park, PA: Pennsylvania State University Press, 1990), p. 8.

2. V. V. Ramanadham, "Privatization: Constraints and Impacts," in V. V. Ramanadham, ed., *Constraints and Impacts of Privatization* (New York: Routledge, 1993), p. 6. Also see Gwynne, op. cit., p. 68.

3. Svetozar Pejovich, *The Economics of Property Rights: Towards a Theory of Comparative Systems* (Norwell, MA: Kluwer Academic Publishers, 1990), p. 41.

4. Ibid.

5. Ibid., p. 27.

6. See Gwynne, op. cit., p. 68.

7. Robert W. Campbell, *The Socialist Economies in Transition: A Primer on Semi-Reformed Systems* (Bloomington, IN: Indiana University Press, 1991), pp. 105–197.

8. Ibid., p. 196.

9. Ibid.

10. Ibid.

11. Gwynne, op. cit., p. 68.

12. Jozef M. van Brabant, "Divestment of State Capital," in Kazimierz Z. Poznanski, ed., *Constructing Capitalism: The Reemergence of Civil Society and Liberal Economy in the Post-Communist World* (Boulder, CO: Westview, 1992), pp. 118–119.

13. Gwynne, op. cit., p. 68.

14. Kazimierz Z. Poznanski, "Property Rights Perspective on Evolution of Communist-Type Economies," in Poznanski, ed., op. cit., pp. 118–119.

15. Stephen Breyer, "Regulation and Deregulation in the United States," in Giandomenico Majone, ed., *Deregulation or Re-Regulation?: Regulatory Reform in Europe and the United States* (London: Pinter Publishers, 1990), pp. 7–8.

16. Ibid., pp. 9–10.

17. Ibid., p. 10, and also John Kay and John Vickers, "Regulatory Reform: An Appraisal," in ibid., pp. 227–228.

18. Kay and Vickers, Ibid., p. 227.

19. Ibid., p. 228.

20. Ibid.

21. Quoted from Breyer, op. cit., p. 11, with minor changes.

22. Kay and Vickers, op. cit., p. 228.

23. Breyer, op. cit., p. 10.

24. Kay and Vickers, op. cit., p. 226.

25. Breyer, op. cit., p. 10.

26. Kay and Vickers, op. cit., p. 228.

27. Ibid., p. 230.

28. Breyer, op. cit., p. 11.

29. Ibid., pp. 11–12.

30. Rob Van Tulder and Gerd Junne, *European Multinationals in Core Technologies* (New York: John Wiley and Sons, 1988), p. 201.

31. Ibid.

32. Kay and Vickers, op. cit., pp. 242–243.

33. Ibid., p. 243.

34. Ibid., pp. 243–244.

35. Ibid., p. 244.

36. Murray Weidenbaum, "Antitrust Policy for the Global Market Place," *Journal of World Trade* (February 1994), pp. 27–31.

37. Tulder and Junne, op. cit., p. 198.

38. Ibid., p. 198.
39. Ibid.
40. Ibid., p. 199.
41. Quoted from ibid., pp. 200–201, with minor changes.
42. Ibid., p. 201.
43. Peter T. Jones and David J. Teece, "What We Know and What We Don't Know About Competitiveness," in Antonio Furino, ed., *Cooperation and Competition in the Global Economy* (New York: Ballinger Publishing Company, 1988), pp. 301–302.
44. Quoted from Alfie Kohn, *No Contest: The Case Against Competition,* rev. edn (Boston: Houghton Mifflin, 1992), p. 76, with minor changes.
45. This section draws heavily from Jan Tinbergen, "Should All Markets Be Free?" in Soumitra Sharma, ed., *Development Policy* (New York: St. Martin's Press, 1992), p. 81.
46. John Stopford and Susan Strange, with John S. Henley, *Rival States, Rival Firms: Competition for World Market Shares* (New York: Cambridge University Press, 1991), p. 122.
47. L. Gray Cowan, *Privatization in the Developing World* (New York: Greenwood Press, 1990), p. 6.
48. Because most privatizations in the developing world have been recent, they do not appear fully in the 1991 data. See UNDP, *Human Development Report 1993* (New York: Oxford University Press, 1993), p. 48.
49. Cowan, op. cit., p. 52.
50. Quoted from Ramanadham, ed., op. cit., p. 9, with minor changes.
51. Cowan, op. cit., p. 51.
52. UNDP, op. cit., p. 51.
53. Quoted from ibid., p. 44, with minor changes.
54. Ramanadham, ed., op. cit., p. 16.
55. UNDP, op. cit., p. 51.
56. Cowan, op. cit., p. 51.
57. Ramanadham, ed., op. cit., pp. 6–16.
58. Quoted from ibid., p. 16.
59. Cowan, op. cit., p. 52.
60. This section draws heavily from UNDP, op. cit., pp. 49–51.
61. John Wanna, "Business Options in Industrial Relations Policy," in Stephen Bell and John Wanna, eds., *Business-Government Relations in Australia* (Marrickville, NSW: Harcourt Brace Jovanovich, 1992), p. 255.
62. Annemieke J. M. Roobeek, *Beyond the Technology Race: An Analysis of Technology Policy in Seven Industrial Countries* (Amsterdam: Elsevier, 1990), p. 202.
63. C. K. Prahalad, *Globalization: Pitfalls, Pain and Potential,"* Rajiv Gandhi Institute for Contemporary Studies (n.d.), p. 24.
64. Quoted from Chan Suo Chang, "Human Resource Management in Korea," in Kae H. Chung and Hak Chong Lee, eds., *Korean Managerial Dynamics* (New York: Praeger, 1989), p. 203, with minor changes.
65. John Middleton, Adrian Ziderman, and Arvil Van Adams, *Skills for Productivity:*

Vocational, Education and Training in Developing Countries, A World Bank Book (New York: Oxford University Press, 1993), p. 96.

66. Ibid.
67. Ibid. See also E. P. Lazear, "Job Security Provisions and Employment," *Quarterly Journal of Economics,* vol. 105, no. 3 (1990), pp. 669–726.
68. UNDP, op. cit., p. 37.
69. Quoted from ibid., with minor changes.
70. Middleton, Ziderman, and Van Adams, op. cit., p. 96.
71. Seiji Furuta and Ichiro Kano, "The General Account Budget," in Tokue Shibata, ed., *Japan's Public Sector: How the Government Is Financed* (Tokyo: University of Tokyo Press, 1993), p. 71.
72. Quoted from Ira Magaziner and Mark Patinkin, *The Silent War* (New York: Vintage Books, 1989), pp. 354–355, with minor changes.
73. Quoted from UNDP, op. cit., p. 42, with minor changes.
74. Ibid., p. 43.
75. Ibid., pp. 43–44.
76. Chang, op. cit., p. 203.
77. UNDP, op. cit., pp. 43–44.
78. Ibid. See also Gay W. Seidman, "Facing the New International Context of Development," in Jeremy Brecher, John Brown Childs, and Jill Cutler eds., *Global Visions: Beyond the New World Order* (Boston: South End Press, 1993), p. 176.
79. UNDP, op. cit., p. 41.
80. Quoted from ibid., p. 44, with minor changes.
81. Ibid., pp. 43–44.
82. Vito Tanzi, *Public Finance in Developing Countries* (Brookfield, VT: Edward Elgar, 1991), p. 10.
83. This section draws heavily on Michael P. Todaro, *Economic Development in the Third World,* 5th edn (White Plains, NY: Longmans, 1994), pp. 165–169.
84. Assar Lindbeck, et al., *Turning Sweden Around* (Cambridge, MA: MIT Press, 1994), pp. 56–57.
85. Todaro, op. cit., pp. 165–169.
86. Ibid.
87. Quoted from Tokue Shibata, "Japan's Special Features," in Shibata, ed., op. cit., p. 6, with minor changes.
88. Quoted from UNDP, op. cit., pp. 37–38, with minor changes.
89. Todaro, op. cit., pp. 165–169.
90. Ibid.
91. Ibid.
92. Tanzi, op. cit., p. 55.
93. This section draws heavily from *The Economist,* Sept. 2, 1995, p. 74.
94. This section draws heavily from Elise Boulding, "Ethnicity and New Constitute Orders," in Brecher, Childs, and Cutler, eds., op. cit., pp. 213–227.
95. Quoted from ibid., pp. 220–221.

Chapter 15: Bridging Corporate Strategy with the Nation's Wealth-Building Strategy

1. Quoted from Peter Dicken, *Global Shift: The Internationalization of Economic Activity* (New York: The Guilford Press, 1992), p. 372.
2. Quoted from Sheridan M. Tatsuno, *Created in Japan* (New York: Harper & Row, 1990), pp. 162–163.
3. Quoted from *The Economist,* June 13–19, 1992, pp. 73–74.
4. Quoted from *The Economist,* Jan. 18–24, 1992, pp. 67–68.
5. See Robert Ballance, "Industry-Specific Strategies in a Protectionist World," in H. W. Singer, Neelambar Hatti, and Rameshwar Tandon, eds., *Trade Liberalization in the 1990s* (New Delhi: Indus Publishing, 1990), pp. 247–250.
6. See *Tokyo Business Today* (November 1991), p. 48.
7. Quoted from *The Economist,* Jan. 18–24, 1992, p. 67, with minor changes.
8. Quoted from H. William Ebeling, "Positioning Strategies in the New Europe," in Liam Fahey, ed., *Winning in the New Europe: Taking Advantage of the Single Market* (Englewood Cliffs, NJ: Prentice Hall, 1992), pp. 125–126 (including the figure), with minor changes.
9. Kae H. Chung and Hak Chong Lee, "National Differences in Managerial Practice," in Kae H. Chung and Hak Chong Lee, eds., *Korean Managerial Dynamics* (New York: Praeger, 1989), p. 171.
10. Malcolm S. Salter and Wolf A. Weinhold, *Diversification Through Acquisition: Strategies for Creating Economic Value* (New York: The Free Press, 1979), p. 62.
11. Quoted from Fumio Kodama, *Emerging Patterns of Innovation: Sources of Japan's Technological Edge* (Boston: Harvard Business School Press, 1995), p. 71.
12. See Salter and Weinhold, op. cit., p. 61.
13. Quoted from *The Economist,* Aug. 12, 1989, pp. 59–60, with minor changes.
14. Salter and Weinhold op. cit., p. 62.
15. Quoted from Alfred D. Chandler, "The Enduring Logic of Industrial Success," *Harvard Business Review* (March–April 1990), pp. 138–140, with minor changes.
16. Ibid., p. 140.
17. Dong Sung Cho, "Diversification Strategy of Korean Firms," in Chung and Lee, eds., op. cit., p. 99.

Chapter 16: Nourishing Company Growth

1. Quoted from C. K. Prahalad and Gary Hamel, "The Core Competence of the Corporation," *Harvard Business Review* (May–June 1990), p. 82, with minor changes. Reprinted by permission.
2. Quoted from ibid., p. 82, with minor changes.
3. O. Bertrand and T. Noyelle, *Human Resources and Corporate Strategy: Technological Change in Banks and Insurance Companies* (Paris: OECD, 1988), pp. 40–41.
4. Prahalad and Hamel, op. cit., p. 86.
5. Fumio Kodama, "Technology Fusion and the New R&D," *Harvard Business Review* (July–August 1992) pp. 70–78.
6. Ralph Gomery, "The Technology-Product Relationship: Early and Late Stages," in

Nathan Rosenberg, Ralph Landau, and David C. Mowery, eds., *Technology and the Wealth of Nations* (Stanford, CA: Stanford University Press, 1992), pp. 383–394.

7. Quoted from Gary Hamel and C. K. Prahalad, "Strategic Intent," *Harvard Business Review* (May–June 1989), pp. 70–71.

8. Treacy and Fred Wiersema, "Customer Intimacy and Other Value Discipline," *Harvard Business Review* (January–February 1993), pp. 84–93.

9. Quoted from Calvin L. Hodock, "Strategies Behind the Winners and Losers," *Journal of Business Strategies* (September–October 1990), p. 7.

10. This section draws heavily on Al Ries and Jack Trout, *Positioning: The Battle for Your Mind* (New York: Warner Books, 1982).

11. Ford S. Worthy, "Japan's Smart Secret Weapon," *Fortune*, Aug. 12, 1991, pp. 52–55.

12. Many theories have been offered to explain Japan's global success. Some point to its unique business practices, such as lifetime employment, quality circles, consensus management, and just-in-time production. Others point to the supportive role of government policies and subsidies, the existence of powerful trading companies, and businesses' access to low-cost bank financing. Still others view Japan's success as based on unfair dumping practices, protected markets, and almost zero defense industry costs.

13. Philip Kotler, Liam Fahey, and Somkid Jatusripitak, *The New Competition* (Englewood Cliffs, NJ: Prentice Hall, 1985). See also John K. Johansson and Ikvjiro Nonaka, *Relentless: The Japanese Way of Marketing* (New York: Harper Business, 1996).

14. See Kenichi Ohmae, *Triad Power* (New York: The Free Press, 1985), and Philip Kotler and Nikhilesh Dholakia, "Ending Global Stagnation: Linking the Fortunes of the Industrial and Developing Countries," *Business in the Contemporary World* (Spring 1989), pp. 86–97.

15. "Survey of the Global Economy," *The Economist*, Oct. 1, 1995, p. 10.

16. See Ohmae, op. cit.; also Kotler and Dholakia, op. cit.

17. "Survey of the Global Economy," *The Economist*, op. cit., pp. 13–14.

18. Quoted from J. Boddewyn, "International Political Strategy: A Fourth 'Generic' Strategy?" Paper presented at the Academy of International Business meeting, London, 1986.

19. Philip Kotler, "Megamarketing," *Harvard Business Review* (March–April 1986), pp. 117–124.

20. Pat Choate, "Political Advantage: Japan's Campaign for America," *Harvard Business Review* (September–October 1990), pp. 87–89.

21. Quoted from John Kao, "The Worldwide Web of Chinese Business," *Harvard Business Review* (March–April 1993), pp. 24–36, with minor changes.

22. Briance Mascarenhas, "Transnational Linkage and Strategy," in Anant R. Negandhi and Arun Savara, eds., *International Strategic Management* (Toronto: Lexington Books, 1989), pp. 62–63.

23. Jean-Pierre Jeannet and Hubert D. Hennessey, *Global Marketing Strategies*, 3rd edn (Boston: Houghton Mifflin 1992), pp. 94–95.

24. Ibid., p. 94.

25. Ibid., p. 95.

26. Ibid., p. 94.

27. David K. Tse and Gerald J. Gorn, "An Experiment on the Salience of Country-of-

Origin in the Era of Global Brands," *Journal of International Marketing,* vol. 1, no. 1 (1993), p. 57.

28. Ibid.

29. Gold Peak also makes batteries, but has recently spun this operation off into a separate company, GP Batteries International, listed in Singapore.

30. "Asian Firms Seek to Produce Own Brand Goods: Brands for Hope," *Far Eastern Economic Review,* Oct. 3, 1991, pp. 52–53.

31. Quoted from Jeannet and Hennessey, op. cit., pp. 457–458, with minor changes.

32. Quoted from Bradley K. Martin, "Japanese Seek to Be Moscow's Middlemen," *The Wall Street Journal,* July 13, 1984, p. 18, with minor changes.

Chapter 17: Strategic Development Through Cooperative Strategies

1. Bo Hellgren and Leif Melin, "Corporate Strategies in Nordic Firms Facing Europe," In Lars-Gunnar Mattsson and Bengt Stymne, eds., *Corporate and Industry Strategies for Europe* (New York: North Holland, 1991), pp. 329–330.

2. J. Johanson and L. G. Mattsson, "Interorganisational Relations in Industrial Systems," *International Journal of Management and Organization,* vol. 17., no. 1 (Spring 1987), pp. 34–38.

3. Hans B. Thorelli and S. Tamer Cavusgil, *International Marketing Strategy* (New York: Pergamon Press, 1990), pp. 432–435.

4. G. C. Cainarca, M. G. Colombo, and S. Mariotti, "Agreements Between Firms and the Technological Life Cycle Model: Evidence from Information Technologies," *Research Policy,* 21 (1992), pp. 45–62.

5. See Gary Hamel and C. K. Prahalad, "The Core Competence of the Corporation," *Harvard Business Review* (May–June 1990), pp. 79–91. Reprinted by permission.

6. Cainarca, Colombo, and Mariotti, op. cit., pp. 45–62.

7. Yves Doz, "Partnerships in Europe: The 'Soft Restructuring' Option?" in Mattsson and Stymne, eds., op. cit., pp. 305–309.

8. Quoted from Thorelli and Cavusgil, op. cit., pp. 432–435, with minor changes.

9. Quoted from Peter Lorange and Johan Roos, "Why Some Strategic Alliances Succeed and Others Fail," *Journal of Business Strategies* (January–February 1991), p. 25, with minor changes.

10. Quoted from Thorelli and Cavusgil, op. cit., pp. 432–435, with minor changes.

11. Subhash C. Jain, "Perspective on International Strategic Alliances," in S. Tamer Cavusgil, ed., *Advances in International Marketing* (Greenwich, CT: JAI Press, 1987), vol. 2, pp. 106–108.

12. This section heavily draws from Doz, op. cit., pp. 314–318. See also Cainarca, Colombo, and Mariotti, op. cit., pp. 45–62.

13. Quoted from Thorelli and Cavusgil, op. cit., p. 76, with minor changes.

14. Quoted from Joel D. Glodhar and David Lei, "The Shape of Twenty-First Century Global Manufacturing," *Journal of Business Strategy* (March–April 1991), p. 39, with minor changes.

15. This section draws heavily from Joel Bleeke and David Ernst, "The Way to Win in Cross-Border Alliances," *Harvard Business Review* (November–December 1991), pp. 127–135. Reprinted by permission.

16. Quoted from ibid., pp. 128–129.
17. Quoted from ibid., pp. 129–130.
18. Quoted from ibid., pp. 130–131.
19. Quoted from ibid., p. 131.
20. Quoted from ibid., p. 133.
21. Peter Dicken, *Global Shift: The Internationalization of Economic Activity* (New York: The Guilford Press, 1992), p. 213.
22. Lorange and Roos, op. cit., pp. 26–27.
23. Thorelli and Cavusgil, op. cit., p. 432.

Chapter 18: National Wealth-Building Strategies: From Strategic Vision to Strategic Implementation

1. Hugh Mosley and Gunter Schmid, "Public Service and Competitiveness," in Kirsty S. Hughes, ed., *European Competitiveness* (Cambridge, UK: Cambridge University Press 1993), pp. 204–205.
2. Stephen Bell and John Wanna, "Business and Government: Context and Patterns of Interaction," in Stephen Bell and John Wanna, eds., *Business-Government Relations in Australia* (Marrickville, NSW: Harcourt Brace Jovanovich, 1992), p. 17. Reprinted with permission from *Business-Government Relations in Australia,* ed. Stephen Bell and John Wanna. Copyright © 1992 by Harcourt Brace and Company, Australia.
3. Michael P. Todaro, *Economic Development in the Third World,* 5th edn (White Plains, NY: Longmans, 1994), p. 585.
4. Martin Janicke, *State Failure: The Impotence of Politics in Industrial Society, trans. Alan Braley* (University Park, PA: Pennsylvania State University Press, 1990), p. 33.
5. This section heavily draws from Bell and Wanna, op. cit., pp. 22–23.
6. C. K. Prahalad, *Globalization: Pitfalls, Pain and Potential,* Rajiv Gandhi Institute for Contemporary Studies (n.d.), p. 24.
7. Henry Kissinger, *Diplomacy* (New York: Simon & Schuster, 1994), pp. 23–24.
8. Joshua S. Goldstein, *International Relations* (New York: HarperCollins, 1994), pp. 333–350.
9. Quoted from Klaus Schwab and Claude Smadja, "Power and Policy: The New Economic World Order," in Kenichi Ohmae, ed., *The Evolving Global Economy* (Boston: Harvard Business School Press, 1995), pp. 110–111, with minor changes.
10. Quoted from Jagdish Bhagwati, *The World Trading System at Risk* (Princeton, NJ: Princeton University Press, 1991), pp. 74–77, with minor changes.

INDEX

ABOUT THE AUTHORS

PHILIP KOTLER is the S. C. Johnson & Son Distinguished Professor of International Marketing at the J. L. Kellogg Graduate School of Management, Northwestern University in Evanston, Illinois, where he lives. Professor Kotler is a world-renowned authority on marketing and has consulted for such companies as IBM, General Electric, AT&T, Honeywell, Bank of America, Merck, and others in the areas of marketing strategy and planning, marketing organization, and international marketing. He is the author of several books, including *Marketing Places* and *Social Marketing* (both published by The Free Press), as well as *Marketing Management* (Prentice Hall)—the most widely used marketing textbook in graduate business schools worldwide.

SOMKID JATUSRIPITAK is Professor of Marketing at NIDA in Bangkok, Thailand. He entered his Ph.D. from the Kellogg Graduate School of Management where, with Dr. Kotler, he co-authored *The New Competition*. He is well known in Thailand as an authority on marketing. In addition, he has been chairman and member of the board of directors of several companies, as well as an advisor to the Foreign Minister.

SUVIT MAESINCEE is a consultant for Booz • Allen & Hamilton Inc. in Chicago and Bangkok. He earned his Ph.D. in Marketing from the Kellogg Graduate School of Management. He lives in Bangkok.